Village Life in Modern Japan

JAPANESE SOCIETY SERIES

General Editor: Yoshio Sugimoto

Lives of Young Koreans in Japan
Yasunori Fukuoka

Globalization and Social Change in Contemporary Japan
J.S. Eades, Tom Gill and Harumi Befu

Coming Out in Japan: The Story of Satoru and Ryuta
Satoru Ito and Ryuta Yanase

Japan and Its Others:
Globalization, Difference and the Critique of Modernity
John Clammer

Hegemony of Homogeneity:
An Anthropological Analysis of Nihonjinron
Harumi Befu

Foreign Migrants in Contemporary Japan
Hiroshi Komai

A Social History of Science and Technology in
Contempory Japan, Volume 1
Shigeru Nakayama

Farewell to Nippon: Japanese Lifestyle Migrants in Australia
Machiko Sato

The Peripheral Centre:
Essays on Japanese History and Civilization
Johann P. Arnason

A Genealogy of 'Japanese' Self-images
Eiji Oguma

Class Structure in Contemporary Japan
Kenji Hashimoto

An Ecological View of History
Tadao Umesao

Nationalism and Gender
Chizuko Ueno

Native Anthropology: The Japanese Challenge
to Western Academic Hegemony
Takami Kuwayama

Youth Deviance in Japan: Class Reproduction of Non-Conformity
Robert Stuart Yoder

Japanese Companies: Theories and Realities
Masami Nomura and Yoshihiko Kamii

From Salvation to Spirituality:
Popular Religious Movements in Modern Japan
Susumu Shimazono

The 'Big Bang' in Japanese Higher Education:
The 2004 Reforms and the Dynamics of Change
J.S. Eades, Roger Goodman and Yumiko Hada

Japanese Politics: An Introduction
Takashi Inoguchi

A Social History of Science and Technology in
Contempory Japan, Volume 2
Shigeru Nakayama

Gender and Japanese Management
Kimiko Kimoto

Philosophy of Agricultural Science: A Japanese Perspective
Osamu Soda

A Social History of Science and Technology in
Contempory Japan, Volume 3
Shigeru Nakayama and Kunio Goto

Japan's Underclass: Day Laborers and the Homeless
Hideo Aoki

A Social History of Science and Technology
in Contemporary Japan, Volume 4
Shigeru Nakayama and Hitoshi Yoshioka

Escape from Work: A Lifestyle Choice of Japanese Youth
Reiko Kosugi

Social Welfare in Japan: Principles and Applications
Kojun Furukawa

Scams and Sweeteners: A Sociology of Fraud
Masahiro Ogino

Toyota's Assembly Line: A View from the Factory Floor
Ryoji Ihara

Village Life in Modern Japan: An Environmental Perspective
Akira Furukawa

Social Stratification and Inequality Series

Inequality amid Affluence: Social Stratification in Japan
Junsuke Hara and Kazuo Seiyama

Intentional Social Change: A Rational Choice Theory
Yoshimichi Sato

Constructing Civil Society in Japan:
Voices of Environmental Movements
Koichi Hasegawa

Deciphering Stratification and Inequality: Japan and beyond
Yoshimichi Sato

Social Justice in Japan: Concepts, Theories and Paradigms
Ken-ichi Ohbuchi

Advanced Social Research Series

A Sociology of Happiness
Kenji Kosaka

Frontiers of Social Research: Japan and beyond
Akira Furukawa

MODERNITY AND IDENTITY IN ASIA SERIES

Globalization, Culture and Inequality in Asia
Timothy S. Scrase, Todd Miles Joseph Holden and Scott Baum

Looking for Money:
Capitalism and Modernity in an Orang Asli Village
Alberto Gomes

Governance and Democracy in Asia
Takashi Inoguchi and Matthew Carlson

Village Life in Modern Japan

An Environmental Perspective

Akira Furukawa

Translated by
Kikuko Onoda

Trans Pacific Press
Melbourne

First published in Japanese in 2004 by Sekai Shisōsha as *Mura no seikatsu kankyōshi*

This English language edition published in 2007 by
Trans Pacific Press, PO Box 120, Rosanna, Melbourne, Victoria 3084, Australia
Telephone: +61 3 9459 3021 Fax: +61 3 9457 5923
Email: tpp.mail@gmail.com
Web: http://www.transpacificpress.com

Copyright © Trans Pacific Press 2007

Designed and set by digital environs, Melbourne, Australia. www.digitalenvirons.com

Printed by BPA Print Group, Burwood, Victoria, Australia

Distributors

Australia and New Zealand
UNIREPS
University of New South Wales
Sydney, NSW 2052
Australia
Telephone: +61(0)2-9664-0999
Fax: +61(0)2-9664-5420
Email: info.press@unsw.edu.au
Web: http://www.unireps.com.au

USA and Canada
International Specialized Book Services (ISBS)
920 NE 58th Avenue, Suite 300
Portland, Oregon 97213-3786
USA
Telephone: (800) 944-6190
Fax: (503) 280-8832
Email: orders@isbs.com
Web: http://www.isbs.com

Asia and the Pacific
Kinokuniya Company Ltd.

Head office:
Shin-Mizonokuchi Bldg. 2F
5-7 Hisamoto 3-chome
Takatsu-ku, Kawasaki 213-8506
Japan
Telephone: +81(0)44-874-9642
Fax: +81(0)44-829-1025
Email: bkimp@kinokuniya.co.jp
Web: www.kinokuniya.co.jp

Asia-Pacific office:
Kinokuniya Book Stores of Singapore Pte., Ltd.
391B Orchard Road #13-06/07/08
Ngee Ann City Tower B
Singapore 238874
Telephone: +65 6276 5558
Fax: +65 6276 5570
Email: SSO@kinokuniya.co.jp

All rights reserved. No production of any part of this book may take place without the written permission of Trans Pacific Press.

ISSN   1443-9670 (Japanese Society Series)

ISBN   978-1-876843-32-8 (Hardcover)
ISBN   978-1-876843-40-3 (Paperback)

The National Library of Australia Cataloguing-in-Publication entry

Furukawa, Akira.
  Village life in modern Japan : an environmental perspective.
  Bibliography.
  Includes index.
  ISBN 9781876843328 (hbk.).

  1. Villages – Environmental aspects – Japan. 2. Country life – Environmental aspects – Japan. 3. Country life – Religious aspects. 4. Japan – Social life and customs. I. Title. (Series : Japanese society series, 1443-9670).

307.720952

Cover illustration: A *dōsojin* festival in Nagano Prefecture, a celebration to worship the rural deity believed to protect the village community, ensure prosperity for offspring and guard travelers in the area.

Contents

Figures	viii
Photos	viii
Tables	viii
Acknowledgements	ix
Introduction: Rural and Small Communities	1
1 Life-environmentalism and Environmental Sociology Methods	16
2 The Village as an Independent Body	62
3 Rural Community Structure and Family System	129
4 Modernization of Villages and Transformation of Everyday Life Knowledge	170
5 Techniques of Forest Management and Philosophy of Living	218
Conclusion: Towards Neo-Communalism	261
Notes	270
Bibliography	278
Name Index	295
Subject Index	297

Figures

2.1	Map of Lake Biwa and surrounds	68
2.2	The seating arrangements at *okonai* rituals	85
4.1	Various uses of the Mae River	174
4.2	*Suimon* and *suikomi*	175
4.3	The areas relying on different types of water sources in Kaizu Higashi district	177
4.4	Transformation of the lagoons	188
4.4	continued	189
5.1	A map of Higashi-hagidaira District in Asahi-chō in 1867	224
5.2	A map of Higashi-hagidaira District in Asahi-chō around 1980	225

Photos

5.1	A view of a mountain hamlet in the 1950s	220
5.2	A photo taken in December 1998 from approximately the same location as that used to take Photo 5.1	220
5.3	A view of a mountain hamlet in the 1950s	221
5.4	A photo taken in December 1998 from approximately the same location as that used to take Photo 5.3	221
5.5	A *mandala* (*thanka*, or Buddhist painting)	248

Tables

4.1	Account Book, Mori Ike Renchū (company)	181
4.2	Events and occurrances in the *mura* in 1970	208
5.1	Clan composition in Solu and Khumbu	254
5.2	Aid to Khumbu	259

Acknowledgements

I am grateful to the 21st century Center of Excellence Program for the Study of 'Social Research for the Enhancement of Human Well-being,' Kwansei Gakuin University, for its intellectual, moral and financial support. The COE is funded by the Japanese Ministry of Education, Culture, Sports, Science and Technology. This study represents a scholarly achievement of the COE.

Thanks are due to Ms Kikuko Onoda for her excellent translation of a difficult Japanese text into lucid English and to Ms Miriam Riley and Dr Karl Smith for their superb editorial work at various stages of production. I also wish to express my gratitude to Ms Takako Morino for her efficient and conscientious administrative support.

Akira Furukawa

Introduction: Rural and Small Communities

This work is an attempt to critically analyze the significant changes occurring in modern society from the perspective of the everyday life of rural communities. Using concrete examples, this work discusses how rural communities have emerged from crises situations as self-determining entities, with hidden potential to guide modern societies towards better ways of life.

Countless researchers have discussed the myriad ways in which the drastic changes in postwar Japanese society have undermined the capacity of agriculture, forestry and fisheries to provide sufficient sources of livelihood, threatening rural farming, mountain and fishing communities with collapse and extinction. This issue requires no further explanation. Few have offered analyses, however, of how structural changes in Japanese society have inspired widespread nostalgia for these primary industries, thus giving them new value. This revaluation can be seen, for example, in the current 'rural boom' as well as a more general longing for the virtues of rural life.

This work focuses on the plasticity of Japanese rural communities as traditional social and cultural units and discusses: the creativity exercised in adapting to and resisting ever-changing situations; the extent and effectiveness of their power to modify existing social conditions; and the processes through which local initiatives develop.

In modern Japan, rural communities have typically been understood to be controlled by state authorities aiming to construct a modern nation-state. They have been understood as sources of labor and military manpower, and as subject to the state's ideological system which has infused national morality through national education in rural communities. In other words, rural communities have been understood by modern researchers to have been subsumed under the strong imperial state and the capitalist economy, thus transforming the modern state's rural communities even while retaining vestiges of feudalism.

This work departs from the depiction of rural communities as passive, inactive entities. There can be no doubt that the relationship between rural communities and the powerful central government has been grossly inequitable, or that various systems and ideologies have been imposed upon rural communities by the government. However, these imposed systems and ideologies have been negotiated and modified in the process of being incorporated into the everyday life of rural communities. While we must refrain from overrating rural communities' capacities and autonomy to modify and adapt such external impositions, we must nevertheless properly assess the significance of local initiatives.

Rural communities have sustained their reproductive activities by sometimes complying with national initiatives and sometimes redefining them in accordance with local values and knowledge. This work explores the initiatives of rural communities from the perspective of these reproductive activities. Rural communities' reactions to macro-level social changes are perhaps most readily apparent in the transformation of local ritual organizations, changes to their water supply and sewerage systems, and in their forest management practices. This book discusses each of these phenomena in turn, with the aim of reevaluating the social adaptability of rural communities. I contend that such an evaluation will reveal that rural communities might potentially provide a sufficient foundation for formulating new ways of living in this ever-changing world.

I begin with an overview of the difficult situation confronting rural communities today before outlining the typical urbanites' view of the situation.

Challenges facing rural communities today

Contemporary Japan appears to be increasingly 'nature-oriented,' with an ever-expanding 'nostalgia for rural life' among the Japanese people. Browse through almost any bookstore in town and you will find a section of how-to manuals that valorize rural life and offer guidance on how to enjoy a life of farming activities surrounded by nature. Many people readily accept that it is important to live in a comfortable, relaxed manner surrounded by nature in order to enjoy a satisfactory existence. Agriculture, forestry and fisheries have been rediscovered as meaningful activities for people who coexist with nature. In fact, when local governments announce invitations with incentives for people to relocate to their areas they are typically inundated with applicants. Correlated with this is an increasingly critical appraisal of the modern way of life that prioritizes productivity and efficiency.

Of course, Japan is not the only country that has witnessed stark changes in people's values. There is no doubt that the catalyst for this change was a growing awareness of the consequences of modern industrial society, consequences that have become increasingly apparent and have had ever-increasing effects on everyday life over the course of the twentieth century. The social form and lifestyle that emerged in Western Europe between the late eighteenth and early nineteenth centuries has swept across the world in less than two centuries. This modern civil society is associated with a series of inventions, including the nation-state, the market economy, and free, independent individuals, coupled with a historical view that supports social development and progress. But the environmental destruction wrought by this industrialist and consumerist lifestyle has become too pervasive to ignore any longer, and has forced a reconsideration of the values of progress and development that underpinned modern society, especially the ways in which these values were founded upon a belief in the human capacity to conquer and exploit nature. The growing recognition of the past few decades that we must reorient ourselves towards a more 'nature friendly' way of life demands a radical reevaluation of the central tenets of modern societies, especially the value of continuous growth in terms of both production and consumption.

There is currently a growing trend towards 'coexistence with nature.' This emerged from trial and error attempts to create a new social system to replace modern industrial society. From the viewpoint of cultural history, it is necessary to criticize the institutional fatigue of modern societies, as well as the widespread destruction of the environment, with an aim towards enhancing public awareness of the importance of nature. However, to date, these discussions have largely failed to give due consideration to the local knowledge and perspectives of the inhabitants of rural communities, namely, the people who actually live in coexistence with nature. Rural dwellers are primarily 'ordinary people' who worry about the declining capacity of their farming, forestry or fishing industries to offer satisfactory means of making a living and who are therefore sometimes attracted to various proposals made by developers. All discussions should start with understanding the reality of these rural people. We should be aware that our valorization of nature often tends to mystify the lives of the inhabitants of rural communities, obscuring them beneath the urbanites' romanticized view of rural life constructed in response to the dark shadows of industrialization. This is one of the foundations for the present critical appraisal.

My objective is to enrich and preserve the rural life-world. This objective is wholly compatible with the need to find ways of coexisting with nature, a need that is beginning to be advocated by both governments and the private sector. There are countless examples of large projects that purported to aim at local development and prosperity but resulted instead in serious environmental destruction and further deterioration of local standards of living. This experience reinforces the importance of a broad societal environmental consciousness – an understanding that all social undertakings must be 'nature friendly.'

We must ask, however, 'Why did the rural communities invite projects that destroyed the natural environment and endangered the community's way of life?' Some would argue that large-scale projects came to rural communities uninvited, imposed by the logic of capitalism irrespective of local desires or sentiments. From a macroscopic perspective, in fact, it is often the case that development projects are initiated and driven by giant capitalist firms and/or regional and national governments. Yet we must also take the local residents' attitudes and responses toward such macro-level decisions into account. Certainly, from the perspective of macro-level social structures, the affected residents are innocent people who have been victimized by forces beyond their control. But such a perspective is overly narrow, overlooking the attitudes and actions of the affected people, portraying them as passive objects who are helplessly subject to externally imposed conditions, rather than as active, independent subjects.

My objective is to consider from the micro-level why rural communities make decisions to allow development projects that may cause environmental damage. For example, a certain settlement in a mountain village located near the boundaries of Aichi, Gifu and Nagano Prefectures was inhabited by more than forty families immediately after World War II. It has only six families now, comprising only elderly members. Until relatively recently, forestry was their primary industry, but today they cannot even cover the costs of logging because market prices are suppressed by imported lumber. The elderly residents cannot even provide sufficient labor to clean their water source and its supply pipes. When someone requires urgent medical care, they must ask a man in his fifties from the neighboring settlement to drive them to hospital.¹ For people living under such difficult conditions following the long-term depopulation of rural settlements, urban messages such as those advocating 'resort development' and 'coexistence with nature' are interpreted and transformed so as to improve (or be seen to improve) the convenience of rural life.

The potential of rural communities as active bodies

This study focuses on the life of rural communities which comprise the majority of Japan. It is a review of activities such as rural development and environmental protection from the perspective of preserving the rural way of life, which entails preserving the natural and social systems that make such lifestyles sustainable and desirable. In the modernization of Japan and its transformation into a modern civil society, numerous structural contradictions have accumulated in the lives of rural communities. In an effort to improve the situation in rural communities, the national government has initiated and implemented various measures.

The first steps in this direction were taken in the 1960s, in the formulation of the first national plan for rural development. Until then, rural communities had been regarded primarily as a source of labor for industrial growth in the large cities while providing jobs for the unemployed in times of economic recession. The Comprehensive National Development Plan (CNDP) announced in 1962, though, designated fifteen new industrial cities and six rural areas for specified industrial development. The intent was to reorganize local communities around these new developments.

The plan went totally awry. Its intention to urbanize the countryside by incorporating rural areas into urban living spheres was unsuccessful. Despite huge investments, many of the designated cities failed to attract large chemical plants or other heavy industries. The Toyama Prefecture government, for example, concluded that their failure in this regard was not because the physical environment was unsuitable, but rather the availability of (highly-trained, diligent) labor was inadequate. In response, the local government reorganized its secondary education system, dividing its high school students into career-bound (70%) and university-bound (30%) students, in an effort to develop a 'highly-skilled' labor force. However, these efforts were not successful, either. Overall, the CNDP failed to realize its objectives of resolving the rural depopulation problems by providing stable employment in rural areas.

Thus, in the 1970s a revised New Comprehensive National Development Plan was adopted. Unlike the original CNDP which had attempted to develop rural areas by constructing similar industrial cities in each region, the new plan accepted that wealth and population would be concentrated in centralized metropolitan zones and aimed to promote an inter-regional division of labor. Specifically, the new CNDP aimed to locate urban industries and administrative functions in the central zones – Keihin (Tokyo and Yokohama), Keiyō (Tokyo and Chiba), Tōkai, Chūkyō, Keihanshin (Kyoto–Osaka–Kōbe), Setouchi and Kitakyūshū – while developing the remaining northeast and southwest regions as huge industrial bases or tourist resorts. Former Prime Minister Kakuei Tanaka's efforts to 'remodel the Japanese archipelago' were based on this plan. According to the new plan, rural communities would generate income by providing land for huge industrial facilities, as seen in the Mutsu Ogawara and Shibushi Bay projects, or by providing recreational facilities for workers residing in metropolitan areas.[2] However, the large-scale projects suffered a severe set-back due to the oil crises of the 1970s. Thus, rather than alleviating the suffering and problems of the declining rural areas, pollution and other social dysfunctions were exacerbated by these initiatives. Nevertheless, during that period rural areas were seized to serve primarily as sources of labor for metropolitan areas and came to be increasingly seen as a locus for physical and mental recreational areas for urban residents. That is, tourism emerged as a viable option for rural development.

The recreational function of depopulated areas expanded during the resort boom in the late 1980s. As the focus of the urban lifestyle shifted from production to consumption and leisure, resort development boomed, providing city people with lush natural environments in which to relax and rejuvenate. After the Resort Law (Comprehensive Resort Area Development Law) was enacted in 1987, each of Japan's forty-seven prefectures formulated a local 'resort plan,' which soon became the centerpiece of its efforts to develop depopulated areas. The Resort Law identifies its own objectives, including: increasing domestic demand by utilizing private enterprises; developing local regions that suffer from depopulation and the declining value of agricultural products; and providing city residents with leisure facilities. This law's emphasis on the importance of recreational developments opened the way to the prefectures significantly relaxing environmental protection regulations. The ensuing environmental destruction was exacerbated by the subsequent enactment of the Special Measures Law for the Further Utilization of Forests to Advance the Public Health, which enabled the elimination of forest reserves, and revisions to the National Park Law, which encouraged the construction of ski resorts, golf courses and marine sports facilities in designated national parklands.

By the end of 1989, up to 19.2% (7,250,000 hectares) of the nation had been covered by resort developments. This included somewhere between 1,500 and 2,000 new golf courses that were either already under construction or scheduled to begin soon, in addition to the 1,600 courses already in operation. It was as if the entire archipelago was dancing to a *capriccio* for resorts.

When the 'bubble economy' collapsed in the early 1990s, numerous developers were bankrupted and many who survived did so by withdrawing from or suspending their development projects. This had a profound impact on the nature of subsequent resort development projects. Large-scale resort projects – including the construction of new golf courses and ski slopes – disappeared. New projects tended to be smaller, including family resorts and rural resorts located in farming or mountain communities. In 1994, the National Land Agency published a report which recommended that resort development in rural areas should be oriented towards giving tourists a chance to experience rural life and facilitating exchange between urban and rural people (Yorimitsu and Kurisu 1996: 17).

The frenetic activities of the resort boom included numerous cases where huge developments destroyed precious forest resources, or where pesticide-saturated golf courses caused health problems in the adjoining areas. In hindsight, the suspension or discontinuation of these projects following the collapse of the bubble economy prevented further destruction of the natural environment. But nothing was done to rectify the damage that had already been done to rural ways of life. For example, there was no change for those rural people who had previously sold significant portions of their mountains and forests for golf course developments. Thus, once the nightmare of the resort boom was over, rural dwellers were forced to make other choices.

In 1998, the Grand Design for National Land in the Twenty-first Century (the fifth CNDP) was adopted. In the history of CNDPs, this was the first attempt of the national plan to reflect the rural communities' desires to maintain their lifestyles. It was also the first to emphasize the choices and responsibilities of local residents. The plan went so far as to actively approve the initiative of 'natural villages' (as opposed to administrative villages), for the purpose of enhancing local creativity and initiatives. In this respect, the plan was a clear departure from previous rural development plans which had invariably aimed for greater centralization. The fifth plan sought to create 'New Hometown Industrial Systems,' which aimed to nurture compound industries in each region based on agriculture, forestry or fisheries and including downstream processing of products and the provision of related services. It also recommended 'green tourism' for farming and mountain communities and 'blue tourism' for fishing communities. These changes were highly significant in that they, for the first time, acknowledged the initiatives that rural communities generate for change and cease to treat these communities as passive objects.

Nevertheless, the local communities' initiatives continued to be circumscribed by the central government's macroscopic structure. The Grand Design recognizes that the circumstances of these communities are inseparable from macroscopic social changes, including globalization and advanced information technologies. Specifically, each community is given a range of choices that could avoid their own trial and error initiatives; these choices are provided by the central government within a uniform system for the nation as a whole, in which a choice made by a particular community can enhance the centralized system. Let me discuss this point by taking green tourism as an example.

Green tourism is a means of rural development and is emphasized in the fifth CNDP. Although the term 'green tourism' has acquired many and diverse meanings, in Japan it basically refers to spending leisure time in rural communities. It aims to instill among city people an awareness of humanity's embeddedness in nature – a sense that is often lost in urban culture – while, at the same time, protecting the natural environment and developing depopulated areas. The development of green tourism has been embraced by both urban and rural dwellers. In 1970, the Rural Development Basic Issues Advisory Committee (Sanson Shinkō Kihon Mondai Shimon Iinkai) submitted a report on rural development which states: 'Rural areas must preserve and conserve precious nature for the long-term, thereby playing a major role in contributing to the sound development of the Japanese economy and society.' In addition to traditional functions such as supplying agricultural and forestry products, or recharging water, the report demands that rural areas 'provide green spaces and places for recreation and relaxation for most people, but mainly for urban residents.' The emphasis on providing recreation resources for urban residents suggests that the report's primary objective is to reproduce/rejuvenate the labor force, rather than to preserve the natural environment as precious in its own right. There is no indication that the report's authors value the initiatives and creative efforts of rural communities to construct and maintain unique communities. Hence, while green tourism is presented as necessary for both urban and rural communities, its implications suggest that it is primarily geared towards the needs of cities and their residents.

Rural communities as decision-making bodies

Many rural communities and municipalities have turned towards green tourism or ecotourism as their preferred means of rural development. It is certainly not my intent to suggest that they are somehow mistaken in adopting this course of action. Small communities all over the country are suffering from the effects of depopulation, aging, and the steadily declining economic value of their primary industries. Under these circumstances, green tourism provides a ray of hope. My concern in this work is that the efforts of small communities in these directions should not be absorbed into macro-level systems of urban knowledge, such as environmental protection or coexistence with nature. Although the critiques of modernity entailed in these buzzwords are certainly valid and important, we should not use them as the sole bases from which to define, evaluate and interpret the activities of small communities. Nor should we consider their activities simply as objects of consideration and conceptualization in the history of thought. Instead, we must attempt to understand their activities on the level at which they are carried out. That is, we must discuss these activities from the perspective of rural life.

Recent discussions about the independence of rural communities have tended to respect the community residents' positions and to defend their cultural identities. This approach seems to respect the residents' perspective. Yet, upon closer examination it appears to be their economic or consumerist identities rather than their identities as members of rural communities and cultures that is being respected, in which case there is little difference between this approach and calculating prospective economic effects on the local community. That is, their views are not respected as members of a local community worthy of being preserved in its own right, but rather as economic units capable of rationally maximizing costs and benefits. Of course it is necessary to consider how each member of a depopulated community should be economically compensated when the community embarks on various attempts at economic development. Failure to do so is likely to result in perfunctory volunteerism, precluding friendly exchanges among the community members and placing excessive burdens on the community. But the value and logic of rural life cannot be wholly reduced to economics, nor the merits of development projects evaluated simply in terms of the financial proceeds that might flow to the community as a whole. The consequences of this economic reductionist approach to community development became blindingly obvious in Japan's intermediate and mountainous regions during the 1960s and 1970s.

My argument is that we should use the rural dwellers' everyday life-world as the basis for understanding the specific measures taken to revitalize rural communities and their culture through rural development. The following situation provides a good starting point for understanding the merits of this approach.

Let us assume that a mountain village has terraced rice paddies that have increasingly been neglected due to the depopulation of the region. In discussing their options, some villagers propose incorporating these paddies into an exchange program with city dwellers, wherein the latter would participate in the revitalization and maintenance of the paddies. Others extend the first proposal, suggesting that visitors from the cities should also have access to local cuisine and folk art and be given the opportunity to learn about local nature-friendly lifestyles. They choose to start the exchange program surrounded by nature. The program is geared towards activities that heal city dwellers suffering from the strains of their industrialized communities while enhancing their environmental awareness. At the same time it introduces new activities that stimulate the local community. In other words, the program is positioned in the new stereotypical lifestyle that seeks to redress the illnesses of modern society through coexistence with nature.

Examining this program from the perspective of the everyday life-world of the rural residents, however, provides a completely different account. Rural residents are well-versed in the arguments about environmental protection and the malaises of modernity. They understand, on the same level as urban dwellers, the scientific arguments for environmental protection and the social values of the natural environment in depopulated areas. Yet we cannot directly or necessarily link the development of the exchange program to this understanding. Having carefully considered their particular situation and concluded that something must be done, they begin to explore numerous options. A wide range of options are available, from less plausible ones such as attracting industry or constructing an express highway, to green tourism and rural education programs. From these options, one or more are chosen based on what appears to be most convenient, or least intrusive, from the perspective of their local life-world. Once options are chosen, the residents begin moves towards their realization. In the process of developing and establishing their new scheme(s), various explanations are created to justify the choices that were made. Plausible and convincing arguments are formulated by manipulating various facts and theories, from ecology, modern economics and critiques of modernity, to existentialist and utilitarian philosophies. The consistent reasoning typically found in local communities to justify their endeavors is often merely *ex post facto* justification for choosing the most convenient means of maintaining their everyday life-world. We should therefore not search for substantive meanings in such reasoning, nor imagine that it has a fixed, absolute meaning. Adopting the perspective of the rural dwellers' everyday life-world means accepting the centrality of 'convenience' in collective decision-making and refraining from attaching unwarranted logic or excessive meanings to it.

This book hypothesizes the everyday life-worlds dynamically constructed by rural dwellers in small communities. It treats Japanese villages as one type of actor in modern Japanese society. Since the 1950s, these villages have been increasingly understood to be breaking down, a process that is perceived as having restricted the free action of community residents. There have, however, been various attempts to more positively evaluate these villages as small communities, rather than simply criticizing, denouncing or ignoring them. For example, Hiroyuki Torigoe was an early advocate of recognizing the importance of small communities in dealing with environmental issues, whether at a macro- or micro-level. Torigoe's position is based on the reports of researchers who have conducted fieldwork in Asia and Africa. For example, citing Masakazu Yamazaki, Torigoe argues that the best way to resolve the contradiction between freedom and stability in modern society is to restore the functions of small communities (1997a: ii–iii).

Behind this community-ism we find disputes between Rawls (1971), Nozick (1974), Sandel and others, over the basic characteristics of human beings and society in modernity.[3] The sharpest contrast in this debate is between liberals and communitarians, where the former emphasize the importance of individuals, their equality and freedom of choice, while the latter maintain that individuals can only be defined in the context of a community. The present work adopts a 'small community-ist' orientation that clearly overlaps with both the liberal and communitarian views.

However, the small community-ism hypothesized in this work differs from communitarianism, in that it is based on concrete observations of the everyday life-world. This small community-ism may be called communalism. Disputes over the independence of small communities constitute an important problematic in the history of social thought. However, the aim of this book is to develop new perspectives based on an analysis of the complex, multilayered realities of small communities.[4]

Each chapter of this book examines a different facet of the everyday life-world of the inhabitants of small rural communities. Each chapter depicts some of the ways in which the members of rural communities reinterpret urban views of the rural life and use the information and views available in the modern world to take action in their local community. Under the circumstances of systematic depopulation, the potential of rural communities as independent actors working to transform their ritual organizations, adopt environmental theories, and recreate local knowledge in order to protect their local ways of life, will be made apparent.

The composition of this work

Chapter One begins with a discussion of the philosophy of life-environmentalism, elucidating its key concepts, methodology and approaches. Life-environmentalism is a means to clarify rural residents' everyday life-world and provides the theoretical and methodological foundations for the present work. Once this foundation is established, the chapter surveys studies in environmental sociology conducted during the past two decades, with a view to finding a place for life-environmentalism in the arguments of environmental sociology. Approaches made in environmental sociology can be roughly divided into two directions. One is the 'sociology of environmental issues,' which regards the deterioration of the natural and living environments associated with industrialization and modernization as environmental issues and attempts to elucidate the social consequences of this damage and the victims' responses in various social movements. The other is a 'sociology of coexistence with the environment,' which focuses on small communities and attempts to elucidate each community's practical processes of creating its everyday life, from the perspective of its relationship with the environment. This latter approach also focuses on each community's local knowledge and their mechanisms for environmental protection as well as the processes whereby such knowledge and mechanisms can be changed. The present work belongs to the latter category, in that it focuses on small communities, on people's everyday life practices.

Chapter Two discusses the small community's formation as an 'independent body.' The term 'independent body' as used here should be understood not in the sense of an individual person, but rather as the system governing the small community's everyday life. In the first section I consider the relationship between rural community studies and environmental sociology. In the process, I introduce the *Kiroku* (Records) of Chinai Village (hereinafter referred to as '*Kiroku*'), the main research materials for this work, and discuss its relevance as research material. In the second section I examine the structural characteristics of Chinai Village by tracing the changes in its administrative structure during the Meiji and Taishō Periods. The third section reviews these changes from the perspective of Shinto (religious) affairs. Traditionally, these affairs were fully integrated with agricultural and administrative affairs and constituted the foundation of the village's administrative system until the Meiji Period. Furthermore, village affairs and individual household affairs were deeply integrated in the daily activities of the village. My argument is that this was precisely because Shinto affairs integrated administrative, agricultural and personal affairs. This relationship between household and village affairs would not have been sustainable if it had not ensured the underlying security of the individual households. In the fourth section I discuss an institution referred to as the 'poor's fishing system' that was created to ensure the wellbeing of the village and each of its member households. This entails a discussion of the concept of ownership underpinning this system. In the fifth section the focus is on who was responsible for conducting river improvements and other public works in the village during the Meiji and Taishō Periods. From this perspective, I discuss the variability and plasticity of the rural community as an 'independent body' in the context of relationships between the village and the local and national governments.

Chapter Three reviews the history of sociological and anthropological studies of rural community structures, aiming to position the structural characteristics of Chinai Village within this history. This chapter also explores studies and debates about the family (*ie*) or quasi-kin group (*dōzoku*) – arguably the most important element in rural community structures. This discussion aims to clarify the theoretical background of the 'village' and the 'family' when considering the village as an independent actor. The first section of this chapter reviews the ritual organization called *miyaza* (*okonai*) from the perspective of the rural community structure. *Miyaza* are prevalent in the villages of Shiga Prefecture where I conducted most of the fieldwork for this work. The classification of rural community structures in the Kinki region into 'horizontal (*kōgumi*) systems' rather than 'vertical (*dōzoku*) systems' has been widely accepted in rural community studies in Japan. I argue, however, that the structure of rural communities in the Kinki regions is better understood as a third category, in which the key factor is *miyaza*. This categorization, I believe, provides a better historical and theoretical understanding of the meanings and mechanisms of everyday life in rural communities.

Chapter Four outlines changes in the everyday life of Chinai Village to clarify the logic of this way of life. It considers: the impact of scientific knowledge on rural communities in the process of modernization and industrialization since the beginning of the Meiji Period; and alterations in everyday life practices to accommodate this scientific knowledge into the everyday life knowledge that underpins village life. The first section describes the traditional water supply and drainage systems that developed to ensure the cleanliness of waters, and how these uses and systems changed following the introduction of modern water supply services. The intent of this section is to clarify the meanings of everyday life knowledge and scientific knowledge in everyday life. The second section reconsiders the same subject matter through a discussion of changes to an annual event called '*mushi okuri*' – a torch procession for driving away noxious insects. This discussion deepens our understanding of the conflict between everyday life knowledge and scientific knowledge. The third section illustrates daily life in the village by examining the significant events of a single year and then comparing these events to occurrences over many years, using the records of *Kiroku*. Most of the normal activities in the village have been routinized and repeated for decades, if not centuries. Yet the village today is quite different than it was even a decade ago, much less a century ago. The central point, however, is that external pressures do not directly change the village. There are at least two significant internal forces that seem to be involved in any response to external pressure. One seeks to minimize the broader society's impact on the village, while the other seeks to maximize the benefits to be derived from the same society. These forces appear to constitute directly opposed vectors, which are both supported by the everyday life knowledge of the members of small communities and their everyday life practices.

Chapter Five reviews the same subject matter in the context of other communities, exploring the conflict between everyday life knowledge and scientific knowledge by describing changes in local forest management practices. Traditional forest management practices based on local knowledge have been overturned by modernization – the external imposition of so-called 'scientific' forest management systems. These examples raise questions about problems in current concepts of development assistance. The first section explores these issues in the context of Japanese mountain villages, focusing on changes in mountain and forest landscapes. Japanese mountain villages traditionally maintained symbiotic management systems where various resources circulated in long cycles, creating what I call a landscape of symbiosis. The forest policies implemented during the rapid economic growth of the later twentieth century, however, drastically shortened these cycles in the promotion of monocultures, resulting in a loss of the landscapes of symbiosis. The second section describes similar problems and changes in Himalayan communities brought about by social movements and government policies aimed at 'protecting' the Himalayan forests, which have come to be seen around the world as a precious natural heritage. This section clarifies the external logic of environmental protection and contrasts it to the local people's logic for protecting their everyday life, thus highlighting the importance of local practices developed in the everyday life of small communities for environmental protection.

In short, this work seeks to clarify the logic and importance of small communities' local activities. Of course, there are systematic pitfalls in the small community activities discussed in this work. I choose, however, not to analyze these pitfalls from the perspective of the history of thought. Instead, my intent is to focus on small communities' capacities to knowingly adapt to changing conditions and circumstances, occasionally falling into the pits, but then using local creativity and knowledge to relativize them. My objective is to emphasize the significant potential of small communities for dealing with the very real problems of the twenty-first century, without excessively romanticizing the small community way of life.

1 Life-environmentalism and Environmental Sociology Methods

Life-environmentalism as a method: Introduction

At the beginning of the twenty-first century, global environmental issues feel much closer to our everyday lives. Only a few decades ago, environmental issues were typically framed within a stereotypical dichotomy of perpetrators and victims; namely, between those who produce noxious odors or excessive noise or toxic waste, and those who suffer from such pollution. The strength and persistence of this stereotype derived from the fact that it did adequately explain many of the pollution issues that arose during Japan's rapid postwar economic growth.

Today, however, environmental issues are seen from perspectives that go far beyond this perpetrator-victim dichotomy and beyond the boundaries of the regions and countries in which such dichotomous relationships must be located. There is now a growing consensus that the life-sustaining natural resources of the Earth are rapidly and irreparably diminishing in such a way as to threaten life itself, including (but not limited to) human life. The most prominent example of this is widespread concern about the 'greenhouse effect,' one of the most important causes of global warming, caused by extensive deforestation of tropical rainforests, ever-increasing carbon-gas emissions from motor vehicles, and other consumption of fossil fuels. The understanding that this is a *global* problem has stimulated a much greater and more widespread awareness that each human being is a 'member of the Earth community.' Awareness of this rapidly growing problem had reached a critical mass by the early 1990s, as can be seen in the scope and substance of the Earth Summit (United Nations Conference on Environment and Development) held in Rio de Janeiro, Brazil, in 1992. The primary aim of this summit was to construct an 'environmentally sustainable world.' This, in a nutshell, is the central doctrine of global environmentalism, which regards the maintenance and protection of *all* forms of life on Earth as equal priorities.

Global environmentalism has subsequently begun to exert significant influence on governments around the world. The 1997 International Summit on Global Warming held in Kyoto is both an example and further evidence of such influence. Global warming is perhaps the 'flagship' issue of global environmentalism, as it clearly illustrates the need for perspectives that go beyond not only the perpetrator-victim dichotomy, but also every other type of social division (including nation, race, gender, generation or class) if we are to cope with the environmental issues caused by human activities. We have thus come to discuss these issues in terms of environmental theories that have been developed from a universal, transcendental perspective – the perspective of mankind *sui generis*, rather than of this or that specific group of people. From the perspective of these theories, the conflicts within a community and the local customs of residents can be disregarded as narrow-minded parochialism, regionalism or self-interest. In other words, it is simply outdated to focus on minor local conflicts or differences of opinion, when the very survival of humankind is at stake. In this sense, though, the global environmentalists' slogan, 'think global, act local,' invalidates the significance of 'thinking locally.'

Hence, my first objective here is to discuss (and re-validate) the significance of 'thinking locally, acting locally,' by focusing on how environmental consciousnesses have been generated in local communities and exploring how we might understand them through research. This will entail criticism of a dangerous spirit behind global environmentalism, which on the surface seems to be quite a reasonable perspective.

Approaches to environmental sociology can be broadly categorized into a 'sociology of environmental issues' and a 'sociology of coexistence with the environment' (see, for example, Iijima 1998). The approach followed here is derived from (and contributes to) life-environmentalism, a sub-category of the 'sociology of coexistence with the environment.' I focus on life-environmentalism because the sociology of environmental issues remains trapped in the perspective of the perpetrator-victim dichotomy, while sociology of coexistence with the environment, in contrast, recognizes and explores the diversity of relationships between people and their environment. The concepts and methodologies of these two fields of sociology are therefore quite different from one another. In short, life-environmentalism represents the concepts and methodology of the sociology of coexistence with the environment and is distinct from the sociology of environmental issues.

Environmental issues as ideology

Facts and justice as power-creating agents

The 1998 edition of *Kankyō Hakusho* (White paper on the environment in Japan) shows that the characteristics of environmental issues have changed significantly over the past three decades or so. Simply put, the focus of environmentalism has shifted from industrial pollution issues, where the perpetrator-victim stereotype was clearly visible – big businesses pursuing maximum profits irregardless of the cost to others, and innocent local residents victimized by the actions of these businesses – to urban/lifestyle-related issues, where the relationship between perpetrators and victims has blurred, if it has not been destroyed altogether. Indeed, the problems experienced by urban people, who are both the victims and the perpetrators at the same time, have become the central, and perhaps most pressing, environmental issues.

Let me take for example the significant contribution of motor vehicle emissions to global warming. By driving his/her own car, an individual may both damage the global environment and be a victim of the resulting climatic changes. What must we do to preserve life under these circumstances? *Kankyō Hakusho* appeals to the public to correctly understand the effects of human activities on the global environment and to act with such effects in mind. In other words, it urges people to modify or abandon lifestyles that simply focus on consumption and lack a global perspective.

Modern lifestyles are characterized by mass production, mass consumption and mass disposal. The central message and underlying tenet of global environmentalism is that this lifestyle is destroying the planet, and we therefore must break away from it. Global environmentalism asserts that the common target of human society for the twenty-first century must be a transition from a globalized society that places enormous burdens on the global environment to a society based on principles of recycling and coexistence with the environment. This argument is very persuasive. There can be no doubt that the globe is actually warming. Since the nineteenth century, the mean global surface temperature has risen by as much as $0.3–0.6°C$, and scientists are predicting that it will rise by an additional $2°C–5°C$ by the end of the twenty-first century. Furthermore, they calculate that this will cause the sea level to rise by around fifty centimeters. This data suggests that global warming is a real, extremely urgent problem that needs to be dealt with.

In fact the evidence supporting this hypothesis appears to be incontrovertible; and yet, there is a major fault in both the diagnoses and the prescribed remedy. That is, arguments mounted from the perspective of global environmentalism entail very specific conceptions of justice and ethics. From the perspective of global environmentalism, it is self-evident that the Earth is getting warmer and that it is the duty of humankind to deal with it promptly. Lurking within this apparent self-evidence, however, is a pattern of judgment that dismisses any questioning, criticism or denial of it as simply 'wrong,' 'outdated' or narrow-minded. In other words, what global environmentalism sees as self-evident objective facts are grounded in ethical judgments of right and wrong. In fact, any opinion that seems right and reasonable to anybody and everybody creates a space where power can be exercised in an extremely efficient manner. For a genuinely objective perspective, however, there must be a considerable distance between the fact of air pollution or rising surface temperature and the judgments of whether this is right or wrong, good or bad.

Of course, I certainly do not intend to deny or gloss over the fact that air pollution etcetera exist and significantly contribute to global warming. It is unquestionable that these are serious problems that must be addressed. But I do want to point out that global environmentalism has assumed many of the characteristics of a social ideology, in that judgments on these natural phenomena are made in the total absence of criticisms and questions. It can therefore appropriately be called a modernist ideology that mystifies its claims under the rubric of natural facts.

My point is that neither diagnostic analyses nor corrective prescriptions can be adequately derived from theory alone, but must instead be based on solid empirical research. Let me now discuss how to achieve this.

Ideology behind the creation of an environmental issue

The processes through which various natural and social phenomena come to be conceptualized as environmental issues are ideological in that they incorporate pre-established judgments of right and wrong, good and bad. These pre-established judgments, or rather the standards or norms that they entail, constitute the framework for understanding that a given phenomenon is a 'problem.'

For example, odor, noise, air pollution and rising temperature are typical categories of environmental 'problems.' This seems to be a completely reasonable way of understanding the associated phenomena. But is it? For just one example, there is no absolute and objective point at which sound comes to be regarded as noise. More concretely, crickets chirping on a long autumn night might be regarded as noise by some people, but as pleasantly musical by others. For another example, consider human waste, which today is understood to be an unhygienic source of noxious odors, but until the early 1960s in Japan was universally understood to be a resource 'too good to throw away.' What changed has nothing to do with the phenomena itself, but is rather social attitudes or beliefs, such that what was once too good to throw away has become too dangerous to keep around. The hegemonic social attitude to human waste in the modern world emphasizes only its negative aspects and demands that it be chemically treated and discharged somewhere safe. This perspective has completely forgotten, or refuses to acknowledge, the value of human waste as fertilizer, or in cultural terms. In short, what constitutes a 'problem' in the living environment differs significantly between cultures and individuals.

To overcome these differences and achieve a general consensus about the particular definition of various phenomena as 'problems' requires a strong ideological power. This (modern scientific perspective) power has encouraged us to ignore cultural or subjective value judgments to favor supposedly universal, rational standards. From this perspective we have precisely defined the point at which sound becomes noise (seventy decibels) as well as establishing absolute and quantifiable standards for E. coli bacteria and other organic matter content in our drinking water. Regardless of differences in specific circumstances, this ideological power draws absolute lines between what matters and what does not by measuring environmental phenomena in quantitative terms. The ideological power I refer to can be called modern science. This is integral to the driving force that created modern industrialized/mass-consumption society as well as, in its broadest sense, civil society. For our purposes, it can also be called the modern European way of thinking.

The 1998 edition of *Kankyō Hakusho* says that we should 'correctly understand the effects of our activities on the environment and act with such effects in mind' in order to redress environmental issues arising from contemporary urban lifestyles. This perspective represents the typical modern European way of thinking; it was born of the scientific approach in which the subject is objectified and understood according to supposedly universal and rational criteria. Modern society takes this way of thinking for granted because we have been taught that it is the one-true approach by our modern school education. It is not, however, self-evident that we should create 'issues' of certain observable phenomena. That is, the scientifically rational outlook is not the only correct way of thinking.

Thinking of environmental issues, of course, requires dealing with the actual environment. At the same time, however, we must recognize the often unconscious role of ideological principles and the exercise of power in our judgments that particular phenomena amount to environmental issues. As discussed, the construction of 'issues' always entails value judgments of right and wrong, good and bad – the same judgments, or standards, by which we tend to unconsciously regard ourselves as the 'just people' or the 'good people.' To be aware of the power of these unconscious frameworks on our judgments, it is important to adopt a way of understanding our environment that is different from the modern European scientific one. One alternative way of understanding the environment can be found embedded in our everyday life-worlds, as I discuss in the next section.

Modern knowledge and the everyday life-world

Thinking in the everyday life-world

According to the modern scientific paradigm, when we think about environmental issues we first categorize the various phenomena in our environment according to supposedly objective criteria, then establish quantifiable standards of normality for each phenomenon, and finally judge whether or not a particular phenomenon is normal or an 'issue.' But how did people make judgments about their environment before this way of thinking was established?

In pre-modern Japan, rural villages had developed very ingenious environmental management systems over long periods of time, by which they controlled irrigation and drainage as well as mountains and forests. Let me illustrate this briefly through the example of the water management practices in a village on the shore of Lake Biwa in Shiga Prefecture (Torigoe and Kada, 1984). I discuss the case in more detail in Chapter Four.

Until a small water-supply system was built in 1957, the village had been entirely dependent on the river running through it for water. Villagers drew their drinking water from the same river in which they washed their dishes and clothes. They believed that the river water was cleansed by the god of water in a three-*shaku* (about ninety-one centimeter) run, and had only a few unwritten rules restricting their use of the river. These included things such as: 'do not wash underwear in the river; use a ditch in a different water system,' and 'do not urinate into the river, or you will have a swollen tummy banana.'

Each household drew its water from the river and drained its wastewater into a wastewater tank. Each house had its own wastewater tank and a wastewater osmotic cell (called '*suimon*' and '*suikomi*,' respectively). When the osmotic cell was full, the clear upper portion was mixed with manure and used as fertilizer for fields. Algae growing in the river was eliminated each year on the annual *tokobori* (river dredging) day by all of the villagers working together. The algae itself was then auctioned for use as fertilizer in the rice fields. These are just some of the ways that the villagers both used and protected the river at the same time. This water management system was seamlessly integrated into their everyday lives.

The important point of this example for present purposes is that it clearly demonstrates that an efficient and effective set of practices can exist entirely independently of any rational or logical explanation of the system or the problems that it addresses. To put this another way, the rationality of the system of practice is totally independent of the rationality of the way of understanding/ thinking. It follows that even communities that are lacking in the rationally organized knowledge of environmental protection and explicit frameworks for understanding their environment, are not automatically lacking in effectively organised practices of environmental protection or management. Communities have their own working knowledge and frameworks for understanding, which are not always rationally organized or lucidly explicated. This simple point is frequently overlooked by researchers who adhere to modern scientific hegemony. In such communities, the 'place of everyday life' has not been divided into separate fields, such as the economy, politics and the environment, that are understood to exist independently of each other. Instead, these fields are actually 'embedded' in the everyday life-world.

To understand this, we must begin our research by detailing every aspect of the daily lives of community members and then retrospectively trace their memory of the past. We interview people to learn of the individual events and activities in which their daily routines are depicted. Only through this process can the economic, political or environmental conditions embedded in their everyday life-worlds be revealed. Now let me explain what this means for our framework of understanding.

Merits and demerits of modern knowledge

The modern framework of understanding severed the aforementioned fields of the everyday life-world from each other in order to treat them as independent systems and then produced an explicit, rational system of knowledge for each field. This has generated floods of specialized theories and explanations in fields such as modern economics and sociology. Our knowledge of the environment has also been subject to the segregation of this modern knowledge system. This system of knowledge was originally born of expediency – to deal with increasingly complex fields in a rational and efficient manner. It was more convenient to identify and separate individual fields in order to understand them rationally. But this way of understanding that was originally born of expediency soon came to be regarded as absolute (objective) truth. From this perspective then, it appears to be obvious that all of our knowledge of everything must be organized in an explicit, logical manner.

In many respects, this modern way of understanding was quite appropriate for categorizing the phenomena of the world and understanding it in a rational manner. This was not only expeditious, but also highly effective. As mentioned above, however, the rational scientific approach is not the only way of understanding the world, and our current environmental situation suggests that it is no longer (if it ever was) adequate to the challenges facing us. So, what kind of methods can we apply to recognize the various fields embedded in the everyday life-world that are not organized into explicit systems? To do this, we need to focus on practices that are neither explicit nor logical. A prime example of this is the practices that are rooted in a community's customs and conventions. Customs and rules such as 'you must clap your hands when you worship at a Shinto shrine' or 'you may wash vegetables only at this watering place' are not accompanied by rational explanations. When asked why they maintain such customs, the practitioners can only reply that 'it's our tradition,' or 'that's just the way we do it.' These kinds of customary practices that have no explicit explanations are typical of the veins of knowledge embedded in a community.

The scientific approach to understanding phenomena entails reducing them to their constituent elements, analyzing these elements independently, and then attempting to reconstruct the overall structure by logically recombining our understanding of the relationships among them. This approach to knowledge is definitive of the natural sciences, such as chemistry and medicine, but has also played a dominant role in the social sciences, such as sociology and economics. As suggested above, this approach, which is often called positivism, has become the 'officially sanctioned' way of thinking in modern civil society. In our everyday lives, though, we often use other ways of understanding, in which it is common to understand a complete phenomenon as a single entity (i.e. without reducing it to constituent elements), and to deal with matter in traditional ways rather than in an explicit, logical manner. In everyday life, it is not uncommon to take actions that are logically contradictory or inconsistent.

Local concepts for understanding and managing the environment typically fall into this latter category. The everyday life-world is rife with wisdom and practices that often lack rational, systematic explanations and are often accompanied by contradictory explanations, but which have nevertheless resulted in the creation of effective systems for protecting the local environment. Although this wisdom and these practices are not accompanied by advanced scientific theories or lofty conceptualizations, as is global environmentalism, they have nevertheless fulfilled their objectives of protecting the local environment, often in extremely ingenious and clever ways, as described later. Importantly, they were created free of the ideological demands for universal standards of justice or similar. This wisdom and these practices, which in many ways can contribute to overcoming the limitations of modernism, are born in the 'place of everyday life.'

We must, however, carefully refrain from attempting to organize this way of understanding, and its potential, in a scientifically logical manner. Organizing inexplicit, non-rational knowledge into explicit, rational knowledge would nullify its fundamental essence. The delicacy of this problematic has been concisely described by Yoshiyuki Tsurumi, who criticized the one-dimensional understanding of modern science and pioneered the attempt to see the world from the perspective of the 'place of everyday life.' He says:

> It seems that discussions about the economy in the Third World have largely revolved around the perspective of "spontaneous development." This concept attempts to ascertain the Third World's course of history, assuming that it must have been different from that of the modern

Western world. I broadly agree with this concept, but the question of how we should define the "spontaneousness" of spontaneous development is quite difficult...Although I agree that we should seek to understand more about spontaneous development, I think we should refrain from theorizing it in too much detail. In the course of theorization, part of the real wealth is often overlooked. Excessive theorization may turn out to be a mere judgment by the outside world. (1990: 107–8)

The concept of 'place of everyday life'

Development as virtue

I have thus far discussed modern civil society's way of understanding through segregating the subject from its context and reducing it to its constituent elements before attempting to grasp the overall structure in terms of 'natural laws' or 'universals,' and then to explain these 'laws' in a consistent, rational and logical manner. Furthermore, I have argued that knowledge so obtained underpins the concept of global environment and corresponding environmental issues. Finally, I have argued that while this 'scientific' knowledge system has become the dominant paradigm in the contemporary world, other ways of understanding have been formed in the everyday life-world.

Let me discuss these two ways of understanding in more detail through a case where both were put into practice. The case takes place in a mountain village community in Nepal named Namche Bazaar (hereinafter referred to as 'Namche') where I conducted fieldwork using the methods mentioned above. Namche is a village of Sherpas on a mountainside in the Himalayas (Furukawa 1992) (described in more detail in Chapter Five).

This beautiful village was made known to the 'outside' world by a New Zealander, Sir Edmund Hillary. Hillary is best known as the first person to reach the summit of Mt. Everest, the world's highest mountain. He first visited Namche in 1951. Amongst his notes that described his impression of the village, he wrote: 'The whole region was dense with greenery. Below the village, giant conifers soared.' But when I first visited Namche in 1989, there were scarcely any trees to be seen near the village except for some recently planted saplings. I was told that they had been planted about a dozen years earlier, so the village must have been surrounded by logged areas instead of forests before then. The radical change in the beautiful highland setting 'discovered' by

Hillary was an enormous change in the community's everyday life-world – the development of tourism.

Hillary claims that the development that led to the region's deforestation was primarily his fault. After becoming the first man to reach the summit of Mt. Everest, he had wanted to repay the Sherpas for their role in his great achievement. When he visited Namche, he witnessed villagers who lived in poverty, with no access to the outside world, or to proper medical care or education. Hillary decided he had to do what he could to improve the lives of these villagers. By the mid-1960s, he had water supplied to the village and bridges constructed in and around the village. He also established local schools and hospitals. And he had an airport built near the village so that building materials for river improvement works could be flown-in to the village. All of these were part of his village development project driven by his passion to help the villagers to enjoy at least some of the benefits of a modern life.

Hillary's identification of an 'issue' and his conception of the type of development that could 'address' it begin with a judgment that the village of Namche was lacking in something that a community *should have* in the modern world. In other words, Hillary's conception of development was grounded in the standards of modern (scientific) knowledge, where any subject is regarded as part of a larger (global) system and its value is judged by (supposedly) universal criteria. From this perspective, introducing certain elements of modern civilization into a poor undeveloped village is indisputably a virtuous act. Indeed, Hillary raised donations in the West from many lovers of the Himalayas and worked hard to modernize the Namche community from a genuine sense of what is right, just and virtuous.

Nature conservation as justice

Over time, however, Hillary began to question this approach to development. He could see that the development of Namche, born of his affection for and gratitude to the Sherpas, resulted in a rapid change in the local community. A boom in Himalayan mountaineering in the 1970s and another in trekking in the 1980s brought large numbers of tourists to Namche. This resulted in a situation where nearly half of the 140-odd households in the village ran lodges for tourists and earned an income as trekking guides. The rapid increase in the number of tourists brought a corresponding increase in the demand for fuel, which resulted in cutting down the trees around the village for firewood. As the demand continued to grow, the forests around the village gradually disappeared. Thus, contrary to Hillary's intention to protect the beautiful village and help the villagers, this precious environment was lost through reckless deforestation.

Faced with this totally transformed situation, Hillary radically revised his development policy to focus his efforts on nature conservation. He sought help from the New Zealand government. The New Zealand government had been conducting basic research for forest resource protection in the Himalayas during the late 1960s and early 1970s. Hillary put a proposal to the New Zealand government to establish a forest national park in the region including Namche Village.

The New Zealand government immediately dispatched an investigation team, which subsequently reported that the uncontrolled exploitation of the forests might lead to the destruction of the Sherpa community and would be a great loss to humankind. Based on this report, in 1975 the New Zealand government decided to provide financial support for five years to create a national park and invited five Nepalese to New Zealand for training in forest protection. In 1976, a national park was established in the region, including Namche Village – the result of the collaboration of the New Zealand and Nepalese governments, with the former supplying financial aid. Thus, Hillary converted from a developmentalist to a conservationist, a defender of forests, standing on the side of the national administration that prohibited and prosecuted locals logging in the park for building materials and firewood.

The establishment of the national park confronted the Namche villagers with a completely new, imported concept – the idea that their forests are the common property of humankind and must therefore be managed by the state. The mountain scenery that they had always taken-for-granted was 'discovered' as a natural resource in-itself, and they were now expected to play a front line 'role' in the global battle for environmental protection. They were no longer free to fell trees or graze their livestock in the surrounding area. This idea of 'common property' and the expected 'role' of the Sherpas derives from universal conceptions of justice, the violation of which may be regarded as 'evil' and is often 'illegal.'

The programs offered to the community to help to realize this conception of justice were also formulated on the basis of universal and scientific frameworks. The local wisdom that had developed in the community over many generations for managing the environment was disregarded, considered to be 'behind,' because it consisted of unsystematic knowledge that was neither explicit nor scientific. New standards and strictures based on modern science were imposed upon the villagers. Local knowledge was supplanted by imported concepts.

Traditionally, Sherpa communities such as Namche recognized men called '*nawas*' who played a unique role in their community (further detailed in Chapter Five). The *nawa* system can be regarded as an environment management system embedded in the everyday life of the community. Some *nawas* controlled tree harvesting activities while others managed livestock movements, for example. Each village appointed several experienced men to each of these roles. Forests and livestock, or environment and economics, were controlled by one integrated system.

By contrast, global environmentalism regards forests and livestock as separate fields, independent from one another. Global environmentalism prioritizes forest protection and natural resource management, thus only producing theories and procedures for the protection of forests. This was precisely the objective of sending Sherpas to New Zealand for education in forest management. These educated foresters played important roles in introducing a modern warden system to the Namche community as the 'right' technology. Under this new warden system, access to the forests was restricted by laws and governed by formal systems to manage the trees in an efficient manner. Namche villagers were taught that only modern technology and universal concepts could protect this precious natural resource for the good of all humankind. In the process, the *nawa* system was rejected and replaced. The environmental protection system embedded in the community's everyday life was undermined and destroyed.

Wisdom in the everyday life-world

Enchanted by the natural environment of the Himalayas, and concerned for the Sherpas, Hillary did an about-face from development to protection after he witnessed the environmental destruction and the effects on the local people's everyday lives that followed his development initiatives. As indicated above, though, the underlying understanding upon which these two alternatives were based had not changed at all, despite his apparent change of direction. Whether he intended to develop or protect the community, his practice was grounded in rational, systematic concepts, at the center of which were the values of universal justice. In other words, his modern European worldview was not shaken at all – in both approaches Hillary remained true to the concept that a rational understanding is the only universal and absolutely correct way of understanding.

The Sherpa community was forced to accept this powerful worldview and its associated practices. The traditional *nawas* of the forest were transformed into forest wardens appointed as rangers in the national park, who were supposed to be responsible for supervising or prohibiting the locals' access to the forests. In the process, the *nawas* of livestock were abolished. Hence, the traditional forest management practices that were based on the local knowledge of the *nawas* of forests and livestock in each village were supplanted by a modern, centralized forest protection system. That is, forest management was taken out of the hands of the villagers and the local community.

Were these Sherpas, then, simply subjected to the external forces of development and protection? Did they passively submit to these external impositions? Detailed research into the villagers' reactions has revealed that they have actively and firmly established the 'place' of their everyday lives even while accepting the conditions imposed on them by external powers. The practices through which they create an everyday life-world between development and protection are inherently critical of the modern way of thinking described above. The Sherpas have employed innovative and clever practices in response to the national park system and the forest protection measures introduced by Hillary and others.

For example, the national park regulations strictly limited the number of trees a villager was permitted to harvest during his/her lifetime to three. Violations of these regulations were subject to punishment by national law. Yet compliance would leave the villagers with too little lumber to build even minimal housing, much less to meet their daily demands for firewood. These regulations, which effectively prohibited the villagers from maintaining their existing living conditions, were imposed on them in the name of abstract principles such as 'protecting the common property of humankind.' Yet the villagers did not openly object to or resist these regulations. Instead, they developed ways of being seen to comply with the regulations while effectively nullifying them to protect their livelihoods and ways of life. One of the ways in which they manipulated the new regulatory system took advantage of the fact that there was no limit to the number of dead trees that the villagers could collect; they would cut a tree halfway through, and then wait until it died to cut it down as a dead tree. Another method (frequently used when someone wanted more than three trees) was to secretly ask an 'outsider' to fell a tree and leave it in the forest for the villager to collect later. Through these and other similarly desperate measures, the villagers effectively undermined the regulations imposed from above.

Importantly, the villagers' disregard for these regulations does not necessarily result in reckless deforestation or wanton development. The logic of capitalism regards human beings as seekers of maximum profit, from which it follows that if we leave people without strong external regulations and sanctions for deviation, society will plunge into anarchic chaos and be threatened with collapse. Communities, though, are naturally endowed with their own control systems. This is exactly what enables each community to protect their community life by managing their resources, including water, forests and fields. Wherever these indigenous community-based control systems have been replaced with centralized, rationalized systems various problems have arisen. And, of course, the displacement of localized knowledges and practices by rationalized scientific knowledge and practice is a central characteristic of the general trend towards modernization that has engulfed communities around the globe in the latter half of the twentieth century. In this sense, they are part of irreversible changes in history. Clearly, rejecting modernization and its impact on communities and demanding a return to traditional lifestyles would be a romantic, utopian approach that is intrinsically inconsistent and unrealistic.

Namche's experience indicates that modern forest management systems can prove to be obstructions to the way of life of local communities, and that the local people's efforts to circumvent imposed regulations need not result in reckless deforestation or rampant development. Communities only exist because they have developed various arts and techniques for protecting their member's daily lives, even though these may not be organized in a logical and systematic manner. The *nawa* system is but one example of this. By reevaluating the wisdom with which a community has sustained itself, we can begin to explore the possibility of environmental protection practices based on local knowledge. We need not travel far down this road to realize the importance of discussing the environment from the perspective of maintaining and developing the everyday lives of local peoples, rather than severing and segregating the various parts of their daily lives in order to deal with 'issues.'

Concept and methods of life-environmentalism

Birth of life-environmentalism

As described above, everyday life-worlds were once defined by various wisdoms and systems that differ from the rational, scientific knowledges and systems that dominate the modern Western world. It is true that everyday life-worlds were typically neither explicit nor 'scientific.' Through these seemingly non-rational, non-articulated local knowledges, however, we have been able to find effective ways of protecting communities and their environments. The starting point of life-environmentalism is to re-evaluate these local wisdoms and practices and to incorporate our findings into approaches to dealing with today's environmental issues.

Responding to his concerns for the people of a small village in the Himalayas, Hillary pursued two diametrically opposed agendas – economic development and environmental protection. In pursuit of economic development, forests were cleared and tourist lodges were constructed, providing the villagers with various opportunities to earn money. Then, in an effort to redress the environmental impact of this development, he adopted a protectionist approach that essentially consisted of designating the region a national park and prohibiting any logging in the forest to conserve the ecosystem. For the local Sherpas, both approaches were manifestations of enormous forces from the outside world. The villagers continued their everyday lives in the shadow of these external forces, at times lightly parrying them and at other times being almost totally immersed in them. But along the way, using their own long-established forestry management practices, the villagers compensated for the protectionist approach's neglect of their everyday lives, by putting the brakes on excessive development and cleverly evading laws and regulations. The ideas and practices that prioritize their own long-established living systems provide the bases of life-environmentalism.

Note, however, that the Namche villagers' practices are not exceptional. We find similar practices, for example, in rural Japanese villages. There is a growing trend among fieldworkers to look for the abundant potential of the 'place of everyday life,' which has been ignored by more rigorously 'scientific' researchers. This trend originated among those fieldworkers who encountered such practices in rural Japanese villages; namely, researchers specializing in rural sociology and cultural anthropology. One of the earliest and most recognized of these works is *Mizu to hito no kankyō-shi* (The history of the environment for water and people), which reports the findings of Hiroyuki Torigoe's research group from their intensive research in a village near Lake Biwa, the unique techniques of environmental protection embedded in the local community's everyday life, and the history of the villagers' attempts to improve their quality of life, including initiatives to actively tamper with nature (Torigoe and Kada et al. 1984). The group adopted the title 'life-environmentalism' to refer to an approach that gives priority to local living systems. This term also refers to the theory guiding this research where, as described above, all aspects of the everyday lives of community members are described, followed by recording their memories of the past.

What is life-environmentalism?

Based on their fieldwork experience, Torigoe and his colleagues reject the way that environmental issues are conventionally understood in scientific discourses – that is, framed in the dichotomy between development and protection. Their approach would attempt to find a place for the Sherpas' traditional way of life in Namche in efforts to deal with pressing environmental issues. Importantly, they recognize the Sherpas' traditional way of life as one that prioritizes the maintenance and protection of itself and its native environment. One extreme view of environmental issues considers 'untampered' nature to be the most desirable. This perspective regards humans as merely one part of the environment and focuses on the maintenance and restoration of ecological systems, regardless of the impact on local people's everyday lives. At the other end of the spectrum, others consider economic development to be the highest priority, regardless of its impact on the environment or local people's everyday lives. This perspective is firmly grounded in a scientific worldview which believes that the application of modern technology will eventually but inevitably solve any environmental issues that arise along the way. This is the perspective that underpins, for example, the large-scale 'River Basin Sewerage System' project for Lake Biwa, which will collect all of the wastewater in the lake basin in a single place for treatment.

Recognizing that modern conceptions of environmental protection dissociate nature from the everyday lives of the people who live in any given environment, Torigoe et al. (1984) developed a new conception that gives the highest priority to 'protecting everyday life' of the local residents *in order to* protect the environment. From this new perspective, 'protecting everyday life' means safeguarding customary living systems. Here, 'living systems' signify social systems related to people's everyday lives, including families and the various groups and organizations of a local community. In other words, life-environmentalism regards small communities as being the strategically most important living system.

One of the characteristics of life-environmentalism emphasized by its advocates is to think from the 'perspective of the everyday lives of people living in the local community.' This approach is subject to the following criticism: thinking from the 'perspective of residents' lacks any substantial meaning, because residents' perspectives vary and cannot be regarded as homogenous. Yet life-environmentalism seeks a 'perspective from the *everyday lives* of residents,' not a homogenous 'perspective of residents.' More specifically, it prioritizes protecting the everyday life of residents *in order to* protect the environment. Hence, to the extent that the 'perspective of residents' and the 'perspective of the everyday lives of residents' are in agreement, there is no conflict here. But where these two perspectives diverge – more specifically, if residents choose to destroy their everyday lives – then life-environmentalism will criticize residents from the 'perspective of the everyday lives of residents.' It is impossible to represent the perspectives of all residents, since each individual is different. It is, however, possible to develop a view that attempts to protect their everyday lives.

Torigoe (1997) explains this approach in terms of three main characteristics of life-environmentalism: empiricism, an organization theory, and a theory of power. Of these, empiricism is at the core of life-environmentalism's breakthrough in modern knowledge. From the perspective of life-environmentalism, empiricism means that when we attempt to predict the effects of extant human activities and potential future activities, we must delve beneath the apparent surface phenomena and probe deeply into the past experiences that underlie those activities in order to conduct analyses based on these experiences. More specifically, when we observe that some people behave in certain ways, we cannot take their behavior at face-value but must evaluate it in terms of the experiences that underlie the behavior.

This approach considers people's action or behavior as products of the forces of circumstance. In other words, they must choose their course of action from a limited menu of potential choices. The option they have chosen emerges as observable actions or behaviors. At the same time, the other potential choices remain unrealized. But any of these may emerge later, depending on circumstances. If we focus solely on the chosen option, we fail to see the other, unrealized, possibilities. And we thus fail to recognize the true depth of the everyday life-world of the people who exhibit particular actions or behaviors, resulting in a total misunderstanding of the community in question.

Of course, community members' opinions and perspectives on their particular environmental issues differ. In fact, it often seems that their opinions are so sharply divided that there is no scope for mutual understanding. Yet communities do typically manage to reach some sort of consensus on the issues confronting them, through processes that often entail some of the members drastically changing at least their behavior, if not also their opinions. The process by which these behaviors and opinions change is not solely attributable to the binding social forces characteristic of rural communities. Drastic change is only possible in the first place because the original choices were selected from a limited menu of options under a given set of circumstances. Clusters of differing opinions among community members can be used to identify different groups within the community. Yet communities do not continue to exist if their members are incapable of resolving their differences through some set of procedures or another. With this understanding, life-environmentalism draws a clear line between the disagreements or disparities in understanding among community members and the mutual understandings collectively created by the community as a whole, and deals only with the latter. For convenience, life-environmentalism chooses not to deal with the inner struggles of individuals within the community, focusing instead on the consensus that they actually do achieve. As Torigoe explains: 'I cannot tell what a person is thinking, but I can tell what *people* are thinking' (1989: 45).

Our research method

Our research method is not original or unique, but is based on well-established fieldwork methods in rural sociology and cultural anthropology. Our primary method is to adopt the perspective of the people living in the target community by participating in their everyday life-world. Importantly, we must be ready to conceptualize the entire, comprehensive world of their everyday lives, rather than simply interviewing individual people or collecting materials relating to a specific issue. For example, let us suppose that in a certain local community the residents' opinions are divided on the proposed construction of a garbage or industrial waste treatment plant in the community. From the perspective of life-environmentalism it is not sufficient to conduct a formal, house-to-house survey *exclusively* on this issue. Instead, we must also ask residents various details about their life stories, such as how they customarily managed their water supply system, or details of their traditional shrine festivals, or what hardships they had endured during wartime. These stories may appear on the surface to have nothing to do with the issue in question, but are necessary to uncover important facts about the ways in which residents have constructed their everyday lives. The wisdom, systems and values embedded in their everyday lives can be revealed only through a comprehensive approach. What is conventionally called social research has been conducted by isolating the particular subject matter in question from the entirety of people's everyday life and discussing it as a logical unit. A critique of this methodology is the starting point for our research methodology.

While there is nothing particularly novel about the methodology employed in this work, there is nevertheless a significant difference vis-à-vis conventional social research methods. The view of human beings – the anthropology – upon which our research is based, is markedly different from the one that underlies conventional, positivistic methods of social research. In conventional research, researchers collect various kinds of information by interviewing informants and analyze the collected information within a rational, logical framework. In this approach, researchers are puzzled if one informant answers the same question differently when asked by different interviewers or at different times or places. When this occurs, these researchers can only conclude that the informant is not adequately qualified and that any information that he or she provides is unreliable. For these researchers, a reliable informant is one who gives the same answer to each question time and again, regardless of who asked it and of the time or the social setting in which it was asked. This is the positivist anthropology upon which modern science is based. From this perspective, human beings do not lie, do not respond vaguely to questions, do not become emotionally disturbed regardless of how insensitively the questions are put, and do not discuss the politics of the situation. The ideal informant has a near-perfect, chronologically-organized memory.

In our experience of fieldwork, however, such an informant is very rare. Each of our informants seems to have a rather selective memory of the past and told a different story in each interview, depending on his/her mood or circumstances. Sometimes they had emotional outbursts, and sometimes they explicitly framed their responses in terms of their political attitudes, beliefs and interests. In fact, these informants are far more likely to conform to what Matsuda (1989) identified as a 'turnaround culture' than the consistent, linear reporters expected by positivism. Matsuda uses the term 'turnaround culture' to refer to the ways that villagers frequently, for example, present a strong developmentalist position in one interview and then in the next interview eloquently advocate a protectionist position, or they might present as a staunch supporter of a reformist political party in one interview and as a strong conservative party supporter in the next. These turnarounds, which are far more common than the hypothetical alternative (consistency regardless of context), have not been properly accounted for in social research.

From the perspective of life-environmentalism, the particular opinion(s) expressed by an informant in a particular interview at a particular time are not considered to be fixed attributes. Rather, we accept that the particular opinion that was expressed was selected from several potential choices in accordance with the informant's subjective assessment of the particular circumstances in which the interview occurred, and for his/her own convenience. Demanding logical and/or chronological consistency in the expression of opinions and behaviors is to attach too much meaning to them. In fact, we can safely say that the positivists' over-emphasis on transient opinions and behavior has significantly occluded our vision of the creativity of the everyday life-world.

Environmental sociology and life-environmentalism

In this section I trace changes in environmental issues while providing an overview of how environmental sociology has dealt with those changes, and seek an appropriate place for life-environmentalism within environmental sociology. In the process I also discuss the methodologies characteristic of environmental sociology in relation to changes in the nature of environmental issues.

Environmental sociology deals with environmental issues in a broad sense. That is, it deals not only with social problems arising from environmental issues, such as negative health impacts or the destruction of the natural environment, but also with our continuous involvement in environmental management in our everyday lives.

As discussed in the Introduction, the social problems arising from environmental issues are dealt with by the 'sociology of environmental issues,' while our involvement in environmental management is addressed by the 'sociology of coexistence with the environment.' Environmental sociology is composed of these two distinct and separable fields.

What follows here is an overview of changes in environmental issues with an emphasis on an holistic picture of the environment – from specific environmental pollution issues to our more general involvement in environmental management in everyday life. This is followed by a discussion of the characteristics and research fields of environmental sociology, and finally a brief mention of some specific studies that reveal the types of topics dealt with by environmental sociology.[1]

Environmental issues and changes in people's awareness

Establishment of 'environmental sociology'

Changes in people's awareness of environmental issues are inseparable from the gradual emergence of environmental sociology as a field of study. For example, the Environmental Sociology Workshop was established in the 1990s, and soon developed into the Japanese Society for Environmental Sociology. The emergence of this field is in part due to the realization that sociology cannot be limited by social relationships among people, but must also take into account the relationship between people and their environment. Further adding impetus to the development of environmental sociology was the worldwide growth of environmental awareness at the end of the 1980s that positioned environmental issues as a major concern to people, resulting in a rapid increase in the number of studies on environmental issues and nature conservation.

Sociology typically aims to elucidate social phenomena in terms of relationships between persons, between a person (or persons) and a group (or groups), or between groups – in other words, social relationships. Everyday life, however, is not composed solely of such relationships. That is, while sociology conventionally posits society as being outside of nature, a significant proportion of human enterprise entails dealing directly with nature. For a start, our bodies cannot be sustained through social relationships alone, but are always also part of the natural ecosystem. As our modern way of life has increasingly had a negative effect on the natural ecosystem, we have become more acutely aware of how our everyday lives are grounded in the logic of this ecosystem.

Although we are 'naturally' embedded in the natural ecosystem, the growing awareness of this situation has been brought to our attention by specific effects in our living environment. For example, the increasing incidence of pollen allergies in the population are manifestations of various changes that have occurred in our everyday life-world. Other examples include the increasing importance of taking specific measures to treat the waste products generated by urban lifestyles, and the poor urban living environment, which becomes starkly apparent when residents shift their focus from the city to the world outside. As these phenomena have become tangible at the level of everyday life they have been defined and explained as 'environmental issues.' In the process, theories of environmental issues have been formulated to explain the various problems that are being experienced.

Of course, even before the general public became widely aware of these environmental issues, human industry had created numerous environmental problems – most commonly pollution – and caused widespread damage around the world. In Japan, incidents of such damage began to be frequently reported by newspapers and had become a major social issue by the late 1960s. This damage, though, was understood at the time to inflict suffering only on particular individuals or communities, like typhoons or earthquakes, and was thus not an issue of concern to the everyday lives of others who were at a distance from the residents of the affected communities. As mentioned above, we became increasingly and more generally aware of these environmental issues as they began to have more concrete effects on our bodies and our living environments. But we must not underestimate the important role that the categorization of the changes taking place as 'environmental issues' had on the development of our growing understanding that they might affect any or all of us. And as mentioned, the dominant factor in the development of this common understanding was the conceptualization of 'global environmental issues,' as typified by global warming.

Against the backdrop of this rapidly expanding understanding, sociological studies of environmental issues such as pollution were brought together in a new sub-discipline called environmental sociology. For example, the following four books were published between 1983 and 1985: Daikichi Irokawa (ed.) (1983) *Minamata no keiji* (Revelation of Minamata) (two volumes), (see in particular Kazuko Tsurumi's chapter in volume one); Hiroyuki Torigoe and Yukiko Kada (eds) (1984) *Mizu to hito no kankyō-shi* (The history of the environment for water and people); Nobuko Iijima (1984b) *Kankyō mondai to higaisha undō* (Environmental issues and victim movements); and Harutoshi Funabashi et al. (1985) *Shinkansen kōgai* (Shinkansen pollution). These four social studies each deal with environmental issues. According to our typology, the first two books can be categorized as sociology of coexistence with the environment, and the latter two as sociology of environmental issues. These works provide important tools to environmental sociology, including: the spontaneous development theory, life-environmentalism, the perpetrator-victim dichotomy, and beneficiary/affected zones. When they were published, the field of environmental sociology did not yet exist, at least not in Japan. Hence these tools were originally produced as applications of theories of social change, rural sociology, regional sociology, organizational sociology, or social movement theories.

These were among many works published in the first half of the 1980s that generated momentum towards the creation of a new sub-discipline of sociology, called environmental sociology. The establishment of environmental sociology as an academic discipline began with the formation of the Japanese Association for Environmental Sociology in 1990, was consolidated by the foundation of the Japanese Society for Environmental Sociology in 1993, and was completed by the launch of the *Journal of Environmental Sociology* in 1995. In the process, studies that were originally conducted in fields such as regional sociology or social movements acquired new meaning and were repositioned in the 1990s as the nascent works of environmental sociology.

Among the four books listed above, Iijima's work primarily reports the results of her research conducted in the 1970s, when pollution was rampant. The other books typically report on original research conducted in the years immediately preceding their publication. These books all have something in common: they all develop original theories based on long-term research, which allows them to create theories in accordance with Merton's notion of a middle range theory. Briefly, Merton argued that in the development of environmental issues and sociological theories, we should not simply apply existing theories and search for evidence that supports them, but should instead modify our theories as required by individual case studies, and in the process, create new theories. This process is characteristic of these four books.

Periodization of the history of environmental issues

Let me now briefly review how environmental issues have changed over time. In Japan, as in many other countries, many environmental problems began to arise along with modernization (Andō 1984). And, as elsewhere, these environmental issues have become more serious with the steady advance of industrialization.

Researchers have therefore made attempts to classify changing environmental issues chronologically, focusing on the impact of advancing industrialization. The most significant of these attempts in Japan is Nobuko Iijima et al. (1997) *Kōgai/rōsai/shokugyō-byō nenpyō* (The chronological table of environmental pollution, industrial accidents and occupational disease) published by Kōgai Taisaku Gijutsu Dōyūkai (Association of Environmental Pollution Control Technology). This is a revised edition of the 1970 publication *Kōgai oyobi rōdō saigai nenpyō* (The chronological table of environmental pollution and industrial accidents) by the same association.

These chronological tables were compiled with data accumulated in answer to the following questions: 'How have the life and health of residents/workers been destroyed under the capitalist system? What were the reactions of capital and the government to this destruction?' This table was not originally intended to divide the history of environmental issues in Japan into periods; it only broadly distinguishes the history of the feudal age, the modern age and the present age. We can, however, identify changes in environmental issues and in people's awareness of them from the chronological table, which is organized into six grouping axes: 'environmental pollution/destruction,' 'residents/supporters,' 'business and industry,' 'national and local governments,' 'industrial accidents/occupational disease and workers,' and 'remarks.' The table makes it clear that changes in environmental issues have resulted from the sum total of: the occurrence of specific environmental damage, in addition to the reactions of residents, their supporters, business and industry, and national and local governments to this damage. Changes in people's awareness of environmental issues can also be deduced by comparing the two editions of this table.

Based on this chronological table and her own research, Iijima (ed.) (1993) proposed that the history of environmental issues in Japan might be periodized by: types of source and victim; the government's reactions; and the action and behavior of victims and/or residents.

From this perspective, the history of environmental issues in Japan can be periodized as: (1) Changes in source of problems, as the focus of environmental issues shifted from the pollution produced by local heavy industries, as typified by the four major pollution cases[2] and Mizushima Industrial Complex in Okayama Prefecture, to more various and widespread issues, such as air pollution, well-water pollution, land subsidence, and noise pollution around airports and along Shinkansen (bullet train) lines, and then to pollution produced by the everyday lifestyles of ordinary citizens, such as photochemical smog, the dust pollution produced by studded tires, and garbage disposal problems in megacities; (2) at the same time, the affected 'victims' of specific incidents expanded from local residents in close proximity to the source of the pollutants to larger populations; and (3) in line with these changes, victims broadened their outlook from campaigns denouncing pollution, such as the four major pollution lawsuits, to wholesale reviews of modern consumerist lifestyles, as seen in recycling campaigns, and to environmental movements with broader objectives for natural or historical conservation.[3] These movements developed into campaigns aiming to prevent the destruction of the natural and living environment by public works projects, such as the construction of the Nagara River estuary weir in Mie Prefecture and the reclamation works at Isahaya Bay, Nagasaki Prefecture. In response to such campaigns, the Japanese government enacted pollution regulations setting relatively strict standards during the late 1960s and early 1970s. In the late 1970s, however, the government began to relax these standards. Hence, with the exception of a few years before and after 1970, the Japanese government was consistently reluctant to enact significant measures against environmental problems.

This gives us the understanding that, amid the ongoing environmental problems (pollution) resulting from consistent industrialization and its contradiction, people's lifestyles had changed by the late 1970s to such an extent that consumers were recognized as part of the source of environmental problems along with industry. Speaking of types of environmental issues, the initial form was pollution. In pollution issues, the contradiction between environment protection and the consistent industrial policy – which had been pursued since the Meiji Period – erupted in geographical areas where the causative industries were based, due to the rapid expansion of production during the rapid economic growth of the early postwar years. This has been overtaken (but not supplanted) by a new type of problem – everyday life-related environmental issues which are significantly generated by the lifestyles of ordinary citizens.

From an absolutist or universalist scientific perspective, the environmental problems generated by governments and businesses pursuing industrialization, and those generated by everyday life-related factors have essentially the same nature. This understanding is necessary when discussing environmental issues, but so is a perspective that maintains that everyday life-related environmental issues should be clearly distinguished from pollution issues.

Summarizing this history of environmental issues we can see that there are significant differences in the nature of environmental issues between the period before the mid-1970s – when everyday life in Japan was completely industrialized – and the period thereafter. Specifically, before the mid-1970s, environmental issues had the following characteristics: (1) each case had a single source; (2) the perpetrator-victim relationship was relatively clear; and (3) damage was localized. As industrialization continued to pervade every aspect of social life, this period was followed by the frequent appearance of environmental issues whose sources were more generalized and more difficult to identify. Hence, from the mid-1970s, environmental issues increasingly assumed the following characteristics: (1) the source is difficult to identify; (2) the perpetrator-victim relationship is unclear; and (3) larger areas are affected. This is what I call the change from industrial-pollution issues to everyday life-related issues.

Iijima (1993) states, 'a considerable part of the originality of environmental sociology compared to other fields of science lies in the fact that it has methods and techniques to approach environmental issues as a whole from the perspectives of residents and victims.' This suggests it is important for researchers to maintain and clarify their localized perspectives when looking at environmental issues from a variety of approaches.

What, then, are the perspectives of residents, dwellers and victims? This is a sociological question that must be repeatedly asked. In everyday life-related environmental issues, and global environmental issues, the question 'who constitutes residents or victims?' must be answered in order to solve the problem. Even in industrial pollution issues where the perpetrator-victim relationship seems clear enough on the surface, when we delve deeper we soon discover that it is very rare for either side to be homogenous in itself. Which means that the perpetrator-victim relationship cannot be taken-for-granted, but must always be reconsidered.

Other perspectives on the periodization

From the perspective of people's awareness of environmental issues, these changes in the nature of environmental issues in postwar Japan can be summarized into three periods. First came the period of postwar rehabilitation and rapid growth when environmental issues emerged as clear and localized pollution. This was the pollution period, represented by the four major pollution-related diseases, subacute-myelo-optico-neuropathy (SMON), and noise pollution near the Osaka International and Itami Airport. Second came the period of slow economic growth following the first oil crises in the early 1970s, when environmental issues became more widespread and people came to a more generalized understanding that these issues were integral to some of their personal problems. This was the period of everyday life-related environmental issues, typified by the pollution of Lake Biwa by domestic wastewater, garbage disposal problems in various parts of Japan, and photochemical smog caused by the exhaust emissions of motor vehicles. The third period began in the latter half of the 1980s, when environmental issues became more widely recognized due to the activities of the environmental protection movements, such as the campaign for global environmental issues. During this period the word 'environment' became one of the principle terms employed to explain social trends. This was the period of global environment issues, characterized by global warming caused by the destruction of tropical rainforests (for consumer products) and carbon dioxide emissions, compounded by ozone depletion from the production and release of CFC gases, in addition to expanding desertification caused by deforestation and overgrazing and an ever-expanding number of species either extinct or threatened with extinction.

This periodization can also be explained in terms of the shift from a denunciation model to a self-enlightenment model, and later to an everyday life practice model. The former model was evident in the campaigns against industrial pollution during the industrial pollution period. The self-enlightenment model came to the fore in the everyday-life related environmental issues period, underpinning energy saving and recycling campaigns. Finally, the everyday life practice model is manifest through environmental consciousness in terms of consumption and all aspects of daily life during the global environmental issues period.

We must bear in mind that these categories are merely working assumptions to aid in understanding the whole picture, and that the issues typical of the industrial-pollution period remained in the everyday life-related environmental issues period. Similarly, today, in the global environment issues period, some of the newly occurring environmental issues are typical of the industrial-pollution period, while everyday life-related environmental issues become increasingly more serious.

At the same time, the failure to resolve many of the issues that arose during the earlier periods has made numerous issues increasingly onerous and their resolution more urgent. Examples include natural destruction by public works projects, safety issues arising from the disposal of household and industrial waste, and the radioactive waste generated by nuclear power plants. In this context, it is important to understand these various environmental issues as a continuous series of events, all part and parcel of the same process, rather than as individual or separate events.

Environmental issues and environmental sociology

Environment and environmental issues

I have thus far used the terms 'environment' and 'environmental issue' without defining their meanings. From the perspective of environmental sociology, these terms should be primarily understood according to their practical usage in everyday discourse as well as in particular academic discourses. Hence we should review differences in their usage in various fields of study.

When defining the term 'environment,' Iijima (1993) does not include the 'cultural or social environments, which have traditionally been signified by this term in sociology,' as 'independent subjects of study.' Instead, she employs the term 'environment' to refer directly to the 'physical, chemical or natural environment, which has seldom attracted attention in traditional sociological studies. To study an issue in a sociological manner, its position in the social and cultural environment is primarily important.' Then building on this limited definition of the 'environment,' Iijima defines 'environmental issue' as 'various effects and problems occurring in human life, human groups, social relationships and the like in connection with changes or deterioration in the physical, chemical or natural environment.' This is quite similar to Yoshikazu Hiraoka's (1993) definition of an environmental issue, as 'a situation in which the destruction of the natural environment changes a local community and, in turn, causes damage to people's lives.' Iijima's narrow definition of 'environment' to exclude cultural and social dimensions was necessary at the time to establish environmental sociology as a distinct sub-discipline within sociology. In hindsight, however, this definition is perhaps overly restrictive.

It seems more practical to define the term 'environment' in a less restrictive manner, as does Minoru Nakata (1995). Nakata defines 'environment' as (1) physical nature (2) in which human activities take place or which has resources to support such activities and (3) can be divided in broad terms into 'artificial' or 'modified' environments – those created by humans – and 'natural' environments. Using this definition, Nakata defines an 'environmental issue' as a situation in which the environment as per (1) poses difficulties to the present or future survival of humans due to the negative impact of the community's use of the environment as per (2), in any of its various aspects as per (3). Nakata's definition, however, is perhaps overly restrictive, in that an event does not constitute an environmental issue unless it poses 'difficulties to survival.' Environmental issues cannot be limited to difficulties in human survival, but must also include situations in which normal everyday life is disturbed. That is, an environmental issue is any negative impact on either the natural or socio-cultural environment's various aspects. This is my preferred definition of 'environment' and 'environmental issues.'

Classification of environmental issues

To date, each researcher in Japanese environmental sociology has classified environmental issues in their own way in their attempts to find a legitimate place for their research in the field of sociology. Hence there is as yet no general consensus on how to classify environmental issues in Japanese sociology.

For example, Harutoshi Funabashi (1993) divides environmental policy into three fields: (1) pollution control measures; (2) nature conservation and amenity measures; and (3) measures to reduce damage to the environment arising from changing the socioeconomic systems and lifestyles. Importantly, he does not treat these three fields as separate from each other, but rather as overlapping. From this perspective, environmental issues can be classified broadly into: (1) pollution; (2) destruction of nature; and (3) urban/lifestyle-related environmental destruction and global environmental issues (i.e. issues not covered by pollution or destruction of nature).

This classification is based on the following understanding. On the one hand, pollution control measures are implemented in order to 'avoid adverse consequences, such as loss of life or damage to health' for any type of pollution. On the other hand, nature conservation and amenity measures aim to 'realize the positive values of the environment.' Until the late 1970s, these two directions were the core of environmental policy. Then in the 1980s, people began to pay closer attention to urban/lifestyle-related environmental effects, typified by garbage problems, the air pollution caused by motor vehicles, and global environmental issues – such as ozone depletion caused by CFC gases and the global warming resulting from carbon dioxide emissions. These issues are not addressed by pollution control measures or nature conservation measures. To deal with these issues, we must take more broad-ranging measures such as 'changing the socioeconomic system so as to systematically reduce damage to the environment' and 'changing everyday lifestyles.' This new situation could not be dealt with by the existing laws – the Basic Law for Environmental Pollution Control and the Nature Conservation Law. A new law – the Basic Environment Law – had to be enacted. Hence, Funabashi's broad classification – (1) pollution, (2) destruction of nature, and (3) issues not covered by pollution or destruction of nature – is useful for analyzing environmental policies.

From another perspective – the social mechanisms of environmental destruction – Michio Umino (1993) proposes four categories: (1) industrial pollution; (2) lifestyle-related pollution; (3) large-scale development issues; and (4) global environmental issues. Umino divides category (1) further into two subcategories: (a) pollution caused by a single company and (b) by more than one company. The first of these (a) is further divided into two more subcategories depending on whether the specific company can easily be identified or not. Category (2) is also divided into two subcategories: whether the source generates pollution (a) directly or (b) indirectly. Category (4) is divided into two subcategories depending on whether the issue has (a) high or (b) low potential for public awareness. Umino's classification is intended for use in analyzing the social mechanisms that generate environmental issues. Funabashi (1995) later developed a more abstract classification of environmental issues as social dilemmas.

While both Funabashi and Umino classify environmental issues based on where the issues occur, Yukiko Kada (1993) argues that environmental sociology must address not only environmental issues that have already emerged but a wider range of issues as well. To this end he proposes a categorization of: (1) 'environmental issues in a narrow sense,' consisting of environmental issues that arise as social problems; and (2) 'environmental issues in a broad sense,' consisting of those that emerge in the interaction between nature and humans. His 'environmental issues in a narrow sense,' are subdivided into environmental issues that are geographically localized and those that have assumed a global scale. From this perspective, Funabashi's and Umino's classifications both fall into the first category, 'environmental issues in a narrow sense.' Kada's classification of 'environmental issues in a narrow sense' and 'environmental issues in a broad sense' corresponds to my distinction between a 'sociology of environmental issues' and a 'sociology of coexistence with the environment,' respectively.

Kada (1993) created this classification system by 'pondering what social and cultural background lies behind environmental issues and what measures people can take to deal with these issues in their social and cultural activities from the perspective of local residents' – a perspective of 'life and culture studies.' To achieve this aim, Kada had to treat environmental issues as a superordinate concept over and above Funabashi's and Umino's classifications.

By expanding our conception of environmental issues to include the interactions between nature and humans, environmental sociology can perceive a continuity between the 'life and culture studies' approach to the interaction between nature and humans and studies on environmental issues that emerge as social problems.

Before moving on, it is worth briefly comparing these sociological perspectives of environmental issues to a more conventional 'economists' view. For example, the economist Ken'ichi Miyamoto (1989) proposed eight categories to organize our understanding of environmental issues: (1) changes in the global ecosystem; (2) destruction of the natural environment; (3) destruction and stagnation of local communities and cultures; (4) damage to the living environment; (5) ill health – bad shape, general sick feeling, poor physical condition; (6) health problems; (7) pollution-related diseases; and (8) recognized patients. From this perspective, it is clear that sociology attempts to understand interactions between humans and their environment in a much broader sense.

The nature and subjects of environmental sociology

The origins of environmental sociology in Japan are different from, for example, the United States. In Japan, environmental sociology originated from particular analyses of the serious damage caused by concrete instances of pollution. In the U.S., environmental sociology was first proposed by Dunlap (1980) and his colleagues as a paradigm shift to renovate and reinvigorate sociology itself. Although he later abandoned the conviction of a wholesale transformation of sociology itself and accepted that environmental sociology was rightfully a sub-discipline of sociology (Taniguchi 1998: 182–3), Dunlap's original idea was highly stimulating and can still provide important perspectives for thinking about the environment and environmental issues. I will, therefore, briefly introduce Dunlap's idea before turning to a more detailed discussion of environmental sociology in Japan.

In the late 1970s in the U.S., Dunlap and his colleagues began to criticize conventional sociology for its approach to explaining social events. From the standard sociological perspective, social events can only be adequately explained in terms of other social events, and all 'environmental explanations' – attempts to attribute social events to natural (biological and physical) environmental events – were rejected. Dunlap et al. argued that sociology must come to accept the natural environment as an explanatory variable for particular types of social issues. Since the dominant logic of sociology regarded 'society' as being antithetical to the natural environment, this argument required a paradigm shift in sociology. That is, they were not simply suggesting that sociology must accept another, or a different, explanatory variable, but rather that the underlying worldview of conventional sociology must be revised.

Dunlap et al. referred to the worldview underlying sociology as the Human Exceptionalism Paradigm (HEP) and proposed that it should be completely replaced with the New Ecological Paradigm (NEP). The HEP maintains that humans are different from all other living things, and that all human events are determined exclusively by the social and cultural environment, virtually independently of the biological and physical environment. The HEP worldview maintains that culture is cumulative, and thus all social problems that arise can and will be solved through further technological and social progress. In contrast, the NEP worldview maintains that humans, like all other living things, are always dependent on the biological and physical environment of the global ecosystem and always remain subject to ecological rules.

NEP supporters argue that the optimistic HEP worldview, and therefore conventional sociology, is inadequate for analyzing the world of the late-twentieth century and beyond – the world in which resource shortages and environmental problems have become important and pressing social issues. Hence, they argue, modern society can only be correctly understood by environmental sociology, which develops its theories on the basis of the NEP.

This argument provided the basis for the development of environmental sociology in the U.S. in the late 1970s and early 1980s. During this period, its advocates began to research things such as: natural environments that have (as yet) been minimally affected by human activities (wilderness, unexploited mineral deposits, etc.); the damage done to human-affected natural environments (air, water and other undesirable forms of pollution, water reservoirs, etc.); the effects of artificial environments (skyscrapers, traffic systems, etc.); and social measures introduced to redress environmental issues (environmental movements, etc.) (Humphrey and Buttel 1982).

The arguments put forward by Dunlap et al. prompted a barrage of criticisms and failed to achieve a radically new paradigm in American sociology. But we can nevertheless learn much from their attempt, for the distinction they developed between the HEP and NEP highlights the importance of introducing an environmental perspective into sociology.

As mentioned, though, Japanese environmental sociology developed via a considerably different path from its U.S. counterpart, partly because the types of environmental issues faced by these countries are different.

According to Iijima, a pioneer of environmental sociology in Japan, '[E]nvironmental sociology is a field of sociology in which interaction between human society and the natural environment (such as the effects of human society on the physical, biological and chemical environments (hereinafter referred to as the "natural environment") and the resulting reactions of such effects on human society) are studied in both empirical and theoretical manners by focusing on their social aspects' (Iijima 1998: 1–2). Thus, one crucial characteristic of environmental sociology that distinguishes it from conventional sociology is that it 'requires a focus on the interaction between human society and nature, in addition to that between human society and the social and cultural environments.' Another characteristic of environmental sociology is that it is a 'problem-based field of sociology that pursues the resolution of particular problems by conducting fieldwork aimed at understanding the actual circumstances of the society' (Iijima 1998: 2).

For Iijima (1993) this 'problem-based field of sociology' is 'of an extremely practical nature.' This characterization implies that Japanese environmental sociology does not merely attempt to develop an understanding of the environmental issues confronting society, but actually strives to find appropriate ways to resolve environmental issues. In other words, for Iijima, environmental sociology is a field of study where interactions between humans/societies and the environment are studied in a 'practical' manner. This becomes clearer through a more detailed description of the research subjects undertaken by environmental sociologists.

Iijima broadly divides current research in environmental sociology into a 'sociology of environmental issues' and a 'sociology of coexistence with the environment,' and argues that these categories intersect with two other fields: a 'sociology of environmental behavior' and a 'sociology of environmental awareness and environmental culture' (Iijima 1998: 2–3). As previously discussed, the 'sociology of environmental issues' focuses on the mechanisms by which damage is suffered or inflicted, and deals mainly with the 'social systems that may amplify damage, the reactions of existing systems and organizations to the issues in question, and the reactions of the scientific or technological community or the media and their effects.' In contrast, the sociology of coexistence with the environment focuses on discussing the 'characteristics of communities that have harmoniously coexisted with their natural environments at various times in history, via diverse cultures in different parts of the world.' Hence, this field of sociology more actively deals with matters of environmental reclamation or rehabilitation, such as the protection of the historical environment and town planning. As mentioned, these two fields intersect with two other perspectives – a 'sociology of environmental behavior' and a 'sociology of environmental awareness and environmental culture.' The former focuses on social movement theories, while the latter primarily addresses the formation, meaning and effects of the values and attitudes involved in the formation of environmental awareness and environmental culture. These subjects could be subdivided further, but are sufficient as they stand for classifying studies currently in progress.

Iijima (1993: 216) identifies two distinct directions for environmental sociology: (1) the 'sociology of environmental issues' deals with environmental issues that are clearly social problems, including those with serious health consequences; and (2) the 'sociology of environment' consists of sociological studies concerning social phenomena that are related to natural, chemical and physical environments. In the former, Iijima argues, 'actual or potential perpetrator-victim relationships' constitute the 'core of the issues,' while in the latter, 'perpetrator-victim relationships are incidental phenomena.' This distinction is indicative of Iijima's clear intention to locate perpetrator-victim relationships at the center of environmental sociological studies. Japanese sociological studies of environmental issues began with research into the damage that resulted from pollution, and has continued to accumulate this type of research material.

As mentioned earlier, as environmental issues have accumulated and become ever more intrusive problems for human life, various analytical perspectives have been proposed that differ from the conventional perpetrator-victim perspective. Nakata's (1995) description of environmental sociology reveals some of the breadth of these analytical perspectives. Nakata identifies five distinct questions that guide environmental sociology enquiries into various phenomena at the different stages of the emergence of environmental issues as social problems: (1) What are the social mechanisms through which have they appeared?; (2) What is their hierarchical structure?; (3) Where can we find measures to resolve or prevent them, and the agents and resources necessary for such implementing such measures?; (4) What environment is considered comfortable and needed?; and (5) How we do establish our analyses and prescriptions for the common property that is our environment? Nakata also argues that foundations for such studies can be established by: (6) studies that identify the minimum criteria for sustainability. To tie this to Iijima's distinction, we might suggest that questions (1) to (3) belong to the sociology of environmental issues and (6) belongs to the sociology of coexistence with the environment, while questions (4) and (5) apply to both fields.

Nakata characterizes the place of environmental sociology within sociology as follows: 'while other hyphenated-sociologies represent vertically divided fields of sociology, environmental sociology represents a cross-sectional field of study. Environmental sociology aims to sum up and integrate all of the various studies into the interaction between humans (society) and the environment from across the various fields of sociology.' This idea of a cross-sectional field that summarizes and integrates all of the other fields of study in sociology is developed on the basis of Dunlap's argument for a paradigm shift in mainstream sociology described above. Although Nakata's proposal is interesting, like Dunlap's, it has had no lasting impact on mainstream sociology.

Research topics in environmental sociology

Trends in environmental sociology

The most important topics addressed by Japanese environmental sociology thus far have included: What caused pollution and deterioration of the environment? How did damage occur (theories on mechanisms of generation of environmental issues and social dilemma theories), and how did affected residents, individuals and the relevant local government agencies react to the damage (environmental movement theories and arguments over policy)? How were the relationships between perpetrators and victims structured (theories on the structure of damage and beneficiary/affected zones)? When those concerned by these questions were later confronted by the rise of global environmental issues, Japanese environmental sociology developed new perspectives that extended beyond the borders of Japan to become involved in the broader world, particularly the developing world.

Studies concerned with the deteriorating environment have not been limited to negative health impacts, but included concerns with the destruction of nature (such as forests and rivers), and even expanded to incorporate the destruction of historically significant built environments. Researchers have not only attempted to elucidate the mechanisms that underlie or cause environmental damage, but also the relationships between people or groups of people and the environment (regionalism, spontaneous development theory, and life-environmentalism). At the same time, they have initiated various social movements that aim to resolve environmental issues by creating new modes of production or new social organizations (organic farming and recycling, for example). Further research has attempted to identify the concepts and beliefs that have initiated and sustained changing relationships to the environment (environmentalism and environmental consciousness), while others have investigated how these changes have been taken up as issues (constructionism and creation of issues). These are all important research topics that contribute to our capacity to see environmental issues from a relativistic perspective.

These research topics have not been clearly distinguished or studied in isolation from one another. In environmental issues such as pollution, it is impossible to separate the issues of damage – negative health effects suffered by individuals, and damage to the everyday lives of families and communities – and the efforts of social movements to solve these issues (i.e. damage issues and solution strategies). Furthermore, any discussion of solution strategies must produce policy proposals, such as reforming the existing lifestyle or restoring traditional ways of managing the natural environment that are specific to the individuals or community involved. It is therefore essential to ascertain the logic of life that traditionally maintained the environment of the community; and, hence, these topics must be conducted in association with each other.

It is safe to say that these research trends, which have intersected at various stages, define environmental sociology in Japan. It is worth repeating that the boundary between the two categories of research – environmental issues and coexistence with the environment – is tentative, and that these are perhaps more correctly understood as dealing with the same issues from different perspectives. Let us now look at some concrete examples of such studies.

Two lines of study in environmental sociology

The majority of the research conducted to date in environmental sociology has been concerned with environmental issues, rather than with coexistence with the environment. This sociology of environmental issues has dealt with industrial pollution and everyday life-related environmental issues that emerge as problems when they negatively affect people's health or a community's living environment. As mentioned previously, these problems vary from industrial pollution issues, where the distinction between perpetrators and victims is clear, to everyday life-related environmental issues, where the relationship between perpetrators and victims is typically blurred and the damage is often, in a sense, self-inflicted.

The first sociological sub-disciplines to turn their attention to pollution were rural and regional sociology. Notable examples of early research on this topic include studies of mineral poisoning in Annaka-chō, Gunma Prefecture conducted by Tadashi Fukutake, Minoru Shimazaki and others (Nihon Jinbunkagaku kai (Japanese Society for Humanities) ed., 1955), a study of the circumstances behind the continuing industrialization of Mishima, Shizuoka Prefecture conducted by Takayoshi Kitagawa and Kiyoshi Ishikawa (1965), a study of the Yokkaichi and the Mishima/Numazu area edited by Fukutake (1965), and a study of anti-pollution social movements edited by Haruo Matsubara (1971). Each of these studies begin with the fundamental sociological insight that negative health effects are not merely personal problems but are related to social structures in the affected regions; and each concluded that these social structures were inseparable from particular corporate ethics. These two insights remain cornerstones of environmental sociology to this day.

As pollution became more severe, its impact on the everyday life of affected communities was felt more deeply and had increasingly devastating consequences. In regional sociology – which had previously focused primarily on changes in political structures and local communities – and more particularly in rural sociology, changes to communities brought about by industrial development and the damage caused by pollution began to attract greater levels of attention as their impact on lives in rural communities intensified. While researchers in the sociology of health focus on the impact of such developments on individuals' health, regional and rural sociologists focus instead on the broader impact on life in the community, drawing on data previously acquired from more generalized studies of families and rural communities. This approach aims to clarify the real effects of pollution on communities, rather than simply elucidating the mechanisms of pollution. Hence, this approach leads into discussions about the structure of damage and of victims' movements.

Perhaps the most important contribution to sociological research to develop out of these studies is the damage structure theory first proposed by Iijima (1984b). Iijima 'specifically took up issues of damage that [had been] neglected by the offending enterprises, as well as by the [government] administration and researchers in general' (1984b: 80). She studied the experiences of victims in numerous pollution cases, and proposed a damage structure theory, which consisted of the type and extent of damage and the social factors involved. Clearly, research into the structure of damage requires consideration of the structures through which the damage was inflicted, and hence these two structures must be researched in parallel.

The damage structure theory was elaborated and elucidated in an edited collection by Iijima and Funabashi (1999) titled *Niigata Minamata-byō mondai: Kagai to higai no shakaigaku* (The issue of Niigata Minamata disease: Sociology of perpetrators and victims). As the title indicates, rather than a theoretical treatise, this was a concrete sociological study of Niigata Minamata disease which elucidated the structure of the disease as a social problem through research consisting primarily of long-term, detailed interviews.

Organizational theory and social movement theories have also been employed by researchers examining pollution issues. These researchers recognized that, when faced with environmental problems, people are flexible and attempt to maintain their everyday lives by modifying their way of life and the systems that sustain it. Yet even while adapting to the changing situation, they often vigorously protest against perpetrators and governments. Hence, researchers have employed organizational theories in attempts to understand the processes and principles by which protests are organized and sustained. Similarly, social movement theories help to explain how and why protestor's activities are joined by other people from (non-affected) neighboring or more distant areas?

For example, Harutoshi Funabashi and Kōichi Hasegawa (1985, 1988) examined a new type of pollution – Shinkansen (bullet train) pollution – which is distinctively different from that caused by the chemical industry; the primary focus of all previous environmental sociology research. They identified the 'various entities involved in this problem' as thoroughly as they could before commencing their field research. They identified the central issues as: the social problems created by the construction of large-scale social infrastructure and public facilities; conflicts between economic and environmental values and between 'high speed civilization' (quantity of life) and 'quality of life'; and how to harmonize the conflicting interests of a large number of beneficiaries with a small number of specified victims and achieve consensus between them. Funabashi and Hasegawa analyzed these three points from perspectives such as the beneficiary/affected zone theory. The results of their analyses are highly suggestive. Particularly remarkable is the successful achievement of the principal aim of their study – to 'organize conceptual tools and discover their sociological meanings in Merton's "middle range" level through individual case studies.' For example, the concept of 'publicness' was reconsidered from the perspective of Control System theory and was redefined as 'universal public convenience.'

The concepts developed in these studies were then employed by Funabashi, Hasegawa and Iijima (1998) in another groundbreaking study, this one of large-scale community development. In this work, large-scale community development projects were analyzed in terms of regional disparities, community development, nuclear power policy, and democratic decision and democracy. Notable here is the use of the conceptual relationship between the 'center' and 'periphery' in considering regional disparities as well as in their theories of decision-making and social movements. Furthermore, their recognition of the bullet train passengers' roles as indirect perpetrators was significant for the later development of social dilemma theory. For our present purposes, what is most important here is that the studies mentioned above all demonstrate environmental sociologists' orientation towards formulating theories only on the basis of thorough empirical research and analysis. Then, based on these sociological theories, the studies discussed above elucidate the causal relationships among social factors, the environmental problem and the resulting damage in addition to other factors that render finding a solution more difficult.

Research into community development issues had begun in the fields of rural and regional sociology in the 1950s. Combined with the aforementioned studies on pollution by Iijima and others, these studies led to important developments in environmental sociology, such as the studies by Funabashi discussed above and Teruyoshi Ukai's (1992) *Okinawa: kyodai kaihatsu no ronri to hihan* (Okinawa: The logic and criticism of large-scale development).

Social movement theories, such as Matsubara and Nitagai (1976) *Jumin undō no ronri* (The logic of public movements), can be included in the sociology of environmental issues since they are concerned with finding solutions. In this work, the concept of publicness is explored through case studies, such as the antinuclear movement and campaigns opposing the construction of freeway bypasses, the Jōetsu bullet train line, and various shopping centers. Social movement theories later developed into 'resource mobilization theory' and theories of 'new social movements.' Shinji Katagiri's (1995b) *Shakai undō no chūhan'i riron* (Middle range theory on social movement), for example, employs resource mobilization theory to analyze a variety of development issues. In recent decades, social movements have acquired new characteristics that distinguish them from the classic social movements, such as the labor movement or the women's movement, and have formed new types of groups (e.g. NGOs and NPOs) and new systems of expression (e.g. local referendums), so that researchers have had to find new ways of analyzing them. These research topics have brought new dimensions to traditional movement theories.[4] For example, Kōichi Hasegawa's (1996) *Datsu genshiryoku shakai no sentaku* (A choice for a post-nuclear society) vividly describes the successful processes by which environmental NPOs in the U.S. stopped the further development of nuclear power in certain locales. This work suggests one possible course for environmental sociology to take in the future, including research methods and descriptive style.

From a different perspective, Hideo Nakazawa et al. (1998) provide a quantitative analysis of the cycle of environmental movement protests using two variables: 'structural strain' and the 'structure of political opportunities.' The indicators of structural strain are industrial and GDP growth rates. The indicators of the structure of political opportunities are the number of progressive local governments and the increase in the number of pollution control ordinances. The authors conclude that the cycle of environmental movements is not affected by 'structural strain' but is determined by the 'structure of political opportunities.' Their analysis reveals an important dimension in the relationship between environmental issues and environmental movements.

In the sociology of environmental issues, the perpetrator-victim dichotomy has been a significant concept. As described above, however, this relationship has not been clearly dichotomous in an increasing number of environmental problems since the latter half of the 1970s. Thus, when the social dilemma theory appeared, it provided a clear and crisp explanation of these problems – it elucidated the mechanisms underlying these problems and offerred solutions.

A social dilemma is a 'situation with a structure in which there are multiple actors, who have mutual relationships in which each actor can pursue their own interests without restricting the others, and each acts in an individual, reasonable manner, but the accumulated results of their actions cause deterioration of the collective property that is their environment and generates consequences that are undesirable for each and every actor' (Funabashi 1995: 6). Umino's group, for example, sees the garbage problem as a social dilemma and attempts to elucidate the mechanisms that underlie it, analyzing quantitative data in pursuit of possible ways of controlling the problem (Nakano et al. 1996).

The sociology of coexistence with the environment aims to elucidate the everyday interactions between people and their environment in order to discover ways and systems for protecting the environment. This field of sociology has revealed ways of maintaining the environment and of solving environmental problems that were actually used by community members – whether or not the environmental issues had actually become social problems in those communities – by canvassing the opinions of local residents and adopting various techniques and social structures that they had developed to maintain their everyday lives. These research methods are quite similar to the methods employed by rural sociology and folklore studies, but also incorporate the methods of regional sociology in the 1970s, the spontaneous development theory that subsequently emerged, a unique methodology proposed by Yoshiyuki Tsurumi and his colleagues (see for example, Tsurumi 1982, 1990), and the theory of commons (see for example, Nakamura and Tsurumi (eds) 1995; Inoue 1995; Miyauchi 1998).

Rural sociology became involved in studies of the environment because, as Akira Kawamoto (1983) put it, it basically regards a rural community as an organization that aims to protect its territory as both its living environment and the primary source of its livelihood. In the process of explaining a community's techniques for maintaining their territory and the processes by which that territory had been transformed, rural sociologists were actually elucidating the ways and means of environmental protection.

The life-environmentalism advocated by Torigoe and others (Torigoe and Kada (eds) 1984; Torigoe (ed.) 1989; Kada 1995; Matsuda 1996; Torigoe 1997a) also derives from these methods. In their analyses of the environmental deterioration around Lake Biwa, Torigoe et al. chose particular lakeside villages as their research zone, rather than the broader geographical areas in which pollution had become a serious problem. Their research continued over a three-year period, mainly through interviews, and investigated all aspects of the villagers' everyday lives. From the beginning, their approach was similar to the methods used in writing oral history. As well as interviews, they conducted archival research of documents concerning the area from early-modern times to the present. Their research uncovered many facts, such as a close relationship between changes in the villages' water use patterns and pollution of Lake Biwa.

This research did not begin with either a question or a hypothesis. The researchers carefully collected evidence of problems generally embedded in the villagers' everyday lives. Based on this research, Torigoe et al. elucidate the role of residents in environmental deterioration as well as the effect of environmental deterioration on the residents and the measures taken by residents in response. They found that residents take a variety of measures in response to environmental deterioration in order to protect their health and way of life, but some of these measures are contrary to environmental protection in a general sense. Yet Torigoe argues that these seemingly contrary measures should not always be denied (e.g. residents' saying 'No' to forced emigration for the so-called conservation and protection of Himalayan forests), as the importance of residents maintaining their own living systems is critical from the perspective of life-environmentalism. This approach is called 'life-environmentalism,' which, as discussed earlier, attempts to analyze environmental issues from the perspective of community life.

Life-environmentalism is similar to regionalism and the spontaneous development theory in several respects. Regionalism stresses the autonomy of local communities and the importance of recycling resources (see for example, Tamanoi, Kiyonari and Nakamura 1978). The spontaneous development theory encourages community development by fostering connections between available resources and the social systems already existing within a community, rather than by external forces (see for example, Tsurumi 1996). These concepts also bear similarities to the 'community co-management theory' proposed by Minoru Nakata (1993), Shūichi Kitō's (1996) 'social link theory,' Takao Inoue's (1996) 'environment-society system theory,' and Kazunori Matsumura (ed.) (1997) 'practical sense theory.'

Another important trend in the sociology of coexistence with the environment can be found in studies of movements to change production systems and community lifestyles. These studies have analyzed social trends toward re-creating local systems for recycling and environmental protection, which had suffered from the external imposition of significant changes during Japan's rapid economic growth in the 1950s and 1960s.

Regionalism can be regarded as one of the sources of this trend, which also includes the spontaneous development theory and the theory of commons. While the sociology of environmental issues is based on the perpetrator-victim dichotomy and is concerned with communities in which an environmental problem has already occurred, these studies in the sociology of coexistence with the environment are based on the relationships between humans and nature and focus on recycling, the distribution of resources and the creation of appropriate systems for these purposes.

This trend also includes moves to create a wide variety of different values. These range from organic agriculture movements, which aim at securing food safety (see for example, Tabeta et al. 1986; Matsumura and Aoki (eds) 1991), to movements for resource/ waste recycling (see for example, Yorimoto 1990; Taniguchi 1996) and alternative (renewable) energies (Terada 1995), and movements for the protection of the natural environment and conservation of historically significant sites.

New topics of study

Finally, let us review recent developments in the two major fields – environmental issues and coexistence with environment – by reviewing the contents of the *Journal of Environmental Sociology*.

The *Journal of Environmental Sociology* was first published in 1995 by the Japanese Society for Environmental Sociology, and has published articles on the various topics discussed above. In its first four issues, the journal ran feature articles titled 'Perspectives in Environmental Sociology,' 'Fields in Environmental Sociology,' 'Forests, Rivers and Seas as Commons,' and 'Environmental Movements and NGOs,' in that order. Its approach to environmental issues has always been fresh and responsive to developments in environmental issues. Although many of the articles published in the journal can be roughly classified into the sociology of environmental issues and the sociology of coexistence with the environment, it has also published numerous articles that do not fit into either of these two categories. For example, a study of second generation victims of Minamata disease (Rie Harada, Issue 3); the development of local referendums as a new social movement (Yūko Takubo, Issue 3; and Atsushi Yamamuro, Issue 4); the concept of social arenas and analysis of the social forces leading to the enactment of new environmental protection laws (Yūko Takubo, Issue 2); the relationship between environmental protection and the commons (feature articles, Issue 3); and a discussion of how environmental problems develop into social issues (Yoshiki Ōtsuka, Issue 4). Furthermore, the regional approach to environmental issues in Asia taken by Yoshikazu Hiraoka and his colleagues (Issue 2) indicates an awareness of the increasingly global characteristics of environmental issues.

It is worth repeating that the methods and objectives of these studies developed from the accumulated results of studies in other fields of sociology. They can only be summarized as trends in environmental sociology with the benefit of hindsight. We should also note that, due to the nature of environmental issues, most sociological studies of environmental issues tend to rely on the results of research from both other social sciences and the natural sciences.[5]

Although there has been a gradually increasing number of studies specifically in environmental sociology, to date there have been too few monographs published on the basis of extensive fieldwork. It is time for us to stop simply testing and modifying theories developed in other fields and begin to formulate theories on the basis of our own detailed monographic studies.

Practicality of studies in environmental sociology

Studies in environmental sociology must include proposed solutions to the problem and must monitor any measures implemented to this end. This may be done at various stages and to different degrees, but it is safe to say that a study is not genuinely environmental sociology if it is not directly involved in both the identification/analysis of a problem and its solution in one way or another. We must remain constantly aware not only that our research continuously changes as we learn more about the problem at hand, but also that our involvement is highly likely to become one of the factors affecting the nature and extent of the problem. This is in no small part due to the fact that as the social scientist begins to elucidate the perspective of the local residents, that perspective inevitably changes. While this situation pertains to the social sciences in general, it is perhaps more acute in environmental sociology due to the grave potential of environmental issues.

As the frequency and severity of environmental issues continue to increase, so too will the field of environmental sociology. In the process, the practical/problem-based approach of this field of study has the potential to bring it closer to policy studies and to break down the barriers between sociology and other fields of science. To realize this potential, though, environmental sociology will have to extend beyond the methodologies and theories of sociology in its attempts to solve environmental problems, and develop new and unique theories that will be useful for other fields of study and for solving specific problems.

2 The Village as an Independent Body

Environmental issues and rural community studies

Two trends in rural community studies

The environment and environmental issues have become important subjects in many fields of study. One major paradigm that is increasingly embraced by researchers in many diverse fields is that human beings are dependent upon the circulation of other life forms and the physical world ('environment' in a narrow sense) and cannot survive as a privileged life form in isolation. This understanding requires all fields of study to abandon traditional anthropocentric structures and to seriously consider the relationships between humans and the surrounding environment.

In rural community studies, two trends have emerged that are directly related to the environment: studies aiming to elucidate the mechanisms by which rural communities protect their living environment,[1] and those aiming to find some bases for the continuing existence of rural communities in increasingly urbanized societies – typically through elucidating a new relationship between towns and rural communities, as seen in organic agriculture movements.[2] Both of these trends have emerged through the long-term accumulation of rural community studies, rather than as hasty responses to the more recent explosion in environmental awareness.

Put simply, agriculture, forestry and fishing are all dependent upon the mechanisms that sustain life. Producers in these industries are only productive if they operate in accordance with these mechanisms and have therefore developed various social systems for production over long periods of time. Rural communities, however, have been gradually but steadily alienated from these life sustaining mechanisms, and in the process have lost or forgotten their roles as protectors of the living environment.

The two research trends mentioned above might be regarded as efforts to restore this life-sustaining mechanism to the central place in rural communities with the help of the knowledge accumulated through rural community studies. These efforts do not simply aim to restore the rural communities' role as protectors of their particular living environments, but seek new mechanisms for environmental protection on a global scale.

The present work pursues the same objective. To this end, this chapter reviews the role of rural communities as the protectors of their living environments using locally maintained historical documents to review the transformation of the relationships between rural communities, government administrations and the living environment with a view to restoring traditional ways of protecting the living environment.

Rural communities as the protectors of the living environment

The idea that a rural community is the protector of its living environment entails two dimensions: a rural community conducts certain activities that are necessary for the protection of its living environment and it acts as a single entity when conducting these activities. These, of course, are not separable, but interact with and transform one other.

More specifically, the rural community must protect its living environment because individual households and persons are incapable of doing so independently. Conversely, the fact that a rural community is the protector means that the community's living environment must be controlled by something other than individual ownership.

In Japanese law, a rural community's territory was clearly divided into private, communal and public domains by the Land Tax Reform in 1873. In principle, only the communal domain was subject to the community's control, with the private domains controlled by private land owners and the public domains controlled by the government. In practice, however, the community's involvement in irrigation and all other aspects of farm management was indispensable to the private land owner. In other words, the community had to assert control over the entirety of its territory in order to sustain its member's lives.

Akira Kawamoto referred to this aspect of the rural community as the 'duality of land ownership' (private and collective ownerships). Kawamoto says,

> in terms of space, a rural community's territory consists of land that is the private property of each "household" and the mountains, forests,

wilderness, roads and waterways that are the collective property of the community. A rural community's territory as its collective property does not only mean mountains, forests, wilderness, roads and waterways as collective property of the community. The whole territory is collective property of the community. (1972: 138–44)

This mode of operation in a rural community, he says, is

supported by three properly working functions of a community – resident protection, territory protection, and product protection. Among these, resident protection and territory protection are essential to community members' living. A community's production activities are conducted based on protection of its territory and products. Resident protection means coordination of the living environment and personal relationships. Territory protection means protection of the territory as the basis for production and life, since it goes without saying that people can live and conduct production activities only on land.[3] Product protection means protection of farm products (including livestock) produced on the territory. These three functions are performed by community members in three different roles: as residents, as owners, and as farmers. (1983: 283)

Before World War II, these three protective functions were typically controlled by the *sōdai* (community representative), who was a landowner (landlord) or an upper-class owner-farmer. After the war,

the three protective functions were differentiated from each other; resident protection became the responsibility of the chairman of the district association or the residents' association, product protection the responsibility of the president of the farmers union...and only territory protection remained under the jurisdiction of the community representative...(Kawamoto 1983: 283)

This was due to factors such as agrarian reform and the increasing number of non-farming households in rural communities. Finally, the government administration has attempted to supplant the landlords' responsibility for taking care of farmers, 'from their production activities to life in general.' Resident protection became the responsibility of general administrative bodies, while product protection was taken over by agricultural administrative bodies and agricultural cooperatives. However, 'the administrative bodies responsible for territory protection have only an old-fashioned understanding of rural communities' and have therefore established administrative channels that do not distinguish between the head of a ward and the community representative. This has confused Japanese farm policy. Furthermore, the destruction of rural territory by urbanization has been entirely neglected by urban administrative bodies and inadequately dealt with by agricultural administrative bodies. Hence, rural communities remain ultimately responsible for protecting their territory, despite the fact that, due to factors such as a trend towards much larger-scale farms and the increasing number of part-time farming households, they are no longer capable of doing so (Kawamoto 1983: 283).

Although this is Kawamoto's analysis as of 1983, it remains valid today, although the continuing development of cultivated land improvement projects has probably achieved a more definite separation of the three protective functions since then.

Yukiko Kada also analyzed the transformation of rural communities' territory protection function, albeit from a different perspective, taking river management as his example. Drawing on Kawamoto's theory on territory protection, Kada states:

> Environment management in a rural community can be roughly divided into: (1) "protective management," which aims to maintain certain conditions, as seen in draining; and (2) "investing management," which aims to ensure the original living standards by introducing new factors, such as the creation of a fish farm. In addition, labor provided for environment management was appreciated and rewarded. In this sense, a rural community was a "management body that had conducted environment management using a labor organization which consisted of members whose labor was individually rewarded and which worked on other members of the community [in conducting the aforementioned two styles of management]." Since the beginning of the Meiji Period, however, the space managed by a rural community has gradually been narrowed and placed under administrative control, by such means as designation of first-class rivers. Space so placed under administrative control has been neglected without a management body, as a domain not belonging to the community even though it exists within the community. This is one social aspect of modern environmental issues. (Kada 1991: 89–110)

Kada then concludes,

> If we can in some form realize a rural community's independent aspect, or intention as a local management body, then a community will be able to fulfill its functions as the body in charge of protecting the environment within its territory. I cannot think of any other body that is appropriate to take responsibility for protecting the environment of the rural community. (Kada 1991: 106)

Kawamoto and Kada share an understanding that responsibility for the management of a rural community's territory/environment was taken away from its residents and given to a government administrative body. In analyzing who performs the three protective functions identified by Kawamoto, Kada notes the absence of any management body responsible for protecting particular regions within the community's territory that do not 'belong' to the community, such as designated rivers. This is similar to the situation that Kawamoto observed, in which rural communities must ultimately bear responsibility for protecting their territory, despite no longer being capable of doing so. Although one researcher approaches the problem from the perspective of the rural community and highlights the extremely vague limits of its territory and territorial responsibilities, and the other approaches the problematic from the perspective of environmental protection and points out the absence or inadequacy of the management body, both appear to reach similar conclusions.

So, why is Kada's perspective so much more hopeful and optimistic than Kawamoto's? One reason is that Kada approaches the rural community as the 'place of everyday life,' while Kawamoto approaches rural community management from a perspective of agricultural production. For Kawamoto, then, resident and territory protection are only of concern to his research insofar as they relate to product protection. This is his logic of a rural community. In practice, however, product protection is no longer solely within the domain of a rural community's self-management. Kawamoto himself admits that in the current economic climate, individual farms can be, and increasingly are, managed without any help from the local community. In this sense, product protection, territory protection and resident protection have been radically separated.

Nevertheless, even today, very few rural communities exist as groups of individual households with absolutely no sense of unity. As has always been the case, a rural community must be managed as a whole in order for its residents to live in it. If Kawamoto's 'product protection function' is more abstractly conceived as a 'management protection function,' and the three functions are combined into the 'living environment protection functions,' it becomes clear that a rural community is a management body for protecting its living environment.

How, then, was a rural community able to become the protector of its living environment? To discuss this in a way that is continuous with the present, we need to focus on a period in the history of rural communities sometime during or after the Meiji Period. Considering that rural communities are not at present capable of acting as the protectors of their living environment because the protective functions have been assumed by the government administration, we must begin by reviewing changes in the relationship between the state and rural communities.

Rural communities experienced three major turning points in this regard during and after the Meiji Period. The first came with the establishment of the local government system in 1888, with the government's promulgation of the act establishing the *shi-chō-son* (city-town-village) system. During this period, rural communities each established their own ways of protecting their living environments. Then, during the 1920s (between the two world wars), rural communities were threatened with the loss of their roles as the living environment protector through disputes between landowners and tenant farmers. Then during the period of rapid economic growth after World War II (primarily in the 1960s), many rural communities lost their status as independent actors, due to the pressures of urbanization and the increasing numbers of non-farming households in rural communities, on one hand, and the rapid individualization of farm management combined with the massive depopulation of rural areas on the other.[4] There are a large number of issues in each of these three periods to discuss in terms of protecting the living environment in rural communities and who is responsible (or empowered) to do so. In the next section I focus on the first period in order to describe changes to the living environment protectors,[5] taking Chinai Village (currently, Chinai District in Makino-chō) in Shiga Prefecture as an example.

Chinai Village and village diary

The principal materials in this account are documents called *Kiroku* (literally: 'records'), consisting of sixteen volumes which have been

Figure 2.1: Map of Lake Biwa and surrounds

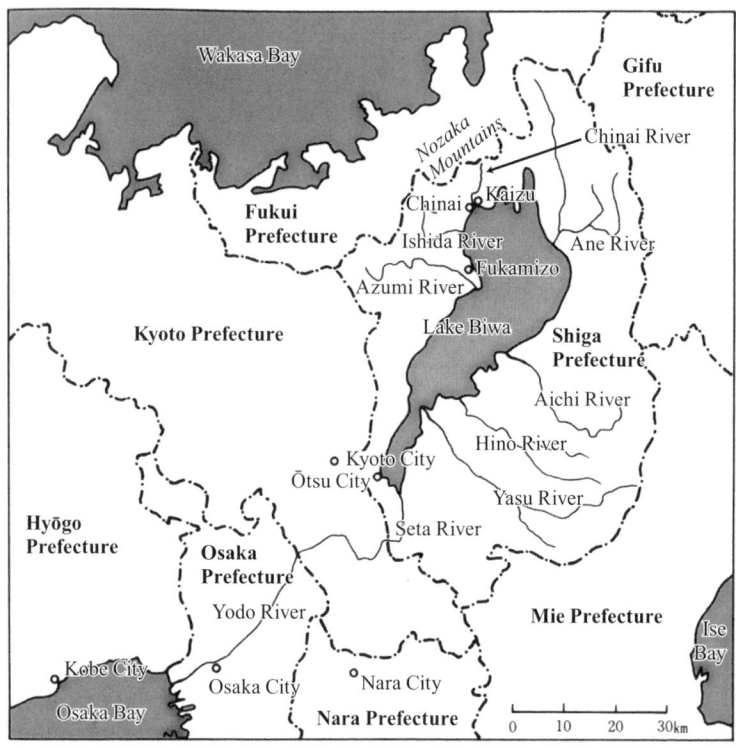

Source: Torigoe and Kada, eds, 1984

continuously maintained for more than 250 years in Chinai Village.[6] The Chinai *Kiroku* has been maintained by village representatives, such as the village headman (*shōya*), the district chief (*kochō*) or the district head (*kuchō*), as routine memoranda distinct from official documents. It describes not only the village's official activities but also actions taken by villagers in response to natural disasters (such as floods) and personal comments about such events, and may therefore be thought of as a 'village diary' of sorts. Around the Taishō Period (1912–1925) there was a change in the nature of the matters it recorded: prior to this period it had reported the results of the elections of village officials as well as incidents and events; after this period it is more like a diary, containing descriptions of daily events.

Chinai Village is a farm village located northwest of Lake Biwa (Figure 2.1). Before the Meiji Period, it had belonged to the Kōriyama feudal domain. Subsequently, there were a series of changes in the village's position in the Japanese local administration system: under the ward-district (*daiku-shōku*) system in 1872–1879, it was the First District of Takashima County (Dai-1-ku of Takashima-gun); in 1879–1885 it was simply Chinai Village again; in 1885–1889 it was consolidated into a six-village association; in 1889, in the midst of a flurry of town-village mergers, it was incorporated into Momose Village; and in 1955 it merged with three other villages to become the Chinai District in Makino-chō. Thus, Chinai Village no longer officially exists. However, since the village bylaws remain in effect after numerous revisions, for all practical purposes (including ours) Chinai Village still exists today.

Chinai is divided into a lakeside area (Shimo-chinai) and an inland area (Age-chinai). According to *Kiroku*, there have been no significant changes in the number of households in Chinai Village since 1872: 105 households (521 persons) in 1872; 124 households (610 persons) in 1925; 125 households (592 persons) in 1940; and 134 households (602 persons) in 1970. Most villagers are farmers. In 1872 the village's cultivated land consisted of sixty-six *chōbu* (about 162 acres) of rice fields and eleven *chōbu* (about thirty acres) of other fields. Some villagers engage in fishing in the Chinai River and Lake Biwa.

The Hira Mountains lie to the west of the village and Lake Biwa to the east, but it is only a short distance from the mountains to the lake. The rivers through the village have raised riverbed levels due to historical circumstances. For example the Momose River, which runs through the middle of the village, has a national road running underneath it through a tunnel. Due to these circumstances, the entire district, including the village, is regularly flooded. *Kiroku* contains a large number of entries about collapsed river banks and the use of the water from the Momose and Chinai Rivers (the latter is also referred to as the Ōkawa River in *Kiroku*).

In the next section, I discuss the structure of Chinai Village (hereinafter referred to as 'Ōaza'[7] or 'Chinai' unless otherwise required, since the village is now called Ōaza Chinai).[8]

The structure and transformation of a rural community

The transformation of a rural community's management body

In 1889, the year following the introduction of the town-village system, Chinai Village was incorporated into Momose Village along with six neighboring villages. In 1890, Chinai Village established its village bylaws, which were revised in 1897 and 1902. The bylaws are interesting in that they show two sides of Chinai – as a subordinate of the Momose administrative village and as an autonomous body that had been maintained until the incorporation. Let me outline the community structure of Chinai Village as it appears in the three versions of bylaws and some of the entries in *Kiroku*.

The 1890 bylaws are titled 'Bylaw by Agreement among the Residents of Ōaza Chinai, Momose Village' (Momose-village Ōaza Chinai Jūmin Moushiawase Kisoku). Its preamble states that Ōaza must maintain its own conditions even after the incorporation.

> The town-village system was enforced in April 1889. Accordingly, residents have the right and obligation to comply with all of the rules and regulations to be issued by the public office, and citizens must make efforts to promote public works projects. Unlike towns, however, a rural community is surrounded by various special circumstances. Therefore, each of the residents hereby agrees to establish this bylaw, with which all residents shall comply for six years starting this year.

Maintaining Ōaza's own bylaws effectively means maintaining the autonomy and dominion of Ōaza itself, even after it was incorporated into Momose Village.

There were only two administrative posts defined in the 1890 bylaws: managers (*sewagakari*) and councilors (*kyōgiin*). The managers referred to here are effectively the same as the traditional community representative (*sōdai*). The councilors (*kyōgiin*) are substantially the same as the traditional members of the Chinai *osabun* (the decision-making body; hereinafter, the 'council of elders,'[9] to be discussed in more detail shortly), although the qualifications for being one are somewhat different, such as being subject to a certain amount of land tax.

> Article 1: Ōaza shall have two managers (*sewagakari*) (one principal and one vice), who shall administer administrative, legal and other affairs related to the Chinai community.
>
> Article 3: Ōaza Chinai shall have several councilors (*kyōgiin*). A councilor shall be at least twenty-five years of age, shall have set up his own household, and shall have paid land tax of at least ten yen.

As early as 1892, the title of manager (*sewagakari*) in this bylaw was changed to district head (*kuchō*) and deputy district head (*kuchōdairi*). For example:

> With regard to the posts that have been titled manager, as from April 1892 Mr. Nakagawa and Mr. Maekawa were appointed district head and his deputy, respectively, as announced in the notice of results of the recent district head elections for Ōaza Dai-4-ku (Fourth District) of the seven districts in Momose Village.

Despite these minor changes, the subsequent revisions to the bylaws in 1897 make it clear that the 1890 bylaws basically confirmed the existing council of elders (*osabun/kumigashira*) system. The 1897 bylaws are titled 'Ōaza Chinai Bylaws (Ōaza Chinai Kiyaku).' The preamble states, '[d]ue to the expiration of the Agreed Ōaza Bylaws…these bylaws intend to revise the bylaws for Ōaza Chinai as a result of discussion among council of elders members…' In short, the council of elders (*osabun*) reappears here as the body empowered to revise the bylaws.

Furthermore, in marked contrast to the 1890 bylaws, the 1897 bylaws contain relatively complete descriptions of the various administrative posts in Ōaza. The 1890 bylaws, which were enacted upon Chinai's incorporation into the administrative village, kept the national government at a distance. In contrast, the 1897 bylaws have a group of provisions that clearly demand that the village be managed locally, by Ōaza's own residents/officers. These provisions seem to cover virtually everything – what must be done by locals, who should be in charge, the rights and obligations of community members, affairs delegated by the national government, and so forth. Let us take a closer look at the provisions on administrative posts.

First, Ōaza's decision-making body is the council of elders (*osabun*). To this day, the 11th of January is called 'First Meeting Day' in Chinai. On this day, the council of elders decides when to hold Ōaza's events and who will assume Ōaza's administrative posts. The meeting is attended by councilors only. A general meeting of residents can only be convened by a resolution passed at a council of elders (*osabun*) meeting. Paragraph three (as below) of the bylaws details the qualifications for becoming a councilor – for example, he must own land of a certain minimum value. Paragraph four is contradictory to Paragraph three; it states that a person who owns land equivalent to that of a councilor must assume obligations equivalent to those of a councilor. This shows that councilors are appointed not solely on the basis of the value of land they own but that membership in the council of elders is exclusively held by certain families. Following are excerpts from the bylaws, renumbered by the author.

1. At the council of elders (*osabun*) meeting held on the 11th of January, the *nengyōji* [literally: 'annual event manager'; discussed in more detail below] shall be replaced, decisions shall be made on official events, and the health union president and other officers shall be elected to a one-year term./At the council of elders meeting held on the 3rd of April, the accounts for the preceding year and the budget for the current year shall be discussed and agreed upon.
2. Upon notice from the district head (*kuchō*), all councilors shall attend council meetings punctually. A council of elders meeting is empowered to decide various matters related to Ōaza.
3. A council of elders (*osabun*) member shall be at least twenty-five years of age, shall have set up his own household, and shall own land of at least 400 yen in value;/provided, however, that even if such person is not married, he shall be eligible for election to an official post.
4. A non-council member who owns land of at least 400 yen in value and has set up his own household shall have obligations equivalent to those of a councilor.
5. A person who gains admission to the council of elders shall pay one yen as membership fee.
6. A councilor shall be disqualified from membership of the council of elders at the age of sixty-five. Any councilor under the age of sixty-five may not resign his membership in the council of elders barring accidents;/provided, however, that the foregoing shall not apply if his heir is under the age of twenty-five.
7. No general meeting shall be convened unless a resolution to do so has been passed at a council of elders meeting.

The district head (*kuchō*) and his deputy (*kuchō-dairi*) are designated by the council of elders. The district head may hold many other posts concurrently, including some for conducting services delegated by the village administrator.

Election of the district head and deputy district head shall be held on the 11th of March./The district head and deputy district head shall serve for two years./Remuneration, travel expenses and daily allowances shall be paid to the district head and deputy district head.

In the subsequent bylaw provisions, the title *moroto* appears in addition to *osabun* (council). *Moroto* are members of *miyaza* (a religious union, as explained in more detail below). *Moroto* are worthy of special mention here because they are an important component of the community structure. A detailed explanation of *miyaza* activities is unnecessary here, as the present focus is on how the rural community's role in protecting its living environment has changed through the interventions of the national government. Hence I simply outline the relationship between *moroto* and the community structure.[10] Excerpts from the bylaw focused on *moroto* follow, renumbered by the author.

1. On the morning of the 24th of March each year, one person per *moroto* family shall be sent for cleaning the Hiyoshi Shrine.
2. A *moroto* member shall be disqualified from *moroto* membership at the age of sixty-five;/provided, however, that the foregoing shall not apply if his heir is under the age of twenty-five.
3. All charges to be collected pursuant to the *moroto* rules from a person who gains admission to *moroto* shall be collected together with community membership dues.
4. Of the expenses required for Karasaki Shrine festivals, those for food and drink for representatives of shrine parishioners, the annual event manager (*nengyōji*), other officers, sumo wrestlers and police officers shall be borne by Ōaza. All other expenses shall be borne by *kannushi* (shrine guardian).

A religious body called *miyaza* can be found in many rural communities in Shiga Prefecture. There have been numerous studies on *miyaza*, dating back at least to the early 1940s (e.g., Higo 1941). Today, *miyaza* membership in most communities is open to all villagers, and *miyaza* have effectively become *muraza* (village union),[11] the ritual-performing group for the Shinto ritual known as *okonai* (literally: 'event'). The original *miyaza*, however, was not merely a religious body; it overlapped with the governing body in communities where it maintained privileges. Where there is *miyaza*, the community structure is characterized by its division into two classes – *miyaza* members and non-*miyaza* members – that are generally equal (for further explanation see Chapter Three, Introduction). Members of each class are equal, and the equality between the two classes is maintained by rotational duty systems. The two classes are not equal in terms of Shinto rituals but are generally complementary to each other. Major inequalities in this system have been eliminated in many communities, including Chinai, by opening *miyaza* membership to all villagers. Hence, in Chinai Village and elsewhere, *miyaza* and its members are both called *moroto*[12] (members of *miyaza* and *miyaza* itself) and appear as such in the Chinai *Kiroku* from early on.

More than half of the entries in *Kiroku* written in the late nineteenth century are about shrines and Shinto rituals, which suggests that religion played a much larger role then than it does today, not only in Chinai but in rural communities in general. Shinto rituals appear to have been extremely important, and were exclusively controlled by *miyaza*.

In Chinai, the council of elders (*osabun*) members and the *moroto* members were substantially the same.[13] The council of elders was the village's administrative (governing) body, while *moroto* conducted Shinto rituals. But despite this formal separation of the management of secular and sacred affairs, the fact that the membership of these two governing bodies was substantially the same suggests that in practice there was little separation of these two spheres.

Another administrative post that appears in the 1897 bylaw is the annual events manager (*nengyōji*). This office has primary responsibility for annual events and, in Shiga Prefecture, generally exists wherever *miyaza* exists. In some research *nengyōji* is understood as a village handyman who first appeared during the Meiji Period. But Higo argues that the position has existed since ancient times and was always an important component of Shinto rituals (1941: 351–2). In Chinai, the annual events manager (*nengyōji*) later played a very important role, but in the 1897 bylaw, it appears only in provisions concerning Shinto rituals.

Thus, until 1897 Chinai was managed by the council of elders (in charge of administrative affairs), which was substantially composed of the same people as the *moroto* (in charge of Shinto affairs). The basic structure of this framework had not changed since at least the final years of the Edo Period (approx. 1860s).

In the 1902 bylaw, however, the council of elders disappears as the governing body. Let us take a look at the preamble.

In this bylaw, the *osabun* (council of elders) has traditionally been called *kumigashira* (head of the village), and used to decide on all matters by discussion. Ōaza's general meeting on the 26th April 1902 passed a resolution to abolish the aforementioned *kumigashira* and elected six drafters, who prepared a draft amendment. Upon approval at the general meeting on the 8th of May 1902, the amended provisions of this bylaw came into force. The provisions are as follows.

In place of the council of elders (*osabun*), a representative system was introduced, under which councilors (*kyōgiin*) were elected. The right to vote in council elections was opened to all households in Ōaza – technically, only to 'all Ōaza residents who are men at least twenty years of age and are the head of a household.' As for the eligibility for election, a person was eligible for election 'if and only if the person is a male of at least twenty-five years of age, is eligible to vote and has set up his own household.' In addition, councilors were divided into two categories on the basis of land they own, as seen in the following provisions:

> Article 18: Councilors shall be elected pursuant to the following paragraphs:
> 1. All persons whose entire household owns land of at least 350 yen in value shall be classified into Class A.
> 2. All remaining persons shall be classified into Class B.
> 3. Class A voters and Class B voters shall elect an equal number of councilors separately. A person eligible for election may be elected by all voters regardless of whether he belongs to Class A or Class B.

This classification into Class A and Class B is intended not only to protect the privileges of landowners but also to include the following provisions:

> Article 42: Class A shall have the obligation to serve as annual event managers (*nengyōji*).

> Article 43: The number of annual event managers (*nengyōji*) shall be three, who shall take turns serving in a conventional manner.

This bylaw put an end to the traditional community management by the council of elders (in charge of administrative affairs). Although a new elected council of community management was created, it no longer overlapped to the same extent with the *moroto* (responsible for Shinto affairs).

But note that the new bylaw stipulates that the manager of annual events (*nengyōji*) is restricted to Class A councilors – those who had previously been members of the council of elders, and continued to be, for the most part, *moroto* members. Although the new bylaw does not specify the functions to be performed by *nengyōji*, the later

1924 bylaw revisions dedicate a special chapter to detailing these functions. According to these bylaws, the manager of annual events (*nengyōji*) is not only responsible for managing Shinto rituals but also various other events in Ōaza and, indeed, during an emergency, is responsible for managing the whole of the Ōaza village. It also stipulates: '*Nengyōji* shall not resign.'

The 1924 bylaw also dropped the provisions that divided councilors into classes A and B, but retained the requirement that only 'those who own land of at least 300 yen in value' could serve as the annual events manager.

Administrative, Shinto, village and household affairs

As we have seen, although Chinai 'village' has been subject to various changes in its administrative framework, it seems to have continuously existed as an autonomous unit of one sort or another. Despite the continual encroachment of centralized administrative controls, to this day many of the villages in Shiga Prefecture have retained many important characteristics of an autonomous village community. This kind of rural community, although no longer formally 'villages' in administrative terms, will nevertheless be referred to as villages in this work.

The existence of genuinely autonomous villages is an impediment to a centralized government's attempts to directly control individual households. It has been frequently observed that, in Japan, villages are the most important of the intermediate organizations between the national government and the individual household. Neither villages nor households have remained unchanged in the process of rapid modernization since the Meiji era. There have been numerous and extensive changes in the relationships between households and villages, between households and the national government, and between the national government and villages. These have been detailed by countless studies in rural sociology.

As discussed in the previous section, in Chinai, the body managing local religious affairs (*moroto/miyaza*) significantly overlapped with the local council of elders until the early twentieth century; that is, it was effectively a theocratic system of local governance. Through a variety of both internal and external pressures, however, the local administration of secular and sacred affairs was gradually separated, radically transforming the traditional local governance structures. This transformation had ramifications for the relationships between individuals, between households, and between the local and national governments, as mentioned. Hence it is worth examining how households had previously been involved with one another and in the affairs of the village shrine and the village itself. For example, how did the village respond to an individual's death? How were 'household affairs' related to 'village affairs?' How have these relationships changed? The general trend since the Meiji Reformation has been that 'village affairs' have been divided into 'household affairs' and centralized government concerns as the villages have lost much of their significance.

Village duties versus household duties

As discussed, although there were significant changes in Chinai's administrative structure during the century beginning in the late 1860s, this does not mean that Chinai was entirely absorbed into a centralized administration unit or lost its independence. For example, the compulsory service in village affairs stipulated in the 1924 bylaws indicates its continuing independence. Indeed, these provisions for compulsory service remain virtually unchanged until 1968, and even then the change merely differentiates the obligations of farming (five days) and non-farming households (three days). A brief look at the provisions in the various revisions of the bylaws bears this out:

> [1924] Article 4: Compulsory service shall be imposed for the following categories:
> 1. Paid service: Each year, each household shall provide four persons for paid service. The amount of payment shall be five *bu* for a household owning land of fifty to 100 yen in value and an additional three *bu* for each 100-yen increment in land value, with any value less than 100 yen being discarded./A household failing to provide the aforementioned number of laborers shall pay compensation.[14] The amount of such compensation shall be determined by a councilors' meeting./A household may be requested to provide more than the aforementioned number of laborers if necessary. In this case, no compensation shall be paid for any shortfall in the number of laborers provided./The following persons and households shall be suspended from the obligation of compulsory service:/The community representative (*sōdai*) and his deputy (*dairisha*), the Ōaza messenger (*Ōaza kozukai*), households where soldiers stay or which provide for soldiers (during the term of such stay or provision), the annual events

manager (*nengyōji*), the boiler man (*yuwakashi*), and persons who pay construction charges.
2. Unpaid labor: (1) dam construction; (2) cleaning of Karasaki Shrine before regular festivals; (3) cemetery cleaning; (4) work at construction sites; (5) clearing of snow from streets; and (6) snow fencing (including materials)./Any other work specifically determined./The obligation to provide (1) through (4) shall not be imposed on the community representative (*sōdai*) and his deputy (*dairisha*), the Ōaza messenger (*Ōaza kozukai*), and shrines and temples; and (6) shall not be imposed on shrines and temples.
3. Emergency service: Upon signal of emergency, all men between seventeen and sixty years of age shall be mobilized with appropriate protective gear.

[1957] Paid compulsory laborers, five; 30 yen per laborer; 100 yen penalty for failure to provide a sufficient number of laborers; an additional 20 yen for each additional laborer provided; the number of days of service, five days.

[1967] Compulsory laborers, five; 50 yen per laborer; 500 yen penalty for failure to provide a sufficient number of laborers; an additional 400 yen for each additional laborer provided; subsidy for the fire brigade increased from 4000 yen to 6000 yen.

[1968] Compulsory laborers, five for each farming household and three for each non-farming household; shortfall and additional laborers are treated in the same manner as previously (400 yen for each additional laborer, and 500 yen penalty for shortfall)

Subsequently, Chinai Village was placed under the control of a board of councilors, which has substantially the same form as the current system. However, as evidenced by changes in the religious body to be reviewed in the following section, the village's class structure was taken over by the board of councilors. Even after the post-World War II agrarian reforms, some systems seem to have retained traces of the former council of elders system. Yet, to understand the continuity of the village's role as the protector of everyday lives, it is necessary to understand that the village's management framework, which retained traces of the feudal landlord system in the head/branch family system, was more dramatically affected in the postwar period.

Let us explore the changes in the religious body in order to more fully understand these transformations.

Transformation of the independent body

The rotating shrine guardianship

The entries in *Kiroku* from October 1872 include the following:

> In 1872, the year of *mizunoe* (the ninth of the ten calendar signs) monkey,[15] Nakagawa Gentarō had been serving as the rotating shrine guardian (*kannushi*). The Kaizu branch office then informed us that the shrine guardian must always be one and the same person and that the rotating guardianship was not acceptable. Therefore, after consultation with all villagers, a ballot was held in late May in an attempt to appoint a permanent shrine guardian. The winner was Torii Sajirō's family. After a while, in October, Mr. Torii was summoned by the Kaizu office to sit an examination, and was licensed as a shrine guardian. Immediately, village officers proceeded to deliver implements as had been agreed. In mid-October, the rotating shrine guardian Nakagawa Gentarō and his relatives, accompanied by village officers, delivered all of the shrine guardian's implements to Torii Sajirō's house. The Toriis thus became the permanent shrine guardian family. (October 1872, the year of *mizunoe* monkey: Incumbent Village Head)

Here we can see the Meiji government's intervention in the villages systems of maintenance and operation. The post of the village's shrine guardianship had traditionally been served by different village families in rotation by casting lots. Following the government's intervention, the Torii family became the village's permanent shrine guardian.

The government's decree affected villages all over the country, with effects that have continued for more than 130 years now. When I first read this record, I was led to wondering as to how the rotating shrine guardianship had been maintained. This was what prompted my research on the *miyaza*. Rereading the Chinai *Kiroku* from this perspective, it appears to be an entirely different history of this village, whose *miyaza* had broken down. The *Kiroku* traces the process of the *miyaza*'s breakdown, during which the community structure that had traditionally supported and been supported by the *miyaza* repeatedly disappeared and was recreated in attempts to compensate for the *miyaza*'s breakdown. Reading the *Kiroku* from this perspective also revealed a rural community that does not conform to the classical rural studies typology of communities in the Kinki region.

Although the *miyaza* in Chinai Village has broken down, there are still some communities where the Shinto rituals continue to be conducted by *miyaza*. In order to understand how these *miyaza* are maintained and the structures of the communities that have managed to sustain their *miyaza*, let us compare the community structures of rural communities with *miyaza* and those without one.

Typology of rural communities and *miyaza* in the Kinki Region

Miyaza are religious bodies that still exist in many rural communities throughout the Kinki region with various names and forms. In the area north of Lake Biwa in Shiga Prefecture they are often called *okonai* (literally: event). In the area west of the lake they are often called *moroto*. The name *okonai* seems to refer to the fact that the *miyaza* conducts Shinto rituals, while *moroto* seems to refer to its membership.

One of the roots of the terms *miyaza* is *za* (union), which implies a clear distinction between members and non-members. Hence, there must be obvious inequalities between members and non-members of the union. Yet rural community typology has traditionally understood rural communities in the Kinki region to be alliances of households that are on a relatively equal footing with one another. Clearly, this understanding is contradicted by the presence of *miyaza* in these communities.

It seems that the conventional rural community typology has misunderstood these rural communities in the Kinki region in one way or another. But perhaps we must allow that these communities do indeed have characteristics that led researchers to the conclusion that they are alliances of households on a relatively equal footing with one another. This might derive from the fact that in most of the villages that still have a viable *miyaza*, it consists of all of the villagers, and hence, the villagers appear to be on a relatively equal footing.

One way to approach this dilemma is to ask whether every *miyaza* began as a privileged union that gradually opened to all villagers, or if they originally included all villagers, among whom a privileged group gradually formed in some cases. Researchers specializing in *miyaza* are sharply divided over this issue. Conventionally, *miyaza* whose membership is exclusively reserved for certain villagers are called *kabuza* (exclusive union) and those whose membership is open to all villagers are called *muraza* (village union). Whether the earliest *miyaza* were *kabuza* or *muraza*, it is generally agreed that *miyaza* were established before the end of the medieval period. It has also generally accepted that *miyaza* were more like *kabuza* during the medieval period, and gradually opened, so that those that have not been lost are currently more like *muraza*. My concern here, though, is whether a loss of *miyaza* means the breakdown of the governing structure operated by the union, and what has happened to communities in which a *muraza* continues to conduct religious rituals. To this end I examine Village N in Kohoku-cho, Shiga Prefecture, a community where Shinto rituals are still conducted by *miyaza*.

The Shinto ritual '*okonai*' and its framework

Framework for the *okonai* ritual

In general, the main part of the Shinto ritual *okonai* (event) is to offer food and sake to the gods and to dine together as a community. In these activities, an important role is played by the 'head family' (*tōya*), which is appointed at the annual *okonai* ritual. Several 'managers' (*sewakata*) conduct the proceedings of the ritual. These staff members and *okonai* members carry out the ritual under the supervision of the shrine guardian (*kannushi*). Interestingly, in some villages the head family (*tōya*) is also the shrine guardian, while in other villages these two roles remain separate. In addition, some villages have both a professional, or permanent, shrine guardian and a rotating guardianship, resulting in double shrine guardianship. In such cases, the post of the professional/permanent shrine guardian was created to satisfy the Meiji government's requirements, while the villages maintained their rotating shrine guardianship in a conventional manner.

In addition, many villages in Shiga Prefecture have an annual events manager (*nengyōji*), as previously mentioned. The *nengyōji* plays various roles in the *okonai* ritual. The important point here is that the *nengyōji* performs these religious roles despite being a (secular) village officer. This issue will be discussed in more detail later.

The *okonai* rituals vary widely from village to village. But in each case, it is generally overseen or officiated by the shrine guardian, the head family (*tōya*), the head facilitator (*sewakata*) and the (secular) annual events manager (*nengyōji*).

Village N has three *okonai* groups: Higashigumi, Nakagumi and Nishigumi (literally: East Group, Middle Group and West Group). To become a member, when a boy is born, his family invites six village elders to enter the boy's name in the '*yoboshi*' (literally: traditional Japanese headgear which indicated the wearers' social class) register. When this formality (called '*yoboshi-gi*': *yoboshi* capping) is completed, the boy is formally a member of his family's *okonai* group. Each *okonai* group in this village has six elders, six junior-elders, and other members. The oldest and the second oldest of the elders are called *kannushi* (shrine guardian) and *waki-kannushi* (assistant shrine guardian), respectively. The elders are the six oldest surviving members registered in the *yoboshi*, in the order of entry. Thus, some men may serve as an elder for a long time while others may not serve at all. The head family (*tōya*) is appointed by the shrine guardian each year by casting a lot (drawn out of a hat) at the annual *okonai* ritual.

The *okonai* ritual is conducted by six *sewakata* (head facilitators) members. *Yoboshi* registrants serve as the head facilitators (*sewakata*) by turns in the order of entry. The head family (*tōya*) plays its part in accordance with instructions given by the *sewakata* (the head facilitator). In addition, the (secular) village annual events manager (*nengyōji*) plays an important part.

Apart from this quite rigid seniority system, members of an *okonai* group are categorized into the Major, Middle and Minor (supervisor, intermediate and subordinate) categories according to the families they are from (currently only the Major and Middle categories remain, but the details of the ritual below are from the period before this changed). Although a *tōya* is appointed from each category, effectively resulting in three *tōya*, the Major *tōya* (*tōnoya*) is the ritual *tōya*, while the others are expected to assist him.

Village N's *okonai* ritual reaches its climax when each of the three ritual groups places their offering of *kagami-mochi* (a stack of round rice cakes piled according to size) on their portable shrine and brings it to the village shrine as their offering. The offerings are made by all three groups, and in the predetermined order of arrival, their offerings are called 'Flower Mountain,' 'Second Mountain,' and 'Third Mountain.' This order of arrival is determined on a rotating basis, so that each group makes an offering of Flower Mountain once every three years. The offering of *kagami-mochi* is the only occasion upon which the village's three *okonai* groups come into contact during a Shinto ritual.

The Shinto ritual 'okonai'
In general, the *okonai* ritual is held in mid-February, although this may vary from village to village. In Village N, the *okonai* ritual is usually held between the 13th and 17th of February. The three *okonai* groups in Village N each conduct their rituals separately, but what they each do is basically the same. In the following, I describe the ritual proceedings in detail by referring to the Middle (Nakagumi) group's *Shinji ni kansuru sho gyōji oboe chō* (Book of memoranda on events related to Shinto rituals) for 1961.

On the 7th of February, 'the head facilitators (*sewakata*) gather at the Major head family's (*tōnoya*'s) home from around eight in the morning.' First, they 'assess what things require repair due to damage suffered during the previous year's Shinto ritual and things which need to be made anew according to resolution.' In the process, they 'work out the budget for the [year's] Shinto ritual and decide on the allocation of the costs of food and drink to adult males [family heads according to the *yoboshi* register], families, etcetera, and produce tickets for each family.' They then 'prepare a table of allocation' and deliver it to the annual events manager (*nengyōji*). The 1961 table of allocation states: 'glutinous rice for *kagami-mochi* to be offered to the shrine, 180 cc per family; soybeans for tōfu, 180 cc per *yoboshi* registrant (per family); *amazake* (sweet drink made from fermented rice or sake lees), 180 cc per female child of a *yoboshi* registrant's family; white rice, 90 cc per *yoboshi* registrant and 900 cc per family in its turn for providing it (three families, 2.7 liters in total).' The annual events manager (*nengyōji*) then visits each *okonai* member's house to 'deliver the tickets, and collect glutinous rice, soybeans and rice from each family.' He then delivers the 'glutinous rice to the Major *tōya*'s house, the soybeans to the head facilitator (*sewakata*) house, and white rice to the Nagahama *kōji* (rice malt) store and requests that the product be delivered on the morning of the 16th.' In addition, orders are placed for gibel carp, sake and other food necessary for the ritual.

On the 10th of February, 180 cc of soybeans per *yoboshi* registrant, totaling 15.3 liters, are to be collected by the *nengyōji* and brought to a tōfu maker, with whom an order for thirty-two tōfu is to be placed.

The 13th of February is the day to 'collect glutinous rice for *kagami-mochi*'; '360 cc of glutinous rice are collected per family, totaling 12.6 liters (from thirty-five families), and are placed in four new buckets in equal amounts by weighing them precisely. After being washed, the rice is placed at the alcove and covered by newspapers.' Additionally, the *okonai* group whose turn it is to offer the Flower Mountain for the year, will provide '3.6 liters of glutinous rice...which is then divided into four equal parts and placed in buckets (900 cc of glutinous rice in each bucket) and soaked in water, to make *futae*.' *Futae* (literally: 'two-layered') is an 'offering for the goddess Benten and Lord Maitreya.' Unlike other offerings, this offering is 'consumed exclusively by the Major *tōya*'s family without being distributed to all villagers.'

On the 14th of February, the heads of all the *tōya* families in full dress (wearing *haori* (a Japanese half-coat) and holding a folding fan) report the 'condition of soaked rice for *kagami-mochi*' to 'each village elder at his [own] house' (*Nakagumi go-shinji chōrō jūrai reishiki kinen* (Records of traditional procedures for the Nakagumi Shinto rituals for the elders)).

The 16th of February is the day of rice cake pounding to make *kagami-mochi*. Rice cake pounding is of central importance to the *okonai* ritual. In another village in the same area of Kohoku, each group makes its own *kagami-mochi* – typically more than one meter in diameter – in competition with each other. 'In the presence of the head facilitators (*sewakata*), the Major *tōya*'s family members and helpers complete the rice cake pounding.' During this work, they are 'prohibited from drinking or eating.' After the rice cake pounding, the managers have a lunch of 'tōfu and pickles only' prepared by the Major *tōya*'s family. They also have dinner 'at the Major *tōya*'s house.' The rice for this dinner is from the collected rice. The dish accompanying the rice is to be the 'shallow bowl dish to be served at the dinner party' on the 17th. For the soup, both tōfu and deep-fried tōfu are provided by the managers, which are 'cooked and eaten.' That evening, the 'eve party' (*yoimiya*) takes place. Prior to the eve party, *yoboshi* members[17] arrive and deliver '540 cc of rice per person, always measured using the group's 540 cc measuring cup.' Halfway into the party, the head facilitator (*sewakata*) asks the most senior village elder to 'announce the casting of lots to appoint the *tōya* members for the following year.' At the eve party, food and drink are served 'on a high one-person table to each village elder only, with the rest of the members eating from their one-person round trays.' They sit as shown in Figure 2.2. At this party, the most senior village elder casts a lot to appoint the following year's Major *tōya*. The assistant shrine guardian then draws a lot to appoint the

Figure 2.2: The seating arrangements at okonai *rituals*

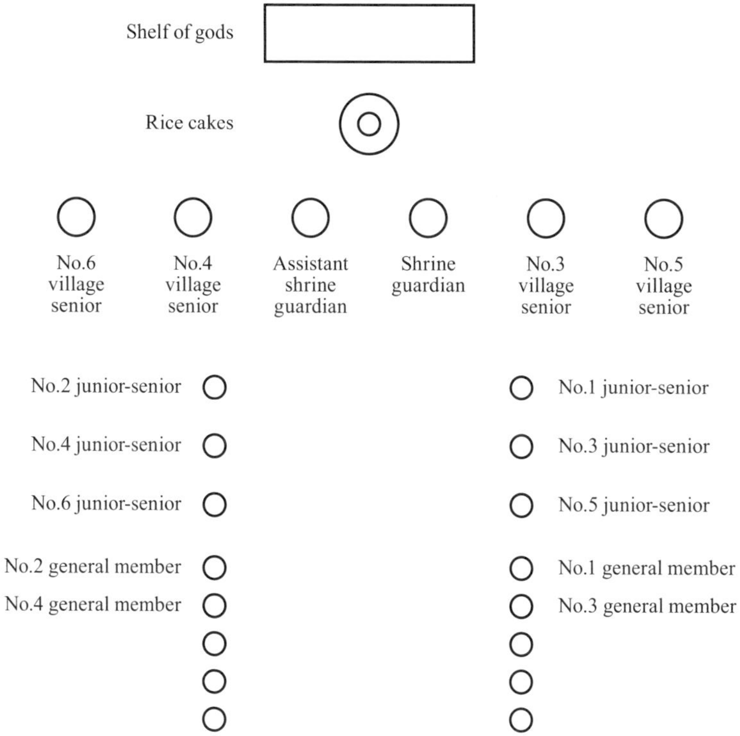

Shelf of gods					
Rice cakes		◎			
○	○	○	○	○	○
No.6 village senior	No.4 village senior	Assistant shrine guardian	Shrine guardian	No.3 village senior	No.5 village senior

Left side		Right side	
No.2 junior-senior	○	○	No.1 junior-senior
No.4 junior-senior	○	○	No.3 junior-senior
No.6 junior-senior	○	○	No.5 junior-senior
No.2 general member	○	○	No.1 general member
No.4 general member	○	○	No.3 general member
	○	○	
	○	○	
	○	○	

tōya from the Middle category. When a family's name is drawn, the assistant shrine guardian shows the lot to the other village elders one at a time, followed by the head facilitator's (*sewakata*) report of the result to the general congregation. During the party, *tōya* (the head man), in *kamishimo* (traditional ceremonial dress), sits next to *sewakata* (the head facilitator). Earlier, at the rice cake pounding, the *tōya* wore a crested kimono and simply greeted his guests at the door of the drawing room.

The 17th of February is the day of the shrine visit and dinner party.

The six *sewakata* and the *nengyōji* arrive at the Major *tōya*'s house at four-thirty in the morning and 'work out a plan for arrangements.' The *nengyōji* then goes around to 'wake village members at five (the elders are to be woken first, followed by others).' At the Major *tōya*'s house, meanwhile, *yoboshi* members gather one after another. They are provided with 'tōfu soup first, followed by sacred sake (7.2 liters).' On this occasion, the Major *tōya* greets his guests with the humble phrase, 'please have a drink of my family's poor sake.' Again, food and drink are served 'on a high one-person table to each village elder, with the remaining members eating from their one-person round trays.'

After they have enjoyed the breakfast party for a while, a bell is rung to announce that it is time to visit the shrine. The head *sewakata* 'notifies the village elders thereof and serves tea.' The book says that on this occasion, the *'nengyōji* is in charge of entertaining the village elders in all aspects.'

After the rice cakes have been offered to the shrine, *yoboshi* members go home and wait. After a while, the dinner party starts, at a time 'set by agreement by the *sewakata* members.' And, again, the *'nengyōji* goes around to each house' to notify the time. Meanwhile, at the Major *tōya*'s house, the *sewakata* members cut the rice cakes (returned from the shrine) into blocks using rulers and put the members' names on them to share the cakes equally among members. These blocks are later distributed among the *yoboshi* members.

The dinner party starts with an 'opening address,' followed by '1. Solemn greeting (by the Major *tōya*); 2. Offering of poor sake (by the Major *tōya*); 3. Offering of sake to the incoming *tōya* members (by the head *sewakata*).' When the *sewakata* offers sake to the incoming *tōya* members he marks the succession. On this occasion, the shrine guardian offers a cup of sake to the Major *tōya* and the assistant shrine guardian offers one to the Middle *tōya*, 'in cooperation with the *nengyōji*.' Meanwhile, the outgoing 'Major *tōya* and the head *sewakata* sit and wait in attendance.' Then they chant a typical festive Noh song, *Shikainami*.

The party proceeds to '4. Distribution of the rice cake blocks (by the incoming Major *tōya*); 5. Offering another cup of sake...(by the Major *tōya*).' Then, all three *tōya* members sit next to each other and finally conclude the party. The entire Shinto ritual is completed by the following: '6. Request not to leave after chanting *Senshūraku* [a typical closing Noh song] as tea will be served (by the Major *tōya*); 7. Invitation for tea by succeeding *tōya* members; 8. Closing address (by the Major *tōya*).'

The *nengyōji's* role and transformation of the ritual framework

It is necessary to briefly elaborate the roles played by the various offices described in the ritual above. The *sewakata* members are in charge of matters in the Major *tōya*'s house, as well as all communication with the village elders, while the *nengyōji* serves as the link between the Major *tōya*'s house and the other members. The *nengyōji* is typically understood to be a (secular) village post, rather than an official appointed for the (sacred) *okonai* ritual. This understanding is supported by the fact that the *tōya* (head families) give the '*nengyōji* a white fan as a token of their gratitude' following the completion of the ritual. This formality seems to symbolize the role of *nengyōji* as the link between the Shinto rites and village affairs. Before we can pursue the question of why the secular office of the *nengyōji* is so closely involved in the *okonai* ritual, we need to return to the case of Chinai Village; but before we do that, we should first outline some of the more recent changes in Village N's *okonai* ritual.

As previously mentioned, the *okonai* ritual in Village N continues to this day, although there have been several changes. To begin with, there was a change in the ritual's proceedings in 1966: 'soybeans for tōfu shall no longer be collected [but instead] the cost of the tōfu shall be collected together with the cost of food.' In 1967 they decided to reduce the 'tōfu levy for the eve party…from two boxes to one.' Then, in 1969: 'the cost of the sacred sake to be collected from the village elders, junior-elders and *sewakata* members shall be increased from 1.8 liters to 3.6 liters starting this year.' Despite these minor changes, though, it is safe to say that there have been virtually no changes in the ritual proceedings.

There was, however, a major change in the ritual framework in 1978. *Shinji ni kansuru sho gyōji oboe chō* (Book of memoranda on events related to Shinto rituals) states, 'starting from the Shinto ritual for 1979, there shall be two *tōya* members, of which the following person shall be the supervisor: [name omitted].' This is the point at which the traditional three-level *tōya* system (appointed from the Major, Middle and Minor categories) changed to the current dual system. In each *okonai* group of Village N, the Major category roughly consisted of head families, while the Middle and Minor categories consisted of branch families. Changing to a dual system meant integrating the Middle and Minor categories and adjusting the number of families belonging to the Major and Middle (supervisor and subordinate) categories.

As a matter of fact, this change resulted from changes in the practice of *yoboshi* registration. In earlier times, families had registered all of their sons in the *yoboshi* register – not only the firstborn. Later (it is not clear precisely when), they began to register only the firstborn son. Those sons who were not registered could never become *tōya*. This broke down the head/branch family structure in the *miyaza* (ritual union). The balance between the

Major category and the Middle and Minor categories was thus lost. This created the situation in 1978 mentioned above where it became necessary to integrate the Middle and Minor categories.

At the same time, there was a change in the prerequisites for filling the post of *nengyōji*. Until then, the *nengyōji* had been appointed from *yoboshi* members belonging to the Major and Middle categories.[18] This was changed as follows: 'In and after 1979, members of the Middle category shall serve as *nengyōji* in the order of seniority.' To organize this new system, the following provisions were formulated for newcomers: 'any person who joins Nakagumi from elsewhere or another group and goes through *yoboshi* capping shall be, if he is older (than the person currently serving as *nengyōji*), entered [in the *yoboshi* register] immediately below the place of the *nengyōji*. If the person is younger (than the person currently serving as *nengyōji*), he shall be entered immediately below the members of the same age; provided, however, that if he served as *nengyōji* in or before 1978, he shall be placed immediately below the places of *sewakata*.' Thus, the post of *nengyōji* was incorporated into the seniority system.

There was yet another change in 1982. The following inquiry on a newcomer from elsewhere was received: 'Mr. N has gone through *yoboshi* capping and has become a member of Nakagumi. Which category should he belong to, the Major or Minor?' The answer was 'he shall belong to the Minor category,' according to Mr. N's wishes. At that time, eighteen families belonged to the Major group and fourteen to the Minor group.

These changes may have occurred in the process of the village's adaptation to broader social changes, such as the steadily increasing number of part-time farmers. The point is that the Major/Middle/Minor category system had been maintained until the time of these changes, and that specific administrative posts had been linked to certain categories, independently of the seniority system. In other words, these classes – the Major, Middle and Minor – had been maintained for a long time within the *miyaza* (*okonai* group) of this village, in which membership in the group appears to have been equally open to all villagers.

The unity and separation of Shinto affairs and village affairs

Moroto

In Village N's case, as we have seen, its *miyaza* has a dual internal structure, although its membership is open to all villagers, giving

The Village as an Independent Body 89

the impression of a single-layered structure. Let us now review the situation in a village whose *miyaza* has dissolved. We return now to Chinai Village for our example, examining the relationship between the *miyaza* and the community structure. The main reference materials used here are the 1890, 1897, 1902 and 1924 versions of the village bylaws.

In Chinai Village, *miyaza* was called *moroto*. Its members were also called *moroto*. The eligibility requirements for membership in the *moroto* are not clear. According to Chinai's *Moroto* register, twenty-two families were members in 1933. Considering that the village had more than 120 families at the time, it is clear that the *moroto* membership was quite restricted. Let us now examine developments in the history of the Chinai *moroto* from the perspective of its position in the community structure, particularly with regard to the villages system of governance.

Unity of Shinto and administrative affairs
The 1897 bylaw begins with the following statement: 'Due to the expiration of the Agreed Ōaza Bylaw dated the 16th of March 1890, this bylaw intends to revise the bylaw for Ōaza Chinai as a result of discussion among council of elders (*osabun*) members...' The bylaws define the term '*osabun*' (council of elders) in this statement as follows: 'A council of elders member shall be at least twenty-five years of age, shall have set up his own household, and shall own land of at least 400 yen in value.' The following provisions clearly indicate that Chinai Village was governed by this council of elders at the time: 'Upon notice of *kuchō* (district head), council of elders members shall attend a council meeting punctually. A council of elders meeting is empowered to decide various matters related to Ōaza.'

The bylaw includes provisions on *moroto* as well as those on the council of elders, as follows:

1. A council of elders member shall be disqualified from council membership at the age of sixty-five. Any council member under the age of sixty-five may not resign his membership in council barring accidents; provided, however, that the foregoing shall not apply if his successor is under the age of twenty-five.
2. A *moroto* member shall be disqualified from *moroto* membership at the age of sixty-five; provided, however, that the foregoing shall not apply if his heir is under the age of twenty-five.
3. A person who gains admission to the council of elders shall pay one yen as membership fee; provided, however, that a person who

gains such admission for the second or more time shall provide two *shō* of sake as a donation to the after-rice-planting party.
4. All charges to be collected pursuant to the *moroto* rules from a person who gains admission to *moroto* shall be collected together with community membership dues; provided, however, that a person who gains such admission for the second or more time shall provide 3.6 liters of sake as a donation to the after-rice-planting party.

The first half of the 1897 bylaw includes provisions on the eligibility for membership on the council of elders (*osabun*) and the *moroto* as well as for the post of the *nengyōji*. The remaining provisions in the first half may be applied to all ordinary families, for example: '*Ohimachi* (sunrise-waiting party)...shall be attended by family heads only' and '[a]ll persons who have set up a household in Ōaza shall join the *Shinpū* association (one of the widespread local Shinto associations).' The latter half of the bylaw includes provisions on administrative posts, including *kuchō* (the district head). The last provision of the bylaw is: 'No general meeting shall be convened unless a resolution to do so has been passed at a council of elders (*osabun*) meeting.'

As described above, these provisions indicate that the village (secular) administration was governed by the council of elders (*osabun*) and the religious organization was governed by the *moroto*. These two bodies, though, consisted of substantially the same members, as evidenced by the actual records of membership. Therefore, it would be safe to say that at least until this period, the village was governed by effectively the same body in both its administrative and religious affairs.

The same version of the bylaws also includes the following provisions for the post of *nengyōji*:

At the *osabun* meeting held on the 11th of January, *nengyōji* shall be replaced and (the health union president and other officers) shall be elected to a one-year term.

In these provisions, '*nengyōji*' seems to be one of the village officers (along with the health union president, for example). The only provisions for the *nengyōji* in this bylaw, however, are as follows: 'Of the expenses required for Karasaki Shrine festivals, those for food and drink for the representatives of shrine parishioners, the *nengyōji* and other officers, sumo wrestlers and police officers shall be borne by Ōaza. All other expenses shall be borne by the *kannushi* (shrine guardian)'; and '[t]he sunrise-waiting party on the 13th of January shall only be attended by family heads; provided, however, that the district head, the deputy district head and the *nengyōji* shall attend and conduct affairs during the night.' Similarly to Village N, these provisions treat the *nengyōji* as a link between Shinto affairs and village affairs.

I return to the issue of the *nengyōji* later. For now I simply note that at that time (1897) in Chinai Village, the *osabun* and *moroto* administered village (administrative) affairs and Shinto affairs, respectively, and that these bodies consisted of substantially the same members. In other words, up to at least 1897 when the bylaws were established, village affairs (administration) and Shinto affairs were inseparable. Furthermore, it is safe to say that the *moroto* at that time had characteristics of the early-modern *miyaza*, in that it was in many important respects a *kabuza* (exclusive union) and existed as the ruling class. For the time being, let us consider this to be the original form of *moroto* in this village and follow the subsequent changes in *miyaza*.

Separation of *moroto* and *osabun* rules

Before the 1897 bylaws, Chinai Village had enacted the *Jūmin Moushiawase Kisoku* (Bylaws by Agreement among the Residents of Ōaza Chinai, Momose Village) in connection with the village's incorporation into Momose Village in 1889 as previously mentioned. Its preamble reads as follows:

> The town-village system was enforced in April 1889. Accordingly, residents have the right and obligation to comply with all regulations and rules to be issued by the public office, and citizens must make efforts to promote public works projects. Unlike towns, however, a rural community is surrounded by various special circumstances. Therefore, each of the residents hereby agrees to establish this bylaw, with which all residents shall comply for six years starting this year.

Curiously, the terms *osabun* and *moroto*, which seem to be what the phrase 'various specific circumstances' refers to, never appear in this bylaw. The only posts appearing in this bylaw are *sewagakari* (managers), who are in charge of administrative affairs, and *kyōgiin* (councilors), who are restricted to those who 'shall be at least twenty-five years of age, shall have set up his own household, and shall have paid land tax of at least 10 yen' (as mentioned above). These bylaws specify the duties of these officers and the procedures of their meetings. Considering that the qualification for election to the prefectural assembly was payment of a specified amount of land tax, the above provisions were probably formulated to align the membership requirements of *osabun* in with the provisions applicable to the Momose administrative village. As described above, however, when the bylaws were revised in 1897, provisions on the *osabun*, *moroto* and *nengyōji* were added to the preceding 1890 bylaws. Why did they need to add these provisions, which seem to have been intentionally excluded from the earlier bylaws?

As discussed above, the 1897 bylaws also indicate some degree of breakdown of the original form of community rule – wherein there was some integration of administrative and religious affairs, as indicated by the overlap of *osabun* and *moroto* members. It was not until 1897 that the *osabun* and *moroto* were specified in the village bylaws. Yet, of all the duties of *moroto* members, only one is mentioned in the bylaw: 'On the morning of the 24th day of March each year, one person per *moroto* family shall be sent to clean the Hiyoshi Shrine.' There are no provisions that specify how *moroto* members should administer Shinto affairs.

Thus, it seems that the village was under pressure to separate the *moroto* from administrative affairs and to clarify its role in Shinto affairs, despite the fact that the *osabun* and *moroto* members continued to be substantially the same. This may have had something to do with flood damage in the village in two consecutive years (1895 and 1896), followed by an outbreak of dysentery that resulted in huge expenditures and impoverished many of the villagers. The *Kiroku* describes these circumstances as follows.

1. Due to the storm that had continued since mid-July 1895, an embankment at Aza Inoshiri became loose and its surface collapsed on the 28th of July – about 315 meters of the embankment collapsed. To repair it, stakes (one *jō* two *shaku*; about 3.6 meters) were put up and the embankment was sandbagged...This has brought hardships beyond description to people.
2. From the 1st of August 1895, Mr. T suffered from dysentery. On the 23rd of August, his family members showed symptoms...As of the 1st of September, there are twenty-five patients in Ōaza Chinai.
3. The outbreak of dysentery has caused a considerable expenditure of Ōaza's money and considerable hardships to people.

4. Due to financial difficulties, Ōaza borrowed 150 yen from the village's fundamental property reserve.
 5. It rained continuously from the middle of July 1896, and around the 10th of August Aza Ōkawa River overflowed and flooded residential lands. By the 30th of August most of the residential lands in Ōaza had been flooded. In addition, the strongest southeast wind on record blew and caused damage to houses, resulting in two completely destroyed, six half-destroyed, and ten seriously damaged houses. The heavy rain on the 6th and 7th of September caused river flooding everywhere in the village...Due to the circumstances described above, not a single grain of rice was harvested. We looked in every corner of the village for surviving rice plants, but all survivors were found unacceptable because they had been under water for a long time. Barley, wheat and rye were successfully harvested, but pulses produced no crop because of night crawlers. Ōaza had no vegetable crop at all.
 6. Families staying with relatives or friends: sixty-eight families.
 7. Families which have put up a shed: forty-three families.
 8. Families which cannot afford to put up a shed: thirteen families.
 9. Families which temporarily received financial aid from emergency savings: fourty-six families.
 10. In response to the worst wind and flood damage on record, on the 10th of October 1896 all residents of Ōaza agreed on and read aloud a set of proposed measures, and all of the villagers agreed to accept them to save expenses and, in witness thereof, prepared a written agreement to which people affixed their seals.

These descriptions seem to indicate that in the face of such emergencies, the *osabun* members had shown what they could do, while, at the same time, the 'people' were clearly exhausted. The bylaws were revised under these circumstances. Nevertheless, it seems clear that independent of these emergencies, there was a struggle between maintaining and transforming the traditional system of local governance. This period should therefore be regarded as the time when the control of administrative and Shinto affairs began to be separated.

From *osabun* (*kumigashira*) to *kyōgiin*

The 1902 bylaws begin as follows: 'In these bylaws, *osabun* (council) had traditionally been called *kumigashira* (head of the village), which decided on all matters by discussion. Ōaza's general meeting on the 26th of April 1902 passed a resolution to abolish the aforementioned *kumigashira* and elected six drafters, who prepared a draft amendment. Upon approval at the general meeting on the 8th of May 1902, the amended provisions of these bylaws came into force.' Subsequently, neither the term *osabun* nor *moroto* has appeared in the village bylaws.

In the 1897 bylaws, only twenty-two of those who 'own land of at least 400 yen in value' could be councilors. And these councilors were both *osabun* and *moroto* members. In the 1902 bylaw, the requirements for councilors were relaxed as follows: 'A person shall be eligible for election if and only if the person is a male of at least twenty-five years of age, is eligible to vote and has set up his own household.' These provisions should not, however, be taken at face value as relaxing the requirements for *osabun* and *moroto* membership, for they also establish the following classification: 'Councilors shall be elected pursuant to the following paragraphs/1. All persons whose entire household owns land of at least 350 yen in value shall be classified into Class A./2. All remaining persons shall be classified into Class B./3. Class A voters and Class B voters shall elect an equal number of councilors separately. A person eligible for election may be elected by all voters regardless of whether he belongs to Class A or Class B.' This classification is referred to in the section titled 'Obligations of Class A' in the latter half of the bylaw, as follows: 'Class A shall have the obligation to serve as *nengyōji*.'

In this way, *osabun* and *moroto* disappeared from the village's administrative system. Yet their former members continued, to some extent, to maintain their privileges, although far more in Shinto than administrative affairs. This was achieved by restricting the post of *nengyōji* – the link between village affairs and Shinto affairs – to a privileged class, so that only (former) *moroto* members could hold the post of *nengyōji*.

Relaxing requirements for councilors and the role of the nengyōji

In the 1924 bylaws, the requirements to run for councilor remained unchanged, while the eligibility to vote was changed to one male of at least twenty years of age per household. In addition, the land value requirement for *nengyōji* was changed to at least 350 yen. This requirement was eventually deleted in 1933 and replaced by the phrase, 'the standard amount plus one yen.' The meaning of this is that the qualification of *nengyōji* is given to all persons whose payable community membership dues (classified according to land price, income, estimate, etc.) are one yen higher than the average amount of community membership dues for the entire village. This system was maintained until very recently, in which the basic qualification for *nengyōji* was that his payable community membership dues were higher than the average.

However, the membership requirements for *moroto* were never relaxed. The 1943 *Moroto Register* records twenty-two members at that time. This number decreased substantially during World War II and the chaotic days that followed. Although the second and third sons of families were admitted at this stage, the *moroto* eventually dissolved soon after the war. Except for this admission of younger sons, the *moroto* seems to have dissolved without any attempts to save it by opening its membership to all village households. Factors that led to the *moroto*'s dissolution are not clear, though, since there are no details of its religious services discernible in the records.

These trends in Chinai Village seem to differ from other villages, such as Village N, whose *okonai* has been maintained until the present. And yet, the structure of Chinai Village remains quite similar to Village N, in that it appears to have adopted a single-layered structure, but has actually maintained a double-layered structure by reserving the post of *nengyōji* for the privileged class.

To make this clear, then, I must provide a brief explanation of the post of *nengyōji* in Chinai. Similar to Village N, the *nengyōji* in Chinai were officers who formally moved back and forth between village administration and Shinto affairs. Let us examine the specific bylaws for details.

Chinai Village's 1902 bylaws simply state that the duties of the *nengyōji* were to be performed in a 'conventional manner.' It was not until the 1924 bylaws that these duties were specified in detail. As was the case in Village N, the Chinai bylaws reveal that the *nengyōji* conducted not only religious affairs (such as making arrangements for Shrine festivals and Buddhist temple services) but also village affairs (such as supervising construction sites, collecting rice paid as rent, and making arrangements in the event of disaster). Villagers in both villages give the same explanation when asked why the post of *nengyōji* is still maintained and retains traces of an outdated feudal type hierarchical structure: the office of the n*engyōji* requires a lot of time and money, so you must be of a certain social status to fulfill the duties. Granted that these practical considerations still hold today, I contend that the historical post of the *nengyōji* is in many respects a distinctive response to the modern processes of imposed separation of religious and administrative affairs in a *miyaza*-village, a community-type in which religious and administrative affairs were traditionally administered by one and the same body.

Summary of the discussion so far

Let us return now to the original task of attempting to find the key for discussing villages in the Kinki region. In conventional rural community typology, Kinki villages have either been intentionally excluded from consideration or they have been regarded as generally having a single-layered, egalitarian structure of the *kōgumi*-type (a type of Japanese rural community, defined as a horizontal union consisting of generally equal households). This is how they are represented through the concept of 'a tōya system' community as proposed by Masao Gamō, which is also a single-layered community. (This was the framework I had in mind when I begain my research into *miyaza*.)

But as we have seen, although these villages seem to be single-layered and egalitarian, they are in fact double-layered (upper and lower) through *miyaza*. This double-layered structure remains deeply entrenched through local Shinto rituals. Indeed, today this hierarchical characteristic can only be seen in Shinto rituals. In Chinai Village, the double-layered structure was generated in the process that broke down the traditional system in which Shinto rituals and administrative affairs had been administered by a single body. I believe this issue has much to do with the fact that Kinki households have high levels of independence, although I did not mention this point above.

Although some commentators have argued for the dismissal of the rural community typology as outdated, I believe it still has some significance, at least as an amplifier of powerful imagery. Yet it is difficult to regard villages with these characteristics as *kōgumi*-type villages, egalitarian and single-layered. We will therefore call such villages '*miyaza*-type' for the time being.

Disaster and safety – The 'poor fishing system'

Introduction

While conducting fieldwork in a certain village, Takashi Uchiyama found that the term '*shizen no buji* (safety of nature)' was used by the villagers in a way that is roughly synonymous with the way we currently use the term 'nature conservation.' The primary difference is that 'nature conservation' tends to imply the protection of nature by humans in a situation where humans and nature are distinctly separated, while the villagers' 'safety of nature' concept implies that nature, the village and 'I' all belong to the same world and interact with each other (Uchiyama 1998: 46–7). According to Uchiyama's understanding of the villager's worldview, the concept 'safety of nature' also includes the sense that 'if this interaction stays safe, the individual parties involved – nature, the village and "I" – will also stay safe.' Uchiyama interprets this to mean that 'in order for "me" as an individual person to stay safe, the "village" and "nature" as our communal space-time, and interaction existing in this space-time, must stay safe' (Uchiyama 1998: 52–3).

My field research in Japanese villages indicates that the same can be said about the relationship between the village and each household. In fact, this relationship appears to be more common between the village and the household than between the village and the individual 'I.' This is at least in part because in the villages I have visited in my research activities – mainly those in the Kinki region – conceptions of 'nature' tend to focus on farmland and water supplies, while the household is the basic unit of labor. It may also be due to the fact that the household is the most commonly used unit of individual activity in the villages' documentary records. Hence, what Uchiyama calls 'me (I)' can be regarded as effectively equivalent to the 'household' in terms of relationships with nature or the village.

Now, if nature must stay safe to keep the village safe, there would have to be techniques for keeping nature safe. There must also be techniques for maintaining and governing the relationships between household and village, and between household and nature. The relationship between nature and the village is discussed in detail in Chapter Four. In what follows here, I focus on the relationship between the village's safety and the safety of individual households.[19]

Documents retained by the Nakagawa family in Chinai District (hereinafter referred to as 'Nakagawa documents') and *Chinai Gyogyō Kumiai enkaku shi* (History of Chinai Fishermen's Association) will be used to supplement the Chinai Village *Kiroku* in this discussion. All quotations in this section are from the *Kiroku* unless otherwise noted.

As discussed, Chinai Village's religious body *moroto* (*miyaza*) and its governing administrative body *osabun* (council of elders) remained substantially unchanged until the Taishō Period (1912–1926). In simple terms, the village was a theocracy. In response to a combination of internal and external pressures, however, the village's administrative and religious affairs were separated from one another, and the traditional rule of the *osabun* transformed. As we have seen, under the traditional rule of the *osabun* (council of elders), Shinto affairs and village affairs were all administrative activities of the village. The village bylaws contained provisions for Shinto affairs as well as 'village affairs.' In the process of rapid modernization, however, 'village affairs' were gradually divided into 'household affairs' and 'village administration' while reducing in scope. Some researchers have gone so far as to claim that village affairs have virtually disappeared. The stereotypical image presented from this perspective is that neighborhood associations and districts function only as the smallest units of administrative functions, while the central government is immediately connected to each household.[20]

In this section I outline how the village was involved with each household before modernization changed these relations by reviewing the measures taken by the village in response to a natural disaster in 1885, on the eve of the rural community system reform. More specifically, I explore the question of how the village treated and supported the families that were affected by the previously mentioned floods. What was the relationship between 'village affairs' and 'household affairs' at this time? Once I have elucidated the pre-modern relationship, I further explore how these matters have changed. If Chinai has survived as a 'village' (*mura*) despite all these changes, what were the mechanisms or systems instituted between the 'village' and 'households' that supported Chinai's sustainability despite the manifold pressures of individualization?

Disaster

> It rained continuously during May 1885, and there still was a lot of rain during June. On the 30th of June Lake Biwa overflowed due to heavy rain and 80% of the rice fields were flooded. My garden was flooded to a maximum depth of thirty centimeters. Seventy-three houses were flooded. (Nakagawa documents)

In July, the head of Takashima County inspected the village and provided a subsidy. This is described as follows:

Ōtsuka Sugizō, the head of Takashima County, came to inspect the village to check whether the floodwaters had receded. Tanaka Ro acted as his guide. Mr. Ōtsuka felt pity to see flooded houses and said that villagers whose house had been damaged and those who lived in a shed should apply for relief. Thus, applications were made through the village head's office. A subsidy was provided: 139 yen 45 *sen* 9 *rin* as relief and 39 yen as shed building costs. The money was distributed to the needy. Details were recorded in the relief register.

In addition, the village succeeded in their request for a subsidy from the county's Industrial Promotion Section to purchase soba seeds for sowing in the flooded fields. The village explained, 'the seeds will be delivered through the San'in route. We requested 126 liters. However, the cost of transport is expensive because of distance, resulting in a 50% increase in purchase price as compared to locally produced seeds.' The village was also given instructions, such as: 'they told us that late-ripening crops are good for flooded fields.'

Further, in March 1886, the village was provided with 'a subsidy from the Imperial Court' for the cost of seeds to be sown in flooded fields. The subsidy was provided to 'owner farmers whose own land is less than 1.2 acres and tenant farmers' at the rate of the 'price for 10.8 liters of seed paddy per *tan* (0.25 acres) of flooded field.' The number of recipients and the amounts provided were: 'seventy-one persons; an amount of 96 yen 6 *sen* 6 *rin*; February of the same year, an amount of 9 yen 75 *sen*.'

The size and scope of these government subsidies indicates how devastating the flood of 1885 was to the village. Yet the village did not passively await government handouts. From the beginning it had taken its own measures, beginning with routine disaster countermeasures as can be seen in the following:

> July: Impoverished people who find it difficult to make a living asked for help. *Osabun* (council of elders) members discussed [their application] and decided to loan seed paddy stored in the emergency storehouse until this autumn.

> September: Villagers had no way of making a living due to the flood. Therefore, the three villages discussed special use of the common land Aza Hiratoyama and decided on when each village may use the land. This village allowed use of the land by all villagers, except *kumigashira* (head of the village) and *osabun* (council of elders) members, as a special relief measure. Two *osabun* members went to

the site every other day to supervise villagers' use of the land [and] to make sure standing trees were not used.

In short, emergency rice stocks were loaned in July, and in September affected residents were allowed access to the common woods to use brushwood and undergrowth, despite the fact that the common land was usually not available for use at that time of year.

It seems, however, that these 'ordinary' local measures were not sufficient for the village to recover from the flood. As discussed in more detail later, the village affected a major reform: it granted the exclusive rights to trap fish in the river to people who had been impoverished by the disaster. That right had previously been the common property of all villagers. Before discussing this major reform in more detail, I need to explain the significance of the river fish trap in Chinai.

The river fish trap

Chinai River runs along the boundary between Chinai Village and Nishihama Village. The river contains extremely fertile fishing grounds, with a large number of fish swimming upstream from Lake Biwa between May (when *ayu* fish [*Plecoglossus altivelis*] start to swim upstream) and November (when Biwa trout [*Oncorhynchus masou rhodurus*] swim upstream). People set traps at places less than 100 meters from the river's mouth and catch seasonal fish swimming upstream. The history of this practice has been dated as far back as the Keichō era (1596–1615) (Ōtsuki: 58–9).

Because these fertile fishing grounds are situated along the boundary between Chinai and Nishihama, there had been repeated disputes over fishing rights between the two villages. These disputes have been extensively studied by Itō (1984: 110–19). I use his work to supplement the information found in the Chinai *Kiroku* to discuss the significance of fish traps in Chinai River for Chinai Village.

The last dispute over fish traps broke out in 1870 and continued until 1875. At that time, the trap fishing right was held by Nishihama Village. The dispute occurred because fishermen from Chinai Village attempted to catch fish by setting another fish trap downstream of Nishihama's trap. Nishihama fishermen argued that fishing downstream of their trap would cause a reduction in their catch because fish traps in Chinai River are intended to catch fish swimming upstream. According to *Kiroku*, in 1873 Chinai Village began to lobby and petition the prefectural office to obtain the fishing rights. As a result, as early as 1874 the prefectural office issued a notification recognizing that both villages had fishing rights in light of the local history and declaring that an exclusive holder of the trap fishing right should be decided on by tender between Nishihama and Chinai. In the tender that soon followed, Nishihama bid 180 yen, whereas Chinai successfully bid 352 yen for the trap fishing right. The bid price is estimated to be equivalent to seven years' proceeds from the village's trap fishing.

Subsequently, in response to Nishihama's complaint of unfairness, the prefectural office proposed a compromise that fishing should be practiced by both villages at the ratio of three to one. Eventually, the dispute was finalized by Chinai's payment of a settlement (115 yen) to Nishihama in March 1875. The circumstances of this dispute are described in *Kiroku* as follows:

> With respect to the right to fish in Chinai River, twenty-five fishermen from Nishihama Village, who claim to have a fishing right, and two fishermen from this village have practiced fishing. This had caused a couple of troubles and I have heard from others that [??] have felt unbearably depressed about this for a long time. Then, to our surprise, along with the Meiji Restoration came an official notice that all roads, lakes and rivers belong to the Imperial Court and not to private individuals. Accordingly, on the occasion of a public event all villagers discussed and decided to sweep away abuses. As a result, in February 1873 our representatives visited the Shiga prefectural office and requested that based on the recent notice which changed the ownership of lakes and rivers, the right to fish in Chinai River be granted to fishermen from this village. Then it was found that fishermen from Nishihama Village also had been lobbying the prefectural government. Once again a dispute arose. This village sent about five representatives and Nishihama Village sent seven or eight representatives to the prefectural office and made daily requests to the office. They held discussions but the situation was too complicated to make a decision. Finally, in 1875, the office ordered that the matter be settled by tender in accordance with the regulations. We had no choice but to offer a bid. It turned out that we successfully bid at 352 yen for the fishing rights from the upcoming autumn onward. Subsequently, in response to Nishihama Village's repeated request, we paid an amount of 115 yen as a settlement. The receipt for it and a certificate of exchange are attached hereto.

In the following year (1876), fishermen from this village repeatedly lobbied the prefectural office and successfully became authorized fishermen in exchange for payment of 30 yen as tax. (1873 Governor Mr. Matsuda, Naoyuki/1875 Prefectural Governor Mr. Koteda, Yasusada; Current administrative official in charge/*Daisakan* [deputy secretary] Mr. Miyata, Yoshimasa)

However, shortly after Chinai obtained the trap fishing right, in 1879, the Biennial Trap Fishing Act was promulgated with the aim of protecting aquatic resources. Chinai was faced with the possibility that the rights they had finally obtained would lose half their value. The village responded quickly. Before the year was out, the Chinai Gyogyō Kumiai (Chinai Fishermen's Association) had been established under the banner of preventing overfishing and protecting resources. This was soon followed by the establishment of the Chinai Kyōritsu Yōgyo Jō (Chinai Public Fish Farm) in 1883, which established aquaculture activities. Against the backdrop of these efforts, the village negotiated with the prefectural office and, in 1885, an exemption was finally granted to the village under the Biennial Trap Fishing Act. The village's joy at this success is described in *Kiroku* as follows.

> In 1879 the Biennial Trap Fishing Act was enforced. This caused much distress to this village's fishermen. The village thus conducted aquaculture activities. In the presence of Mr. Nakagawa Gengo, fingerlings were released at the fish trap. In recognition of these and other successful activities, the village obtained a special license for trap fishing in 1883. All fishermen were delighted. This year (1885), due to the unavailability of the fish trap, the village made a petition for a lease of a fishing zone. This was approved as shown in the attached document.
>
> > *Bo No.133/Chinai Village, Takashima County*
> > This is to certify that the above village has been allowed to lease the zone as specified below.
> >   Provided, however, that the village shall be reminded that no Class I activities are allowed in the zone. The village shall put a mark at the end of No.4 leased zone to define the zone./From the licensed site of fish trap in Chinai River off Chinai Village down to the lakeshore.
> >
> > 21st of April 1885 Nakai Hiroshi,
> > Shiga Prefectural Governor

The Village as an Independent Body 103

This exemption remains valid to this day.

These passages from *Kiroku* indicate the great significance of the fish trap to the Chinai villagers. But less than two months after Chinai finally obtained the long-sought trap fishing rights, it was hit by a major flood.

The poor fishing system

The villagers' plight after the flood in 1885 is described in the Nakagawa Documents as follows: 'Paupers complained of difficulties and even made and ate what they called "straw rice cakes," which are dumplings made of straw and rice.' When the village administration realized that routine emergency measures would not be adequate to deal with the situation they held a general meeting of villagers and passed a resolution to establish the 'poor's fishing system.' The *Chinai Gyogyō Kumiai enkaku shi* (History of Chinai Fishermen's Association; hereinafter referred to as the 'History') provides a more detailed description of this system than can be found in the *Kiroku*, so I will cite it at length.

> Trap fishing in Chinai River had traditionally been called *mura-kasegi* (village business) and had been available to all Chinai villagers, whether rich or poor. Proceeds from trap fishing had been distributed equally to all villagers who participated in it. However, due to the lake flood in June 1885, Ōaza had the misfortune of having most of its residents' houses flooded. In particular, the difficulty experienced by the poor was beyond description. Unless sufficient means of survival were provided to them, it was inevitable that they would face a miserable situation where they would eventually starve and freeze. Accordingly, Nakagawa Gengo and Torii Goyomo, the village representatives at that time, consulted with each other with much heartache and agony and, as a result, assembled Ōaza residents and proposed to them that starting from the latter period of the year the traditional *murakasegi* should be abolished and a system should be established under which only the poor without assets can engage in fishing and obtain proceeds from it, in order to provide them with a means of survival. Their proposal received unanimous approval of the villagers. This resulted in the enforcement of the poor's fishing system, which continues to this day. However, as it was necessary to supervise the operation of the system, they decided to appoint two representatives by village election to administer accounts and various other affairs. In addition, fishing people have been saving deposits

(as prescribed in Article three, Paragraph two of the Code of Savings Association) from their fishing proceeds, as rental charges for fishing equipment and other property, in accordance with the number of non-fishing people with assets (at least thirty-six *sen* per person per year) (the History: 31).

Trap fishing in Chinai River had been called *mura-kasegi* (village business) and had been available for all Chinai residents under so-called collective ownership. They decided to change it to *hinmin-kasegi* (the poor's business referred to as the 'poor's fishing system'[24] hereinafter) and made it available exclusively for those who were impoverished by disaster.

The structure of the system can be understood from 'Chinai mura chochiku kumiai kiyaku (the Chinai Village Code of Savings Association)' (the History: 25–6). The original reason for creating the Chinai Village Savings Association had been to 'support the life of fishermen in case they face the danger of starvation and freezing due to poor catch or disaster.' Article two of the Code makes it clear that the system is intended to ensure the livelihood of all fishermen by stating, 'any and all persons who practice fishing in Chinai Village shall join the Association.'

Article three has a paragraph stating the amounts of savings. This is described at the end of the 'poor's fishing system' section in the History. 'Article three: The amount to be saved shall be deposited each year in accordance with the following minimum requirements.' The following categories were then listed, but note that there are also provisions for reducing these measures under certain circumstances, such as a poor catch:

1. Trap fishermen: At least 2% of their annual fishing proceeds./2. Other fishermen: At least 36 *sen* per year./3.Those falling under both of the preceding two items: The total sum of the amounts specified in the preceding two items.

From this perspective we should revisit the final lines of the extended quotation from the History above: 'fishing people have been saving deposits…from their fishing proceeds, as rental charges for fishing equipment and other property, in accordance with the number of non-fishing people with assets (at least 36 *sen* per person per year)?'[25] If the fishing association is for everyone, who are these '[o]ther fishermen' specified in Item two of Paragraph two of Article three (the quote immediately above).

Let us refer to the Chinai Fishermen's Association Regulations (enforced in 1879, the 1890 revision) (the History: 1–7) which define fishermen in Chinai. Article two of the Regulations defines the association's membership.

> Article two: The Association shall be established for the purpose of protecting aquatic resources and regulating fishing operations. To achieve this purpose, *any and all persons who live in Chinai Village shall join the Association*. For this purpose, members shall be divided into active members and non-active members, and any adjustment shall be made in January each year to determine the active fishing members. (emphasis added)

This entry provides that all residents in Chinai Village are fishermen who must join the Fishermen's Association. But by dividing fishermen into 'non-active members' and 'active members,' these provisions create a system in which all Chinai residents are obliged to protect aquatic resources while any of them are allowed to become active members if their life becomes difficult. Therefore, the statement '...saving deposits...in accordance with the number of non-fishing people with assets' probably means that 'active members' who are making money from fishing in the river are supposed to save money for 'non-active members' who are not doing so. The logic is that since they never know when a disaster occurs and causes 'non-active members' to switch to 'active members,' they need to save money for potential active members as well; however, since potential active members are not currently making money from fishing in the river, active members who are doing so should save money for them. The number of 'active members' as seen in the History fluctuated between forty-four (1902) and sixty-three (1894) persons, meaning that there was mobility between active and non-active members. As one household may only provide one fisherman according to the Association Regulations, these numbers show the numbers of households which lived on fishing.

Village safety and the weak's right to subsistence

Chinai's 'poor's fishing system' was created in 1885. The village obtained the 'trap fishing right' for all of its residents after many years of dispute with the adjacent village and by finally paying a large sum of money as a bid price and a settlement. Why did they then grant nearly exclusive fishing rights to those villagers who had been impoverished by disaster, only ten years after having obtained the rights for the whole village? This question implies that the fishing right was granted as aid to the needy. In other words, this question is asked from the perspective that the village's trap fishing rights were granted by property owners to the landless needy as a relief measure.

Such an interpretation is incorrect. This right was not 'given' to those most needy by those with plenty, but was an allocation of a universal right of the village as a whole to certain of its members. Just as the right to social security is an undisputable constitutional right in contemporary Japan, Chinai's 'poor's fishing system' was created as an undisputable right of every Chinai resident who was recognized as a fully-fledged member of the community. From this perspective, all Chinai residents are fishermen; some households are currently 'active' and others are currently 'non-active' in fishing at any particular time, but all retain the right to switch to the other status at any time.

The example I am discussing involves fishing rights in a river, but similar approaches have probably developed in mountains communities as well. Torigoe (1997b: 5) goes further and argues that the 'weak's right to subsistence' has long been recognized in relation to common lands in Japan. This right gives priority to the weak in the use of a common land. Torigoe argues that 'the right was not created out of kindness but exists as a right in terms of the theory of ownership.'

Torigoe points to the dual nature of land ownership in a Japanese village, where private land is deemed to be sitting on land collectively owned by the village (1997b: 9). Common land is found where there is no private land sitting on the collectively-owned land. From this perspective, those who have no private land or who do not have sufficient private land to sustain a family in the village should have a preferential right to use or occupy common land for private purposes.

Kawamoto has also argued for a dual nature of land ownership theory. According to this theory, a village's common land and private land are connected to each other in the end. A considerable number of examples have been presented to demonstrate this theory. The 'weak's right to subsistence,' however, has merely been asserted by Torigoe. No specific example has as yet been reported that demonstrates this right. But the present example found in Chinai confirms specifically Ōtsuki's description, upon which Torigoe relied: 'The village had control over trap fishing in Chinai River, and many fishermen were villagers who did not own farmland because the village had a policy of giving priority to the needy in the practice of fishing' (Ōtsuki 1984: 59).

When we relate this theory of ownership to our concerns about peoples' approaches to nature (land), it is clear that the correspondence between what Uchiyama calls 'safety of nature,' the 'safety of village' and 'my safety' is only achieved through the interaction between nature (land) and humans. Further, it has always been necessary for villages to continue to create and sustain the frameworks for such interactions.

I began this section with a discussion of the village framework for the protection of life in individual households and ended with a discussion of the 'weak's right to subsistence.' While Torigoe explained the basis for the 'weak's right to subsistence' in terms of the theory of ownership, by elucidating the history of the 'poor's fishing system' in Chinai village I have revealed the concrete mechanisms by which the 'weak's right to subsistence' comes into effect and factors into real people's everyday lives.

The village as an independent body

I now turn my focus to how Chinai Village responded to the Meiji government's reforms of the local government administration system and created a new living system, from the perspective of the maintenance of the community's territory.

Chinai Village and the government in the early Meiji period

Chinai Village meets the national government
On the 5th of June 1868, immediately before the beginning of the Meiji Period,

> as the younger brother of Gendayū, the current shrine guardian, passed away, *kumigashira* held a meeting and cast lots, and the lot fell on Shichizaemon. [Accordingly, the] handover took place…[village magnates] got dressed in full costume…delivered documents and apparel [to the new shrine guardian] according to precedent.

A similar event took place in April 1869, when a baby was born to the shrine guardian's family.

In the meantime, Japan was undergoing an upheaval – the Meiji Restoration. There were very few changes in *Kiroku*, however, which continued to be dominated by entries about whose turn it would be to administer the next Shinto ritual or about river flooding due to heavy rain. Only one single, three-line entry indicates that the Meiji Restoration had reached this village. It says, '[d]ue to the recent reform, *Kumigashira* discussed and decided on personnel changes as follows./*Shōya-yaku* (village headman): three-year term/*Toshiyori-yaku* (village officials): Same as above.'

In February 1872 there was a farewell party for the Lord of Kōriyama who had worked at Kaizu branch office. Even this event was reported simply as follows:

> In November 1871, the year of *kanoto* (the 8th of the ten calendar signs) sheep,[26] the former Kōriyama became a prefecture. On the last day of February 1872, the year of *mizunoe* (the 9th of the ten calendar signs) monkey, a farewell party for the lord at Kaizu branch office was held at Seieiji Temple in Nishihama Village. The village headman and officials from each village were treated.

Then, in May 1872, when it was Mr. Nakagawa's turn to serve as the shrine guardian, the Kaizu branch office notified the village that 'the shrine guardian must always be one and the same person and that the rotating guardianship was not acceptable.' Chinai Village had never had a permanent shrine guardian before then, as the villagers had always taken turns to serve as the shrine guardian who administered Shinto rituals. Since this rotating shrine guardianship was now prohibited by the prefectural government, the village held a ballot and appointed Mr. Torii as the permanent shrine guardian for the time being, apart from the rotating guardian. Then, as discussed earlier, in October the prefectural office told the village that the permanent guardian had to sit for an examination. Mr. Torii sat the exam, passed, and was licensed as a shrine guardian. The village officers immediately delivered 'all of the shrine guardian's implements' to Mr. Torii's house and made him the permanent shrine guardian.

This was the first in a series of events through which Chinai Village was drawn into direct contact with the national government. In 1872, the Meiji government issued 'Ministry of Finance Notice No.118 on Eradication of Old Village Customs' (Umino and Ōshima (eds) 1989: 203–4) to get rid of traditional customs and conventions in villages. Although the notice did not directly order the village to take corresponding measures, the modernization measures taken by the Meiji government gradually influenced village life and structures across Japan.

The Village as an Independent Body 109

I discuss the relationship between the village and the administration (the national government) in more detail in the next section. Here, I provide an outline of the relationship between the local administration system under the Meiji government and Chinai Village.

In 1745, when the first entry was written in *Kiroku*, Chinai Village belonged to the Kōriyama feudal domain. After the feudal domains were abolished and the prefectures established in 1871, among several other changes, in 1889 Chinai Village was incorporated into Momose Village with six other villages under the town-village system which had been promulgated in 1888. Further, the village merged with three other villages (which had come into existence as a result of enforcement of the town-village system) and became Chinai District in Makino-chō in 1955, which is the current status of Chinai. Over the period of these changes, Chinai Village has maintained its framework as a village in both form and substance, except a certain period when it was under the ward-district system. The Chinai *Kiroku* has been continuously kept by the successive heads of the framework (Chinai Village, Aza Chinai, or Chinai District).

The changes made by the Meiji government in the local administration system did not change the framework of Chinai Village (its territory or members' affiliation). However, the governing system and the administration of the village were forced to undergo major changes.

Allocation of cost for territory maintenance

Except for entries concerning personnel changes and meeting minutes, most entries in the *Kiroku* record repairs to embankments and shrines and disasters. There is a particularly large number of entries on flood damage and repairs due to the geographical situation of the village. The first entry concerning flood damage in the Meiji Period was written in 1870.

> 18th of September, 1870: Due to a heavy storm, an approximately fifty-four meter-portion of Kichirōji Embankment in Aza Misoji along Momose River was washed away; in Kaminokuchi, an about 23.4 meter-portion collapsed; and about 70% of 104.4 meter long Kichirōji North Embankment collapsed. This unprecedented disaster was immediately reported to Kaizu office. Then, inspection was promptly conducted and repairs were ordered. Accordingly, at Kichirōji South Embankement *ushiwaku* (wooden structures for bank protection)

were assembled, and other people built up an embankment using these *ushiwaku* and placed yet another line of *ushiwaku* to provide double protection. The embankment was about 5.4 meters high. The north embankment was repaired in the same manner. The entire 104.4 meter long embankment was protected by a double line of *ushiwaku*. Timbers used for these purposes were cedar logs for ships and purchased from loggers. We notified the office that the price was fifty-six *ryō* three *shu*. The number of timbers used was 340 5.4 meter-logs, and some bamboo was used in *sakuwaku* instead of timber. Other than these, bamboo for *jakago* (bamboo baskets filled with pebbles) was purchased from a person named Ichisaburō of Shinjō Village. Some were also purchased from Funaki. We notified the office that the price of bamboo was twenty *ryō*. For construction of the above *sakuwaku*, thirty-four carpenters and handymen were hired. Their wage was three *shu* and 200 *mon* per person. The work took about 830 man-days. All households in the village worked for seven days, followed by independent farmers' service for 6 days and some additional service by rice field owners in Misoji. In addition, along Ōkawa River, an approximately 23.4 meter-section of Kurikoma Mohei embankment, an approximately 21.6 meter-section of Yoshitake Shōgorō embankment, and an approximately 28.8 meter-section of Tonomachi Shichijirō embankment were collapsed. These three portions were repaired at the village's cost. We notified the office that about 847 to 866 liters of sake and about 325 liters of white rice were consumed. Bamboo was kindly collected from [??] along Ōkawa River according to the proportion, and thus no price for them was notified.

At that time, the Meiji government had not yet fully developed its local administration system, and Chinai Village remained under the jurisdiction of Kōriyama domain. A heavy storm caused 'unprecedented' flooding of Momose River and Ōkawa River (Chinai River), and the village immediately reported the disaster to the local magistrate's office and requested repairs. According to the above record, collapsed embankments along Momose River were repaired at the expense of the local magistrate's office, and those along Chinai River were repaired at the expense of the village. The entry says that bamboo used for those repairs was 'collected from [??] along Ōkawa River according to the proportion.' This implies that the embankments along Chinai River were used exclusively by respective persons after whom the embankments were named (e.g. Mohei embankment was used exclusively by Mohei). Momose

River flooded again that year, and Chinai River the following year. On these two occasions, similar repairs were made at the expense of the local magistrate's office.

According to *Kiroku*, however, the Meiji government issued a notice in 1870 as follows.

1. Due to the 1870 notice, of the places which had been repaired at the local magistrate's expense, those related to water supply to cultivated fields must now be repaired at the village's expense. The three sites of underground drainage along Momose River and the two sites along Chinai River must all be repaired at the village's expense.
2. Both repairs and [??] [the reinforcement] of embankments along Momose River and Chinai River will be at the government's expense.

This notice clearly states that of the repairs which had previously been made at the cost of the Lord of Kōriyama, those related to water supply and drainage for cultivated fields would now have to be borne by the village. This became a problem as early as 1875, in connection with repairs of the underground drainage along Momose River.

Aza Rokutanda underground drainage, 36 meters. Internal measurements: 30.3 centimeters wide; 24.2 centimeters high; bottom board, 4.5 centimeters; rim, 6.1 centimeters; and lid, 7.6 centimeters. Other than the above, a 3.6 meter-long site with internal measurements of 27.3 centimeters x 18.2 centimeters.

Contract price: 28 yen 87 *sen* 5 *rin* (allocated among villages at the rate of 1 yen 31 *sen* 2 *rin* 5 *mō* per *koku* (0.278 m^3) of wood).

With respect to the above work, Mr. Kuratsuji of Sawa Village in the 3rd District of this county said that it was difficult for him to undertake the work because of the low price. Thus, drainage workers were sent to his door and promptly made an arrangement with him and on the 13th of July the original contract price was delivered to him. The repair work was conducted by all villagers on the first day, all *osabun* (council of elders) members on the second day, all *osabun* members and two handymen on the third day, and all villagers on the fourth day and was completed. The work was conducted during the rice planting season and caused a lot of trouble. However, the weather had been extremely dry this year and there had been a lot of drought damage. The former drainage had internal measurements of 18.2 centimeters in width and 12.1 centimeters in thickness. After the recent replacement with the above drainage whose internal measurements are 30.3 centimeters in width and 24.2 centimeters in height, there has been no more drought damage and all villagers are happy. The work cost a lot of money, but we will certainly make it up within this year, although village officers are worried. I must mention that no aid was provided from the prefectural office for the cost of drainage.

According to *Kiroku*, all expenses for this drainage work 'were paid from community membership dues.' The author's modest 'mention' of this fact indicates the village's complaint about this change that had occurred only several years preceding the event. The *Kiroku* also provides evidence that during Kōriyama domain's rule, the village had managed to somehow persuade the local magistrate's office to pay for underground drainage works, as early as 1819, as can be seen in the following:

> For the past few years, we have sent written requests for a subsidy increase by ninety-five *monme* and seven *bu* so that the size of underground drainage can be increased a little. However, we were told that the underground drainage should remain the same. We thus made the same request. Subsequently, after a long discussion, we were told to reconsider and make another request. We had not requested any repairs for as long as eight years, so we obtained from the local magistrate's office a copy of a document explaining the circumstances which led us to make this request. Using the document, we repeated the above request as follows.
>
> We hereby most humbly request financial aid for replacement of the underground drainage.
>
> In response to the above request, we were granted 932 *monme* 2 *bu* in silver as the cost of new drainage.
>
> Internal measurements of the drainage: 30.3 centimeters in width, 18.2 centimeters in height. The total length: 37.8 m. The work was contracted to Hachibē of this village.
>
> Carpenters and handymen/Cost of nails; total; in market price of silver/Two monme was given as cost of sake; 557 *monme* 9 *bu* 1 *rin* 1 *mō*.

I have extensively described these repairs to embankments and underground drainage in Chinai Village during the early years in the Meiji Period for several reasons. First, I wanted to concretely illustrate that in the first year of the Meiji Period, the costs of repairing embankments and underground drains were divided between the village and the government, depending on whether they related to cultivation or rivers per se. This was one of the first measures in Japan to place the rivers under state control. Villagers were still allowed to make relatively free use of river-based resources, such as the bamboo on the banks. While the state assumed this responsibility for maintaining the riverways, the villagers remained autonomous in their administration of the water supply and drainage systems for cultivated lands until state control over these systems was strengthened by the Guideline on Subsidies for Improvement of Water Supply and Drainage Systems in 1923.

The second reason is that I wanted to demonstrate how the members of the village's ruling class, who are frequently mentioned in the reference materials – such as *kumigashira*, *osabun* and councilors – are described in the *Kiroku* at the time, and examine their active roles in administering the village and, especially, the way in which they assumed the central role in maintenance activities concerning the community's territory.

The Meiji local administration system and Chinai Village

Let me briefly review how Chinai Village reacted to changes in the local administration system up to the enforcement of the town-village system, by tracing changes in official job titles.

During the feudal period, there were three key village officials. Of these, the one referred to as *kumigashira sōdai* (representative of assistant headmen) or *sōdai* (representative) was typically referred to in the Chinai *Kiroku* as *osabun*, and *osabun* clearly constituted a *de facto* ruling class in the village. It is inferred from the citations above that *kumigashira* members discussed and decided on important matters in the village during the early years of the Meiji Period. As a matter of form, however, a series of persons designated by the government as the village's 'representative' represented the village, assuming different job titles in different periods.

Since the *Kiroku* is a collection of semi-official documents, it includes copies of many letters posted from the village. Each of these letters contains the then-representatives' names and titles. From changes in the local administration system and in the village's official job titles during the early years of the Meiji Period we can see how the village reacted to the local administration system as well as how the village was actually being ruled. Let us begin with a review of the changes in the representatives' formal job titles as they appear in the *Kiroku*.

The last mention of the three key village officials' job titles in the *Kiroku* were in May 1871. The entry concerns the transfer of the village's household registers when the village came under the jurisdiction of Shiga Prefecture, after a series of changes of the village's supervisory body (from Kōriyama domain to Kōriyama Prefecture, Nagahama Prefecture, and then to Inukami Prefecture).

1. This village had been under the rule of Kaizu branch office in the territory of Matsudaira Tokinosuke, the Lord of Kōriyama, Wa *shū* (province). In January 1870, the feudal system was generally abolished. This village remained under the rule of the former Kōriyama domain from January 1870 to July 1871. In July 1871 feudal domains were abolished. From August 1871 to January 1872, this village was placed under the jurisdiction of Kōriyama Prefecture. In January 1872, Kōriyama Prefecture was abolished. This village was placed under the jurisdiction of Nagahama Prefecture in February and March the same year. In March 1872, Nagahama Prefecture was abolished and this village was placed under the jurisdiction of Inukami Prefecture. This prefecture was abolished, and from November the same year this village was placed under the jurisdiction of Shiga Prefecture. /To: Mr. Michiyuki Matsuda (then governor).
2. Household registers subject to handover and persons registered are as follows:/(1) Number of households: 103 households (including three temples)/(2) Total number of persons: 521 persons (including 251 males,/including one permanently disabled/and three priests)/ The End.

March 1872/a certain Nakagawa, *shōya* (village headman)/a certain Torii, *toshiyori* (village official)/a certain Maekawa, *sōdai* (community representative)/a certain Nakagawa (community representative)/ To: Kaizu Branch Office, Inukami Prefecture

In the following year, the *daiku-shōku* (ward-district) system was enforced and a *kochō* (district chief) was appointed for the village. Subsequently, there is no mention of the three key officials' job titles, beginning with the previously cited entry reporting on the farewell party for the Lord of Kōriyama domain. Instead, the names of *kochō*, two *fuku-kochō* (deputy district chiefs) and two *sōdai* (representatives) are listed.

Later, the name of *shoyaku* (secretary) sometimes appears alongside the *kochō*. The names of two *sōdai* are always presented. At the same time, an increasing number of entries were written with no mention of official job titles. Instead, it becomes increasingly common for entries to end with the statement: 'all expenses were paid from community membership dues.' These changes in the nature of *Kiroku* suggest changes in the decision-making body.

In 1878, the so-called Three New Acts were enacted. In 1879, Chinai was converted from a district under the ward-district system to Chinai Village. However, there was no change in the job titles, except that the village subsequently elected a *senteinin* (appointee) in response to the amendment of the Ward, Town and Village Assembly Act in 1884.

In 1885, the government replaced the *kochō* system with the *rengō kochō* (joint district chief) system. The Chinai *Kiroku* describes this as follows.

> On the 1st of July the same year, *kochō* was abolished in all villages and the *rengō kochō* office was established. The member villages are Shinbo Village, Sawa Village, Nakanoshō Village, Ōnuma Village, Tsuji Village, Morinishi Village and Chinai Village; the above seven villages./Accordingly, the former *kochō* Mr. Torii was appointed *rengō kochō*, and the current *kochō* Mr. Nakagawa was appointed the first secretary of *rengō kochō*./Accordingly, all villagers discussed, elected three *sōdai* and decided that affairs be administered as had been by the *kochō* office. Namely, the first position shall be assumed by Mr. Nakagawa, who shall administer the affairs of *kochō*; the second position shall be assumed by Mr. Torii, who shall administer the affairs of the cemetery manager and the secretary; and the third position shall be assumed by Mr. Nakagawa, who shall administer the affairs of the secretary and also serve as the representative of fishermen./Then, according to the existing rules, we were notified that all documents and notices maintained at the office were to be maintained at the *rengō kochō* office. Embarrassed, we made copies of necessary documents and delivered the copies, and produced a list of notices and put it in a bag in case they are needed in the future.

Here we can see that while the state government's intent was to amalgamate a number of villages into one administrative unit, Chinai Village responded to the changes by continuing to maintain their records and the administration of their affairs independently of the *rengō kochō* system. The village took similar measures in response to a notice given the following year that the *mura-sōdai* (village representative) must be abolished.

> According to recent notice *kō* No.48, the traditional *mura-sōdai* is to be abolished. In the morning, this village's *osabun* members discussed and, pursuant to the said notice, decided that the title of *mura-sōdai* be abolished as of the 1st day of this month and that from then on a *sōdai* (representative) be appointed to administer emergency services as necessary. The *osabun* members also decided that such *sōdai* should not basically be paid and when his service is necessary he should be paid on a per diem basis. In the afternoon, the villagers held a meeting and elected one *sōdai* who shall be in charge of emergency services. The following person was elected by majority vote./Representative for Emergency Services: Mr. Nakagawa/1st of July, 1886/Determined as above.

The *sōdai* had been the most substantial, most important representative of the village since the feudal period. The village thus feared that the abolition of the office of *sōdai* might lead to the abandonment of Chinai Village as an administrative unit. This sense of crisis prompted the village to create a new post: the 'representative for emergency services.' We might consider this moment to be the first crisis Chinai Village faced concerning its autonomous framework. In response, the village took various measures to sustain itself, independently of the government's instructions. What we find, though, is that the office reported on in subsequent entries in *Kiroku* using this new job title is the same old '*sōdai*.' For example, an 1887 entry reads as follows.

> 1st of October 1887, Mr. Torii started to work at the *kochō* office. Accordingly, a *sōdai* election was held./Shichirō Nakagawa was elected by majority vote.

Creating an official post such as this strengthened the village's sense of autonomy, which had been maintained relatively consistently since the feudal period. For the village's upper class, in particular, this situation may have appeared to be an opportunity to present the village as an independent body counterposed to the national government. The need to present Chinai as an autonomous entity became more pressing when Chinai subsequently became Ōaza Chinai and was placed under the jurisdiction of a synthesized administrative village due to widespread reforms to the town-village system.

In 1889, the new city system and the town-village system became effective. This marks the culmination of the Meiji government's reforms to the local administrative system. Chinai Village reacted to these reforms in much the same way as it had to the introduction of the *rengō kochō* office. The village's understanding of this change was that the union of seven villages which had been formed under the *rengō kochō* system was renamed Momose Village and became an administrative village. The *Kiroku* mentions this as follows.

> The town-village system was enforced on the 1st of April 1889. Pursuant to Prefectural Order No.13 dated 19th of February 1889, the former Shinbo Village and Six Other Villages District Chiefs' Office was renamed Momose Village. At the same time, this village and all other villages are renamed *aza mura* (community village). On the 18th and 19th of April the same year, twelve members of the village assembly were elected at Chōhōji Temple in Ōaza Sawa Village. On the 18th of April the second-class members of the assembly were elected. A total of six persons were elected: from Aza Chinai Village, Mr. Torii and Mr. Nakagawa; from Aza Sawa Village…; from Aza Shinbo Village…; from Aza Nakanoshō Village…; and from Aza Morinishi Village…. Then on the 19th of April, in the election of first-class members, a total of six persons were elected: from Aza Chinai Village, Mr. Torii; from Aza Sawa Village…; and from Aza Ōnuma Village….

Chinai remained Ōaza Chinai under the jurisdiction of Momose Village for sixty-five years, until it became Chinai District under the jurisdiction of Makino-chō in the 1955 consolidation of towns and villages.

Village as the protector of its environment and economy

Maintenance and establishment of Chinai Village's territory

In response to these changes in the government's local administration system, Chinai Village successfully maintained its internal integrity as a village, even though, as discussed earlier, its governing body was divided into distinct parts performing separate functions. How, then, did this fragmented governing body establish itself as the protector of its living environment and successfully maintain its independence in its dealings with the national government?

Apart from changes in the allocation of repair costs between the government and the village, as discussed briefly above, one of the most important events concerning the village's territory during the early Meiji Period was the determination of boundaries required by the Land Tax Reform. This not only defined the village's territory but also created an economic foundation for the village by clarifying common land.[27]

The first entry in the *Kiroku* concerning the Land Tax Reform was from 1873:

> In 1873, land certificates were to be issued. Accordingly, those who own land in this village surveyed their land, and the *kochō* office prepared a land register and delivered the same to the Shiga prefectural office.

The land register and other documents related to the Land Tax Reform were not, of course, copied into the *Kiroku*. But the circumstances surrounding the precise determination of boundaries are described therein. Let us review some of those descriptions. First, there is an entry dated 1875 reporting on exchanges of land with adjacent villages, specifically Nishihama and Shinbo Villages, which were located on opposite sides of Chinai Village. Boundaries which had previously been unclear, such as burial grounds and embankments, were determined at that time.

1. In 1875, land certificates were to be checked. All villagers discussed, and villagers were divided into four groups and surveyed lands in the presence of *osabun* members. The land register was corrected and delivered to the Shiga prefectural office.
2. The same year, the burial ground in Aza Hamahata (0.5 acres) was found to be extending over part of Shinbo Village. We however have a certificate for the land.
3. The same year, Aza Kurikoma embankment along Chinai River (48 m) was assigned to this village by Nishihama Village.
4. The same year, land tax was no longer to be paid in rice but in money from now on, at the rate of 3%.
5. The same year, the land tax was to be corrected. The office surveyed lands and roads were determined as follows.

From the southern end of Jintsū Bridge in Aza Hattanda to Roku-Jizō in Aza Hamahata, at the end of every 10.8 meter-section of the road a stone was placed at the center of the road. The road was 1.5 meters wide.

Similarly, mountains contain areas where boundaries or ownership is unclear. The following citation says that *go rinzan* (literally: 'wood mountain') that had previously been used by three villages was nationalized and then sold to certain members of the warrior class in the prefecture, and the three villages repurchased the mountain.

> Aza Hiratoyama (Hirato Mountain), formerly part of Kōriyama domain and called *go rinzan*, had been controlled by three villages, namely, Sawa Village, Shinbo Village and this village. As a result of the issue of land certificates, the area was nationalized and then sold to several members of the warrior class in the former Inukami Prefecture. The three villages purchased the land from the warrior members at 205 yen in November 1876. The cost was evenly allocated among the three villages, with each village paying an amount of 68 yen 33 *sen* 4 *rin*.

This Hiratoyama is often mentioned in subsequent entries in the *Kiroku*, many pertaining to maintenance of the mountain. Other entries show, for example, that the mountain was sometimes opened to those who had been affected by a disaster. This means that the village effectively maintained a means to 'make a living' for those who were affected by a flood or other disaster.

> September 1885: Villagers had no way of making a living due to the flood. Therefore, the three villages discussed special use of the common land Aza Hiratoyama and decided on when each village may use the land. This village allowed use of the land by all villagers, except *kumigashira* and *osabun* members, as a special relief measure. Two *osabun* members went to the site every other day to supervise villagers' use of the land to make sure standing trees were not used.

Unlike the case with Hiratoyama, another case described in the *Kiroku* over land ownership was brought to court. This is described in an entry written in 1879, which reports that ownership of a mountain which had been used by the three villages, like Hiratoyama, was challenged and claimed by other villages based on ancient documents.

> Tango Valley in Aza Sasagamine Mountain had been used as a common mountain of Shinbo Village, Sawa Village and this village. In March 1879, Nakanoshō Village, Ōnuma Village and Fukashimizu Village claimed that the area was their common mountain, based on ancient documents. The ancient documents were examined at a meeting of *kochō* and *sōdai* members of the six villages, but there

was no mention of common use at all. Therefore, the villages held negotiations several times, but the other three villages refused to be persuaded. A petition was thus twice filed in the court branch office. The other three villages then understood our claim. Therefore, in October the same year, deeds to the effect that none of the villagers of the three southern villages would enter Tango Valley in Sasagamine Mountain from then on were exchanged between the other villages and us in the presence of *kochō* and *sōdai* members of the six villages at the *kochō* office of Sawa Village. The case was thus settled./The aforementioned documents are shown in Appendix.

As discussed earlier, there had been a long-running dispute over fishing rights on the Chinai River between Chinai Village and Nishihama Village. The Land Tax Reform triggered not only a territory dispute between the two villages over land along the Chinai River but also reignited the dispute over fishing rights. As discussed above, Chinai Village finally obtained the fishing rights from the prefecture by winning the bid and paying a settlement to Nishihama Village. And, as previously mentioned, the fishing rights thus obtained were later used as a temporary relief measure for villagers affected by disaster.[28]

Located on the shore of Lake Biwa, Chinai has a lakeside area which was traditionally used as a meadow and a planting zone. When this area was nationalized by the Land Tax Reform, it created difficulties for the village because it had been the area where 'the poor' lived. The village therefore took the following measures.

> From the 6th of June 1875, houses were built in Aza Nakaze. Jizōhama (Jizō Shore) had been used by this village as land for the poor. The Land Tax Reform caused trouble to all villagers. Accordingly, seven houses were built on the land at the village's cost. For this purpose, each *kumigashira* member contributed three bundles of straw, each independent farmer two bundles, and each of the other villagers one bundle. All other costs were borne by the village, including the cost of 118 bundles of straw, forty-nine folds of rope, eight bundles of bamboo and nine logs for ships, the wages for carpenters and plasterers, and the cost of nails. However, the cost of sake and food was allocated among all households on a daily basis from the 6th until the 22nd (eighteen days). As this was a particularly unusual building program, it was quite an experience that must be recorded. With respect to the houses, owners of the grounds of the houses may obtain plots of land of their choice in compensation for the grounds. The grounds of the

aforementioned houses were thus obtained by the village and provided to the poor as their place to live.

In fact, it was quite clear that Jizōhama had long been used by Chinai Village as we can see in the next citation (1828). But it was nevertheless nationalized as land 'belonging to nobody.'

> This village has wasteland Shin-warihama. Jizōhama is also wasteland. Accordingly, *kumigashira* members discussed and decided to plant Japanese persimmon (*kaki*) trees in these lands. For this purpose, all villagers spent one day preparing the soil and hammering posts in the ground. About 1500 persimmon trees were then planted. We must take good care of these trees in the future.

Further, after the Land Tax Reform, the village increased the amount of its commonly owned land by reclaiming wasteland. The following two examples show that the village strengthened its economic foundation by reclaiming wasteland at a considerable cost to the village and obtaining title to the reclaimed lands.

> In 1881, it was agreed that land in the northwest of Karasaki Shrine and land belonging to Shrine of Mizokuchi (acreage: about 0.38 acres) will be reclaimed upon approval. The reclamation work will be contracted out at the price of 68 yen 22 *sen* 5 *rin*.
> 1. Reedland, 0.23 acres; owner, the village/2. Reedland, 0.26 acres; owner, the village.
>
> The above two sites were reclaimed upon approval in May 1882. Annual rent paid in rice shall be put aside to fund maintenance activities for Hiyoshi Shrine./The cost of reclamation was 10 yen per *tan* (0.25 acres).

This is a typical example of how the village's territory was gradually established. There are too many cases to mention in which disputes over property ownership, whether a riverside area, an embankment, a mountain or a pond, was not directly triggered by the Land Tax Reform but arose later. Nonetheless, the national government's Land Tax Reform, intended primarily to determine taxpayers, clearly defined the village's territory. Admittedly, this process whereby the village's territory was clearly defined, firmly established Chinai's economic foundation and developed a much stronger awareness among the villagers that the village was 'theirs' and not the government's.

So, we have seen how the Land Tax Reform clearly defined the village's territory and firmly established its economic foundation. Next, I discuss how the village became the protector of its territory, with reference to the village's administrative structure already described above.

Formation of the 'protector' of territory and of villagers
As mentioned, Chinai was controlled by *osabun* (*moroto*) members until around 1902. Traditionally, the costs for maintaining the village's territory were primarily borne by these members.

Then, as discussed, in 1870 the Meiji government assumed the costs of certain repairs and deemed the village responsible for others. This decision was followed by the Land Tax Reform, which clearly defined the village's territory and determined what lands in the village belong to the government, what belonged to the village, and what was privately owned. The *Kiroku* implies that these measures increased the burden on the village.

A majority of the *Kiroku*'s entries indicate increased costs that were borne by the village. These include the costs of repairs to the water supply and drainage systems (e.g., 29 yen for drainage repairs in 1875, and 34 yen for drainage repairs in 1876), deaths from drowning in the river, fires, and repairs to the shrines. Approximately half of these expenses 'were paid from community membership dues.' The remainder was covered by donations. And making donations was a duty of the *osabun* members.

This cost allocation system, which was established in the early Meiji period, was basically maintained by the 1890 and 1897 bylaws, as discussed above. In the 1902 bylaws, however, it was substantially changed. Specifically, after 1902, such costs were to be borne by the village as a whole, not just the *osabun* (*moroto*) members. This change affected not only the system of territory maintenance but the entire system for protecting the living environment in Chinai. Part of its significance arises, no doubt, from the fact that the system produced by this reform remains basically in effect today. What happened between 1890 and 1902 to prompt such significant change? Let us review some of the major events that occurred in the village during this period.

From 1890 to 1894 there are entries about drainage repairs in the *Kiroku*, as there had been previously. Then, as we have discussed, in 1895 Chinai was hit by a storm. The magnitude of the disaster was such that Chinai had to hire workers from other communities. This was followed, in 1896, by a truly unprecedented storm which hit the entire prefecture of Shiga, resulting in serious damage. We have already cited the main entries from the *Kiroku* concerning this flood. For quite a while after the disaster, further reports about the flood, the extent of the damage and the results of inspections filled the pages of *Kiroku*. And yet another flood hit Chinai in 1899, before the village had completely recovered from the preceding disaster.

> Heavy rain continued from the 6th of September 1899. From four a.m. on the 8th of September, it rained even harder. The embankments along both rivers were reinforced. Then at three p.m. the same day, [several] sites were destroyed.

This flood damage and the collapsed embankments increased pressure on Chinai's finances. In 1895, Chinai had borrowed 150 yen from Momose Village's fundamental property reserve, an amount roughly equivalent to Chinai's annual budget.

After the 1896 flood, Chinai developed and implemented a set of specific measures to reduce expenses, as seen in the statement, 'all residents of Ōaza agreed upon and read aloud measures to save expenses and, in witness thereof, prepared a written agreement.' These measures are frequently referred to in later *Kiroku* entries, and were repeatedly put into effect.

The three disasters beginning from the 1895 floods imposed a huge burden on Chinai and its *osabun* (*moroto*) members (mainly *kuchō* (district head), *nengyōji* and councilors). The extent of the burden is evident from too many entries in the *Kiroku* to reproduce here.

It is safe to say that the 1897 bylaws are a product of the confusion produced by these floods. The village's existing order was severely threatened by the extent of the flood damage. Yet the 1890 bylaws provide that the bylaws must be revised in six years. Perhaps the confusion following the floods is the reason why the 1897 revisions are rather disordered, are unnumbered, and tend towards stipulating every specific detail of the villagers' everyday lives. In short, these revisions were not well-considered reforms, but instead rather an ad hoc response to external pressures.

If this is the case, then it is reasonable to assume that major reforms that the 1902 bylaws introduced were not simply responses to changes that had occurred in the five years after the 1897 bylaws were issued, but responded to the period before that as well. Chinai had developed a specific administrative system during the feudal period that had carried through the changes of the early Meiji period. This system was disturbed by the town-village consolidation in 1889 which deprived Chinai village of its status and authority as a public body. The reforms enacted by the 1902 bylaws are the village's response to this situation.

The Meiji government amended the Ward, Town and Village Assembly Act in 1884. According to Mitsuko Ōshima, the intention of this amendment was to organize local communities' economic and administrative affairs into a dual structure by dividing such affairs into those closely related to the national government and those primarily concerned with the community members' livelihoods (Ōshima 1990: 115–32; Ōshima 1989: 501–3). Under this scheme, costs closely related to the national government would be covered by community dues[29] (whose payment is required under national law), and those related to community members' livelihoods would be covered by community membership dues. As a result, the costs of many public works projects which had previously been paid by the national or prefectural government were now to be borne by the community. At the same time, a government education subsidy was discontinued. As we have seen, these reforms also affected the official postings – *kochō* (district chief) became the new government-appointed post, which, along with the prefectural governors, was granted much authority. At the same time, the amendment made it a matter of policy that all public projects in towns and villages should be deliberated at a joint community assembly and that matters within a community (such as collaborative work or water supply practices) should be decided by the community's *sōdai* members or assembly.

For communities like Ōaza Chinai, which had lost their status as public bodies in the town-village consolidations of 1889, the amendments to the Ward, Town and Village Assembly Act meant not only an increased burden from floods, but also the creation of a local administration system that could function without independent sources of revenue and a larger labor force. As a result, many communities were forced to surrender their autonomous administrations and be amalgamated into a larger administrative village.

Chinai attempted to respond to these reforms by expanding the governing body to include all villagers and sharing the community's costs and authority among all villagers. Hence, by the time the 1902 bylaws were produced, Chinai had already created a foundation for continuing autonomous administration despite having been incorporated into the administrative village, by creating *sonmin* (villagers) as the community's governing body.[30]

Nonetheless, *moroto* still remained as the religious administrative body, and Chinai's internal double structure did not break down. Only the council (*osabun*) – the decision-making body for community administration – was opened to the villagers. That is, only the formal administrative affairs were opened to all villagers; the rights and obligations of the villagers in their everyday lives remained unchanged. Changing them would have required opening religious, agricultural and other local affairs to all villagers as well, or enacting measures for leveling the villagers' incomes. Apart from temporarily opening the village's mountain or river to the victims of disaster as discussed above, Chinai continued to conduct (at least until the time of my fieldwork) long-term activities in which all villagers participated. Let me briefly review these activities.

Apart from the *okonai* ritual administered by *moroto* members, a practice called *sen'nichi nissan* (one-thousand-day daily visit) continues in Chinai to this day, as can be seen in the *Kiroku* description below. There are two shrines in Chinai. The village has a wooden card inscribed with the names of all families in the village (daily visit card), and every day the card is passed from one family to the family next door. The family which received the card visits the two shrines with the wooden card, on behalf of all families. This continues for one thousand days, and on the one thousandth day all villagers visit both shrines and have a new card made. This practice is, naturally, reported in the *Kiroku* about every three years.

> 24th of August 1903: Upon completion of the one-thousand-day visits to both shrines for guardian gods, the daily visit card was replaced and all villagers in this community had a day off from work and visited both shrines. Food and nine liters of sacred sake were offered and a festival was held. The cost of the event was about 4 yen 80 *sen*./Current *kuchō*, Mr. Nakagawa/Deputy, Mr. Kamikaw

This practice is also referred to in a statement on the *Shinpū* association in the 1897 bylaw. The *Shinpū* association visited the Ise Shrine on behalf of other villagers. According to the bylaws, all families in Ōaza joined the association, and each year the membership appointed representatives by lot, who would then visit the shrine on behalf of the other villagers.

> All persons who have set up a household in Ōaza shall join the *Shinpū* association. Every year, four representatives shall leave [for Ise Shrine] within one week from the 11th of January. On the 20th of

January, we welcomed representatives and received talisman. We chose representatives of the following year by lot.../Provided that 3.6 liters of brown rice shall be collected from each member of the association at the time of settlement and upon departure [for Ise Shrine] the brown rice shall be converted to money at the market rate at settlement and shall be given to the representatives.

Other activities in which all households are obliged to participate include: dam construction; cleaning of Karasaki Shrine before regular festivals; cemetery cleaning; work at construction sites; clearing snow from the streets; and snow fencing (including materials). Chinai's bylaws state, in an almost excessively repetitive manner, these compulsory activities in which all villagers must participate, as well as measures for leveling villagers' income, such as the imposition of heavier burdens on those who own land of higher value. All of these activities and measures have been continued until the present.

By 1903, Chinai had established not only the formal governing body but also a solid economic foundation for community administration. An important aspect of its economic foundation was the aforementioned fishing rights on the Chinai River. Another aspect was Chinai's own lands – not mountains or riverside areas, but farmlands reclaimed for the community, which brought farm rents to the community. These two sources of income meant that despite having lost its public status as an autonomous body in 1889, the Chinai community had virtually established itself and ensured its basis for acting as an independent protector of its living environment.

Conclusion

In this chapter I have described, via a close reading of historical reference documents, how a particular community was able to survive as an independent governing body and as the protector of its living environment (its territory, administration and people), and how its economic foundation was established in the process of complying with the national government's local administration system reforms from the Meiji Restoration until the early 1900s.

Yoshiteru Iwamoto (1985: 7–9) argues that the intention of the Meiji government's local administration system was

> the breakdown of *gōson*, which had been fictitious autonomous communities under the shogunate system, by compiling family

registers in 1872 and conducting the Land Tax Reform, in order to directly control land and people ... What the government wanted to do with respect to the smallest units of its administrative organization was to create the smallest units that were, without exception, greater than the traditional towns and villages in size and extent...

It was for this purpose that the government developed a series of measures to create its local administration system. Iwamoto says, the government's

> concern was how they would be able to establish a political and economic foundation for governing local communities as the frontline bases for national governance. The government did not have any intention of respecting resident autonomy. "Respect for traditional customs" was the term they used to cover up the lack of resident autonomy.

Iwamoto's claim would seem to be supported by numerous inferences in Chinai's *Kiroku*. Yet as we have seen, faced with the national government's strong orientation towards modernization, Chinai Village chose to remain independent from the government's broad intentions. The village did not openly resist but instead transformed its internal structure such that it could resist government pressure, as well as changing those aspects of itself that needed to be changed while maintaining what should be maintained. This is how the community has survived from the Meiji Restoration until now.

According to Ōishi (1961: 338), the 1884 amendment of the Ward, Town and Village Assembly Act, a major turning point for rural communities' autonomy

> lead rural communities, each of which had traditionally been a synthesis of private businesses (i.e. individual daily living) and, at the same time, a unit of the administrative organization, to split into natural villages, which are rural communities as syntheses of private businesses (i.e. individual daily living), and administrative villages, which are districts/towns/villages as units of the administrative organization.

This, too, is reflected in the *Kiroku* entries written after the amendment. However, those who live in the village must live in the village in concrete terms in the present and towards the future. They live in the physical place of their ancestors and must think of their posterity. They live in a place and community named Chinai, not in the administrative village or the natural village. They do not strive for the well-being of the administrative or natural village – the sole purpose of their efforts to maintain the village has always been to protect their *living*. Living includes all kinds of everyday activities, such as securing food, clothing and a place to live, religion, farming or fishing, and education. It also includes consideration of ancestors and posterity, as well as current villagers. In this chapter, I have called measures to maintain these activities 'protection of living environment,' focusing on the village's land and domain (together: territory).

The national government's imposition of external policies and measures on a village provides the village an opportunity to develop self-consciousness, define its territory, and create a system to protect its territory, crops and people. This system is the protector of its living environment. The village is the domain where the living environment is protected. By taking Chinai as an example, I have disclosed how this village formed an 'independent body' to maintain and develop its own living domain, as the macro-social environment changed, as the feudal period gave way to the national government's modern local administration system.

Granted, during the Meiji Period, not all of the land in a village was cultivated by its owner because of the tenancy farming system. But the protective functions of the land were basically performed by the body of the village's landowners. A village was in effect an 'independent body' that protected its living environment by developing, renewing and revising various measures and even changing the criteria for membership of the village to adapt to various changes in the local administration system made by the national government. It appears to me that this village was able to protect its entire territorial environment only by maintaining a policy that prohibited absolute or exclusive land ownership and that recognized land ownership typically belonging to the village. Notably, all of the properties in this village – not just the wider territory – were controlled by multiple, harmonious systems under the village's general control. This general control is maintained and repeatedly enforced by some of the various systems discussed above (e.g. the daily visit card), and many others as well. All of this suggests that an 'independent body' does not exist in itself, but is continuously created.

3 Rural Community Structure and Family System

Miyaza and rural community structures

In Chapter Three, I discussed how a *mura* (a rural community which had once been a village and continues to maintain a framework as such but is no longer recognized as an independent administrative unit) forms itself as an independent governing body. In this chapter I review various arguments about the relationship between families and the village with the aim of clarifying the current public status of such villages (*mura*) from a historical perspective. In the first half of this chapter, I seek to clarify the position of specific rural communities around Lake Biwa (discussed in Chapters Two and Four) within the discourses of Japanese rural communities at large, by analyzing the position of *miyaza* in studies of rural community structures. In the second half of the chapter, I will review the 'Aruga-Kitano Controversy,' a dispute over the definition and priority of family and genealogical formations in Japanese village life. This is also a dispute between two fundamentally different theoretical approaches – a living-based theory and a kinship-based theory. This controversy merits particular attention here, as it serves to lay some of the essential groundwork for the 'living environmentalism' approach that underlies the present work.

Introduction

A considerable number of studies have accumulated about *miyaza*. Yet in sociology and anthropology, *miyaza* has not been significantly addressed to date. These fields of study have tended to regard *miyaza* as 'merely' a religious group and have ignored its significance in their analyses of rural community structures. In this section, I detail the characteristics of *miyaza* as can be deduced from historical studies, and attempt to clarify its position within the rural community structure.

My interest in *miyaza* arose from observations of its close association with the rural community structure in the Kinki region as I attempted to clarify the structural characteristics of the rural communities during my fieldwork there. Hence my description of *miyaza* in this section focuses on its place in the rural community structure and intentionally neglects the procedures of rituals administered by *miyaza*.

In sociology and anthropology, the structure of Japanese rural communities has been classified into two types: the 'vertical (*dōzoku*[1]) system' and the 'horizontal (*kōgumi*) system' ('*kōgumi*' – literally: 'associations and groups'), or the 'vertical system' and the 'seniority (*nenrei kaitei*) system' ('*nenrei kaitei*' – literally: 'age ladder'). Such dichotomies, however, are inadequate for explaining the organization of rural communities in the Kinki region. Recognizing this inadequacy, Masao Gamō proposed a '*tōya*-type system' as a complementary description of rural community structures in the Kinki region, in addition to the two accepted types. As Gamō uses it, the term '*tōya* system' is not necessarily reducible to or restricted to *miyaza*, but he must have created this term from the image of *tōya* as a position in *miyaza*.

Gamō's concept of 'rural communities under a *tōya* system' ('*tōya* communities') refers to rural communities characterized by 'families taking turns in the administration of funeral services, the operation of shrine rituals, public road-works and other activities' and 'maintaining equality among families in the long run' (Gamō 1982: 484).[2] Of course, these characteristics do not overlap with *miyaza*. Furthermore, I do not believe that there are any grounds for assuming these characteristics to be typical of rural communities in the Kinki region. I nevertheless choose to employ Gamō's conception of the *tōya* community as an entry point into a discussion on the relationship between *miyaza* and rural community structures.

First, I conduct a brief literature review of the sociological and anthropological arguments presented on rural community structures. In this review, I position the Kinki rural communities in the discourses of rural community structures, using Gamō's concept of *tōya* community as a lever. Then, I systematically review historical studies of *miyaza* – which are widespread in Kinki rural communities – and extract those characteristics of *miyaza* that relate to community structures. I then clarify the position of *miyaza* derived from these historical studies within the sociological and anthropological studies of rural community structures. I finish the first half of this chapter with a summary of potential topics for future studies of *miyaza* from the perspective of the interlinking structures of *miyaza* in Kinki rural communities.

Kinki rural communities in studies of rural community structures

To analyze *miyaza* in relation to rural community structures, in this section I attempt to clarify, in the context of related studies, the special characteristics of the rural community structure in the Kinki region, where *miyaza* has been most significant in Japan.

In the history of sociological and anthropological studies, many typographic theories have been proposed concerning the structure of Japanese rural communities. Examples from sociology include Tadashi Fukutake's classification into 'villages under the vertical system and those under the horizontal system' (hereinafter referred to as 'vertical communities' and 'horizontal communities,' respectively) and from anthropology Masao Oka's classification into 'rural communities under the vertical system and those under the seniority system' (hereinafter referred to as 'vertical communities' and 'seniority communities'). However, there seems to have been no typography, except for Gamō's, that accounts for the special structural characteristics of rural communities in the Kinki region. Hence, I review these three typographies of rural community structures in accordance with the aim of locating *miyaza*.

In sociology, the typographical distinction between the 'vertical' and 'horizontal' systems has been much used. According to Fukutake, the vertical system can be characterized as:

> consisting of a head family in the village who is a major farmer-landlord and subordinate branch families who are tenant farmers and are not necessarily related by blood to the head family, and the bond between the head family and branch families is vertical which is similar to the relationship of lord and vassal. (1948: 38)

In contrast, the horizontal system is 'a horizontal union which consists of roughly equal families and which is formed when the vertical system is absent or has declined.' In the latter type of village, 'there is no superior-subordinate relationship according to class, and no unilateral dependence is formed because all families are equal' (Fukutake 1948: 38–9).

This distinction between a vertical and a horizontal system has been directly correlated with a geographical classification into the northeastern Japan-type and the southwestern Japan-type. From this perspective, rural communities in the Kinki region have been understood to correspond to the horizontal system. And while an abundance of monographs have been produced about vertical communities, monographs on the horizontal system are scarce. Thus, there are many details of the horizontal system that remain unknown.

Nonetheless, this classification has been widely used, probably because it presents a very clear image – a vertical (hierarchic) versus a horizontal union – and develops it into a geographical classification according to agricultural productivity. In other words, it seems that the clear classification into 'the vertical system = low productivity = the northeastern Japan-type' and 'the horizontal system = high productivity = the southwestern Japan-type' has been generally accepted as a correct representation of the present situation.

I am not yet in a position to judge whether this horizontal system accurately represents the structural characteristics of Kinki rural communities. But from the perspective of a focus on *miyaza* it is worth noting Fukutake's recognition of a problem in the conceptualization of horizontal communities: 'A rural community under the horizontal system is actually equal only within the upper-level village official class or the powerful farmer class, and the relationship between the upper classes and lower classes is similar to the vertical system' (Fukutake 1948: 42). The defining characteristic of the horizontal system has been understood to be equality among the families constituting the union. Yet when one attempts to apply the horizontal system typology to actual rural communities in the Kinki region, one soon discovers that the dual structure that Fukutake identifies – which may be called a 'double equality structure' – is very important.

So let us look more closely at the 'vertical' and 'seniority' systems. As we have seen, the vertical system is complementary to, but also integral to, the horizontal system. The seniority, in contrast, is considerably different from the horizontal system. According to Itsuo Emori, the seniority system is 'a system for securing social integrity by dividing community members into several age classes, with upper classes controlling and ruling lower classes.' In a village of this type: 'Vertical relationships between villagers are determined exclusively by age, and relationships among villagers are bound by so-called seniority'; each villager submits directly to the community's social control beyond the boundaries of families.

Hence, the tendency of families towards closure is considerably weakened, and 'the community tends to be, to put it with some exaggeration, an association of age classes [rather] than of families' (Emori 1976: 144).

We cannot say that all rural communities in the Kinki region are characterized by a seniority system. However, many *miyaza* do have a seniority system, so we cannot ignore it when considering the classification of rural communities.[3] Furthermore, *miyaza*, as we will see, are typically unions of family representatives. Hence, the question of the boundaries between families – although arising in negative terms in this context – is extremely important to the structure of Kinki rural communities. We must consider, among other things, how family boundaries and the seniority system of *miyaza* coexist in harmony with one another.

The distinction between 'vertical' and 'seniority' communities has also been approximately correlated to the 'northeastern versus southwestern Japan-type,' where the seniority system is attributed to the southwestern part of Japan. Of course, there is no real village in Japan that precisely corresponds to the typology of the seniority system. But if there is any validity to the correlation between the geographical classification and the vertical/seniority distinction, the seniority system will be found in Kinki rural communities. To resolve the conflict between this perspective and the one that categorizes Kinki regional communities as 'horizontal,' Emori treats the horizontal system as an 'intermediate (transitional) form' between the vertical system and the seniority system. He argues, from this perspective, that the horizontal system is distributed in geographical areas with higher productivity than those where the seniority system is found (Emori 1976: 53). Considering that Emori's 'horizontal system' includes systems that contain seniority elements and/or vertical elements – since the horizontal system is seen as a transitional form – his argument applies to many rural communities located in the Kinki region, particularly in Shiga Prefecture, the area of my fieldwork.

In contrast to Emori's conception of an 'intermediate (transitional) form,' Masao Gamō argues that they form an independent category, which he calls a '*tōya* community.' For Gamō, *tōya* communities are characterized by the fact that the

> *tōya* who organizes the shrine ritual, the *yamashi* who digs the grave pit for funerals, and all other posts in charge of public service for the village are equally assumed in turns by all of the families

constituting the community...maintaining equality among families in the long run.

This type of rural community does not ignore seniority and head-branch family relationships, but seniority or being a head family member are not regarded as the primary sources of authority. What differentiates the *tōya* community, Gamō argues, is that

> while both [vertical and seniority communities] actively aim at achieving their economic purposes as their primary objective and give lower priority to achievement of their religious purposes, "*tōya* communities" aim at the execution of shrine rituals and funeral services as the primary objective of the village's existence.

According to Gamō, this type of rural community was 'formed based on permanent and stable farming which would allow each family to live on its own' and is often found in 'old villages in the Kinki and Chūgoku regions' (Gamō 1979: 43).

Gamō's concept of '*tōya* communities' is quite similar to Emori's understanding of horizontal communities as intermediate (transitional) forms. The principal difference between these two arguments is that Emori's classification is based on differences in productivity, while Gamō's is based on different forms of production. Specifically, 'while "*tōya* communities" seem to be closely associated with permanent farming culture, "seniority communities" are...[closely associated with] non-permanent, unstable farming culture or fishing culture,' and vertical communities are associated with aggressive, expansion-oriented farming culture (Gamō 1979: 43).

Gamō stresses another important difference between *tōya* communities and the other two types of rural communities. For the latter, achieving their economic goals is their primary objective, while for those under the *tōya* system, achieving their religious objectives is their highest priority. The idea that these rural communities are primarily structured for the purpose of achieving their religious objectives is what links Gamō's conception to my concerns, through *miyaza*. It is safe to say that where communities are structured that way, the body in charge of their religious services is strongly interlinked with their administrative and economic ruling systems.

A detailed comparison of the characteristics Gamō attributes to *tōya* communities and the characteristics of *miyaza* is presented shortly. First, though, we must conclude this section by considering whether the concept '*tōya* communities' represent a genuine or useful type of rural community.

Rural community 'types' are created, as Emori puts it, to 'contrast them as conceptual models that provide perspectives for analyzing actual rural communities' (1976: 53). If, as I have suggested, the seniority and vertical systems fail to provide adequate models for the structure of Kinki's rural communities, a third type is clearly necessary for the purpose of establishing an analytical perspective. However, as soon as we begin to consider whether Gamō's conception of the *tōya* community can fill this need, it becomes apparent that it lacks a strong signifier like 'seniority' in the seniority community or '*dōzoku*' in the vertical community. So we should withhold a discussion of whether the *tōya* community is an adequate third type or not, and focus instead on introducing a strong signifier into the concept of '*tōya* community.'

We have already encountered two interrelated points of departure for this task. First, Gamō's observation that *tōya* communities are primarily orientated towards achieving their religious goals. Second is the 'double equality structure,' which I introduced while discussing Fukutake's argument earlier. Both of these elements are found in the *miyaza* forms distributed mainly in the Kinki region. In the next section, I review the literature on *miyaza* with a focus on outlining *miyaza*'s characteristic relationships to community structures.

Characteristics of *miyaza*

I focus on *miyaza* because I believe *miyaza* is not merely a religious group for a shrine but was once a central group in the rural community and thus strongly reflects the social and administrative structures of such communities. Although rituals administered by *miyaza* sometimes reflect the social ranking or other aspects of its membership, and I may need to refer to them at some point, my focus is on the *miyaza*'s place in community structures, not the details of the rituals and services it administers.

As with many Japanese traditional groups, including *ie,* families and *dōzoku, miyaza* cannot be clearly and conclusively defined. The problem arises in no small part because *miyaza, dōzoku* and such other 'entities' cannot exist independently, but are always embedded in the complicated social relationships surrounding them. Their definitions therefore differ depending on the perspective from which the entity in question is approached.

Of course different researchers have begun their research with different definitions, and have therefore produced different interpretations of the phenomena observed, which have, in turn, led to various arguments. Although many of these arguments remain unresolved, understanding of the entities in question has deepened through the process of argument.

Major controversial topics in the understanding of *miyaza* are as follows: (1) What is the nature of *miyaza* as an organization (the definition of *miyaza*)?; (2) Should religious organizations whose membership has been opened to all villagers (this type of *miyaza* is called *muraza*; the other, exclusive type is called *kabuza*) be included in the category of *miyaza* (the issue of *muraza* and *kabuza*)?; (3) Does *miyaza* have early-modern or medieval characteristics as an organization (the historical character)?; and (4) Does the structural principle of *miyaza* as an organization lie in the *tōya* system or the seniority system (*miyaza*'s structural principle)?. There are other issues stemming from these, but all branch roughly from these four. Of these, issues (1) through (3) are about the historical nature of *miyaza*. Issue (4) is primarily a concern of sociology and anthropology and is of a somewhat different nature than the others.

Although there are many different definitions of *miyaza*, the three presented by Seiichi Andō, Tatsuo Hagiwara and Toshiaki Harada are representative of the field and cover most of the related points at issue. Andō considers *miyaza* to be not only religious but a 'governing body' consisting of members of privileged classes; Hagiwara defines *miyaza* as a closed religious 'association'; Harada defines it as a religious group dedicated to the village's guardian gods, which was originally the community itself. The terms 'association' and 'governing body' as used above are used with considerably different meanings by different researchers.

Andō defines *miyaza* as: 'a body which was mainly based on a shrine and in which members of families of certain classes controlled not only religious affairs but also the community's political circles or held various privileges, and through which powerful farmers ruled the community' (Andō 1984: 172). This definition emphasizes family classes and the privileged ruling body, which is notable also in Andō's criticism of Kazuo Higo. Higo emphasizes 'social aspects of the concept of *za* (union) in the sense that people gather there, instead of administrative aspects as a type of privileged union' (Higo 1941). In this regard, according to Andō (1960: 3):

If you study *miyaza* from religious or folkloric perspectives, Dr. Higo's argument could hold. However, in this work I attempt to discuss early-modern *miyaza* from a socio-economic historical perspective. In addition, I focus more on privileged aspects of *miyaza* in community life rather than seeing *miyaza*'s privileged nature in shrine rituals, as Tarō Nakayama and Chōshū Takeda do.

While Andō regards *miyaza* as a 'governing body,' Hagiwara argues that '*miyaza* was a type of closed body for shrine rituals arising from the development of the manorial system in Japan,' and emphasizes that it 'appeared and was maintained as a body having the nature of "*za*"' (1978: 47). Hagiwara's criticism of Higo is: 'If *miyaza* is broadly defined as a closed religious body, *miyaza* would have existed not only during the medieval period but for an extremely long period of time. This definition constitutes a stretched interpretation of *miyaza* and overlooks its aspect as a *za*-like union' (1978: 37). Hagiwara also criticizes Andō's emphasis on 'family classes' as follows: 'Family classes mattered because a hierarchy formed in a homogenous community consisting of farmers and because in the medieval period the boundary between the warrior class and farmers was unclear and various classes coexisted' (1978: 37). This critique of Andō is based on Hagiwara's view that *miyaza* is closely related to *za*-like unions and is medieval in nature.

Harada traces the meaning of the term '*za*' historically and concludes that in the term *miyaza* it originally meant 'seat.' He explains:

> All people in a geographically defined village gather and form an organization called *za*. Therefore, all living activities of villagers constitute *za*'s events, and all villagers thus gather and take their seat and live their social life. In other words, it may be said that of the various lives of villagers, their life at this *za* constitutes their entire social life. (1976: 13)

In short, Harada argues that originally the members of *za* were the villagers.

The important differences between the three positions reviewed above stem from how they understand the relationships between '*miyaza*, *za* and the village.' Let us discuss this by focusing on the factors that contributed to the foundation and formation of *miyaza*.

As mentioned, Harada argues that *za* originated from each village and consisted of villagers. It later came to be called *miyaza* because it became a privileged group through the processes of differentiation and development in each village. When *miyaza* 'no longer allowed everyone to join, the village as they called it became a village consisting of special people. The village no longer included all people in the same geographical area; it included certain people only' (Harada 1975: 47). As a result, 'the term "*mura*" (village) was no longer appropriate because it does not imply a privileged group, and this is probably why "*za*" was added to "*mura*" and the term "*muraza*" came to be used' (Harada 1975: 47). In short, Harada seems to imply that the origin of what is now called *miyaza* is a village itself and that responsibility for its religious rituals for guardian gods later became the privilege of a subgroup.

Turning, finally, to Hagiwara's view, as we have seen, he understands *miyaza* as closely related to medieval *za*-like unions. What, then, is the basic factor that changes a *za*-like union to *miyaza*? Hagiwara argues it is the '*sō-son*' union which emerged at the end of the medieval period (*sō-son* – literally: 'everybody's village,' defined as rural communities formed in the medieval period and consisting of all people living in the respective geographical area). Hagiwara understands '*sō*' as having a stronger communal nature than *za* and a more lasting body than '*ikki*' (riot or insurrection). He also understands 'the essential factors in the formation of "*sō*"' as follows: 'The first factor was of course the necessity of securing water supply and mountains and forests. The second was the necessity of forming a self-defense group. This was followed by the necessity of establishing and maintaining community control by employing a council system.' From this perspective, Hagiwara argues that '*miyaza* developed as a body to conduct religious events by turns, in many cases in close association with this "*sō*" union' (1978: 48–9). As a result, many of the medieval *miyaza* that developed in association with '*sō-son*' 'transformed, declined or disappeared due to the subsequent development of the *gō-son* communities' (Hagiwara 1978: 90) ('*gō-son*' – literally: 'countryside village,' defined as rural communities formed later than *sō-son* in more remote regions, each covering a larger geographical area, and thus with weaker bonds between members). In short, Hagiwara says that *miyaza* was formed in close association with a *za*-like union during the medieval period and developed based on *sō-son*, which had a strong communal nature.

While Hagiwara points to the medieval origins of *miyaza*, Andō explains several factors that contributed to the formation of *miyaza*. First, 'the feudal lord's power'; if the lord's control did not extend to the inside of the terminal farming community, powerful farmers had to control water supplies and common lands. This controlling group emerged as *miyaza*, and the above situation constituted a factor that contributed to the formation of *miyaza* in the process of breakdown of manors. (Andō 1984: 179)

Second, from the perspective of farmers in general, in western Japan, including the Kinki region: 'small farmers were highly independent and the ruled farmers in the community were powerful; therefore they had to have *miyaza* – a cooperative governing body consisting of powerful farmers – to govern the community' (Andō 1984: 179). Third, from an economic perspective, *miyaza* was necessary as a body for sharing the costs of constructing and maintaining shrines. Fourth, at the same time, the spread of two-crop systems resulted in increased productivity and 'increased the possibility of subordinate farmers becoming independent, which thus increased the possibility of compound families breaking down, and the possibility of newcomers settling from other communities. The bonds within the community changed from blood relations to a combination of blood relations and territorial connections. These factors increased the necessity for forming a *miyaza*.' Finally, the two-crop systems increased the use of water, requiring extensive irrigation and drainage works and improvements in the control of water. Hence, 'in the Kinki and other regions where there were a large number of headmen of small and medium sized villages, there was a growing need to unite powerful farmers, leading to the birth of *miyaza*' (Andō 1984: 179).

Having initially formed in response to these factors, *miyaza* developed rapidly during the sixteenth century. As Andō reads it: 'powerful warrior classes and local ruling families became officers of warlords and then attempted to become warlords themselves. This resulted in less control of villages and increased independence of small farmers. This must have led to the formation of *miyaza*' (Andō 1984: 178). In the middle of the early-modern period (about the middle of the seventeenth century to the late-eighteenth century), however, further improvements in agricultural productivity and the development of commercial farming led to the emergence of villagers who were not *miyaza* members whose economic strength surpassed the *miyaza* members. These new groups of farmers sometimes formed new *za*, intensifying the confrontation between *miyaza* and non-*miyaza* villagers. Then, at the end of the early-modern period (about the late-eighteenth century to middle of the nineteenth century), the development of the manufacturing industry in rural villages initiated a progressive breakdown of the farmer class, which extremely weakened the power of *miyaza*.

As discussed, Andō argues that *miyaza* initially formed during the time when the manorial system was breaking down, and developed rapidly during the sixteenth century. From this perspective, Andō claims that the 'privilege of *miyaza* represents a characteristic of feudal society' (1984: 184). Furthermore, he explains: to say that *miyaza* has a 'feudal nature does not mean that it had a feudal relationship with the feudal lord. It means that *miyaza* controlled not only religious rituals based mainly on shrines but also administrative, social and economic affairs specific to the rural community as a privileged body' (Andō 1984: 184).

This review of the three accounts of the formation and development of *miyaza* does not inquire into the origins of *miyaza*, but rather aims to understand the nature of *miyaza*. Harada understands *miyaza* as originally a religious body for worshipping the village's guardian gods. In contrast, Hagiwara regards *miyaza* as a *za*-like union based on *sō*, and Andō regards it as a feudal-type ruling body that developed in communities during early-modern times.

Andō's position is similar to Hagiwara's in that both locate the basis for the formation of *miyaza* in '*sō-son*.' We can see this in Andō's statement that *miyaza* was 'formed as *shō-miyaza* or *mura-miyaza* in "*sō-shō*"[4] or "*sō-son*" during the time of change in the manorial system' (1984: 178). But they diverge when Hagiwara argues that the *miyaza* system declined in early-modern times and transformed into the *ujiko* (shrine parishioner) system:

> though it is unlikely that the authority to administer religious rituals was opened to all villagers, it seems that as freehold farmers became widespread in early-modern times, people's awareness as community-based shrine parishioners increased, leading to the formation of the concepts of "*ujigami*" (guardian gods) and "*ujiko*" (shrine parishioners) for each rural community as we generally understand it today. (1978: 39)

Andō, in contrast, argues that the *ujiko* system only emerges in modern times, stating:

> based on studies of the *miyaza* that existed during early-modern times, *miyaza* seems to have been a privileged body from the beginning of the early-modern period. Compared to the medieval period, the range

of privilege holders may have been expanded, but the privilege was still held by only some of the people. (1960: 107)

Let us set aside the question of the transition from *miyaza* to the *ujiko* system for now, and focus on whether the early *miyaza* formed on the basis of *sō-son* were medieval or early-modern in nature. Chōshū Takeda (1977) sheds some light on this question, and in the process links the above arguments to the structure of rural communities in the Kinki region. For Takeda, *miyaza* in *sō-son*

> was never a typical form of *miyaza* during the medieval period. Indeed, if we focus on its closed nature and internal equality deriving from the fact that it was an exclusive union of villagers, *miyaza* in *sō-son* was quite early-modern rather than medieval in form... I would also say that the fact that this early-modern form was established as early as the late medieval period shows the historically special position and character of the advanced regions centered on the Kinki region where this type of *miyaza* was formed. (1977: 37)

As we have seen, Harada argues that the original form of *miyaza* was the entire community consisting of all villagers, or *muraza*. In contrast, Hagiwara and Andō claim that *miyaza* was originally formed as a privileged body. Although the original form of *miyaza* is not my concern here, we should pursue the topic a bit further, as it sheds light on the questions of whether the category of *miyaza* should include *muraza*, a union open to all villagers, and thus characterized by a lack of the privilege that defines *miyaza*.

Arguments about the definition or character of *muraza* (open union) and *kabuza* (restricted union) are closely related to the understanding of *miyaza*. Not surprisingly, therefore, authors such as Andō and Hagiwara, who define *miyaza* in a restrictive manner – as privileged groups that existed during a very limited historical period – basically oppose the use of the term *muraza*. In contrast, Harada, who regards the original *miyaza* as the village itself, argues that *miyaza* specifically refers to *muraza*, and that *kabuza* occurred only later. However, although both Andō and Hagiwara reject the term *muraza*, there are subtle yet important differences between their arguments, which warrant a more detailed discussion.

Hagiwara does not directly address the issue of *muraza*. Pointing to two prominent views on the topic, one that takes the term *miyaza* in a very narrow sense and associates it with a *za*-like nature and another that incorporates the *tōya* system into *miyaza*, he states that 'we have no choice but to accept for the time being that there are two definitions – one broad and one narrow' (1978: 5). Nevertheless, he argues: 'If *miyaza* can be defined broadly as a closed religious body, *miyaza* would have existed not only during the medieval period but for an extremely long period of time. This definition constitutes a stretched interpretation of *miyaza* and overlooks the aspect of *miyaza* as a *za*-like union' (Hagiwara 1978: 37). We can conclude from this claim that for Hagiwara the term *muraza* appears to be devoid of historical content and hence the term's usefulness is questionable. On different grounds, Andō argues that 'in so-called *muraza*, the privilege of *miyaza* was opened to villagers at large. Though *muraza* may have administered the same rituals as *miyaza*, from the writer's view, in which *miyaza* is defined as a privileged union, *muraza* was no longer *miyaza* and should be understood as an *ujiko* system' (Andō 1984: 186). Furthermore, he argues, 'It is not appropriate to use the term "*muraza*" just because traditional rituals have been continued' (1984: 175).

Harada, however, rejects Hagiwara's view, proposing to regard *muraza* as a type of *miyaza*, based on the following interpretation of the meaning of the term '*za*':

> If we accept that the term "*za*" originally means "seat," we must admit that [*muraza*] is still "*za*" even if all villagers participate in it. As a matter of fact, such unions are often called "*za*." Further, unions that worship the village's gods, or *ujigami*, and whose membership covers all villagers are often called *miyaza*. (Harada 1976: 9)

Chōshū Takeda also argues for the use of the term *muraza*, emphasizing the religious dimension of *miyaza*. He states:

> The view that *miyaza* in the strictest sense of the word is *kabuza* only and does not include *muraza* where the authority to administer religious rituals is given equally to all villagers is worth paying attention to in a sense. However, as long as *miyaza* is regarded as a religious body, it is by no means a mistake to regard a body like *muraza* as a form of *miyaza*. (1977: 52)

These arguments seem never to mesh with each other because their authors approach *miyaza* from fundamentally different perspectives. Since our aim is to understand *miyaza* in relation to rural community structures, particularly from a sociological perspective, we should not consider a *miyaza* that has been opened to all villagers as merely a holdover from an earlier age; we should instead understand that a surviving *miyaza* has been maintained by changing in response to the changes in people's lives. In this sense, the following comment made by Andō is important, although his position differs somewhat from ours:

> Even if [a *miyaza* is] opened to all villagers, if discrimination remains among members at rituals or otherwise, then the *miyaza* should be deemed to have retained its privileged nature. Even if a *miyaza* is opened absolutely equally to all villagers and seems to have become a *muraza* for the time being, if it rejects members of next-generation branch families or newcomers from other villages, then there is no substantial difference in its privileged nature. Although attention must be paid to the fact that the membership was expanded and the nature of *miyaza* was changing, such *miyaza* was not of a different nature. If a *miyaza* is opened absolutely equally and unrestrictedly to all villagers and gives the same treatment to any and all newcomers, the situation should be understood as a breakdown of the *miyaza* and the establishment of an *ujiko* system rather than specifically using the term *muraza*. (1960: 107)

If we develop this view, we would be able to say that even if a *miyaza* seems to have been opened to all villagers, as long as its rituals are continued it must retain some structural principles that differ from those of an *ujiko* group, such as an internal ranking among member families and restrictive qualifications for *tōya*. This makes it difficult to regard this type of *miyaza* entirely as an *ujiko* group. Andō also distinguishes two types of currently surviving *miyaza*: the 'isolated (secular) type' and the 'fused (village festival) type' (1984: 181). According to Andō, both of these types should be regarded as *miyaza*. They retain characteristics that are quite distinct from the *ujiko* systems that can be found in areas where *miyaza* never existed. Hence, when we discuss *miyaza* in connection with rural community structure, we should regard these types of *miyaza* as different from *ujiko* groups.

I have thus far reviewed the arguments on *miyaza* presented by historians and folklorists, focusing on their points of dispute. In the next section, I discuss how we can link these conceptions of *miyaza* with the structures of rural communities in a sociological manner.

Miyaza and rural community structures

I have discussed some of the key characteristics of *miyaza* above. Of these, the following seem to be of particular importance in terms of rural community structures. First, *miyaza* developed on the bases of *sō* unions. Assuming that the essential factors in the formation of *sō* were the necessity of securing water supplies and mountains and forests (resources), the necessity of forming self-defense groups, and the necessity of establishing and maintaining community control through a council system, and that *sō* had more communal nature than *za*, then it is safe to say that *miyaza* could potentially have developed into a group of an extremely communal nature. Although the *sō-son-miyaza* type of community that developed thus may have subsequently been transformed or disrupted by the development of the *gō-son* system, it must nevertheless have significantly determined the nature of the *miyaza* that appeared later.[5] In this regard, Takeda argues that *miyaza* based on *sō-son* was more early-modern than medieval in form:

> In early-modern times when the manorial system had completely disappeared...a large number of rural communities had been established...in which families were becoming extensively independent and differentiated, it is considered that *miyaza* in rural communities became smaller in form and scale than former times. On the other hand, it seems that their organization became more intensified and their number increased rapidly throughout the nation, making their overall presence denser in both quantity and quality. In this sense, it is safe to say that early-modern times occupy a central position in the general formation and development of the custom of *miyaza*. (1977: 36)

Takeda also argues that the basic characteristics of this *miyaza* were its 'closed nature and internal equality deriving from the fact that it was an exclusive union of villagers' (1977: 37).

This type of *miyaza* rapidly increased in number during the early-modern period in the sixteenth century. The second characteristic that seems important is that this increase occurred through the following process: 'powerful warrior classes and local ruling families became officers of warlords and then attempted to become warlords themselves. This resulted in declined control of villages and increased independence of small farmers. These must have led to the formation of *miyaza*' (Andō 1984: 178). The point is that *miyaza* developed as a body through which ordinary farmers were controlled by powerful farmers, who reinforced *miyaza* as a governing body as small farmers became increasingly independent and thus centralized control of villages was dissipating.

Third, *miyaza* underwent considerable transformations throughout early-modern times (mid-sixteenth to mid-nineteenth century). Andō explains this in terms of the confrontation between *miyaza* and non-*miyaza* member villagers. In the middle of the early-modern times (about mid-seventeenth to late-eighteenth century), 'some ordinary farmers who were not *miyaza* members became economically stronger than *miyaza* members. Those farmers formed new *za*...*Miyaza* members' control and leadership declined, confrontation between *miyaza* and non-*miyaza* villagers intensified, and disputes among farmers over *miyaza* also intensified.' At the end of the early-modern times (about late-eighteenth to mid-nineteenth century), the *miyaza*'s authority declined further. At that time, 'Villagers who had not been *miyaza* members and had fought against the *miyaza*'s privilege did not force the *miyaza* to open up to them; instead, the more powerful non-members joined *miyaza* and reorganized its form' (Andō 1984: 222). This is very suggestive; those *miyaza* so reorganized at that time survived various internal and external pressures during the Meiji Period and continue today in more or less the same form. Many of the *miyaza* currently seen in rural villages are this type of *miyaza*.

As mentioned earlier, Fukutake identifies a characteristic that I have called a 'double equality structure' in horizontal communities. He regards it as a lingering 'feudal nature' that must be overcome. Fukutake is referring to the control of powerful farmers over ordinary farmers, characteristic of early-modern *miyaza*. While this is undoubtedly an important observation, if we assume that the three characteristics outlined above are sufficiently definitive of *miyaza*, we achieve an understanding that is unduly weighted towards administrative and economic dimensions. But as discussed in earlier chapters, the present study begins from a position that regards the various systems in rural communities as living systems, or systems for sustaining the community members' everyday lives. If we approach *miyaza* as a living system, then, we must consider the organizational structures and characteristics of *miyaza* as well as its administrative and economic dimensions.

Let us discuss this point briefly in connection with the issue of '*miyaza*'s structural principle,' item (4) of the major fields to be clarified if we are to develop an adequate understanding of *miyaza*. Tōichi Takahashi conducted sociological research on *miyaza* in

Shiga Prefecture, and identifies the basic organizational elements of *miyaza* as follows: (1) Many of the *miyaza* are based on certain old families as their fundamental units (these are generally called *kabuza*); (2) Men are ranked under a strict ranking system according to seniority (the seniority element); and (3) Members take annual turns in administering shrine rituals (the *tōya* element). In addition, since *miyaza* often shows a twin organizational form (such as a set of *hidari-za* and *migi-za* (left-*za* and right-*za*)), Takahashi adds this twin-style organization as the fourth element (1978: 12). Of these four elements, Takahashi regards the seniority element as the most important. He explains:

> Generally, in an organization that is considered *miyaza* (whether *kabuza* or *muraza*), each family representative (normally the head of a family) is ranked under a strict seniority system and holds a certain place in shrine rituals under a clear hierarchical system with the oldest at the top, and performs his functions according to his place. Under these circumstances, members generally serve as *tōya* or annual rotating shrine guardian in the order of seniority. (1978: 12)

Takahashi further argues that the centrality of the seniority system in *miyaza* means that *miyaza* can be regarded as a type of religious gerontocracy, 'considering the remarkably high proportions of elders' (1978: 11).

In contrast, according to Kazuo Ueno, 'generally speaking, *miyaza*, whether in the form of *kabuza* or *muraza*, is a religious organization based on strong independence of member families as fundamental units and characterized by internal equality among member families and exclusiveness towards non-members' (1981: 57). Ueno thus argues that 'the structural principle of *miyaza* should be found in the *tōya* system as a principle of equality' and rejects Takahashi's claim, stating, 'the seniority system is merely a means to determine who to serve as *tōya*' (1981: 67).

Whether the defining structural principle of *miyaza* lies in the *tōya* system or the seniority system is less important than Harada's observation that the principle of '*za*' as a religious organization lies in the *tōya* system, as Kazuhiko Sumiya (1982: 242) also points out: 'While *tōya* serves *ujigami* on behalf of all *ujiko* members in religious services for *ujigami*, he also acts as an agent of *ujigami* and behaves as *ujigami* himself towards villagers as a whole' (Harada 1975: 166).

Following this line of thought, if *miyaza* is viewed as a living system for religious services, then *miyaza* is a group for serving gods, and *tōya* is a rotating representative of the group. Harada maintains that originally all villagers took turns to serve as *tōya* and it was only later that they became privileged and formed *kabuza*. It is worth repeating here that the fact that the *tōya* system has been basically maintained and the principle of equality has been observed within various *miyaza* is more important than the question of whether the first *miyaza* were *kabuza* or *muraza*. So let us look more closely at the term 'the *tōya* system.' Hagiwara explains:

> As the *sō-son*-like union developed, villages increasingly attempted to administer religious services independently. Many villagers refused to assume the post of *tōyaku* [literally: "head officer"] even if appointed by the central office or the permanent shrine guardian family, making it difficult to maintain the *tōyaku* system. As *miyaza* under the manorial system switched over to *miyaza* under the *sō-son* system, the shrine *tōyaku* system changed…but the concept of *tōyaku* did not disappear in *miyaza* under *sō-son*…While *tōyaku* had traditionally been appointed by the feudal lord or the permanent shrine guardian family, villagers came to serve as *tōyaku* in rotation with the understanding that they were appointed by the will of their guardian gods…The concept of *tōyaku* declined and the post came to be called "*tōnin*" [literally: "head man"], then "*tōya*." After the start of the early-modern times, even the meaning of the "*tō*" [head] part was forgotten, and the terms "*tōnin*" and "*tōya*" were sometimes spelled with a different kanji character with the same pronunciation in the "*tō*" part. (1962: 215)

Although this description differs slightly from Harada's, it nevertheless presents roughly the same understanding of the role of *tōya* in *miyaza*. If we regard this *tōya* system as the key structural principle of *miyaza*, we could say that as a living system *miyaza* is characterized by, as Ueno puts it, being 'a religious organization based on the strong independence of its member families as fundamental units and characterized by internal equality among member families and exclusiveness towards non-members' (1981: 57).

We can now understand this *tōya* system and the historical characteristics of *miyaza* outlined above to be the characteristics of *miyaza* that relate to rural community structures. Let us, then, compare this understanding to Gamō's proposed concept of '*tōya* community' as a type of rural community structure in the Kinki region. The concept of '*tōya* community' emphasizes the principle of equality among families. Equality was, in fact, the basic principle within *miyaza*. Yet *miyaza* also functioned as a closed governing body towards non-members. Even where the principle of equality within *miyaza* was applied to non-member villagers, it must nevertheless have been applied on the basis of a double structure distinguishing *miyaza* and the rest.

Many surviving *miyaza* today have lost their *kabuza*-like structure and have been opened to all villagers. This does not necessarily mean, however, that in such cases the entire community is structured on the basis of the principle of equality. For example, a certain village located in the Kohoku area of Shiga Prefecture has maintained a *miyaza*, which it calls '*moroto*,' for a long time. Its membership includes approximately one-third of the families in the village. Until the early Taishō Period (1912–1926), the membership was restricted to family heads. As the number of members decreased, eldest sons were allowed to join in 1916, and this continued until after World War II. Soon after the war, the *miyaza*'s membership was opened to all villagers in response to the trend towards democratization, but this did not make the village structure entirely equal or single-layered. At present, the village's *ujiko* organization has a manager called *nengyōji*. One of the prerequisites for this office is that the candidate's community dues payable must be more than the village average. A villager's community dues are determined by an aggregation calculated based on the amount of tax payable, land ownership, and what is called 'evaluation.' Similarly, to qualify as a councilor of the village, one's community dues must be above average. This governing principle is totally different from the village's *miyaza*, which is based on family classes, but it is worth noting that the 'double equality structure' exists in this village outside of its *miyaza*.

A rural community with this type of 'double equality structure' may be called a 'trapezoidal-pyramid' structure in contrast to the pyramid structure of the vertical community. Whatever it is called, though, I assume that Kinki rural communities, whose governing structures seem in many respects to be equal, actually have double structures consisting of ruling groups (main families who are entitled to participate in *miyaza*) and other groups and, in an attempt to make up for the inequality, developed a system where 'families take turns in the administration of funeral services, operation of shrine rituals, public road-works and other activities,' as Gamō argues (1982: 484). So it appears that the concept of '*tōya* community' does accurately describe one important aspect of the rural community structure, but it does not seem to fully describe other important aspects.

Summary of the discussion so far

I have reviewed the structural characteristics of Kinki rural communities through the relevant literature on *miyaza*. The main aim of this task was to clarify the place of *miyaza* in studies of rural community structures – particularly sociological and anthropological studies – using Gamō's proposed concept of the *tōya* community as a starting point.

In the second half of this chapter, I consider the issue of *miyaza* and community structure in a somewhat more abstract manner. For example, as mentioned, Ueno describes *miyaza* as an organization characterized by internal equality among member families and exclusiveness towards non-members. In terms of community structure, this characteristic consists of two principles that seem to contradict one another: differentiation of community member families into privileged and non-privileged classes, and equalization of the members within the *miyaza* group. As Takahashi (1978) argues, however, we must accept that the principle of differentiation also applies within *miyaza*, considering that a seniority system is central to many *miyaza*. From this perspective, the structure of *miyaza* seems to be a matter of balancing between the principle of consistent differentiation, as seen in *kabuza* and the seniority system, and a principle of equalization to address the resulting inequality, as seen in the *tōya* system.

The balance between differentiation and equalization is not fixed but seems to vary in response to both internal and external changes; that is, particular *miyaza* have changed their particular forms at various times in response to changing circumstances.[6] There are many forms of *miyaza* – *muraza* and *kabuza*, those with a seniority system and those with permanent or rotational *tōya* – because *miyaza* have adjusted to the changing circumstances of history.

Leaving aside, again, the question of whether this type of *miyaza* should be called *muraza* or not, this historical review clearly indicates that *miyaza* have continuously changed their grounds for differentiation even while maintaining a principle of differentiation and, in the process, have realized the principle of equalization in various forms. In this sense, the 'double equality structure' introduced above is one way of expressing the lingering presence of such differentiation, while many documents show that the grounds for this differentiation have changed in various ways – sometimes based on family classes, at other times on economic status, and so on.

Is *miyaza*, then, merely an institution of differentiation within the rural community? No. It is more fundamentally a religious body, whose chief purpose has been to mystify religious rituals. This is the essential point of my argument. If we accept that *miyaza* were able to exercise control not only over the religious but also the administrative and economic aspects of the early-modern feudal village, and that its organizational principles were highly compatible with the dominant type of community structure in the Kinki and surrounding regions, then *we should not* consider those currently remaining *miyaza* as merely the 'remnants' of an older system, for this suggests a system in decline, one past its prime and promise. Although many, if not most, of the presently extant *miyaza* have lost their economic and administrative functions, these 'losses' have resulted from the creation of new forms of association compatible with changing circumstances and do not necessarily suggest a breakdown of *miyaza* themselves. Of course, we must accept Andō's (1984) qualification, that the concept of *miyaza* should not include any organization that 'is opened absolutely equally and unrestrictedly to all villagers and gives the same treatment to any and all newcomers' and which has no ranking among its members even at rituals. Yet this means precisely that we must ascertain whether a currently remaining *miyaza* is 'truly' a *miyaza* by analyzing the details of its services and rituals, rather than merely according to some abstract periodization of history.

As discussed, the concept of '*tōya* community' is important, but seems to underrate the importance of other structural characteristics of *miyaza*. If one deals with Kinki rural communities,[7] it is not possible to ignore *miyaza*'s administrative and economic characteristics when considering its structural principles. In this respect, sociological and anthropological studies on *miyaza* have thus far tended to overemphasize analyzing the structural principles in the various observable forms of *miyaza*. In other words, they may have treated *miyaza* as merely a religious organization without sufficiently understanding its broader significance for rural community studies.

'Living-based theory' and 'kinship-based theory'

Introduction

In this section, I outline a 'living-based theory' as the basic perspective of this work, by systematically reviewing arguments about '*ie*' – the classical Japanese family system – regarding the composition of a village.

From the 1930s until after World War II, *ie* and *dōzoku* (the vertical kinship system) were the principal subjects of studies in rural and family sociology. There was an understanding widely accepted among researchers that *ie* and *dōzoku* were determinative characteristics not only of Japanese rural communities and families but of Japanese society in general.

Many researchers have analyzed *ie* and *dōzoku* with the aim of identifying their nature, yet many unresolved questions remain, including: (1) the definition of the *dōzoku* bond; (2) the difference between *dōzoku* and the *oyakata-kokata* (pseudo parent-child) relationship; (3) treatment of non-blood-related persons among the *ie*; and (4) the distinction between *ie* as the compositional unit of *dōzoku* and the conventional concept of *kazoku* (family). Some of these issues have been addressed by various studies on *dōzoku*, but most of the early approaches were clarified in the long-running public debate between Kizaemon Aruga and Seiichi Kitano, which began in the late 1960s and became known as the 'Aruga-Kitano Controversy.'[8]

Since the late 1960s, those who conduct theoretical studies on *ie* and *dōzoku* have found it virtually impossible to ignore this controversy, and several researchers have published interpretations of the issues under debate. For the record, note that there is some doubt about whether or not this debate should properly be called a 'controversy' in the strictest sense of the term, yet I use the well-used term for convenience as I review how it has been interpreted by others. After a review of the secondary literature on the controversy, to help clarify our analytical framework, I will examine some of Aruga's and Kitano's first-hand arguments.

Although some researchers limit the scope of this controversy to the debate about definitions of *ie* and *kazoku* waged during the 1960s and later around Teizō Toda's theory,[9] I use the term 'Aruga-Kitano Controversy' to refer to the entire conflict over *ie* and *dōzoku* between Aruga and Kitano. If we understand the Aruga-Kitano Controversy in this broad sense, the core of the controversy has been concerned with defining the nature of *dōzoku*.

Their competing views on the definition of *dōzoku* can be summarized as follows. First, Aruga emphasizes vertical (master–servant) relationships, in which *dōzoku* groups are defined as having 'common ties to the regional community among *ie* which maintain close community life or close connection in everyday living in accordance with the genealogical relationships between the head *ie* and branch *ie*.' Furthermore, he argues, '*dōzoku* bonds can occur only through vertical or master–servant relationships' (1947: 28–35). In contrast, Kitano argues that the true nature of the *dōzoku* bond is 'not found in vertical relationships in social status or master–servant relationships, but should ultimately be found in genealogical relationships' (1951: 8).

Kaoru Ōhashi argues that Aruga's definition 'over-emphasizes aspects of the phenomenal structural forms or social functions, as can be seen in his emphasis on master–servant relationships in life' and 'overlooks the internal principle on which *dōzoku* groups are based,' providing merely a mechanical representation from the outside. In contrast, Ōhashi regards Kitano's position as 'one step closer to understanding the internal principles' (1953: 6). This idea that Aruga's view focuses on the external form while Kitano's focuses on the internal principle is shared by Masao Gamō.

Gamō distinguishes between Aruga's emphasis on common ties between families and the regional community as 'an understanding of the [particular] form of existence,' and Kitano's emphasis on genealogical relationships as the 'internal structural principle.' Gamō concurs with Kitano's position, stating, 'Apart from dealing with *dōzoku* bonds in terms of studies on community structure, if we deal with the true nature of *dōzoku* itself, there is no question that genealogical relationships are an essential part of it' (Gamō 1958: 242–3).

While Gamō's narrow formulation raises the question of whether the 'true nature of *dōzoku* itself' can really be identified separately from the community structure that supports *dōzoku* or not, we can note simply that Kazuhiko Sumiya shares Gamō's view.

Sumiya argues that if one deals with the nature of the *dōzoku* bonds from the perspective of identifying the basis for the superiority of the head *ie* over its branch *ie*, the conclusion should be that Kitano's 'view that [the superiority] derives from the fact that the head *ie* is the origin of branch *ie* in terms of genealogy is more appropriate as the definition of the concept of "*dōzoku*."' Sumiya asks: 'What type of group' is *dōzoku* when seen from the perspective of genealogical relationships between the head *ie* and its branch *ie*'? He concludes that *dōzoku* is 'one type of lineage group seen worldwide as paternal monophyletic kinship organization' (1963: 363–5). This view both supports and further clarifies Gamō's point.

From this brief review we can understand why these researchers see Aruga's definition as external and formal and Kitano's as revealing the internal structural principle. Kitano approaches *dōzoku* by 'reconstruction, using the concept of "kinship," which seems to allow broader and deeper development,' according to Sumiya (1963: 368). Sumiya further notes that only this perspective is open to cross-cultural comparison, and hence, only by reconstructing from the concept of kinship, 'can we compare Japanese "*dōzoku*" from a broader perspective' (Sumiya 1963: 365).

From the perspective of kinship communities, Aruga's definition of *dōzoku* appears to be external and formal. It is not possible to determine the grounds for Aruga's definition of *dōzoku* from the arguments presented above, where Kitano's position is granted much greater credence. In fact, we will not find them by looking for them directly in Aruga's work. I turn now to a review of those debates in the Aruga-Kitano Controversy surrounding '*ie*.' Commentators offer roughly the same conclusions about Aruga's and Kitano's positions concerning the nature of *ie* as the ones we have seen concerning the definition of the *dōzoku* bond – Aruga's position is external and formal, while Kitano's is internal and fundamental. However, the debate over the definitions of '*ie*' and '*kazoku*' achieved much greater clarity than the *dōzoku* question after the 1960s.

Toshiyuki Mitsuyoshi contends that the Aruga-Kitano Controversy over *ie* stems from the fact that

> while Aruga defines *ie* as Japanese *kazoku* and adopts a position that denies any conceptual distinction between *ie* and *kazoku*, Kitano understands *ie* as an institutional, historical form of *kazoku* and adopts a position that accepts a double structure of *ie* by making a conceptual distinction between *ie* and smaller *kazoku* bonds existing within *ie*. (Mitsuyoshi 1970: 145–6).

Mitsuyoshi also observes that the controversy basically derives from a 'difference in perspective or way of thinking.' Specifically, Aruga is negative about applying a cross-cultural concept, while Kitano 'intends to link the structural analysis of *ie* to the concept of *kazoku*' and thereby attempts to elucidate the characteristics that Japanese *ie* has as *kazoku* (Mitsuyoshi 1970: 145–6).

In short, as Shūhei Yamamuro (1970: 210) observes, the basic conflict over *ie* emerges from different attitudes towards the application of a 'cross-cultural' analytical concept. During and after the 1960s, this particular debate took the form of arguments over Toda's theory, which again raised the question of whether it is appropriate to apply the concept of *kazoku* in a cross-cultural sense to Japanese *ie* or not.

I have so far discussed *ie* and *dōzoku* separately, but of course the controversies surrounding their respective definitions have a common basis. This brief review indicates that the common basis lies in Aruga's and Kitano's respective attitudes toward the application of a cross-cultural analytic concept, which in turn results in their different perspectives and methods for discussing *ie* and *dōzoku*.

My aim in reviewing the Aruga-Kitano Controversy is certainly not to resolve unsolved questions about *ie* and *dōzoku*. Rather, it is to ascertain the differences between Aruga's and Kitano's research methodologies in an effort to develop a more suitable methodology for future studies of Japanese society. Remembering that the aim of this book is to clarify the role played by a small community in protecting community life, it is necessary to develop an understanding of the basic structures of the small community, which demands an understanding of the characteristics of *ie* and *dōzoku*, for these are clearly the bases for the communities in question – villages in Shiga Prefecture. The purpose of this review has been to organize Aruga's and Kitano's arguments on *ie* and *dōzoku* and to highlight the differences in their perspectives.

To recapitulate: Aruga attempts to understand community structure and thus the essential characteristics of Japanese society through studying *ie* and *dōzoku*. His attention is consistently fixed on elucidating the basic structures of living. From this perspective, *ie*, *dōzoku* and rural communities are all accumulated institutions of the basic forms of living. In contrast, Kitano strives to incorporate *ie* and *dōzoku* into a unified theory of kinship using a Weberian typology, from the perspective of cross-cultural comparison. From this perspective, he explains all life activities that occur in *ie* and *dōzoku* using a theory of kinship.

Hereinafter I refer to these two perspectives as the 'theory of living' and 'theory of kinship,' respectively. I intend to clarify each by discussing what they reveal about *ie* and *dōzoku*.

Aruga's and Kitano's theories of *ie* and *dōzoku*

Definition of the nature of *dōzoku*

During the 1930s and 1940s, Aruga constructed his theory of *dōzoku* based on his research in Ishigami Village, Iwate Prefecture. Around the same time, Kitano was constructing a unique theory of *dōzoku* based on his research in Nagamasa, Kaneo Village in Saitama Prefecture and Wakamiya, Sarashina Village in Nagano Prefecture.[10] At this early stage, the two researchers' understandings of *dōzoku* were already slightly different. As early as 1939, Kitano published a critique of Aruga's position for not distinguishing between *dōzoku* and the *oyakata-kokata* (pseudo parent-child) relationship.

However, their respective theoretical views were not clearly elucidated until Aruga published 'Nihon kazoku seido to kosaku seido (Family system and tenant-farmer system in Japan)' in 1943 and Kitano published 'Dōzoku soshiki to hōken isei (*Dōzoku* organization and remnants of the feudal system)' in 1951. After Aruga's 'Dōzoku and shinzoku (*Dōzoku* and kinship)' published in 1947 and Kitano's work published in 1951, their publications frequently contain direct criticisms and counter-criticisms of each other's positions. The main points of conflict in their theories on *dōzoku* are: (1) views on the nature of the *dōzoku* bond; (2) views on genealogy; and (3) views on *dōzoku* and the *oyakata-kokata* relationship. I discuss these points in turn below.

Aruga defines the *dōzoku* group as a 'social relationship involving community life centering around religious rituals for common guardian gods, irrespective of turnover of *ie* member individuals, because the basic nature of the *dōzoku* group lies in having a place in the genealogical relationships of head *ie* and branch *ie* and in the common ties to the regional community among *ie*' (1943: 112), or 'common ties to the regional community among *ie* which maintain close community life or close connection in daily living in accordance with the genealogical relationships between the head *ie* and branch *ie*' (1947: 28–9). But he also states that the *dōzoku* bond 'can only occur through vertical or master–servant relationships' (1947: 35), and characterizes it as occurring 'in any age, if *ie* had vertical relationships – specifically, relationships in which one *ie* is relied on by other *ie* in terms of living' (Aruga 1947: 31–2). This begs the question as to how genealogical relationships occur. Aruga says, 'genealogical relationships can occur, at the beginning of their establishment, only through the reliance of branch *ie* on the head *ie* in terms of living, and many of them occurred due to the necessity of establishing close relationships in terms of living with the development of the head *ie*' (1948a: 116–17).

In short, Aruga argues that the reliance of branch families on the head *ie* (vertical relationship) creates genealogical relationships. In this context, Aruga refers to these relationships as the '*dōzoku* relationship,' and seems to distinguish this from the landlord-tenant relationship based on the observation that the former has 'religious rituals for common guardian gods' and the latter does not.[11]

In contrast, Kitano argues that 'to understand the *dōzoku* organization, we should not only discuss its structural form or functions' but should also find out 'the internal structural principle that defines the nature of its bonds' (1951: 8). From this position, Kitano criticizes Aruga, arguing that the nature of the *dōzoku* bond 'should not be found in the vertical relationships in social status or master–servant relationships, but should ultimately be found in genealogical relationships' (1951: 8). In this context, a genealogical relationship is related to each *ie*'s origin and is 'established between the head *ie* and a branch *ie* by, so to speak, the mutual acknowledgement of the existence of an ancestor-descendent relationship between them, at the time of an *ie* branching or the creation of a branch *ie*,' and 'based on this mutual acknowledgment, the head *ie* and the branch *ie* are linked by an *ie* relationship that has a certain place in the genealogical relationships' (Kitano 1951: 8–9). An *ie* branching, or the granting of independence to a branch *ie* from the head *ie*, is the establishment of a genealogical relationship which entails certain obligations, but also involves a guarantee of the livelihood of the members of the branch *ie*. The guarantee generally involves the head of the *ie* providing part of the *ie*'s property as a dependency allowance. A branch *ie*'s head has patriarchal rights independently of the head *ie*, but a branch *ie* is inevitably placed in a 'position subordinate to the authority of the head *ie* in the genealogical order of the *dōzoku* group' (Kitano 1951: 16–18).

Understanding *dōzoku* to have the internal bonding principle described above, Kitano finds that it is 'very close to the patrimonial system that Max Weber explains in distinction from the feudal system.' Kitano, however, then asked what to this day remains an unanswered question: In *dōzoku*, 'genealogic relationships are of foremost significance and being the genealogical origin is the source of the authority of the head *ie*.' Does this apply to Weber's patrimonial system (1951: 23–4)?

At this point in our comparison, it is becoming clear that both Aruga and Kitano stress the importance of genealogy in their definitions of *dōzoku*. Aruga nevertheless seeks the true nature of the *dōzoku* bond in vertical relationships rather than genealogy because Aruga understands genealogy in a particular way.

Dōzoku is a union of *ie* closely related to the establishment of each *ie*. Because the establishment of one *ie* was related to the maintenance of its living, the genealogical relationship between the head *ie* and the branch *ie* was closely associated with the mutual aid organization consisting of member *ie* families. However, 'in recent years, genealogical relationships between the head *ie* and its branch *ie* have been increasingly separated from these living relationships' (Aruga 1962: 71). This is how Aruga understands the term 'genealogy'; clearly something quite different to that in which Kitano argues the nature of the *dōzoku* bond should be found. Hence, it is not surprising that Aruga does not locate the nature of the *dōzoku* bond in genealogy – for Aruga, genealogy has no meaning when taken as something separate from living relationships (or master–servant relationships in this context). In other words, at base, Aruga contends that any particular institutional factor has meaning only if it is supported by the facts of everyday life.

Importantly, there is no inconsistency in the logical structures of their respective arguments. On one hand, Aruga regards vertical relationships to be the basis for *dōzoku* bond because of his unique genealogy and unique view of Japanese culture, in which the vertical or master–servant relationship is understood to be the basic characteristic of Japanese society. On the other hand, Kitano understands genealogical relationships to be the basis because he approaches *dōzoku* as a type of kinship community.

Further clarification can be achieved through a brief examination of the relationship between *dōzoku* and *oyakata-kokata* – another distinction about which the two authors differ. Their differences regarding this relationship appeared as early as 1939, in Kitano's monograph on the practice of *oyakata-kokata* in Ōgaito, Yamanashi Prefecture.

Based on his research in Ōgaito, Kitano argues that 'the two life frameworks – the *oyakata-kokata* relationship and the *dōzoku* organization – should not be regarded as the same thing in nature, but at a certain stage in the development of society…the two may fuse together as an organization'(1941: 162). Yet he also argues that even though it is difficult to separate these two living organizations in form, it is important to distinguish them as two types of superior-subordinate relationships with different principles.

Kitano explains the basis for this distinction as follows, focusing on the motive to enter into the *oyakata-kokata* relationship or *dōzoku*: the motive to enter into the *oyakata-kokata* relationship lies 'more in the substantial protection and services it offers to everyday living.' Thus, it does not require a 'superior-subordinate relationship based on the authority deriving from the *ie*'s genealogy.' The *oyakata-kokata* relationship can therefore be 'established separately from genealogical relationships' (Kitano 1959: 42). Kitano adds, 'if two *ie* are connected with each other only in terms of living – with one protecting and serving the other's everyday living – then there is no need for the latter *ie* to be absorbed by the former *ie*'s *dōzoku*, and they are free to remain in the *oyakata-kokata* relationship.' He argues that *dōzoku* and the *oyakata-kokata* relationship must be distinguished because, although the two relationships 'may not be distinguishable in form, their standards of behavior are different.' These differences manifest themselves in the manners of 'participating in such matters as religious services for the *dōzoku*'s guardian gods conducted by the entire *dōzoku*, succession of the head *ie*, creation of a new branch *ie*, or disposition of the *dōzoku*'s common property' (Kitano 1959: 59).

Thus, Kitano explains the difference between *dōzoku* and the *oyakata-kokata* relationship based on whether or not they are associated with the *ie*'s genealogical relationships. By contrast, it appears that Aruga does not distinguish between *dōzoku* and the *oyakata-kokata* relationship, as suggested in the statement, 'the master–servant relationship manifests itself as the head-branch *ie* relationship or the *oya-ko* (*oyakata-kokata*) relationship' (1947: 35). He bases this argument on the following understanding: 'Genealogical relationships between the head *ie* and branch *ie* in a *dōzoku* group basically occur in cases where there are class distinctions due to which branch *ie* are dependent on the head *ie* for their living,' and 'regardless of whether or not they are related by blood, the head *ie* is *oya* or *oyakata*, and branch *ie* are *ko* or *kokata*.' In such cases, branch *ie* include not only blood-related branches and servants' branches but also 'those that moved from elsewhere into the village and settled there by relying on an influential family when entering the village' and becoming *kokata* of the influential family (Aruga 1952: 288).

Aruga, again, emphasizes living relationships, arguing that 'even when the designations of "head *ie*" and "branch *ie*" no longer apply to the *oyakata-kokata* relationship between non-relatives, we cannot definitely conclude that the living relationship between *oyabun* and *kobun* [i.e. *oyakata* and *kokata*] has turned into a mere formality' (1974: 26), while Kitano argues that an '*ie*'s supporting activities' directed toward its branch *ie*, and 'protection of living of *kobun*' are different (1981: 101).

Aruga's position is that one must deepen one's understanding of the basic characteristics of a phenomenon in life by tracing it back to its original form before interpreting the event. By contrast, Kitano's approach is to form a more general analytical concept and use it to explain the event. This difference can be clearly seen in the arguments above.

Having reviewed Aruga's and Kitano's arguments on *dōzoku* we find that their differences in understanding *dōzoku* lie, at base, in their respective understandings of *ie*. Hence, I analyze their arguments about *ie* in the next section.

The concept of '*ie*' and its members
The points at issue in the Aruga-Kitano Controversy over *ie* can be summarized as follows: (1) The relationship between *ie* and the cross-cultural concept of *kazoku* (family); (2) the nature of *ie* as an organization – specifically, whether *ie* should be regarded as a life community or a kinship community; and (3) the issue of non-blood-related members of an *ie*. Differences between the two researchers on these points have also resulted in the points at issue in their arguments on *dōzoku* described above.

Aruga's arguments on *ie* have roughly the same structure as those on *dōzoku*. To sum up, Aruga argues that *ie* is: a life community or a commune for the management of family property and the operation of family business centered around a married couple; and that its members help each other in a functional manner in performing their everyday living functions, and each has a certain right to the *ie*'s property; and that therefore *ie* members include both relatives and non-relatives (non-blood-related members). However, since the basic nature of *ie* lies in the maintenance of the *ie*'s perpetuity and the provision of a guarantee of the member's livelihood, the members are divided into stem members and collateral members, a distinction made basically by establishing a master–servant relationship between these two types of members. Aruga argues that the development of *ie* with this structure is unique to Japan and, therefore, the concept of family in a cross-cultural sense is not applicable to *ie*.

Kitano criticizes Aruga for failing to describe the nature of *ie* as an organization, developing his argument on *ie* as follows: *Ie* in Japan is *kazoku* (family), based on the tradition of patriarchy, and the bonds of *ie* are based on acceptance of its authority out of filial piety. However, *ie* is nothing other than family in a cross-cultural sense. Therefore, at its core, *ie* is based on small bonds.

From this perspective, Kitano criticizes Aruga for unduly neglecting 'the organizational system of <u>*kazoku*</u> [emphasis original] which constitutes the *ie* and is the entity that actually conducts everyday living activities for the *ie*.' Kitano regards *ie* as a kinship community after all, arguing that it is ultimately 'one historical form of *kazoku* as a kinship community.' Kitano argues that it is for the sake of this kinship community that *ie* has its property and business and requires community life, and that 'this order must not be reversed' (1981: 10–11).

As per their views of *dōzoku*, these arguments about *ie* very clearly reveal the contrast between Aruga, who regards *ie* as a life community, and Kitano, who regards it as a kinship community. This represents the more general contrast between Kitano, who aims to position *ie* in the context of arguments on *kazoku* in a cross-cultural sense, and Aruga, who maintains that *ie* should be properly positioned in Japanese culture before making any comparisons.

An understanding of what defines a member of *ie* is perhaps best achieved through reviewing their arguments about what we might call the 'marginal cases' – the question of whether non-blood-related persons (live-in servants) should be regarded as *ie* members or not.

Aruga regards *ie* as a life community that is centered on a married couple and manages the *ie*'s property and operates its business. He therefore argues that 'non-blood-related servants taken in from the outside' may be regarded as having 'a de facto sense of family if they are aware that they participate in the *ie*'s life with a sense of subordination to the core members of the *ie* under a certain social relationship' (1952: 167). That is, he regards non-blood-related servants under these conditions to be *ie* members. However, since an *ie* not only guarantees the livelihood of its members, but also demands 'dedicated service for the *ie*'s long-lasting existence,' its members are divided into stem members, who are directly responsible for maintaining the *ie*'s continuity, and others (Aruga 1965: 39). In this sense, the non-blood-related servants' position in *ie* is special, as collateral (non-kin) members of the *ie*.

As previously noted, Aruga maintains that the difference between kin members and non-kin members is not very important in the maintenance of *ie*. This also applies to his arguments on *dōzoku*, as follows: some live-in servants are distant blood relatives of the *ie*, while others are non-relatives. Among such live-in servants, some are not regarded as *ie* members. This indicates that 'whether blood relations are near or distant is a matter of degree,' and whether a live-in servant is an *ie* member 'depends on the conditions of the family business management and the length of the period of residence in the *ie*' (Torigoe 1983: 5).

Later, however, Aruga refined his position, no longer regarding non-blood-related live-in servants as '*ie* members in any case,' but adopting a more restrictive stance in which they are regarded as *ie* members 'if they are so defined by certain custom' (1974: 11). Here, 'certain custom' means a common practice of treatment, such as where a non-blood-related person who became a servant at a young age gets married and, after a certain period of service to the master's *ie*, establishes a branch *ie* that maintains a close relationship with the everyday affairs of the master's *ie*.

In contrast, Kitano 'hesitate[s] to regard live-ins (servants), who identify themselves less with the *ie* [than the *ie*'s children would do], as *ie* members,' and argues that servants should be understood as being 'housed with the mutual understanding that they have a position as *kobun* of the master who is also the landlord' (1981: 95). This follows from Kitano's understanding of *ie* as *kazoku*, formed as a kinship community. Regarding *ie* as essentially a kinship community requires distinguishing between the support and livelihood protection the *ie* head's provides to his children and *kobun*. That is, because Kitano understands that '*ie* members are those who are to be supported by the *ie* head because he is responsible for supporting the *ie*, or the representative of the *ie*' (1981: 101), he hesitates to regard servants as *ie* members.

When Kitano focuses, however, on the treatment of servants according to what Aruga calls a 'certain custom,' he finds that it is substantially the same as the support provided to a farming family's children by the family head and concludes that 'live-in servants given such treatment should be regarded, as Aruga says, as fulfilling the qualifications for being *ie* members' (Kitano 1981: 89). Yet Kitano still hesitates to regard them as *ie* members because servants are 'taken in [to the master's *ie*] as a factor in the *ie*'s operation' and that the master 'must treat them in compliance with the "custom" in the treatment of servants already established outside the *ie*' (1981: 98).

As we can see then, Kitano almost accepts Aruga's argument that live-in servants should be regarded as *ie* members, diverging only on a fine distinction about the roots or source of the 'custom' that makes it so. Kitano nevertheless accepts that Aruga's definition of *ie* members is 'a natural consequence of Aruga's concepts and ideas on *ie*, *dōzoku* and *oyakata-kokata*' (1981: 102).

Aruga's and Kitano's perspectives

I have discussed Aruga's and Kitano's arguments on *ie* and *dōzoku* focusing on the theoretical and methodological differences from which their conflicts arise. I have argued that their conflicts arise from a fundamental difference in approach: while Aruga understands *ie* and *dōzoku* as a life community, Kitano understands them as a kinship group.[12] Hence, we must now look more closely at the theoretical orientations that led these two thinkers to such different understandings of the organizational nature of *ie* and *dōzoku*. Thus, I now discuss the relative positions of *ie* and *dōzoku* in their wider studies, and then examine their theoretical and methodological positions in detail.

Aruga's life community theory

Aruga's (1966) study on *ie* and *dōzoku* arose from his study of the practice of tenant farming, which began from the perspective of a critique of Japanese capitalism. He begins from a position that sees sociology as a specialized science that must deal with social relationships as 'forms of human existence.' From this perspective, Aruga intended to 'study the practice of tenant farming...as a social relationship and to clarify its social and historical relations from this angle, and then to understand its ethnic nature.' More specifically, since the practice of tenant farming is a social relationship, Aruga thought that he must 'discuss it in relation to the community's form of life.' To do this, he would have to 'study the life' of *ie* and *dōzoku* as associations of *ie*, which are the most important forms in rural community life, by understanding the form of existence of phenomena in their life practices (1943: 32–3). In other words, Aruga believes that studying *ie* and *dōzoku* is necessary to clarify the basic forms of rural community life in Japan and therefore necessary to any attempt to identify the ethnic nature of Japanese society.

From his studies of the forms of rural community life, in 1947 Aruga proposed two types of *ie* associations in rural communities – *dōzoku* and *kumi* (literally: 'group' or 'team'). In Aruga's opinion, both *dōzoku* and *kumi* are phenomena that appear in rural community life. They differ only in their manner of association to *ie*, having the following frameworks.

Dōzoku is a 'life community based on the genealogical relationship between the head *ie* and branch *ie*, when one *ie*'s livelihood depends on another *ie*, or the two *ie* are linked by vertical bonds'

(Aruga 1948b: 176–7). *Kumi* is a 'life community in which *ie* are linked by horizontal bonds.' *Dōzoku* and *kumi* 'restrict each other, and thus they not only affect each other in characteristics but are also interconvertible depending on the internal and external living conditions determining their characteristics' (Aruga 1947: 50). That is, since *dōzoku* and *kumi* differ only in the manner of association of *ie*, assuming that *ie* has a singular ethnic nature, they have a definite interconvertibility. Conversely, if 'the genealogical relationships among *ie* [in *dōzoku*] are fixed, then the *dōzoku* can never be converted to *kumi*' (Aruga 1948b: 176). Hence, their interconvertibility occurs because both *dōzoku* and *kumi* are life communities, not kinship communities.

As we will see more clearly in the next section, Aruga's life community theory described above is completely different from Kitano's theory, which begins with the attempt to identify the 'nature' of *ie* by directly discussing *ie* and *dōzoku* using cross-cultural analytical concepts.

Kitano's kinship community theory

Kitano's research began as an attempt to elucidate the social stratification of farmers. Like Aruga, he began from a perspective that was critical of Japanese capitalism (Sumiya and Kitano 1968: 143). Kitano explains that his subsequent studies developed in stages: 'Assuming that the first stage was the attempt to understand *dōzoku* as the basis for my study, the second stage was the learning of a typological method to study various relationships that are as important as *dōzoku*.' Kitano's studies then developed to a third stage, which addressed questions of *dōzoku* and *shinzoku* (kinship). The overall direction of his studies was to seek an 'understanding of Japanese kinship organizations at large' (Kitano 1962: 11). From this perspective, Kitano conducted studies to analyze the 'nature of the respective bonds of *dōzoku*, *shinzoku*, *ie* and *kazoku*.' Starting from an interest in Japanese kinship organizations Kitano had already adopted a cross-cultural perspective before he commenced his specific studies on *ie* and *dōzoku*. It is beyond the scope of the present work to argue it here, but suffice to say that in adopting this cross-cultural perspective, he also adopted other Weberian prejudices, such that his arguments on *ie* and *dōzoku* are notably influenced by Weber's typology of patriarchal and patrimonial systems.

Nevertheless, in Kitano's studies of kinship organizations, *ie* and *dōzoku* are both assumed to be based on genealogical relationships and are therefore understood to be historical forms of kinship organizations (Kitano and Masaoka 1971: 6).[13] To sustain this argument, though, Kitano must draw a clear line between *dōzoku*, which is a kinship organization, and the *oyakata-kokata* relationship, which is not. Similarly, Kitano hesitates to regard non-blood-related *kokata* as *ie* members.

As mentioned, the third stage of Kitano's research was marked by a move into studies about the two types of kinship organizations – '*dōzoku*' and '*shinrui kankei*' (kinship relations) – in a rural community (Kitano and Masaoka 1971: 10). The topics he pursued at this stage included: the relationship between rural community structures and kinship organizations focusing on '*ie*'; the symbiotic relationship between *dōzoku* and *shinzoku* in a kinship organization; and the potential conditions affecting the relationship between kinship organizations and rural community structures. Through studying these topics, Kitano has established that 'kinship organizations have an extremely important, or primary, meaning in the formation and organization of the community structure' and that 'kinship organizations beyond the boundaries of *ie* always consist of *dōzoku* and *shinrui* (relatives), which are organizations of different natures, that coexist while performing different functions' (Kitano and Masaoka 1971: 344).

Kitano's research has consistently attempted to identify the 'nature' of the bonds in and between *dōzoku* and *shinrui* by studying them as kinship organizations. This approach is justified by Kitano's view of sociology, which he explains as follows:

> We accept our study subjects which probably have strong ethnic characteristics, such as kinship organizations, as they are. We [also, however] treat them in a so-called "cross-cultural" manner, [and] define concepts and raise and interpret issues by associating them with common theories in sociology to the maximum extent possible. (Kitano and Masaoka 1971: 7)

Here we find an explicit acknowledgement of Kitano's commitment to 'cross-cultural' concepts, a sharp contrast to Aruga's view of sociology presented earlier.

Methodologies in living- and kinship-based theories
Aruga's life community theory ('living-based theory') and Kitano's kinship community theory ('kinship-based theory') each adopt a different methodology for analysis. The life community theory

employs a 'methodology for understanding living' (Torigoe 1977) to study life phenomena from the perspective of their forms of existence, while the kinship community theory uses a 'kinship typology' characteristic of cross-cultural studies.

As Kitano admits, his kinship-based theory is basically a 'methodology based on Weber's typology' (1962: 8). Such typology-based methodologies do not develop conceptual types as a means of defining common facts that can be empirically observed about *dōzoku* bonds, but rather 'conceptually sublimate[s the types] as a means of defining the semantic characteristics of bonds' and then comparing them with *shinzoku* (kinship) as a cross-cultural analytical concept (Kitano 1962: 9). This is the methodology that led to Kitano's definition of the nature of *dōzoku* bond and his argument for the double structure of *ie* as outlined above.

In contrast, the methodology employed in Aruga's living-based theory has been elucidated by Hiroyuki Torigoe and Toshimasa Hirano (Torigoe 1977; Hirano 1981), among others. Allow me to outline it here.[14]

For Aruga, sociology is concerned with 'social relationships as forms of human existence.' According to Aruga, in social relationships, 'the collective whole is the only entity that can fulfill one term of a binary opposition when the other term is the individual person (individual),' and 'as a concept having the meaning of collective whole, the term group (*shūdan*) is used as the opposing binary term of the individual person.' Social relationships are the 'direct intermediation' between the individual and the group (social relations theory).

These social relationships are not fixed, though; hence it is necessary to 'understand the process of formation and the formed facet [that which is formulated] in association with each other.' Specifically, in a social relationship, the process of formation (i.e. the historical nature) and the formulated facet (i.e. the social nature) reciprocate. To understand these two facets, therefore, we must trace the original form of the social relationship (retrospective history method).

Aruga uses the term 'collective whole (group)' to refer to an ethnic cultural area in which particular ethnic characteristics are found (ethnic culture area theory). To understand the specific ethnic characteristics of the social relationships witnessed in the ethnic cultural area, he constructs typological concepts for social relationships (e.g. *dōzoku* and *kumi*).[15] These models are created by 'eliminating specific differences from individual social relationships [that are similar to] a certain extent.' The originality of this typology lies in the way that the creation of types is 'limited by the ethnic cultural area [first] and then by social relationships of the same kind.' By respecting these limits, the types become interconvertible (interconversion theory). According to Aruga this is what makes historical sociology possible, because 'The interrelationship or interconvertibility between different types of social relationships of the same kind remains unchanged throughout historical periods under certain conditions.'

Hence, if we aim to understand and elucidate the ethnic characteristics of social relationships as forms of human existence, or forms of living, an ethnic cultural area must be established as a limitation of scope. The retrospective history method is then used to identify the specific forms of living that have emerged in response to various internal and external conditions. The typology is a means of generalizing these forms of living and is supported by the interconversion theory.

It should be clear now that Aruga's living-based theory attempts to understand social relationships as forms of living using the methodology described above. As we have seen, the conflict between Aruga and Kitano over their conceptions of *ie* and *dōzoku* is at its base a conflict between the living-based theory and the kinship-based theory and their respective methodologies. One manifestation of this conflict is the difference in their definitions of key concepts, and thus in their understandings of the nature of phenomena. One source of this conflict is their different views on the question of Japanese peculiarity or uniqueness – specifically, whether a cross-cultural conception is applicable or not. Let me discuss the conflict in understanding the 'nature of phenomena' first.

Recall that Kitano's primary critique of Aruga stems from Kitano's unwavering conviction that the nature of the *dōzoku* bond is ultimately found in 'genealogical relationships' (Kitano 1951: 8). From the perspective of Aruga's living-based theory, the 'nature' of any such 'bond' is always bound by social conditions and determined in a particular historical context. Therefore, the 'nature' of *dōzoku* cannot be understood simply as genealogy. In Aruga's theory, genealogy is part of what must be explained, not an explanation of how particular relationships are formed or structured. Hence, what each author means by 'nature' is quite different from the other. For Aruga:

> Since the nature of a certain practice in life is related to the nature of cultural phenomena in general, the nature of the practice must include

that it is a social and historical phenomena. Therefore, its nature is nothing other than [the particular way] that the various forms of the practice are socially and historically related to each other.

Therefore, the nature of a phenomenon in life must be defined so as to elucidate the 'social and historical interrelationships among the various forms by identifying the social conditions existing at time of their development' (Aruga 1943: 21). The historical perspective underlying this definition of nature is an important characteristic of Aruga's living-based theory.

In contrast, Kitano seeks to identify the nature of the unique bonds found in *dōzoku* as a community – having already concluded that *dōzoku* is a type of kinship organization. In other words, while Aruga, from the living-based perspective, seeks to elucidate the nature of specific historical and social phenomena as observed in their cultural context, Kitano explores the nature of bonds as a typology of certain phenomena. It is no surprise that there are differences in their positions.

Let us turn now to the second point of conflict – whether to introduce cross-cultural analytical concepts into our arguments about *ie*. This point also becomes clear by understanding it in terms of a conflict between the living-based and the kinship-based theories.

In Aruga's living-based theory, *ie* is a 'life community based on a married couple' (1948b: 164), and *ie* members are those who 'participate in self-rule of the *ie* from the inside' (1948b: 173). By contrast, Kitano's kinship-based theory understands *ie* as 'one historical form in Japan of common *kazoku* as a social group' and discusses 'its position in *kazoku* in general in terms of typology' (1962: 85). In this context, *ie* is regarded as a 'historical social system which is established under the power of *ie* led by the *ie* head's patriarchal power and which contains one or more core *kazoku*' forming small bonds at the core (Kitano 1951: 12). Kitano criticizes Aruga on methodological grounds: 'without defining the nature of *kazoku*, no study of actual *kazoku* can be sufficiently theoretical as long as it intends to lead to a theory on *kazoku*' (1962: 153). Elsewhere, Kitano argues that Aruga's attempt to understand the nature of *kazoku* as a group satisfying a combination of functions is heading in the 'opposite direction from family sociology's past efforts to identify the nature of *ie* bonds' (1962: 142). These criticisms are justified from the perspective of the family sociology-oriented kinship-based theory. But Aruga's interest is not in family sociology; his objective is to identify the nature of *ie* and *dōzoku* as respective social relationships in the overall context of social interrelationships *per se*, which is what rural sociology has generally intended to do.

Conclusion

We can now schematically summarize Aruga's and Kitano's respective 'living-based' and 'kinship-based' theories. Aruga regards *ie* and *dōzoku* as life communities, beginning from the perspective that sociology's task is to understand social relationships as forms of living. This approach prompted Aruga to formulate a 'methodology for understanding living' and to use it in developing his understanding of *ie* and *dōzoku* as life communities. Overall, Aruga's work is a life community study which follows the general direction aimed at by rural sociology.

Kitano, in contrast, is strongly Weberian and thus analyzes *ie* and *dōzoku* through a Weberian typology. This methodological typology led him to the cross-cultural concepts of *kazoku* and *shinzoku* by 'conceptually sublimating' the nature of *ie* and *dōzoku* bonds. Kitano's work has thus generally been recognized as a kinship organization study, which is one of the principal aims of family sociology.

The primary difference between the living-based and kinship-based theories thus parallels the difference between seeing life phenomena from the perspective of those who live it and seeing them from an outside perspective. Aruga's life-based theory strictly focuses on discussing phenomena from the inside, where ordinary people conduct their everyday living activities in their typical place of being. Beginning with the minutiae of everyday life, Aruga's study develops from *ie* to *dōzoku*, then to rural communities and finally to Japanese culture in general. In contrast, Kitano seeks to achieve an understanding of phenomena in a typological, analytical manner, using external concepts and typologies to illuminate what lies within. This has shaped his system of study, which starts from *dōzoku*, followed by *ie/kazoku* and then kinship organizations.

I have argued the difference between the living-based and kinship-based theories derives from the different attitudes towards cross-cultural comparison. This difference has manifested in the expressions: '*ie* is the Japanese kazoku' (Aruga) and '*ie* is nothing other than *family*' (Kitano). This also appoints to a fundamental difference between Aruga, who highlights ethnic characteristics and attempts to understand them (which means also understanding the ethnic characteristics of peoples other than the Japanese), and Kitano, who is content to formulate concepts that can be obtained by sublimating experiential characteristics and may be called analytical concepts. What the two researchers mean by the term '*kazoku*' is clearly different – Aruga argues that *ie* is not like a family in the cross-cultural sense of the term (based on the 1960s understanding of 'family') but is actually a unique Japanese indigenous/original form of organization (so-called 'management body'), and Kitano suggests *ie* is simply a family in the cross-cultural sense of the term.

While Aruga is fully aware of the necessity for cross-cultural comparisons, he points to the risks involved in carelessly applying existing concepts to observed phenomena, arguing that one must identify the basic characteristics of a phenomenon by observing its function and structure within the ethnic cultural area in which it is an everyday lived experience. This is the starting point for Aruga's living-based theory. Although Kitano's stated objective for formulating cross-cultural analytical concepts is similar ('to clarify the characteristics of...a historical fact in Japan') the two researchers' different perspectives have nevertheless produced vastly different results from their studies of *ie* and *dōzoku*.

Through reviewing this controversy over key concepts in village life, I have been struck by the richness and power of Aruga's *seikatsu-ron* (living-based theory) (Torigoe 1977) for discussing *ie* and *dōzoku*. The essence of this theory lies in the understanding that people's lives are invariably processes that are continuously formed in the intermediation between the creativity of individuals and the community's norms. In short, the living-based theory aims to understand social phenomena by analyzing the living activities that constitute each phenomenon in its particular social-historical setting, rather than through comparison with some externally derived forms or pre-existing analytical concepts.

The present work is a study in living environmentalism, which has been substantially derived from this living-based theory. The following chapters elucidate living environmentalism in more detail.

4 Modernization of Villages and Transformation of Everyday Life Knowledge

Everyday life knowledge and water systems

Everyday life knowledge and scientific knowledge

Perspectives for understanding issues

Since Kuhn (1962), our belief in the objectivity of scientists – that scientists are able to view facts 'objectively' – has been shaken. Controversies between objectivism (universalism) and relativism underlie all arguments about science. Even when we are not directly concerned with science, we are unable to use the word 'scientific' without some hesitation. So, what perspective can we use to understand environmental issues that seem to require practical solutions?

Environmental issues, and particularly water issues, have become 'hot topics' in recent years. In the natural sciences, researchers have set pollution standards and repeatedly measured pollution levels, achieving some measure of success. In the social sciences, however, particularly sociology and anthropology, very few researchers have taken up environmental issues, or developed methods for analyzing them. Environmental issues have largely been avoided, tending to be too practical to be dealt with objectively. I tackle environmental issues because I believe their resolution to be extremely urgent, in light of the current status of various environmental problems, including water pollution, around the shores of Lake Biwa over the past several years.

Previous studies of environmental issues have included, for example, elucidating the mechanisms of water pollution, residents' responses to pollution, and residents' movements to combat pollution.

In this chapter, I address environmental issues from the perspective of the gap between the everyday life traditionally maintained by residents and modern scientific knowledge, as embodied by modern technology and introduced to residents' everyday lives.

Everyday life knowledge and scientific knowledge
Environmental issues are often represented as consequences of capitalistic production. Historical studies of environmental pollution, for example, treat cases of mining pollution during the feudal age as issues of the preceding period.[1] While it is certainly important to analyze the mechanisms by which capitalistic production styles cause environmental pollution, pollution itself cannot be attributed solely to capitalism as an administrative/economic system. For one thing, as is well known, environmental pollution also constitutes major social issues under socialist systems.

This means that environmental issues derive from a principle that applies in capitalism, socialism and other ideologies: industrialization (Nakaoka and Hanazaki: 1986). We must understand environmental issues as products of industrialization before we can fully appreciate issues specific to capitalism. Otherwise, we may reach misguided conclusions, for example, that abandoning capitalism will resolve our environmental issues.

How, then, have environmental issues occurred in the process of industrialization? Yōichirō Murakami argues that environmental issues stem from the basic nature of technology. Murakami argues that technology 'starts to function only after "targets" to be achieved have been set,' and it functions best when it is aimed at meeting targets required by external factors, such as economic efficiency, 'disregarding [other] issues such as how [the targets] should be achieved.' Hence, the 'relationship between individual targets' and inconsistencies between them cannot be addressed or resolved by technology itself. Environmental pollution is in effect 'the negative aspect of the nature of technology' (Murakami 1974). Nevertheless, modern technology is characterized as 'scientific,' which means that it is derived from understanding matters through a system in which 'the matter to be understood and the person who attempts to understand it are completely separate from each other, with the former thoroughly objectified and the latter super-subjectified – to the extent of having a god's-eye view, freed from any and all restrictions on its existence.' This system has also been referred to as a 'manipulation system,' under which 'a person existing outside of the matter manipulates and utilizes the matter as he wishes' (Takeuchi 1986). This is not an extreme criticism of how scientific technology develops, but rather the generally accepted understanding of both advocates and critics.

How, then, does everyday life knowledge differ from scientific knowledge? How is everyday life knowledge accepted? And how has it been affected by scientific knowledge?

In modern societies, we have generally accepted scientific knowledge into our everyday lives in a matter-of-fact manner. This does not mean, however, that we have ignored the various conflicts that have arisen through the adoption of various modern technologies, such as the noise pollution produced by airports, the exhaust pollution from automobiles, and the toxic air pollution produced by chemical manufacturing. By developing an understanding of the intersection of scientific knowledge and everyday life knowledge, we will see that these conflicts arise as soon as technology begins to be incorporated into our everyday lives.

In what follows, I discuss how these two lines of knowledge have come together and generated conflicts, by discussing a case of transition from traditional water use to a modern water supply system in a rural community.

Water use and the logic of everyday life

In many Japanese rural villages, modern water supply systems were not constructed until the late 1950s. Until then, water was primarily obtained from wells. Other sources included rivers, lakes, rain and so on. In 1984, a survey was conducted of 295 communities located on the shores of Lake Biwa regarding their water use before the construction of modern water supply systems. The results show that they depended mainly on wells and rivers for their daily water supplies (Kada 1984). Of the 295 sample communities (multiple answers allowed), 224 communities obtained drinking water from wells, twenty-three from rivers, twenty-two from lakes and nineteen from other sources. At the time of the survey, however, most communities had switched to modern water services, resulting in the loss of the diversity of water sources that had existed before the construction of modern water supply systems.

My objective in this section is to clarify the relationship between the use of wells, rivers and the lake and people's everyday lives. There are several reasons for taking this approach. One is that I believe that the current pollution problems in Lake Biwa have been primarily caused by disruptions to the traditional drainage systems. Before the construction of modern water supply systems, the 'traditional drainage systems' were inextricably integrated with the water supply systems, working together to keep water supplies clean. These systems are no longer effective because of the new water supply systems. Yet, the drainage systems remain unchanged, with no specific plan for reconstruction. The current situation in the region is too dire to leave these drainage systems as they are. I am not suggesting, though, that we should 'revert back' to the traditional water supply and drainage systems. People today are solely dependent on tap water, and there is no doubt that traditional drainage systems can no longer work effectively. Yet, understanding the 'idea' of the traditional integrated water supply and drainage systems in everyday life knowledge can shed light on the current situation.

Everyday water use

Age-chinai[2] is located on the northwest shore of Lake Biwa (see map on page 68 in Chapter Two). The village spreads along both banks of the Mae River. Throughout the long history of this village before the construction of modern water systems, the villagers were primarily dependent on this small river for their daily water supplies. Hence, Mae River has been used for a variety of purposes and many facilities were built over a very long period of time to serve these purposes. Many facilities and practices have also been established to maintain and control the river and its water.

For example, to facilitate the river's use as a traffic route, some of the bridges are detachable while others, built of stone, are constructed high above the water level by building up the embankments on both sides. To assist the villagers access to the water (for collecting water, or washing clothes), places called *kawata* (*kabata*) have been constructed at regular intervals along the river banks. Let us divide the elements of the river into (1) space, (2) water, (3) organisms, and (4) flow (Figure 4.1).

The Mae River runs through Age-chinai for less than 200 meters. Nevertheless, villagers were extremely conscious of upstream and downstream (*kami* and *shimo*) and careful not to pollute the river water. Each family's use of the river is significantly characterized by its upstream-downstream (*kami-shimo*) relationships with its neighbors, which imposes restrictions on water use that do not arise in the use of wells or the lake. Such restrictions are incorporated into the village's system for maintaining and controlling the Mae River. Let us discuss these restrictions on water use and their role in river management in more detail.

Figure 4.1: Various uses of the Mae River

Element	Use	Facilities
Uses		
Space	Traffic route	Boats, bridges
	Amusement	Weirs, tubs
Water	Drinking water	*Kawata* (kabata)
	Irrigation water	Weirs
	Water for firefighting	Weirs
Life	Fish (ayu[a], trout, hasu[b])	*Douke*
	Algae	'Auction of algae'
Flow	Washing	Wash stones
	Snow	'Snow melting function'
	Cooling	Tea-cooling place
	(Shōrō nagashi[c])	
Maintenance and management		
Restrictions on water use	Drainage	*Suimon, suikomi*
	Laundry	Ditches
River management		'*Tokobori* (river dredging)'
		'Auction of algae'
	(Belief in the water god)	

a: Ayu: Plecoglossus altivelis
b: Hasu: Opsariichthys uncirostris uncirostris
c: Shōrō nagashi: An annal event in which paper lanterns or votive offerings are placed on straw boats and launched onto the river to see off family ancestors' spirits on the last day of the Bon festival.

Restrictions on water use are naturally restrictions on river use. But because the Mae River has abundant water, there have never been any restrictions on the amount of water that could be used. The village has therefore never been involved in regulating or monitoring water usage, considering this to be strictly a matter for individual families. River management, however, has been understood to be a matter of concern to Age-chinai and, in turn, to Chinai as a whole. Therefore individual families could not alter river management at their discretion. Hence, while water use has been regarded as strictly private, the cleanliness of the river is a community concern, addressed through the village's management system.

There are no written restrictions on water use, and there appear to be only a few unwritten rules, such as, 'Do not wash underwear in Mae River' or 'Do not urinate in the river or you'll catch disease down below.' However, through the long course of its history, countless rules and regulations have been built-in to various facilities to prevent water pollution.

Figure 4.2: Suimon *and* suikomi

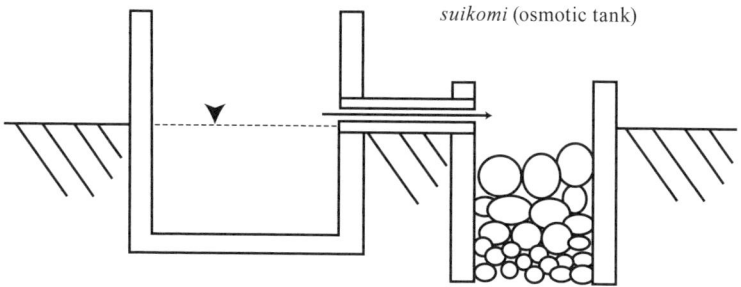

For example, diapers must be washed in a ditch (*mizo*) in a different water system from Mae River. Each household treated its domestic wastewater in a private wastewater tank or an osmotic treatment tank (called '*suimon*' and '*suikomi*,' respectively); a private sewerage system. Wastewater from rice fields was not drained into the river either, but filtered through lagoons sustained for that purpose. These are just some of the private practices through which the Mae River was maintained as a source of clean drinking water.

Although using water is a very private activity, water is a public resource, and its use cannot be simply private. For example, although each family must construct and maintain its own septic system, these are constructed based on an understanding that goes beyond any individual. The everyday knowledge employed here is similar to the understanding that villagers must not wash diapers or urinate in the river. So we should look now at the community management aspects of the situation.

As mentioned in Chapter Two, to this day, each farming family is obliged to provide three man-days of service per year in Chinai. We discussed many of the activities that this labor is allocated to – for the present discussion we only need to consider the annual river dredging, called *tokobori* (literally: riverbed digging). *Tokobori* was conducted on the 7th of August in all of the rivers in the village, through the joint effort of members from every family in Chinai. Another related activity, discussed in Chapter Two, is the day of *yutate* (damming up) in May, when algae were removed from the river and auctioned.

As mentioned, the Mae River changed greatly after 1955, when a modern water supply system was constructed. I want to elaborate on how the river was maintained for centuries until this change, and will begin to do so by examining the water management practices of the nearby village of Kaizu – also located in Makino-chō – where the villagers were reliant on wells and the lake for their water supplies.

Unlike Age-chinai, Kaizu has no river that could be relied upon as a source of water, particularly drinking water. The only rivers running through the district are the In'nai River, which flows from the northwest of the district and 'runs southeastward across paddy fields and flows into the swampland in Ōaza Nishihama,' and the Sōzakai and Naka-no Rivers, which run through the residential areas of Kaizu. Both of the latter are 'merely narrow waterways that run between the swampland and the lake water' (*Aikyōshi* (Hometown lovers' information book) author unknown). The 'swampland' mentioned above refers to the lagoons which once spread across the western parts of the district.

In early-modern times, with the development of the Hokuriku road, Kaizu District (formerly Kaizu Village) flourished as a port town at an important traffic junction. It is not necessary here to detail the history of Kaizu. I will instead restrict myself to quoting a poem from *Aikyōshi* called *Aikyōshi* (A hometown lover's poem), that characterizes the changes in Kaizu, compiled by local historians.

> (1) Having the renowned Lake Biwa at the right forehead,/Claiming the beauty of the lake and mountains as its own, this is my hometown Kaizu./(2) If you ask me how the town started, they say it was more than two thousand years ago/When our ancestors stopped at this place, hoping to flourish like tall pine trees./(3) Later, boat transportation started, using Higashiura as the port./Apart from the port the town was built, to which even the Hokuriku road was drawn./(4) Finally known to people and horses the town became, as an important water and land traffic junction./Frequented by incoming and outgoing boats, the port town flourished more than ever./.../(6) After the Meiji Restoration, the town returned to my old hometown./Civilization is an autumn wind, withering green in the post town./..../(8) Though gone are profits from being an important traffic junction,/Never gone are the blessings of nature, bringing my hometown even more happiness.

After its long and rich history, Kaizu is now a mere transit point along National Route No. 161, its once-thriving commerce now seen only in a few scattered shops.

Figure 4.3: The areas relying on different types of water source in Kaizu Higashi district. (Torigoe and Kada, eds, 1984)

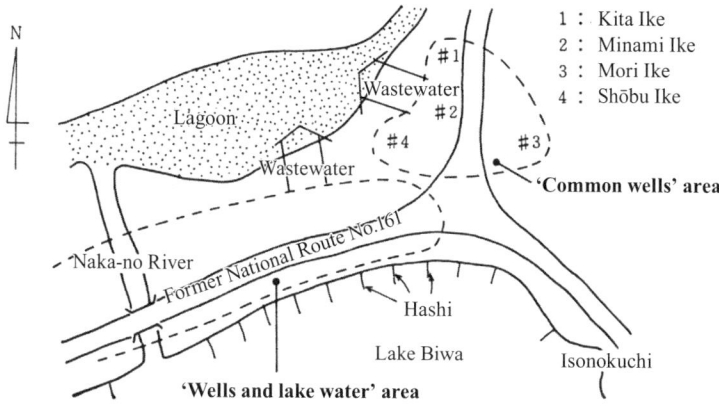

At present, Kaizu is divided into three districts along a north-south axis. Takagi (currently the Third District) is believed to have been established first, followed by Higashi-machi (the First District) near the port, and then Nakamura (the Second District), which was established in between the other two (*Aikyōshi*). Kaizu is also clearly divided by the old main road into a business area and a farming area. The town's *kumi* (groups) are still separated by the old main road. In Higashi district, common wells were only used by residents of the farming area. Residents of the business area use private wells and the lake.

Thus, based on patterns of water use, the Higashi district can be roughly divided into the 'common wells' area, located at the foot of mountains, and the 'lake and private wells' area, located on the lakeshore (Figure 4.3). The well water here was hard – the locals called it *utetenai* (literally: not hit[3]) because of the fairly metallic taste of water – and the lake water was more potable. Hence, there were not many private wells in the district. However, the lake water was not always available, especially on rainy or windy days due to the difficulty of collecting it or carrying it, or due to impurities. The people were therefore flexible, obtaining water from both sources.

Let me turn now to some of the details of the common wells in the Higashi district of Kaizu. The locals call these wells *ike* (literally: ponds). In fact, it is difficult to discern based on appearances whether they are ponds or wells. Indeed, the distinction between wells, ponds and fountains is unclear here where, for example, the local definition of a well is simply 'a hole dug into the ground to accumulate groundwater.' Based on the structure of *ike* in Kaizu, the source of drinking water at the northeast corner could be called a well, while the larger water tank with a place for washing could be called an *ike*. However, I will follow the local custom and call the entire system *ike*.

There were four *ike* in Higashi district until about ten years ago: Kita Ike and Minami Ike near the mountains, Mori Ike located a little way up a mountain in the north, and Shōbu Ike, located within the town. Except for Shōbu Ike, they collected spring-water. Shōbu Ike was created by enclosing part of the flow from a pond, and was reportedly never used for drinking purposes. The other three were constructed by enclosing springs with stone walls and had provided drinking water until the construction of the modern water supply systems.

One characteristic of these four *ike* is that each has an *ike* group (*ike gumi*), which I will discuss in more detail later. First let me describe the structure of the *ike*. Minami Ike is a rectangle measuring seven meters in an east-west direction and eight meters in a north-south direction. There is a three-meter square roof at the northeast corner, under which is a one-meter square well. At the northwest corner is a spot called *koike*, where the spring-water wells up. The entire *ike* is surrounded by a concrete structure called '*araiba*' (place for washing) which varies between 0.5 and 1.5 meters in width, except at the southeast corner where the water discharges. Each of the other corners has a stairway leading to the *araiba*. The discharge is designed such that the water is always about level with the *araiba*. The water is about fifty centimeters deep. Carp are kept in the *ike*. There was once a small shrine for Jizō (the Buddhist guardian deity of children and villages) in the *ike*, but it has been moved to a location near the well, under the roof, due to the danger of falling into the *ike*. Its original pedestal can still be seen in the *ike*, though.

Kita Ike is roughly the same size and has the same overall structure as Minami Ike, except that the Jizō shrine is still located on the surface of the water. Mori Ike is much smaller; only about three meters by 1.5 meters. It has no roof or well. This is reportedly because it is located part way up a mountain and its water springs directly to the surface without running under houses, and thus it was unnecessary to construct a separate well for drinking water. This explanation seems plausible, considering the geographical features of the area. The structure of Shōbu Ike is not clear, since it no longer exists. It seems, though, that it did not have a well for drinking water and was used exclusively for firefighting purposes. Like the others, Shōbu Ike had a Jizō shrine, which still stands on the *ike*'s remains.

While the water sources in Age-chinai were the river and private wells, those in Kaizu Higashi district were the *ike* and the lake, which were used in quite different ways by different families. In Age-chinai, where houses stood along the river, the river was the center of water use. In contrast, houses in Kaizu Higashi district stood at different distances from the nearest *ike* and the lake. Hence, water use by households in Higashi district was more varied than in Age-chinai.

In Kaizu Higashi district, while the Kita Ike and Mori Ike groups primarily obtained daily water supplies from their respective *ike*, Minami Ike and Shōbu Ike groups obtained water from both Minami Ike and the lake (since Shōbu Ike water was only for firefighting purposes, the Shōbu Ike group was allowed to use Minami Ike).

Members of the Minami Ike group typically used water as follows. Drinking water was obtained from the well located at the corner of the *ike* and the *ike* itself was used exclusively for washing food (although the well was apparently not constructed until the Taishō Period, before which the *ike* was also a source of drinking water). Laundry was done mainly at the lake shore.

In contrast, Shōbu Ike group members who had access to Minami Ike would go to the lake shore in the morning to obtain drinking water on clear days. This water was stored in large pots for drinking and cooking throughout the day. During the warmer months, they were more likely to do their laundry at the lake shore than at Minami Ike. In winter, however, they preferred to do laundry at the *ike*, since the water there was warmer than the lake. But they generally preferred the lake water when it was clear, because the *ike*'s spring-water was *utetenai*. When they did do laundry at the *ike*, they usually did so in the afternoon, after food and dishes had been washed. Diapers were either washed at home or at a place on the lakeshore called *isonokuchi* (literally: the shore's mouth).

This pattern of water use remained virtually unchanged from the establishment of the village until World War II. It began to change after the war. First, people stopped drinking the lake water from around the end of the war, because 'people started to say something about hygiene,' although they did not feel that the lake water had become 'really bad' until the early 1960s. They also stopped drinking *ike* water in 1959, when a modern water supply system was constructed.

The *ike* are currently used almost exclusively for firefighting purposes, except, according to the locals, on the rare occasions when they are used to wash the dirt off *daikon* (Japanese radishes) or Chinese cabbages. Yet whenever I visited one of these *ike*, I always saw someone washing something there. Sometimes *daikon*, but at other times, for example, I saw people washing the frames of *shōji* (paper sliding doors).

Regardless, the *ike* are still there, and the group members still perform a general *ike* cleaning once a year. Let me now describe how these *ike* have been maintained by *ike* groups (*ike nakama* – literally: *ike* company).

Each *ike* has an *ike* group (called *ike nakama*),[4] which is responsible for the maintenance and management of the *ike*. Each *ike* group has simple rules. For example, the Kita Ike group has the following rules:

1. Each year for the general *ike* cleaning, 2.7 liters of *sake*[5] shall be contributed from the First District, as has been agreed for a long time.
2. The *ike* group owns one plot of field in Higashi Shibahara./The land tax[6] on this field has been agreed to be eighty *bu* each year.

(General *ike* cleaning, 7th of August 1928./Kita Ike group, *Nenchū gyōji hikae* (Memoranda of annual events))

These *ike* groups are social groups with common ties to the surrounding areas. These areas are different from administrative districts. Each *ike* group not only uses and manages the *ike*, but also maintains the Jizō enshrined at the *ike* and conducts a Jizō Bon festival each year.

The numbers of members (families) of these *ike* groups at the time of survey in 1983 were: Kita Ike, sixteen; Minami Ike, seventeen; Mori Ike, four; and Shōbu Ike, thirteen. Mori Ike had had as many as twenty-five member families during the Taishō Period, while Kita Ike had twenty-eight member families in 1903 according to one record. Each *ike* is also used by a number of non-member families. For example, as previously mentioned, Minami Ike is used by a majority of the members of the Shōbu Ike group.

A general cleaning is conducted at each *ike* once a year, on the 7th of August, in addition to simple daily cleaning. Only group members take part in the general *ike* cleaning, while the daily cleaning is conducted in turns by the housewives of families using the *ike*. Since the *ike* have fallen into disuse, daily cleaning

Table 4.1: Account Book, Mori Ike Renchū *(Company)*

1938	Income	Expense
7th of August		
Amount received	1 yen 50	
2.7 L of *sake* from First District	1 yen 80	
1.8 L of sake from Mr. X of Nishihama (for woodland path)		
XX (for use of *ike*)	1 yen 50	
XX (for entering the group)	0 yen 50	
Donation from Shōukōin (for general *ike* cleaning)	0 yen 30	
24th of August		
Payment from XX	0 yen 37	
Donation to Hōtōin		0 yen 20
Cost of offerings	1 yen 15	
Payment from XX	2 yen 88	
Payment to XX		0 yen 31
1939	**Income**	**Expense**
23rd of August		
Donation from Shōkōin (for general *ike* cleaning)	0 yen 30	
Mr. XX (for entering the neighborhood)	0 yen 50	
(The remaining items are similar to those for 1938 and are omitted.)		

is no longer conducted, but the general cleaning continues to be conducted each year. Members also clean the temple (Shōgyōin and Hōdōin in Kaizu) on the general *ike* cleaning day.

After the general *ike* cleaning on the 7th of August, a Jizō Bon festival is held on the 23rd of August, when accounts are settled for the previous fiscal year.

For example, the settlements of accounts for Mori Ike in 1938 and 1939 were as shown in Table 4.1.

I refer to the Mori Ike account book here simply because this group is the smallest, and hence has the simplest accounts. The Kita Ike and Minami Ike account books are similar, but with more entries.

As shown in the above document, non-member families were charged 1 yen 50 *sen* for using the *ike*, the equivalent of 1.8 liters of *sake*. Another account book shows a payment of '1 yen for failure to participate in general *ike* cleaning.' These incomings were spent on the party after a general *ike* cleaning and on drinks served at the Jizō Bon festival. Of these items, '*ike* use fees' have not been seen since the 1959 accounts – the year when a small modern water supply system was constructed in Kaizu.

The document cited above includes entries 'for entering the group' and 'for entering the neighborhood.' These are two different ways to express the same thing, for moving into the area of an *ike* group also meant entering the *ike* group. In earlier days, the procedures for entering an *ike* group (or neighborhood), which were known as *kinjo no hirō* (announcement to the neighborhood), consisted of handing out 360 cc of *sake* and one or two dried squid to each family in the neighborhood and paying 50 *sen* to the *ike* group (*ike gumi*) as an entrance fee (at the time of my fieldwork, the procedures consisted of handing out matches or towels). Apart from this, a newcomer needed a sponsor to be accepted by the village.

Whatever the requirements for entry, the fact that 'entering the group' and 'entering the neighborhood' mean the same thing indicates that an *ike nakama* is a social group with common ties to the area around the *ike*. In fact, the Mori Ike account books since 1845 give the strong impression that the *ike nakama* is not only a management body for controlling the use of the *ike* but also a social club that is based on members' common ties to the area and whose main event is the annual Jizō Bon festival.

There are no legends, much less records, as to when these *ike* were constructed. According to *Aikyōshi*, Higashi-machi, where these *ike* are located, was formed at the end of the Nara Period (710–794). As mentioned, this area has no rivers or other sources of water other than these *ike* – the lake being too far away to provide daily water needs. Hence, it is quite plausible that from the beginning of Higashi-machi, residents obtained water from these *ike*, although the structures were probably different in the beginning than they are now.

There are seven shrines for Jizō in Higashi-machi. The annual Jizō Bon festival takes place at five of them: in Kita Ike, Minami Ike, Mori Ike and Shōbu Ike, and at the shrine for Yotsutsuji Jizō. Of these, the festival for Shōbu Ike Jizō and Yotsutsuji Jizō are both organized by the former Shōbu Ike group. The other three festivals are organized by the respective *ike* groups.

In the latter three groups, the accounts of the *ike* and of the Jizō Bon festival are entered in the same series of account books. Examples of the titles of the account books include, *Mori Chū* (Mori Company) (1845), *Mori Jizō Chū* (Mori Jizō Company) (1923), *Mori Ike Renchū* (Mori Ike Company) (1938). Similarly, Kita Ike's account books include *Kita Ike Nakama* (Kita Ike Company) (1928) and *Kita Ike Jizō* (1973). These titles indicate that *Jizō chū* (Jizō companies or Jizō *nakama*) and *ike renchū* (*ike nakama*) are exactly the same.

Originally, an *ike* group's member families took turns holding the post-festival party, and the *ike* account book was kept by the family that had held the previous year's party. In the Kita Ike group, however, the party organization continues to rotate through the families, but the bookkeeper has become fixed. The *ike*'s account books are kept by *ike sōdai* (the *ike* representative).

It is unknown when the *ike* group and the corresponding Jizō group meshed. Assuming that the Jizō Bon festival started sometime during the Edo Period (1615–1868)[7] and that the *ike* were most likely already well established by then, it is probable that the Jizō groups derive from the corresponding *ike* groups.

Regardless of which came first, though, the fact that the two groups coincide must be significantly associated with the continuous maintenance and management of each *ike* up to this day. The reason why an *ike* group still exists even if its members no longer use the *ike* frequently is because it now works as a group of families who take turns holding the after-festival party, or a Jizō group. A group of people linked to an *ike* would have a chance to feel their identity as a group only when they conduct a general *ike* cleaning. As members use the *ike* less often, their identity as a group weakens. However, the presence of a Jizō in the *ike* gives the members an identity as a religious group. The *ike* have been maintained and managed by respective *ike* groups, which are also Jizō groups.

I believe that this overlap between the *ike* groups and the Jizō groups was just as significant during the long history preceding the dramatic change as after the dramatic reduction in the use of the *ike*.

So far, I have described how the locals use the wells in their respective areas, but as mentioned previously, Kaizu Higashi district is a 'wells and lake water' area. Let us now discuss their use of the lake. In the discussion below, I refer to the lakeshore as '*hama*,' as the locals do.

At the *hama* of Kaizu, one can still see today a number of boards protruding over the lake surface from the sandy shore. These boards are called '*hashi*' (literally: pier). People draw water or wash clothes from the board. A *hashi* consists of a single pine board, with legs at the water end, and tied to a rock or tree with a rope at the shore end to prevent it from being carried away by waves.

Hashi are generally constructed and installed by families situated along the *hama*, but anyone can use them. Unlike *ike*, there are no fixed groups responsible for caring for respective *hashi*, and users do not need permission to use a specific *hashi*.

Looking at a map, one finds many roads crossing the former National Route No. 161 at right angles. These roads extend straight from the *hama* across the highway to inland areas, each leading to a *hashi* at the lakeshore. According to the locals, these roads are straight for firefighting purposes, rather than to make water-drawing labor easier.

When I asked a local to name the *hashi* installed by particular families in the Higashi district, he instantly listed more than ten *hashi* and the names of their respective owners. Except for rainy days, locals would go to the *hama* with a bucket (*tago*) early in the morning, wash their faces, have a mouthful of water, and bring a bucketful of water home to pour into the big pot that each family had at home. Then they would return to the *hama* for more water. In this way, people used to go back and forth between the *hama* and their house five to ten times a day. The locals say that children used to do most of this work for their families.

Water at the lakeshore was locally considered to be tasty as it was *utete* (literally: well-hit). In summer, water from the *hama* was good for bathwater because it heated quickly. Hence, people would come from a distance to get water from the lakeshore.

After most families had drawn water for the day, people started to do laundry on the *hashi* (piers). The distance between any two adjacent *hashi* was typically less than ten meters and hence housewives could chat to each other from neighboring *hashi*. In summer, children would swim nearby.

After the modern water supply system was built in the area, locals stopped going to the *hama* for water, but they continued doing their laundry there. One can still see them doing so today. During the 1970s, however, swimming at the shore was banned due to the risk posed to the community following the construction of a nuclear power plant near Obama city. A swimming pool was constructed at the local primary school as a compensatory measure. Thus, one can no longer see children swimming at the lakeshore.

As per the *ike*, I never visited the lakeshore without seeing locals doing laundry there. But clearly, both the *ike* and the lakeshore now represent only a very small portion of the locals' daily water use. They claim that what they do at the *ike* and the lakeshore is only prewashing; they wash the clothes 'properly' at home.

Drainage systems and transformation of the lagoons
In Age-chinai, where the main source of daily water was the river, the main drainage arrangements consisted of two systems. One

was the domestic purification system run by each family, and the other was a community drainage system through which domestic wastewater re-entered the natural waterways through specific paths designed to keep wastewater separate from fresh water supplies.

The domestic purification system run by each family consisted of either or both a private wastewater tank and an osmotic treatment tank (Figure 4.2). These were constructed in each family's garden. The wastewater flowing out of these tanks drained into specific 'ditches' that did not join the river supplying fresh water. Diapers and other underwear had to be washed in these ditches, which constituted the drainage system.

It is a matter of commonsense that when the river was the primary source of fresh water, if a family upstream drains its wastewater into the river, all families downstream would be affected. Because the impact of such practices is direct and visible, drainage in this area was more tightly restricted than it was in areas where fresh water was obtained from wells.

In Kaizu Higashi district, where locals could depend on both wells and the lake for water, the drainage system was simpler. Since the *ike* were situated at a distance from the houses, there was no concern that domestic wastewater would flow directly into the *ike*'s water supply.

Domestic wastewater flowed from each house's kitchen, but not directly into Lake Biwa. As mentioned, there is a vast swampland (series of lagoons) in the western part of Kaizu district. Most of the domestic wastewater flowed into these lagoons through ditches. Only after settling in these lagoons did the domestic wastewater flow into Lake Biwa through the Naka-no River. Or rather, since the lagoons had the same water level as the lake, it may be more correct to say that water in the lagoons and in the lake went back and forth through the Naka-no River. The same drainage system had been adopted by the families using lake water, except for those situated along the lake shore.

Considering that families in Kaizu Higashi district used more groundwater than surface water, it may not be surprising that they did not have osmotic treatment tanks (*suikomi*) like the families in Age-chinai. Similarly, families in Higashi district did not need wastewater holding tanks (*suimon*) because the lagoons were directly available to them.

Residents of Higashi district did not wash their diapers or underwear at the *ike* or the *hashi*, either washing them at home or at a place specified on the lakeshore called *isonokuchi*. This is similar to residents of Age-chinai washing diapers in a specific ditch, called *shitashirota*. In fact, the place for washing diapers may be characteristic of each area's drainage system.

In the wells and lake water area, the restrictions on drainage were not as strict as in those areas that depended on rivers for water. Still, the wells and lake water areas complied with two common rules: not to contaminate permeating water, and not to drain domestic wastewater directly into the lake. In Kaizu Higashi district, the lagoons in the west served as a natural wastewater holding and treatment system. Lagoons typically played a similar role in villages all around Lake Biwa.

The above descriptions apply to water-use practices before the construction of modern water supply systems. Currently, both Age-chinai and Kaizu Higashi districts are equipped with modern water supply systems. Since their construction, these systems have supplied most of the everyday water supplies in these areas. But it seems that the introduction of these water supply systems brought about significant changes in the drainage systems in each area.

As mentioned, a modern water system was constructed in Age-chinai in 1957, where residents had previously depended on the river for their fresh water. The introduction of the modern fresh water system effectively reduced the Mae River – which had previously been their sole source of fresh water – to a drainage canal. The seemingly limitless supply of fresh water through this new system directly into their homes led to far greater levels of water consumption, and the performance of *suimon* and *suikomi* rapidly deteriorated. Eventually, these wastewater treatment systems were abandoned and, in their places, the Mae River gradually became primarily a drainage canal. Algae began to grow and filth began to accumulate in it. In an attempt to deal with these problems, the river was paved with concrete – to prevent algae growth and to facilitate cleaning.

The use of the Mae River as a drainage canal undermined the entire series of drainage systems that had been established over many generations to maintain its purity as a source of fresh water. It is safe to assume that similar dramatic changes were occurring in many other parts of Japan at that time.

On the shore of Lake Biwa, the changes to the river effectively meant that domestic wastewater ditches ran directly into the lake. More specifically, rivers around Lake Biwa did not flow directly into the lake, but flowed instead into the lagoons which then flowed into the lake, with the lagoons functioning as natural settling tanks extracting effluent before the water flowed into the lake. However, the lagoons had begun to be reclaimed a decade earlier, during World War II, in an effort to increase food production. This reclamation work had continued throughout the 1950s, when the river underwent the changes described above. This resulted in both domestic wastewater and wastewater from rice fields flowing directly into Lake Biwa.

The reduction of the size of the lagoons is obvious from a comparison of maps of the northwestern part of Lake Biwa from 1895 to 1976 (Figure 4.4).

The Kaizu district originally had Shimizu Numa (lagoon) in the northeast, Hasuhori Numa and Tsuboe Numa in the north, and Funairi Numa and Hashikawa Numa in the northwest (*Aikyōshi*). After 1955, a quarry was constructed upstream of these lagoons, which resulted in a huge amount of dirt flowing into them. As a result, algae – which had never grown in the lagoons – began to grow thickly, and the lagoons steadily became shallower. Finally, through the accumulation of silt, Shimizu Numa was reduced to one third of its original size. Hasuhori and Tsuboe lagoons were reclaimed. The only lagoons that show traces today of their former appearance are Nishiuchi Numa and Funairi Numa (the latter can be seen on the map, Figure 4.4).

After the transformation of the lagoons as described above, the traditional drainage systems in Kaizu district, in which the lagoons had played a central role, no longer functioned. At present, the greater part of the district's wastewater flows directly into Lake Biwa through concrete gutters.

Traditional and modern water systems
As described above, the construction of modern water systems resulted in the discontinuation of the use of the river, wells and lake for fresh water. At the same time, the drainage systems that had worked in conjunction with the use of these water sources broke down. However, it seems more correct to say that the traditional water supply and drainage systems disappeared than to say that they were transformed into a new water supply and drainage system with the construction of the modern water supply system, since no substitute was constructed for the traditional drainage system.

Traditionally, a water supply system and its corresponding drainage system existed as a single, integrated supply/drainage system. Arguably, such systems can only function properly if they exist as a single integrated system. This is because under

Figure 4.4: Transformation of the lagoons. (Torigoe and Kada, eds, 1984)

(1) 1895

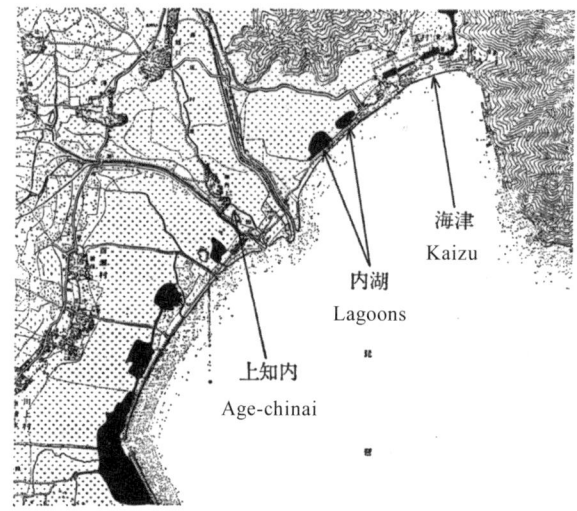

Source: Land Survey Division, *Kaizu Mura*, a one-to-twenty-thousand topographic map surveyed in 1893 and published in 1895.

(2) 1912

Source: Land Survey Division, *Kaizu Mura*, a one-to-twenty-thousand topographic map surveyed in 1893, revised in 1910 and published in 1912.

Figure 4.4: continued

(3) 1947

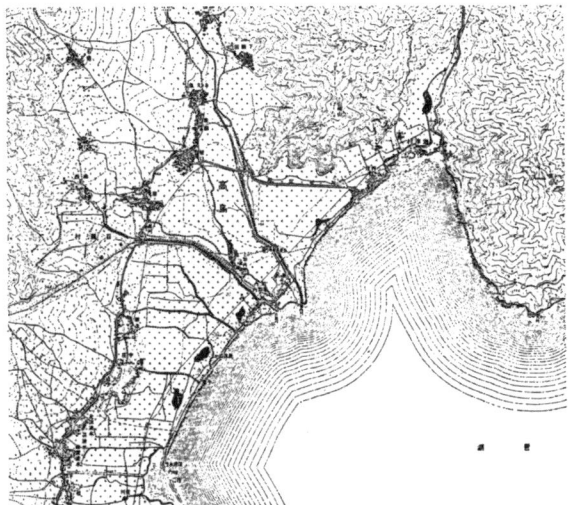

Source: Geographic Survey Office, *Kaizu*, a one-to-twenty-five-thousand topographic map surveyed in 1920 and published in 1947.

(4) 1976

Source: Geographical Survey Institute, *Kaizu*, a one-to-twenty-five-thousand topographic map surveyed in 1920, resurveyed in 1971, revised in 1975 and published in 1976.

the traditional system, wastewater will contaminate fresh water supplies unless people separate their wastewater from fresh water sources more carefully than they do now. One family's wastewater can directly flow into their downstream neighbor's fresh water source, and their wastewater into their downstream neighbor's supply and so on in an endless chain. In the traditional system, though, this chain was clearly visible.

In the modern system of everyday life, where most people now obtain their fresh water from a tap connected to a centralized water supply system, the water supply and drainage system continue to be linked by a similar chain. But this chain is now largely invisible, and many people now live without any understanding of it.

In the 1970s, city water began to smell unpleasant in Japan's major urban centers. This has prompted us, perhaps for the first time since the introduction of modern water supply systems, to begin to recognize the link between fresh water supplies and the drainage system.

The problem is not, however, with the construction of modern water supply systems but with the neglect or even abandonment of the corresponding wastewater drainage systems. Modern water supply systems supply fresh water independently of the drainage systems' capacity to dispose of it. When a modern water supply system is constructed in an area where a traditional integrated water supply and drainage system has functioned properly, the traditional drainage system in the area will be abandoned. Hence, when each area lost its traditional water supply system, its traditional water drainage system was also lost. The ensuing problems would have been minor if the lost drainage systems had only affected an individual area. I suspect that when we lost our traditional drainage systems, though, we also forgot that the water supply system and the drainage system are inextricably linked. To put it more precisely, I suspect that we choked off the set of water supply/drainage systems which had worked properly, although unnoticed.

What kind of drainage system do we need, though, to counterbalance the modern water supply system? Do we need a uniform, characterless drainage system to counterbalance a uniform, characterless water supply system?

Traditional drainage systems have disappeared from virtually every area in Japan. It is probably impossible to restore these systems, and even if we could, they would be inadequate to cope with the modern water supply systems which are entirely different from their traditional counterparts. This conclusion would be supported by a simple calculation of the drainage volumes produced by the modern water supply systems. I believe, however, that the 'idea' of the traditional, integrated water supply/drainage systems provides the proper direction for new drainage systems that will counterbalance the present water supply systems.

Changes in water use and everyday knowledge

Modern and traditional water use

Let me summarize the characteristics of the traditional water-use practices described above. First, the traditional water supply was diverse and mixed in form. No single aspect of the traditional water use system could have existed alone. Second, traditional management consisted of an integrated system covering both water supply and drainage within each particular area. From these characteristics of traditional water use, we can infer characteristics of everyday life knowledge in the local communities. Let us then review the introduction of the modern water system with reference to Atsushi Sakurai's (1984) work.

As mentioned, the modern fresh water supply system was constructed in Age-chinai in December, 1957. According to Sakurai, the incentive to construct a small water supply system in the area stemmed from two major factors. Firstly, as pesticide use began to spread, there was growing concern that the river, the only source of fresh water for the area's residents, might become contaminated. Secondly, the people learned that modern water supply systems were being constructed in many parts of the nation. Chinai's *Kiroku* confirms this, reporting that the villagers had started to use pesticides, including BHC and PCP, as countermeasures against blast or rice stem borers (*Chilo suppressalis*). Sakurai further suggests, based on interviews with locals, that the direct cause of the community's decision to construct a water system was that Councilor N read an article in the *Ie no Hikari* ('Light of Family: Improvement in living and happy home making' magazine of Japanese agricultural co-operatives) magazine about a certain village in Hyōgo Prefecture where such a system had been built, and promptly went to the village on a study tour with the district head and other important village members.

By December 1957, families in the area had begun to use tap water. The availability of tap water changed the use of water in the village very rapidly. First, tap water replaced river water as drinking water, and then as bath water as well. Then, as sinks were gradually installed in each house, tap water became the main source of cooking water. At the same time, the energy revolution resulted in a rapid reduction in the use of firewood as household electrical appliances became increasingly widespread. All of this resulted in the loss of the diversity in the use of the river. Meanwhile, the use of tap water – as people began to do laundry at home instead of in the river, and the ditch for washing diapers no longer had a reason to exist – also resulted in a rapid increase of domestic wastewater which, in turn, resulted in the failure of the *suimon* and *suikomi* system. In the process, the river, which had once been the center of village life in Age-chinai, became a mere ditch. Drainpipes soon began to be installed running from houses to the river – although the residents had never before even dreamed of draining domestic wastewater into the river – and the river began to function as a new drainage canal.

This situation was typical of many villages around Lake Biwa at that time. All of these rivers-turned-drainage canals flowed into Lake Biwa, and began polluting the lake. Perhaps domestic wastewater was not the primary direct cause of the pollution of Lake Biwa, but I suspect that the developments above share the same root cause as the problem of industrial wastewater discharge – that is, the change in local consciousness about the integrity of the water supply/discharge system. I now discuss this point focusing on the philosophy of water systems as a technology.

The philosophy of water systems
What, then, are the characteristics of a water system? It is difficult to imagine a modern water supply system that is as multifunctional and complex as the traditional water supply system. A modern water supply system is a technology that has been made possible by the pursuit of a single function – to supply fresh water whenever and in whatever quantities are desired. Furthermore, a modern water supply system can only exist by being detached from, or maintaining independence from, the local community, in the sense that the water system is used by each and every family and must thus at all times provide clean water to each, no matter how others use the system. Another characteristic in Age-chinai is that the modern water supply system was introduced from the outside – the impetus for the initiative inspired by a magazine article read by a local.

The main (acknowledged) reasons for the construction of a water system in Age-chinai were the 'concern' that the river might become contaminated by pesticides and the 'information' on modern water supply systems obtained from a magazine. I assume that there were many other practical reasons as well. For example, drawing water from the river was hard work. When it rained, the river became muddy and unfit for human consumption. Above all, however, the modernization of Japanese rural villages during the decade between 1955 and 1964 – which started with a movement for better living – can be seen in the fact that the direct causes of the construction of a water system were 'concern' and 'information' obtained from a magazine article. More specifically, residents had directly coped with and accepted the existence of the traditional problems – including the hard work of collecting water from the river and the unavailability of river water whenever it rained. While traditional water use/management had developed from within the community, the modern water supply system was introduced from the outside. When it was introduced, the modern water supply system had the sole function of supplying water.

The introduction of the modern water supply system to Agechinai, coupled with the energy revolution and the broad social movement for 'better living' that were happening concurrently, resulted in the breakdown of the traditional patterns of water use in the community. This amounted to a breakdown of the community's integrated system of water use, which had been inseparable from the traditional use of the river.

However, assuming that it was the local residents' everyday life knowledge that had supported the philosophy of traditional water use, I do not believe that their everyday life knowledge – which had developed over their very long history – could have broken down simply because a new water system was introduced. Hence, it seems necessary to attempt to ascertain the continuities and discontinuities between the residents' everyday life knowledge – which had supported the traditional philosophy of water use – and the everyday life knowledge of the people who live under the philosophy of a modern water supply system.

Although I do not have the means to complete the above task now, I would like to consider the issue from a somewhat different angle. To begin with, I would like to consider the differences between the ways that researchers deal with the issues of water supply systems and the ways that residents do. I suspect that there might be a problem in the understanding itself that changes the structure of residents' knowledge. So let us put aside the issue of water use for the time being, and discuss how environmental issues come to be recognized.

Environmental issues and everyday life knowledge

Environmental deterioration may be recognized as a problem at two different levels. At one level, residents of the affected area become aware of deterioration in their environment as a problem in one form or another, such as water pollution or noxious odors, and recognize it as a local issue. I shall refer to this as 'recognition as a local issue.'

At another level, researchers or local activists become aware of water pollution or noxious odors in a certain area and recognize it as an environmental issue. I shall refer to this as 'recognition as an environmental issue.' At this level, we must distinguish between cases where researchers or local activists recognize an issue that has already been 'recognized as a local issue' and cases where researchers or local activists otherwise obtain information about pollution and recognize it as an issue.

For the purpose of analysis, I consider 'recognition as a local issue' and 'recognition as an environmental issue' to be cognitive activities conducted at two different levels. Specifically, at the level of 'recognition as a local issue,' what needs to be analyzed is limited to the residents' system of knowledge. In contrast, at the level of 'recognition as an environmental issue,' we must analyze researchers' and activists' systems of knowledge, or, more specifically, the modern scientific system of knowledge.

Hiroyuki Torigoe (1985) has attempted to elucidate, from the perspective of the residents' system of knowledge, how residents create an issue from a local event. Torigoe refers to the factors forming the lifeworld as 'everyday life knowledge' and divides them into three types: (1) Personal experience (knowledge obtained through personal experience); (2) Common sense in everyday life within the community (such as *mura*) (accumulation of the community's knowledge necessary for its members to live a peaceful life); and (3) Public morals brought from outside the community (morals that have been created by the state authority and accepted by people).

Torigoe asserts that a community member makes decisions based on these three types of knowledge – having discussed their options with others – and these decisions are expressed as social behavior. *Iibun* (argument) is the term Torigoe uses to refer to the logic roughly agreed upon by the residents as a whole to justify their action. This 'logic' is not necessarily the consensus of the residents; in fact, many residents may object to or question it. Thus it is a logic of justification, formed for the time being within the 'world of self' as opposed to the 'world of others' – two worlds separated by a very unstable (fluid) boundary.[8] Though it may often be somewhat ambiguous, Torigoe's concept of *iibun* represents the residents' opinion on a local issue.

When it comes to dealing with an environmental issue, Torigoe's approach may appear to merely express his stance on the subject matter. But, quoting Hiroshi Nagasaki, Torigoe states, 'I cannot tell what a person is thinking, but I can tell what *people* are thinking.' From this perspective, in the context of an environmental issue, Torigoe has conceptualized *iibun* to indicate that we must attempt to understand the collective mentality that forms under particular circumstances, rather than focusing on sociological action. In other words, the aggregate of individual actions does not always reveal how to deal with a local problem.

Is it true, though, that through the residents' system of knowledge and the combinations and manipulations of this knowledge, that residents express a sense of discomfort about their environment and formulate their *iibun* in one form or another?

If we accept that Torigoe's understanding of the system of knowledge is correct, and that *iibun* is formed through combinations and manipulations of different types of knowledge, the question remains as to how those types of knowledge are drawn from the system and are combined. Torigoe considered the residents' system of knowledge to be a representation of his assertion that sociologists should deal with a collective mind rather than individuals' minds, based on an understanding that individuals do not understand each other. It would be rather stoical, though, to suggest that sociology should limit itself only to this 'collective mind.' Although I am sympathetic to Torigoe's intent, I believe we must consider another type of knowledge that exists at a different level than those proposed by Torigoe: the 'tacit knowledge' referred to by Michael Polanyi, which suggests that 'We can know more than we can tell' (1983: 4).

Dealing with tacit knowledge enables a more dynamic approach to residents' everyday lives and the ways they perceive local issues. Torigoe's identification of three types of residents' knowledge does indeed enable us to understand the processes by which *iibun* is formed. The problem seems to lie in how to use tacit knowledge as a basis for developing the 'concept of *iibun*.' It is obvious that the concept of tacit knowledge is not compatible with our argument. However, it is essential to introduce tacit knowledge into our argument in order to explain that the system of 'knowledge' and '*iibun*' are closely related and that this relationship is involved in the process of how residents recognize local issues.

Polanyi (1983) proposed the following concepts in relation to tacit knowledge. For example, public morals taught by moral education are internalized by the people who receive such education. In this context, to 'internalize' means that morals function as a proximal term of tacit knowledge, integrating the moral teaching into ourselves. Polanyi refers to this as 'interiorization,' and argues that we understand the meaning of these morals through a tacit process called 'comprehension.' Then – and this is the important point – Polanyi argues that it is through a process called 'emergence' that we deal with a problem and form a consensus about it based on the morals. 'Emergence' is a tacit process to create new, comprehensive understandings, which Polanyi suggests is similar to Bergon's notion of 'élan vital' (life force).

In short, what Polanyi means is that it is impossible to explain a certain *iibun* created under certain circumstances using the knowledge of individuals involved, because you cannot explain a function operating at one level using principles that govern lower levels, just as one cannot ascertain the principles underlying the game of chess from the rules of the game. This is what Torigoe means when he says, 'I cannot tell what a person is thinking, but I can tell what *people* are thinking.' Yet we cannot understand 'what people are thinking,' either, without first acknowledging tacit knowledge.

Hence, we must develop our conception of *iibun* using such tacit knowledge as the premise for the system of knowledge and its entire dynamic process. Torigoe did not include tacit knowledge into his system of residents' knowledge, because his main concern was to consider logical compositions that can be investigated, and this, for him, excludes the individuals' knowledge from consideration.

Let us then consider the system of knowledge upon which researchers identify an environmental issue. Let us assume that, for example, a researcher specializing in chemistry checked water quality for whatever reason and found that (1) the water contained a high level of Substance A. The researcher will make the following assessments based on (other) accepted knowledge: (2) Substance A is harmful to humans; (3) it is hazardous to allow a harmful substance to enter the human body; (4) this river water is used for tap water consumed by people; (5) Substance A cannot be eliminated by the purification process at the purification plant; (6) Substance A is thus likely to enter the human body; (7) Substance

A is contained in pesticides; and (8) it is dangerous to use pesticides. Based on this assessment, s/he will (9) issue a warning. Although the only data that this chemist directly obtained from primary research is the level of Substance A, he will instantly be almost sure that statements (1) through (8) above are true. Statements (2) through (8) are information s/he has obtained from others. No positivist can prove everything based on positive evidence. Still, a positivist behaves as though everything he says is based on positive evidence. This is because, according to Polanyi: 'The acceptance of scientific statements by laymen is based on authority, and this true to nearly the same extent for scientists using results from branches of science other than their own. Scientists must rely heavily for their facts on the authority of fellow scientists' (1983: 64). This is deemed to be true on the basis of the authority derived from the myth that science is objective.

Comparison of the processes of 'recognition as an environmental issue' and 'recognition as a local issue' reveals that the respective systems of knowledge involved in these two processes are similar in that, to some extent, both regard modern scientific knowledge to be absolute. Why, then, is it not uncommon for a certain problem to be recognized as a local issue but not as an environmental issue, and vice versa? The difference seems to be whether the factor 'living' is included in the process of reconstructing knowledge. That is, when residents recognize a problem in their surrounding environment, even if they successfully apply all available knowledge to dealing with the problem, the knowledge can only be reconstructed by incorporation into their 'living.'

Let us assume, for example, that a farmer who uses pesticides read a newspaper article warning that pesticides should not be used because they contain a very hazardous substance called A. The farmer follows the process described in Statements (2) through (6) above – the process followed by a chemist checking water quality – until he understands the information. This can be understood as the process of accepting a statement supported by authority. However, his decision about whether or not to continue to use the pesticide is not as simple as the chemist's quick decision that they should not be used to avoid the hazard, because a farmer must make his decision on the use of 'pesticides' rather than Substance A. Pesticides containing Substance A are reducible to the hazardous Substance A from the chemist's perspective, but the farmer understands them in terms of increased yield or labor saving. In other words, the pesticides are located in the farmer's life and knowledge system, and the decision to quit using pesticides means that he must reorganize this system.

Thus, whether 'life and knowledge' are included in the process determines whether or not a matter may be recognized as an issue. This is why there is a gap between 'recognition as a local issue' and 'recognition as an environmental issue.'

Sub-conclusion

People have always acted in line with their respective *iibun* when faced with a problem. Let us now reconsider the construction of the modern water supply system in Age-chinai, once again with reference to Sakurai's work.

As mentioned, after the construction of modern water supply systems, the river in Age-chinai was reduced to a drainage canal. Surely no one was happy to see the river steadily becoming dirtier, yet no effort was made to prevent it. Then, after almost twenty years of degeneration, one man took a stand and voiced a strong protest when he learned that the prefectural government was planning to fill in the river. This was the aforementioned Councilor N, who had previously led the campaign to construct a modern water supply system in Age-chinai. The plan to fill the river was eventually abandoned. Councilor N later established an organization devoted to cleaning the river as part of his the campaign to protect the river from further pollution.

Councilor N also objected to the government's plan to line the riverbed with concrete, on the grounds that a concrete riverbed would prevent groundwater from being absorbed by the river, undermining the ground between houses and the river, and would prevent *ayu* fish (*Plecoglossus altivelis*) from swimming upstream to spawn. He succeeded in preventing the riverbed from being lined by concrete. Thus, the same man who had promoted the construction of a modern water supply system later initiated action to protect the river. From his viewpoint, the construction of the modern water supply systems and protecting the river are not at all incompatible. He knows that the construction of the water system led to the river becoming polluted, but it does not necessarily follow that he must deny the modern water supply system. Residents need water supply systems, but they also need to protect the river. This is their *iibun*.

In the above, I described characteristics of everyday life knowledge as complexity and that it is embedded in local contexts. Observing the development of Councilor N's knowledge reveals another characteristic of everyday life knowledge that was not mentioned above: residents' knowledge is embedded in a historical context. While technology is the opposite of history, life is history itself. Everyday life knowledge is formed via complex processes in space (the local context) and time (the historical context). The construction of water systems and protection of the river – these two actions that seem to seek 'survival and effectiveness of activities for the time being' (Matsuda 1985) – are not incompatible seen from Councilor N's time axis, in contrast to the time axis along which scientific knowledge develops. Here again, we may be able to see a gap between time running in everyday life knowledge and in science.

Mushi-okuri and everyday life knowledge

Everyday life, nature and worldviews

Our everyday lives are based on certain regularity. The regularity of time and space are the most typical examples. Work or school starts at a certain time in a certain place and ends at a certain time, and we return to a(nother) certain place. We cannot live without the regularity of time and space, which we have learned as the natural order of things in the process of growing up. In other words, we have always internalized these rules to maintain the regularity of time and space.

These internalized rules form the axis of our worldview. We recognize other people and things by positioning them along this axis. In this context, our worldview means our perception/conception of our environment. Our worldview is personal and, at the same time, communal (shared). The rules that an individual learns in the process of growing exist to allow people to live in a community, at least to 'some extent.' In other words, we are able to live our everyday lives (in a village, for example) only because we have shared our respective worldviews. A village is a good example of a community, because we understand a village to be a relatively homogeneous community. In this context, being 'homogeneous' means that the regularity of time and space, which forms the axis of the residents' worldviews, is clear and shared by the majority of residents.

A shared worldview is expressed in technology, social organizations and norms, annual events, and various other things. This is what makes a village a community as we understand it. In fact, however, our worldview has been shared beyond this. In particular, our current worldview seems to have expanded to the maximum extent to which information can be disseminated, due to modern communications technology, the mass media and the ever-expanding growth in personal travel.

Has the entirety of human information, then, been homogenized? No. It is more correct to say that worldviews have multilayered structures. Worldviews change according to the information we receive. This creates differences not only between individual worldviews but also between shared worldviews. These differences often generate inconsistencies between newly developing worldviews and existing technology, social organizations, annual events and so on. Changes thus occur all the time. In this context, a 'change' means homogenization of different worldviews.

As is often said, changes typically occur before we notice them. It should be necessary to describe when and how a change occurs, before discussing why. Yet it is impossible to comprehensively describe our worldview, or our view of nature. It must instead be read from events, technology, or forms of social organization.

In the following, I ascertain, using Chinai Village as an example, the bases upon which villagers share a worldview, particularly as concerns the natural environment associated with farming. I also elucidate the villagers' worldview and view of nature by briefly describing the circumstances through which the farming village's traditional *mushi-okuri* (annual torch procession for driving away noxious insects) came to an end.

Village and outside world

When I stated that the residents of a village have a shared worldview, I certainly do not mean that all individuals have an identical worldview, but rather that their worldviews overlap with one another to form a high degree of consensus. What, then, is the bases upon which their worldviews overlap or are shared?

From the perspective that time and space form the axes of our worldview, the most important basis must be the fact that production and everyday life were inseparable from one another in a farming community, as has been frequently observed. This refers to the fact that workplaces were not separated from homes and that, as a result, agricultural, religious and administrative affairs were integrated, not separated.

As discussed in Chapter Two, in Japanese rural communities, agricultural, religious and administrative affairs were conducted in an integrated manner until the Meiji Period (1868–1912). Then, beginning with the separation of religious and administrative affairs, the integration of these affairs gradually declined. By the Shōwa Period (1926–1989), a system had been established in which agricultural, religious and administrative affairs were overseen by distinct organizations.

These changes in the administrative system were not separate from, but paralleled, changes in the residents' worldviews and views of nature. This can be seen from an examination of Chinai's bylaws from 1902 and 1924, which indicate the increasing separation of those affairs. Both of these bylaws were drafted during times when the central government of Japan was seething over popular elections.[9] It is easy to imagine that the residents of Chinai revised their bylaws in response to these events. But I do not mean to suggest that they took measures simply in accordance with movements in the central government. We must therefore look for the reasons that drove Chinai to take the measures that it did at those times.

Needless to say, there was more than one reason. A careful examination of the Chinai *Kiroku* reveals some of them. In 1897, Chinai Village was recovering from the major flooding that had occurred the previous year. An increasing number of *Kiroku* entries from this period describe persisting flood damage, recovery efforts, and preventive public works. As discussed in Chapter Two, Chinai is located between the Chinai and Momose Rivers, which run along its northern and southern boundaries. Improvement works on these two rivers were a matter of urgency for the village.

An entry written in 1900 notes that improvement work on the embankments had been completed for the time being and that all people concerned 'offered sacred sake to the two shrines and had the New Year holidays.' The total cost of the improvement work was '1837 yen 28 *sen* 2 *rin*.' Of the total amount, '1311 yen 73 *sen* 2 *rin*' was paid, but the 'balance: 525 yen 55 *sen*' could not be paid from the village's budget. This deficiency was allocated to and collected from '116 families' in Chinai as follows: '420 yen 24 *sen*: allocated according to land prices'; '78 yen 83 *sen* 2 *rin*: allocated according to ranks'; and '26 yen 27 *sen* 7 *rin*: allocated equally to each family.' Thus, on the '11th of May 1900,' they completed payment of 'all costs for the aforementioned embankment work.' Subsequent entries indicate the considerable burdens placed on residents. Incidentally, a day's wages for farm work in 1923 was generally 1 yen 20 *sen* for men and 80 *sen* for women.

In addition, Chinai's community membership dues rose from about 150 yen in 1890 to 524 yen in 1904, then to 1630 yen in 1923.

Of various costs paid from these dues, public works accounted for about one-third of the total collected (Kada 1991: 96). The soaring public works costs, of course, strained family budgets as well as the community's. Hence, residents were acutely aware of the difficulty of completing all of those public works at the village's expense alone. The Chinai residents therefore requested that their roads be incorporated into the prefectural roads system. In 1925, they also began petitioning the Taiko Kisen steamship company to have its ships call at Chinai so that local products could be transported to markets. These efforts seem to indicate that Chinai residents' desire to remain self-reliant heightened local consciousness of their relationship with the 'outside world,' transforming the local community system into one that was self-supporting through some degree of integration with the outside world. The local understanding of the universality and usefulness of things and events from outside the area became distinctly different from their sense of values towards the outside. Changes in their relationship with the outside world did not occur all at once, but the changing circumstances at the time provided sufficient impetus for the Chinai community to effect drastic changes to their internal administrative system.

The final demise of the *mushi-okuri* ritual described below occurred around 1955, but the first steps towards it appear to have been taken around this time (the end of the Taishō Period – mid-1920s). Whether changes in the residents' view of nature caused the social changes that led to the demise of the *mushi-okuri* ritual or vice-versa is not important. Most likely the changes occurred in a reciprocal process. What is important is that the demise of the *mushi-okuri* ritual was a symbolic event that indicates changes in the residents' views of nature. Below I describe the circumstances leading up to the demise of the *mushi-okuri*, while reviewing the accompanying social changes.

Changes in the *mushi-okuri* ritual

In the Chinai *Kiroku*, the first entry concerning the *mushi-okuri* ritual appeared in 1911, indicating a change in the traditional route of the event:

> April (1911): It has been decided that the *mushi-okuri* (procession) will begin from the Tonoda Bridge in Naka-no-Chōba and follow the hatchery road to the lakeshore.

The fact that the *mushi-okuri* ritual had never previously been mentioned in entries written during the period of over one hundred years preceding the above entry probably means that the event had been conducted, like many other events, every year at around same time and through the same route without any changes. More than ten years after the above entry, the following statement appears:

> 29th of June 1923: Torch procession for the *mushi-okuri* was called off. Everything else was conducted as usual.

The context provides no information on the circumstances surrounding the sudden cancellation of the *mushi-okuri* event. The next entry on the *mushi-okuri* appears another twelve years later:

> This year (1935) had seen an extremely large outbreak of rice stem borers. Considering this, the authorities ordered all municipalities to conduct the *mushi-okuri* simultaneously. Accordingly, this Aza started it at 8:00 p.m. on the 18th of August 1935 and spent three minutes per block. Namely, all residents were divided into nine groups. Each of the two *sōdai*, the councilors and *nengyōji* led a torch procession throughout his assigned area as determined by drawing lots. Everything was completed at 9:30 p.m.

The *mushi-okuri* had been conducted in late June every year. But in 1935 they conducted it nearly two months later than usual due to the government order to conduct it simultaneously with all other municipalities. The *mushi-okuri* was originally a local event conducted by each village to drive noxious insects away from the village. The entry above, however, indicates that the *mushi-okuri* had changed into a joint pest control effort conducted simultaneously by all neighboring municipalities. At the same time, villagers had departed from the prayer-like attitude that they had customarily displayed toward the *mushi-okuri* – that is, a desire to protect their crops without any wanton destruction of life. This departure is symbolized by the reasoning that they should conduct the *mushi-okuri* because of 'an extremely large outbreak of rice stem borers.' Then, a year later, on the night of the 19th of August 1936, light traps were introduced.

> In fiscal year 1937, the authorities notified the municipalities in the prefecture to exterminate rice stem borers by lighting acetylene light traps. Accordingly, on the first of June in this Aza, all councilors

were mobilized and every arrangement was made for the placement and lighting of 230 light traps [one per about 2975 square meters]. In the evening of the day before, the first lighting was done.

In these activities, we no longer see the prayer-like activity that had previously characterized the *mushi-okuri*. Immediately preceding the entry about the *mushi-okuri* in 1935 is an entry stating that vaccinations were given in the village in response to a major outbreak of typhoid:

> 3rd of August 1935: In the morning, typhoid vaccinations were given in the assembly hall...One hundred persons between six and sixty years of age (six inclusive) living in Chinai received injections.

This event occurred in the same Chinai Village where, in 1918, 'in response to the worldwide flu outbreak...a prayer service for prevention was conducted on the 31st of October at An'yōji Temple. In addition, on the 13th of November a festival in prayer for prevention was conducted at both shrines.' In these dispersed records describing the change from the '*mushi-okuri* and prayer' to 'control and vaccination,' we can interpret major changes in the villagers' view of nature.

It seems that the *mushi-okuri* continued subsequently, although the *Kiroku* does not mention it again until the 29th of June, 1955, when an entry reports that the *mushi-okuri* was conducted by dividing the village into four areas. According to interviews, the demise of the *mushi-okuri* occurred around that time, when they decided to post a talisman in each of the four areas, on the trees standing at the terminal points of the torch procession for the *mushi-okuri*. Still today, new talismans are posted every year.

What, then, became of the pest control activities that had changed from the *mushi-okuri* to light traps? Unfortunately, the *Kiroku* volumes for the years 1947 to 1953 were destroyed by fire, making it difficult to identify any changes that had occurred during those years. However, a report of the neighborhood group leaders' association dated 25th of March 1954 states: 'DDT will be applied on the following dates: The 13th and 14th of April.' Similarly, a 1955 entry states that there would be 'two applications, in April and July. Half of the cost will be paid by the municipality, with the payment being 630,000 yen.'

Hence it is clear that in the post-war period, the *mushi-okuri* was supplanted by light traps, which were then replaced by DDT and BHC applications, which were in turn replaced by using PCP. The application of DDT had probably begun before 1954, since it was widely used by the occupation forces immediately after the war.[10] Hence, it is probably no coincidence that the application of DDT corresponds to the change of the *mushi-okuri* event into the simple posting of talismans. If we assume that the introduction of light traps in 1937 represents the separation of the Shintō *mushi-okuri* (prayer) event from agricultural affairs, resulting in the independent coexistence of Shintō and agricultural affairs in village life, then the further change to DDT usage indicates the discontinuation of the Shintō event, and perhaps also the recession of Shintō affairs from community life.

I have described this change from a religious ritual to the use of pesticides (agricultural chemicals) because it is symbolic of the broader changes occurring in village life. As described in the previous section, this includes changes in water usage.

The change from the *mushi-okuri* ritual to the use of DDT and from the use of river water to tap water were not simply changes brought about by the introduction of new technology from the outside world. They were intertwined with changes in the village's everyday life and administrative frameworks which, in turn, were closely connected to changes in the villagers' worldview.

It may be possible to attribute these changes to a causal chain such as, 'impact from the outside world, led to changes in the villagers' worldview and their view of nature, which led to changes in the frameworks of administration and everyday life.' However, I doubt if such an explanation is of much significance. Much of the research into environmental problems to date has relied heavily on a methodological belief that if we clarify the causal relationship, we might be able to change the situation through reforms at the root-level. My analysis is certainly not free from the influence of this belief. Nevertheless, I began my discussion with the disintegration of agricultural, religious and administrative affairs in the village's administrative and everyday life frameworks to demonstrate that these changes are not simply the result of some causal chain. The villagers' creative agency has clearly affected any causal chains that may have existed. And the particular affects of this creative agency derive from their particular worldview.

Sub-conclusion

Villagers have pursued their livelihoods by assessing the existing situation and predicting the future based on the past. Their worldview is the perspective through which they see their past, present and future. The core of their worldview has been their view of nature. They sometimes had a long-term perspective and sometimes a shorter-term view. When the span begins to shorten, it cannot be easily reversed. Shorter-term perspectives are more susceptible to outside influences. Sometimes the perspective itself is provided by the outside world. This can be described as an expansion of the extent to which their worldview and their view of nature correspond.

The view of nature at the core of the villagers' worldview was inseparable from their business. Thus, their view of nature is currently dissolving into a more general worldview with the 'industrialization' of farming. However, in the present situation it is becoming painfully obvious that a worldview focused solely on development by industrialization – or technology – has failed; we are in need of a new worldview. To resolve our current environmental issues, it will probably need to be a worldview based on the understandings of nature that once existed in communities where everyday life and farming were two sides of the same coin. It must be a worldview that will expand our perspective of everyday life to include consideration of future generations and will thus forsake maximizing immediate convenience. This means that the idea of a single worldview shared by all members of the community can no longer hold. Furthermore, a worldview is no longer a fixed 'good' within the community, but is now seen as a dynamic process in which the worldview is continuously created and recreated in the course of everyday living.

In the next section, I will describe the situation of maintaining everyday life in Japanese villages (*mura*) amid these rapidly changing worldviews, focusing on the post-war period of rapid economic growth.

Transformation of the village and everyday life

Introduction – Our recognition of '*mura*' as an issue

There were countless discussions of rural villages in the 1960s and 1970s, as people came to recognize the significant changes occurring amid the rapid industrialization of everyday life and production. Many of the issues that arose then – including issues of migrant workers, depopulated areas, increasing numbers of part-time farmers, and the reduction of rice acreage – appear to have carried over into the twenty-first century.

Yet we no longer discuss these issues as central topics of concern – or subjects in-themselves. Is this because these issues have settled to some extent, if they have not been resolved? One possible response may be that rapid changes are more likely to be recognized as 'issues' because they are more difficult to deal with than gradual changes.

But perhaps the problems are actually worsening in ways that we do not recognize as 'issues' using conventional means of analysis. Needless to say, problems in rural villages have arisen regardless of whether or not outsiders recognize them as issues, and villagers have encountered and had to deal with those problems in the ordinary course of their lives. For the purposes of this discussion, let us understand the primary issues of rural villages to be issues for residents, which can then be appropriately called issues of '*mura*.'

In order to demonstrate the inappropriateness of our (present) means of recognizing the actual issues of a *mura*, allow me to summarize the concrete issues that have arisen in this particular *mura*, and how they have been understood. This will of course entail how the issues and the people's understanding of them have changed.

Once again, I rely primarily on the Chinai *Kiroku* to trace the issues that have arisen and how they have been understood by villagers. First we must note, however, that due to the *Kiroku*'s public nature, there were undoubtedly many issues in the village that were never recorded. Nevertheless, the *Kiroku* is sufficient to reveal general trends in the *mura* for our purposes, which is to understand issues of the *mura* rather than those of individual villagers.

Mura's events and occurrences

To begin, it will be useful to review everyday life in the *mura* during a certain year. As descriptions differ from year to year, I take 1970 as an example, the most recent year with published records (see Table 4.2), in an attempt to see the 250 years of *Kiroku* through the descriptions for this year.

The first annual event of the *mura* was *sōrei* (worship by all villagers together) and the last was *kaisai* (completion of payments). In this respect, there was little change since the end of the Taishō Period (1926). In Table 4.2, the underlined events had traditionally been conducted around the same date every year. Although not mentioned in the table, comparison of similar tables for different

Table 4.2: Events and occurrances in the mura in 1970

Jan. 1st	Sōrei (worship by all villagers together) /7th *Departure of representatives of Shinpū association for shrine visit on behalf of Ōaza.*
11th	*First Ōaza meeting: nengyōji replaced by XX and XX, qualifications satisfied by XX; compulsory labor service - five persons/farming family, three persons/ non-farming family, wages /fifty/person, /400/additional person, /500/ shortfall.* Collection of communal charge from temporary residents moved in from outside: Communal charge of /100/month on those staying for over six months. *The issue of JRC Saruo field*. The issue of road pavement. Use of the remainder of proceeds from sale of the former cemetery.
15th	*First meeting of the Neighborhood Watch.* /16th Prayer service. / 19th Water System Committee meeting. /20th-Jan Damage to water pipe, committee members provide service.
21th	Fertilizer planning. /22th Agriculture and forestry census explanatory meeting. /24th Regular election of district head and his deputy.
27th	Makino-chō mutual aid association meeting. /31st *Collection of membership dues.*
Feb. 1st	*Change of district head and his deputy.* /2nd Neighborhood group leaders (NGLs) meeting (declaration for local income tax, taxpayers' bus trip to Expo, *means to elect comprehensive agricultural policy (CAP) Rural Community Promotion Councilors*).
6th	Meeting of landowners affected by acquisition of land for Chinai River embankment repairs. /8th Implementation of World Agricultural Census.
10th	Regular by-election of councilors. /12th Funeral service for Mr. Nakagawa Kamezō, offering made in recognition of sevice to Ōaza. /15th Neighborhood group leader meeting.
22th	Meeting for appointment of councilors. Order of ranks: *1. ... Committee members: Account Settlement Auditors, 2; Public Works, 2; Agricultural Affairs, 3; Mountains and Forests, 2; Rivers – 2 from North, 2 from South; Statistical Survey, 2; Ujiko Sōdai, 2; Advisors, 2; all Tourism Committee members.* Speech by both district heads. The issue of offering at funerals. *CAP's rice acreage reduction coordinators to be appointed separately.* Municipal head's promise to pave unpaved roads by the end of the current fiscal year (FY). Explanation of the progress of negotiation over acquisition of land for Chinai River embankment repairs. Explanation of uses of proceeds from sale of the cemetery. Accounting report (local share of the road pavement cost, /1,243,688; religious sevice for hungry ghosts at the cemetery, /8,888; cost of operating machines for Age-chinai, /217,339, etc.). *CAP, the issue of rice acreage reduction*. Effective use of land to be created as a result of river embankment repairs.
Mar. 7th	Ōaza Chinai extraordinary general meeting (forty-one participants). Agenda: general agricultural administration rice acreage reduction, meeting adjourned for failure to meet the quorum (two thirds of all members). Resolution passed at rescheduled meeting.
8th	Declaration for local resident tax /19th Representatives of the prefectural tourism department visit to discuss tourist signboards on Chinai Shore. Demise of district head's mother.
21st	Funeral service, provision of offering and wreath. /24th Agricultural Affairs Committee (AAC) meeting. Discussion on coordination of rice acreage reduction issue.
28th	Account settlement rescheduled due to demise of district head's mother. /29th Account settlement. /31st AAC meeting on rice acreage reduction.
Apr. 1st	Joint meeting of Ōaza officers + NGLs on *rice acreage reduction*. /9th AAC meeting on *rice acreage reduction*.
11th	Hiruguchi road repairs. Meeting of parties involved in land leased to Kosai Line.

Table 4.2: continued

21st	AAC meeting on well boring and farm road repairs. Both to be conducted in half a day, on the same day.
26th	*Spring cleaning. Arrangement of order.*
28th	AAC meeting on allocation of service for well boring and farm road repairs.
29th	*On-site revision of service for well boring and farm road repairs.* Committee members, both district heads and secretaries.
30th	Discussion Committee (DC) meeting. Stain removal (Jun. 10th and 11th). Trip to Expo: bus fare to be covered by taxpayers' association reserves; admission fee & lunch at participants' cost. Women's wages to be notified by group leaders based on Women's Club's survey results. Disaster drill. (Jul. 15th: Recruitment of new members of XX (Diet member) supporters' association. The issue of FY 1970 rice price campaign. FY 1970 rice field cultivation survey.)
May. 3rd	*Well boring and farm road repairs.* /23rd NGL meeting on the issue of balancing rice fields.
Jun. 4th	NGL meeting. Stain removal (Jun. 10th and 11th). Trip to Expo: only one person/family. Nonrepresented family may be represented by a member of another family represented by its member. Women's wages: /1188 for rice fields, /1888 for other fields (based on results of Women's Club survey). The issue of disaster drill. The issue of rice price campaign. Rice field cultivation survey.
10th	<u>Stain removal</u>. Tourism Committee (TC): shore opening to swimmers (Jul. 1st); shore cleaning (Jun. 21st); number of invited guests about the same as the preceding year; the issue of outsourcing of on-site manager; <u>the issue of recruitment of extra staff serving in place of committee members</u>; various fees same as the preceding year.
11th	*Stain removal*. Trip to Expo. /13th Explanatory meeting on prefectural emergency drill. /14th NGL meeting, explanation of emergency drill.
15th	*Flashboards removed due to heavy rain. Chinai fire brigade mobilized for river watch. Meals delivered from restaurants.*
16th	<u>Meeting of Council for Control of XX Industry Lead Pollution</u>. /21st <u>Cleaning of Chinai Shore</u>.
22th	Organization and leveling of the shore where prefectural emergency drill would take place (through 23rd).
Jul. 1st	*Shore opened to swimmers.* /10th <u>Confirmation of balancing fields for rice acreage reduction (all day)</u>. /12th Ditch cleaning.
14th	Meeting of parties involved in land leased to Kosai Line. /15th Prefectural emergency drill. /19th <u>Summer cleaning</u>.
21st	Prefectural tourism conference. /27th Aerial pest control
Aug. 2nd	*Tokobori* (river cleaning).
7th	*Cemetery cleaning*. Persons in charge of the above accounting.
21st	DC meeting: <u>the issue of restriction of large-vehicle traffic on prefectural roads (re-submitted by replacing traffic restrictions with speed restrictions)</u>; the issue of submission of a five-year construction plan; other requested matters; Hiruguchi Bridge repairs; reconstruction of municipal bridge over the upper part of Shorai River; construction of Maekawa Bridge on the road along Kosai Line; work for reconstruction of canal providing firefighting water for South; Chinai youth grant program.
24th	AAC meeting.
28th	*Inspection of early-ripening rice plants.*
Sep. 2nd	Preliminary discussion among rice shipping coordinators.
4th	*One-tsubo (3.3 square meters) rice reaping* to facilitate entry of machines into fields. Persons in charge visit from public office.

Table 4.2: continued

	5th	NGL meeting: application for examination (three days before date of examination); name of breeds to be examined in September.
	6th	DC meeting: tourism issues – *XX Industry has expressed its intention through municipal head to visit Chinai to discuss the company's potential cooperation with tourism development of Chinai Shore. As a result of internal discussion Chinai decides not to accept the offer*; request from the fishermen's association – *the change in restrictions on large vehicles is irreversible as all formalities have been completed.*
	8th	*Municipality head and subordinate officers of municipal office visit Chinai to discuss XX Industry's offer. They request acceptance of the offer. Chinai officers explain the series of past events related to and future perspectives of Chinai Shore and explain that they cannot accept the offer.*
	17th	*Chinai is again requested to accept XX Industry's offer. District head repeats Chinai's intention not to accept.*
	20th	Implementation of national census.
	25th	*Account settlement.*
Oct.	1st	Forest survey.
	6th	DC meeting: cost of reconstruction of municipal bridge over the upper part of Shōrai River to be covered by the municipality; the issue of XX Industry; *consideration of Chinai's requests on the sale of XX's rice fields to be made at future meetings with the agent*; the issue of road expansion; implementation of autumn military exercise by the Japan Self-Defense Forces; opinions on invitation of rice dealer XX; the issue of construction of new farm road along the border between Chinai and Hiruguchi.
	10th	Municipal sports day.
	14th	Self-Defense Forces Imazu troop wishes to borrow bass drums.
	23th	Survey conducted for construction of new farm road along the Chinai-Hiruguchi border.
Nov.	5th	Meeting of parties involved in construction of new farm road along the Chinai-Hiruguchi border.
	11th	*Meeting on XX Industry's lead pollution issue.*
	14th	*Meeting of Council for Control of XX Industry Lead Pollution.* (another meeting on 17th)
	25th	Demolition of the municipal bridge over the upper part of Shorai River.
	29th	Shiga Prefectural Governor election. Results of 1970 census: number of families, 134; population, 574 (males 278, females 296); population in 1965 was 682.
Dec.	5th	NGL meeting: Kaisai (completion of payment) scheduled for the 25th; revision of rice drying charges; Shinpu representatives' shrine visit on behalf of Ōaza '5.4L of rice; shrine funds '1.8L of rice; the issue of farmers' pension; the issue of submission of written agreement on units of purchase from Agricultural Cooperative; first seeds from Ōmi Shrine; handful campaign; flu immunization; Japan National Railways; the issue of Kansai Electric Power's construction work; *the issue of protest meeting against XX Industry's lead pollution.*
	7th	*Protest meeting against XX Industry's lead pollution: Participants gather in front of Anraku-ji Temple from respective settlements, hold a demonstration with placards, and engage in collective bargaining in front of the factory. Agreement cannot be reached. Representatives from both sides discuss and the comapny agrees to leave the matter to negotiation with the Council. Meeting dismissed.*
	12th	Reconstruction of the aforementioned municipal bridge. Four compulsory laborers provided.

Table 4.2: continued

13th	TC meeting: Financial results announced; party in recognition of members' service.	
20th	Water System Committee meeting: *Reduction of the number and fresh election of committee members, by integration of small water systems*.	
25th	Kaisai	

Note: Prepared based on *Kiroku* of Ōaza Chinai. Events and occurrences were extracted from *Kiroku* and summarized and listed above. Personal names are omitted. Italicised activities represent annual events and similar activities. Committee meetings are not italicised. Activities italicized and underlined represent matters recognized as issues by the mura. XX represents a personal or company name.

years reveals traditional annual and daily events and quite clearly indicates how the details of those events changed over the years, although their names may have remained the same.

For example, *nissan* (daily visit) is a practice that continues to this day in Chinai. In this daily practice, villagers take turns visiting the two shrines in the village, carrying with them a wooden card inscribed with the names of all the families in the village. *Nissan* is not usually mentioned in the *Kiroku*, but when it is, the description is similar to the following: 'As parishioners completed the prescribed visits to both shrines, the daily visit card was renewed and the entire Aza had a holiday to visit the shrines' (30th of January 1910). The next similar entry thereafter is in 1928. Thus, although *nissan* is mentioned only once in a couple of decades, it is a daily 'event' of the *mura*, which continues unchanged to this day. The *Kiroku* does not mention any of the annual festivals that year (1970).

As mentioned, on the 29th of June 1923 there is an entry that reads: 'Torch procession for the *mushi-okuri* was called off. Everything else was conducted as usual.' The *mushi-okuri* is not mentioned in the 1970 *Kiroku*. However, as described in the preceding section, subsequent records reveal that the event changed to the receipt of talismans from the shrines by the district head, who posts them on the trees standing near the village borders, and that the event continues in this form to this day.

Along with records of these 'events' that have been repeated over the years, sometimes with changes in form and/or substance, the *Kiroku* describes one-off 'occurrences.' These occurrences are indicated in Table 4.2 by a wavy underline. The most significant of these in 1970 were the reduction in total rice acreage and lead poisoning caused by an enterprise that had moved into Makino-chō.

The *Kiroku* entries clearly indicate that these issues were repeatedly discussed at meetings of councilors and neighborhood group leaders and reveal how consensus was formed among residents.

The lead poisoning issue triggered Makino-chō's recognition of industrial pollution as a whole, which developed into an issue of Ōaza Chinai's autonomy as the company's conciliatory measures – primarily an offer to support the development of tourism in Chinai Shore[11] – embroiled Makino-chō's public office.

Otherwise, the main issues that year include: the purchase of a field in Saruo by the Japanese Red Cross (JRC) (11th of January); the recruitment of extra staff to provide service in place of committee members (10th of June); torrential rain in June; the restriction of large-vehicle traffic on prefectural roads (21st of August); and the sale of rice fields (6th of October). Let us review some of these issues to reveal something about their nature.

The JRC purchased the Saruo field for use as a health resort. Residents who had traditionally used a path running through this field in their daily practice complained that they would no longer have access to the path. A councilors' meeting in February 1969 had decided to request 'relocation and reconstruction [of the path] to the edge of the purchased land (in the rice fields).' Then, a councilors' meeting in September 1969 reported:

> Earlier this Ōaza requested [the JRC] to relocate the path to the edge along the boundary between the land and rice fields. However, the path is not relocatable and, if its public use is to be ceased, the JRC must purchase it from the Ministry of Finance because it belongs to the local finance bureau of the Ministry. We will negotiate with the JRC for construction of a road along the border (of the purchased land) to ensure the passage [of residents].

Further negotiations with representatives of the JRC resolved this issue the following year, and the JRC constructed a road along the border according to the villagers' requests.

The issue of recruiting extra staff to provide service in place of committee members derived from a request that had been made several times in previous years – that services which had been provided by the Tourism Committee members (all councilors) during the summer tourist season should be limited to Saturdays and Sundays, abolishing services on weekdays. It was finally agreed that the committee members should provide the service only on weekends, but rather than abolishing the weekday service, they should recruit staff to provide these services. Due to the increasing number of staff with a side job (farming, for instance), discussions about this type of service had continued for quite a while. Around 1970, these matters were gradually settled through, for example, hiring people form outside the area to provide the services.

In Chinai, issues such as the measures to be taken in the event of torrential rains and how to handle sales and purchases of rice fields occurred annually. Although some of these events may seem relatively insignificant from an outside perspective, for the residents of the *mura* they are very important issues of everyday life that must be resolved.

Changes in issues of *mura*

By examining one year of the *mura*'s diary and then tracing changes in particular events over the years we have developed a rough picture of the *mura*. Many routine events have continued for a very long time with only small changes ('ordinary events'), such as the events underlined in Table 4.2, the daily visits to the shrines and the *mushi-okuri*. Between and among these events recurrent issues arise, such as floods, land sales, and conflicts between obligations to the *mura* and to family life (such as the issue of the committee members' service on weekdays), as well as isolated events, such as pollution and the reduction of rice acreage (both recurrent and isolated, 'extraordinary occurrences'). Each of these issues has been a factor in changing the *mura*. More specifically, changes in 'ordinary events' have changed the *mura* very slowly, while 'extraordinary occurrences' have done so rapidly.

We now have an overall picture of the continuously repeated events and the extraordinary occurrences in the *mura*. Let us now examine, in chronological order, the extraordinary occurrences recorded in the *Kiroku*.

The greater part of the *Kiroku* from before the Meiji Period consists of records of construction works, the expenditure of government grants, and requests for reductions or exemptions of land taxes. Those entries written after the beginning of the Meiji Period often record the village's efforts to adapt to significant changes in various systems. For example, the change from a rotating to a permanent shrine guardianship in 1872, as discussed in Chapter Two, would have been a major reform for the *mura*.

In 1873, Chinai was thrown into turmoil due to the Land Tax Reform (also discussed in Chapter Two). The Land Tax Reform affected the use of common forests and fishing rights. Many entries during the following decade record the consequences of this Reform. In 1889, when Chinai was incorporated with six other villages into Momose Village, there is only one entry to this effect. This entry, though, is followed by frequent reports of natural disasters, public works such as river embankment repairs, and repairs to shrines and other facilities. From around the last year of the Meiji Period (1912), entries about war and military exercises are interspersed among reports of disasters and repairs.

The most significant event during the Taishō Period (1912–1926) may be the commencement of regular steamship services at Chinai Port. As mentioned above, in February 1925, the Ōaza Chinai council resolved to petition the Taiko Kisen steamship company for services at Chinai Port. From then until September 1925, there were almost daily negotiations between the village and the company. The village's initial written request begins with the sentence, 'Needless to say, success in the promotion of industry depends on whether the place is conveniently located in terms of public transportation.' It continues: 'In Takashima County, we have no railways. In particular, the areas in the north of Imazu have narrow roads, which prevent mass transportation...[The region relies heavily on] your steamships, but Chinai is halfway between Imazu and Kaizu ports.' The request then emphasizes the necessity of steamship services at Chinai Port, on the grounds that Chinai's access to transportation was too poor to promote industry and, in particular, that 'Ōaza Chinai's most important export items are fish and aquatic products, particularly fresh fish which require quick transport.' The company eventually agreed to commence steamship operations at the port, in exchange for the community's assumption of responsibility for a considerable portion of the expenses involved.

The entry immediately following the February decision reveals that the request for steamship services was part of a strategy to attract a Kanebuchi Bōseki spinning factory to Chinai. Thus, in November, following the agreement to commence steamship services, a written request to construct such a factory was made in the name of Chinai's district head to the president of Kanebuchi Bōseki. Amongst other things, the request points out that,

> as evidence of our good access to transportation, we actually have steamship services by Taiko Kisen at Chinai Port. In addition, a government railway line is scheduled to open along the surveyed line. Thus, we will easily have access to both water and land transportation in the future.

This request, however, was rejected by the company, which replied that it had no such plans, and thus this matter was settled. Nevertheless, in 1929 the Ōaza constructed a pier and steamship services commenced.

Entries written after the start of the Shōwa Period (1926) contain many descriptions of changes in the *mura* resulting from the war. According to an entry of February 1932, four villagers were drafted following the government's 'draft call for the Manchurian Incident.' The Ōaza gave five yen to each of the draftees and decided to 'provide at least ten man-days of labor from the Ōaza to the families who provided soldiers.' This marks the beginning of the *mura*'s move to a war footing. This entry is followed by others about the draftees and mandatory rice quotas delivered to the government.

The entries written around that time frequently report that a person elected to a village office declined to take the post. Refusal to assume such a post had not been uncommon before, but in many earlier cases, the person who initially declined the position was eventually persuaded by others to take it. However, the refusals at this time appear to have been firm and irreversible. In response, the Ōaza adopted a resolution at a general meeting stipulating that 'any and all matters voted for at a general meeting must be absolutely and unconditionally complied with.' Yet the refusals continued until one person stipulated several conditions for assuming the position, including, '1. I take the position only on a tentative basis; 2. Any request for resignation made during the term must be accepted.' In 1941, the Ōaza's general meeting decided to pay 180 yen as remuneration for such positions, but this was not sufficient to curtail the refusals. Although these refusals occurred under special circumstances – that is, wartime – it is clear that the Ōaza's bylaws underwent major revisions during this period. Although some of those revisions were later reversed, many were retained even after the war.

As mentioned earlier, the volumes of *Kiroku* for the years 1947–1953 were destroyed by fire. Considering that this postwar period is characterized by widespread and often radical reforms, including agrarian reform, it is likely that the *mura* experienced further significant changes during this time. The first major event in the *mura* during the decade 1955–1964 was the construction of a modern water supply system. Entries similar to those from 1970 describe the events leading up to the construction of this water supply system. Many of the entries written around 1960 describe changes in agricultural facilities and organizations as well as the consolidation of farmland. In the entries written during the 1960s, the focus shifted to Chinai's tourism development, which brings us back to the year 1970, as per Table 4.2.

Ordinary and extraordinary times in *mura* and cities

By comparing the *mura*'s events and occurrences over the years, we have been able to distinguish between ordinary, routine events and extraordinary occurrences. In addressing the ordinary as well as the extraordinary occurrences, the *mura* has always based its actions on a logic derived from the *mura*'s worldview. The principal element for justifying this logic is local experience.

Our examination of changes in the village reveals that, (1) as described above, in the process of identifying and resolving issues, the villagers have had to take actions requiring new methods and/or different logics than was customary, whether voluntarily or under external pressure; and (2) these new methods and/or logics have slowly and continuously been incorporated into the local worldview. In modern urbanized communities, extraordinary change has typically become routine. In *mura* communities, in contrast, such changes have occurred extremely slowly. As a result of the relatively slower processes, routine affairs, once changed by extraordinary occurrences, settle once again into stable forms.

Kunio Yanagita refers to confusion between *hare* (special occasions) and *ke* (ordinary times) as a characteristic of cities. This is also a characteristic of urbanized communities (e.g., farming villages which have become peripheral suburbs, with new residents leading an urban life). Specifically, these communities are not only unable to make a clear distinction between ordinary times (*ke*) and special occasions (*hare*), but often switch them around. This is the case in rural communities, too, where, as we have seen in Chinai, each year there are more and more situations where extraordinary events occur in everyday life and soon become ordinary affairs. Perhaps we only identify a situation as an issue for the *mura* when some extraordinary occurrence creates confusion in the *mura*'s daily living and the *mura* is at a loss about what to do about it.

It seems to me, however, that the true problem is rooted in ordinary, everyday life. Special occasions have been incorporated into a *mura*'s ordinary life in the broadest sense, and the *mura*'s everyday life thus contains distortions in itself. Needless to say, this is true in cities as well as in village communities. A city, however, as mentioned above, is a community in which the distinction between ordinary times and special occasions has already become unclear. Urbanization might refer to the processes though which a *mura* becomes more like this type of community, but does a *mura* actually get closer to a city to any extent? No. There must be some reason for the fact that one *mura* had, at least until 1970, maintained its local order, at least to some extent, by distinguishing between ordinary affairs and extraordinary events, and has maintained this order to this day. Indeed, in order to maintain agricultural production according to the rhythms of nature, even though many farmers now have 'second' (i.e. non-farm) jobs, and to maintain somewhat stable personal relationships within the community, it is essential that a certain temporal and spatial order that distinguishes between the ordinary and extraordinary is shared and understood by all villagers.

An order based on this distinction is a temporal and spatial order reflecting the relationship that farmers have established with nature in order to sustain their production activities. This order has been embodied in the traditional Japanese calendar as well as in the borders between *mura* communities. I would argue that rural villages would not have been able to conduct their production and everyday life activities without maintaining/embodying such an order.

Based on the above considerations, we can not understand the issues of a *mura* without understanding the order in which its everyday life is conducted and elucidating how its extraordinary occurrences interact with ordinary affairs. This task is also associated with understanding the issues in cities whose residents originate from *mura* communities.

5 Techniques of Forest Management and Philosophy of Living

Mountain villages and development

Introduction

Japanese mountains and forests are in a very bad state. In earlier times, the landscape of a mountain hamlet represented a 'landscape of circulation,' which had been created through the various interactions between people and the mountain forests. Since the energy revolution, however, many Japanese mountain hamlets have seen their forests reduced to mere collections of Japanese cedar and cypress. With the falling economic value of Japanese cedar and cypress, these forests have increasingly been abandoned, and have become overgrown – an initial sign of neglect. In this the first half of this chapter, I discuss the present situation of the landscapes of mountain hamlets, by following changes in the basic way of life of the people of Asahi-chō, a mountain hamlet located along the upper reaches of the Yahagi River, which runs through the eastern part of Aichi Prefecture.

Then and now: comparing photographs

'The mountains have changed. They've been ruined,' said A, a forty-seven year old man, when he spoke to me about changes in the mountain landscapes while comparing a photograph of the mountain across the valley (Photo 5.2) with another taken forty years earlier from the same spot (Photo 5.1). The newer photo clearly shows more trees, densely grown.[1] He has another old photograph (Photo 5.3), looking in the opposite direction, from a location in the direction of the mountains depicted in Photos 5.1 and 5.2 toward the spot from which those photos were taken. We went to the location from which Photo 5.3 was taken to look at the landscape it depicted. Once again, there were more trees in that landscape than there had been forty years earlier.[2]

By comparing these photos, it is obvious that the landscapes captured in the photos are awful. The area has increasingly degenerated, even though it may appear that some of it has been regularly thinned out. 'You can easily see it if you go there,' said A, so we decided to enter the forests. First we entered a wood that A looks after. I brushed aside the fallen leaves around the foot of a tree and picked up a handful of soil, down to about five centimeters deep. I could feel the moisture in the soil, indicating its high water content. Next we entered a forest owned by the prefecture, where I picked up some soil in the same manner. Here the soil felt dry – totally different from the soil in the first spot. I tried soil from other locations a little deeper into the forest, only to find the same dryness. The soil in neglected forests is dry at considerable depths, because it cannot retain much water. The locals say that increasingly more forests have been neglected here in Asahi-chō, particularly over the past decade, causing a rapid decline in the ability of the mountains to retain water.

We returned to the site from which Photo 5.3 was taken and looked at the photos again. It was obvious that the landscapes we were looking at were the same as those shown in the photos. More particularly, each photo shows one area that has scarcely changed – the forest surrounding the shrine. Photos 5.1 and 5.2 were taken of a shrine known locally as Shinmei-san in District T. Photo 5.3 was taken of a small Jizō shrine known as O-dō, located across the valley from Shinmei-san. In both districts, the forest surrounding the shrine – protecting their faith – continues to be well looked after, with the trees trimmed and thinned. What has brought about the changes in the rest of the landscape?

The term *sanson* (mountain village) roughly means a 'rural community which has relatively poor access to public transportation, resulting in limited communication with the outside world and, moreover, which is located in the mountains and where no attempt of an academic living survey has ever been made' (Yanagita (ed.) 1938). In common parlance there is little difference between the meaning of the term 'mountain village' and the term *yamazato* (village hamlet). Both terms evoke a traditional way of life that has been confined and preserved in mountain hamlets, giving the impression of a quiet, peaceful life surrounded by forests on the mountains.

It is only in more recent times that mountain villages have come to be called *chūsankanchi* (intermediate and mountainous area) – a term that strongly suggests continuity between mountain villages and flatland farming villages. Mountain villages, however, have

Photo 5.1: A view of a mountain hamlet in the 1950s

Photo 5.2: A photo taken in December 1998 from approximately the same location as that used to take Photo 5.1

Techniques of Forest Management and Philosophy of Living 221

Photo 5.3: A view of a mountain hamlet in the 1950s

Photo 5.4: A photo taken in December 1998 from approximately the same location as that used to take Photo 5.3

long been neglected in national policy, even though they have underpinned Japan's development. In tracing the recent history of mountain villages, we find too many significant changes to list exhaustively. Examples include: the collapse of the charcoal making industry due to the energy revolution, depopulation, the displacement of villages due to dam construction, the collapse of the forestry industry, moves towards tourism, and pressure to protect the environment. The recent history of the people living in mountain villages can be characterized as a repetition of efforts to find ways to be self-supporting while adapting to changes in the demand for mountain and forest products.

The much-lamented destruction of tropical rainforests has generated a strong impression that any reduction of forests equates to destruction of the environment. This seems to have, in turn, generated a corresponding belief that any increase in the number of trees equates with the recovery of nature. However, the mountains forests in Japan are prime examples of nature that has been developed over very long periods of time by the people who use it. When neglected, these forests degenerate rather than 'returning' to some 'original' or 'pristine' state. Degenerated mountain forests are not merely no longer available for human use; they are no longer able to retain moisture in the soil or to sustain the other processes and cycles necessary for their continued (healthy) existence. That is, they no longer have the self-sustaining capacities of 'natural' forests.

The differences and similarities between the 1950s photos and the present landscapes tell us much about the history of the intervening forty years. In what follows, I aim to elucidate some of the changes in the landscape of this mountain hamlet, and to correlate these with changes in the lives of the people who once maintained the landscapes. For the purposes of this discussion, I assume that the term 'landscape' has two dimensions: the 'appearance' of the environment and what is evoked by this appearance.

Changes in the landscape of a mountain hamlet

The current situation
As can be seen from Shinmei-san, in the district where A's house is located, and from O-dō across the valley, the forests in Asahi-chō have a greater density of trees than forty years earlier and are degenerating. This is not unique to Asahi-chō, but is also applicable to the majority of forests landing Japan, except for some of the areas producing popular, highly valued species such as Japanese cedar.

The Yahagi River begins a short way upstream of Asahi-chō, a hamlet located in the northeastern part of Aichi Prefecture, near the border between Gifu and Nagano prefectures. The middle reaches of this river run through the cities of Toyota, Anjō and Okazaki, before flowing into the sea at Hekinan City. In the cities of Toyota and Nagoya, the uppermost reaches of the Yahagi River, including Asahi-chō, are referred to as the Oku-yahagi (remote Yahagi) area. Out of a total area of 8,216 hectares, 6,761 hectares are forest. After dams were constructed during the decade 1965–1974, there was no more than 260 hectares of cultivated land in the area. In these regards, Asahi-chō is typical of the mountain hamlets designated as *chūsankanchi* (intermediate and mountainous area).

Like other Japanese mountain hamlets, forestry was never the main industry of Asahi-chō. Nevertheless, during the decade 1955–1964, when the aforementioned photos were taken, the hamlet had well maintained forests on the mountains and miscellaneous trees for making charcoal, as well as cultivated land which, although not very large, was sufficient for the community to feed itself. The residents made their living in various ways, working in the mountains, on cultivated land and on the river. During the past four decades, however, their lives have changed significantly due to the collapse of the charcoal industry, the collapse of forestry, depopulation due to migration to the cities, and increasing numbers of part-time farmers who regularly commute to work.

A is one of the few people in this hamlet who continues to be engaged in forestry full-time. He describes the situation of full-time forest owner-managers as follows: 'Trees are waste nowadays. They often tell us to clear our trees for road construction, and those are occasions we are called in.' In other words, he says, they are forest owner-managers in name only; most of what they actually do is similar to what construction workers do. He continues:

> During the decade between 1965 and 1974, there was a period when forestry was strong. Then, after they started importing foreign lumber, many non-brand-name local lumbers became almost unsaleable. Cutting down and planting trees makes no profits. You can get at least some money if you are hired by the day for such jobs as logging or pruning, which are contracted to the forestry cooperative. So, this is how we make a living. I'd rather have the national or prefectural government purchase all my forests on the mountains and be employed and work for them than owning and having to maintain all this. I think this is more or less the case with most forests on the mountains in Japan.

Figure 5.1: A map of Higashi-hagidaira District in Asahi-chō in 1867 (redrawn)

Source: Asahi-chō shi henshū kenkyū kai (Study group for the edition of history of Asahi-chō) (ed.) (1980) *Asahi-chō shi* (History of Asahi-chō), p.321.

History of landscapes of Japanese mountain hamlets

Figures 5.1 and 5.2 are maps of Asahi-chō (Higashi-hagidaira) around 1867 and 1980, respectively. In the 1867 map, we can see the land categorized as: 'settlements; cultivated lands; firewood and charcoal supplying forests; and grassland.' The other map shows that these categories have been simplified, now consisting of 'settlements; cultivated lands; and commercial plantations.' This is not a matter of how meticulously the maps were drawn; but rather reflects the fact that both grasslands and firewood and charcoal supplying forests have become plantations of mostly Japanese cedar or cypress. Let us examine changes in the landscapes of an ordinary mountain hamlet.

According to Toshiyuki Tsuchiya, prewar Japan was rife with 'landscapes with grassy mountains' that were unimaginably vast to the modern eye. Grassy mountains must be looked after as such, or they will soon return to mountains with a variety of self-seeding trees that are not commercially desirable. Grassy mountains were

Figure 5.2: A map of Higashi-hagidaira District in Asahi-chō around 1980

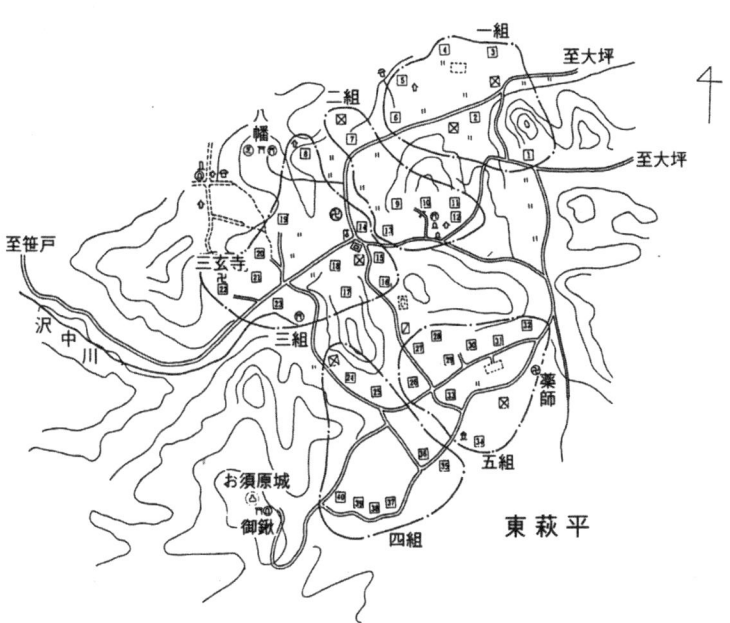

Source: Asahi-chō shi henshū kenkyū kai (ed.) (1980) *Asahi-chō shi*, p.672.

maintained for specific purposes, such as to provide manure and hay, or for use as pasture. In particular, during the Meiji and Taishō Periods, grassy mountains were generally used to obtain grass clippings for compost or livestock feed. They were typically maintained by intentional burning (Tsuchiya 1991).

From the 1920s, however, the extent of grassy mountains began to decrease throughout the country. Passive factors contributing to this decrease were the introduction of commercial fertilizer which made grass clippings for compost unnecessary, in addition to the tighter restrictions imposed upon intentional burning. Active factors included the increasing use of mountains for forestry purposes, such as the production of charcoal and lumber. The conversion of grassy mountains to lumber-producing forests was largely limited to a few regions; the conversion to charcoal-producing forests was more common in most Japanese regions.

Peaking in 1951, charcoal production decreased rapidly from around 1957 due to the so-called energy revolution. By 1965, production was lower than it had been during the early Meiji Period.

In many regions, the forests were converted to lumber-production forests thus and 'landscapes of Japanese cedar and cypress' appeared, particularly during the period 1960–1965. By 1970, the total area of commercial plantation forests exceeded the area at the end of World War II. In other words, what today is understood as the typical landscape of mountain villages has only been so since the war.

Changes in mountain hamlets and the landscape of symbiosis
In Asahi-chō, forestry accounted for less than 10% of the region's industry throughout the Meiji Period. Most of the area was grassy mountains, which are classified as 'wilderness' – an uncultivated landscape where weeds and bushes grow naturally. Much of the forestland in Asahi-chō became communal lands when the Meiji government divided the nation into government-owned and private lands. Ninety-four per cent of all forests became settlement-owned. According to a survey conducted in the late Meiji Period, lumber accounted for 42% of total forestry production in Asahi-chō, while charcoal and other products accounted for 58% (Asahi-chō Shi Henshū Kenkyū Kai (Study group for the edition of history of Asahi-chō) 1981).

Later, though, more and more of Asahi-chō's forests were gradually converted to lumber-production. According to a survey conducted in 1943, 52.2% were coniferous forests, 27.5% were broad-leaved forests, 18.7% were mixed forests, and bamboo thickets accounted for and 1.6% of the total forestlands (5103 hectares). Of these, commercial plantations accounted for 28.4%.

From around 1965, more than 100 hectares of land was afforested each year. By 1975, commercial plantations accounted for more than 60% of all forests. Most of these forests were developed in response to the lumber boom after the energy revolution. Currently, many of these forests have trees suitable for felling, but there is no market demand for them as lumber due to the importation of cheap foreign lumber. Logging full-grown trees now would only result in losses.

Under these circumstances, the local administration enacted measures to promote tree thinning, which A explained as: 'If you bring down one tree, you don't get paid for the tree (the tree does not sell), but the prefectural government and the Asahi-chō administrative body pay you a subsidy of 100 yen and 90 yen, respectively.' According to A, however, this was 'not a clever way' to deal with the issue, no matter how you looked at it. If they pay you a certain amount for one tree, some people will cut one tree into three. Thus, the administration changed their measures and decided to pay 2200 yen per cubic meter. Nonetheless, A still feels that what they are doing is 'far from what can be called forestry.'

Examining these changes in the uses of the fields and mountains of Asahi-chō reveals that they roughly parallel general changes occurring throughout the country. As A puts it, watching the developments in forestry in Asahi-chō gives him a general understanding of the broad trends in Japanese forestry.

However, focusing on forestry does not provide much of an idea about the hamlet's landscape. What is it like to live in a mountain hamlet? Comparing the periods before and after the rapid economic growth of the postwar era – a very recent event – provides a better understanding. As described above, during the period of rapid economic growth, the landscape of mountain hamlets changed from firewood and charcoal supplying forests to commercial plantations consisting of Japanese cedar and cypress through afforestation. Firewood and charcoal supplying industries have relatively short economic cycles. The lifestyles of those engaged in these industries was based on the 'mutual complementarity between the part of life embodied in the process from "wage labor to commodity production and the consumption of commodities," and the part of life in which the necessities of life are made and utilized using life skills' (Uchiyama 1989).

In mountain hamlets at that time, natural cycles and human life cycles had become relatively symbiotic. The landscape of symbiosis so formed was the landscape of a mountain hamlet, laid out in the schema: 'settlements; cultivated lands; grassland or firewood and charcoal supplying forests.' Symbiosis was itself made possible by this layout.

During the period of rapid economic growth, however, the firewood and charcoal making industries collapsed and the forests were rapidly converted to commercial plantations for lumber production. As this process proceeded, 'mountain hamlet communities supported by varied forms of work collapsed, traditional skills became obsolete, and various interactions between nature/forests and villagers were lost' (Uchiyama 1989). Mountain hamlets began to exploit Japanese cedars and cypresses in commercial plantations in tune with the external economy. The landscape of symbiosis was lost, and its layout significantly altered into 'settlement; cultivated lands; commercial plantations.' Now that the external economy no longer demands local lumber, the commercial plantations have been neglected, creating landscapes of 'degenerated' forests.

In short, life in mountain hamlets was once based on an economy of circulation as symbolized by the landscape of symbiosis which, in turn, was based on the use of forests on the mountains as a source of firewood and charcoal, but this is no longer the case.

Tsuneichi Miyamoto's argument on mountain hamlets

Being a *hekichi* (remote rural area)

The conversion to commercial plantations was not the only result of the collapse of the firewood and charcoal production industries. The right to use forests was transferred to the Forestry Development Corporation or local public forestry corporations under the *bunshū zōrin* (proceeds-sharing afforestation) system.[3] In addition, as in A's situation, many forest owner-managers became subcontractors to forestry associations who contract out afforestation work. As these practices became common, it became unnecessary for local landowners to live in the mountain hamlets. Hence, many people moved to cities, severely depopulating the mountain hamlets, such that, for example, District T in Asahi-chō had fifteen families around 1955 but has only six at present.

The Chūgoku Mountains were already in a critical situation in the 1960s due to rapid depopulation. Tsuneichi Miyamoto (1972), who conducted long-term field research in this area described the situation as follows: 'Depopulation problems are occurring in areas called *hekichi* (remote rural areas) or *henchi* (remote areas). Depopulation has been accelerated by the fact that residents living in these areas feel that they live in a *hekichi*.' Miyamoto develops his argument on the following assumptions: 'The remote and rural nature of *hekichi* may lie in the consciousness of residents who live there'; and 'the problem is whether [they] feel that they live in a remote rural area – this is where an important key to the issue of *hekichi* should be found.'

As a matter of fact, the term '*hekichi*' accurately captures the image evoked by the term *yamazato* (mountain hamlet). Miyamoto points out that the term '*hekichi*' evokes: 'poor access to public transportation, low productivity, and an obsolete life culture,' as well as 'low productivity associated with the fact that their production activities take place in primary industry and...these activities go on the same way for ever and ever.'

Why, then, did these *hekichi* remain remote and isolated? For one thing, industry failed to develop in these areas, and trade and transportation systems failed to develop because of their well-developed closed economy. Miyamoto points out that these under-industrialized hamlets 'lived off their fortune.' The Chūgoku Mountains had high production of charcoal and firewood during and after the war, resulting in excessive harvesting of the forests. When the energy revolution occurred, causing a dramatic decline in the demand for firewood and charcoal, it deprived these communities of their primary sources of income. At the time, their trees were not yet tall enough to be harvested for lumber, which accelerated depopulation, because 'they were already cutting down trees recklessly just to survive from one day to the next, and when this no longer worked, the productivity of these mountains became very low' (Miyamoto 1972).

Mountain hamlets had previously overcome many crises, however. Miyamoto argues that the depopulation at this time caused a major crisis because these mountain hamlets lost far more people in the war 'who should otherwise have supported their hamlets in one way or another' than the cities did. Miyamoto points out that the depopulation problem is so serious because people's 'attitude toward their own hamlets' when faced with a crisis has 'changed fundamentally.'

To avoid being a *hekichi*

To avoid being a *hekichi* (remote rural village), villagers need to develop human resources. In schooling, they should 'educate *hekichi*, that is, provide education that deals with the subject matter of how this area should be used and how this hamlet should be improved.' However, in the current school system, teachers only provide 'education (that is common throughout Japan).' Miyamoto criticizes this approach severely, stating that, 'the nurture of successors, which should naturally proceed in a community-based manner, has been replaced by education in general, which has caused depopulation and created *hekichi* and, at the same time, resulted in the overpopulation and pollution of cities.'

Many of these local communities have attempted to attract manufacturing plants by way of addressing this crisis. Miyamoto is harshly critical of these measures: 'Looking at these attempts to attract plants, we have found that those plants are not financed by local resources. They are financed by outside resources. This means that although wages will be paid to the local people, all major profits will go to cities,' which has made these local communities 'colonies to contribute to the modernization of cities.'

These local communities do not lack financial resources, though. As Miyamoto observes, 'Individual people do have money, but their money is not concentrated to finance local industry.'

Importantly, Miyamoto's point is not that local residents should make a living *solely within* their community, but that they should construct their living *based on* their community. In the mountain hamlet of Asahi-chō, the changes in villagers' ways of life described above were shifts in terms of the basis for constructing their living in this sense.

The local people did not expect these changes, but that does not mean they were not ready to accept them. For example, the construction of new roads and upgrading of existing roads is strongly desired by villages and hamlets in the mountains. But, as Miyamoto points out, while new roads may help to overcome their remoteness, 'whether or not this will also bring happiness to the dwellers there is another matter.' Where new roads have been constructed, it has happened without due regard as to how improved access to the outside world is connected to the local people's way of life. This has aggravated the changes to the ways in which local people's lives are constructed.

In his argument, Miyamoto discusses mountain hamlets from the perspective of remoteness, but he seems to reach the same conclusion as arguments concerning the landscape of symbiosis. The breakdown of the basic way of life and the breakdown of the landscape of symbiosis came about through the same route.

Images of three mountain hamlets' landscapes

Eyes on mountain hamlets

Thirty years have passed since Miyamoto published his analysis, during which time it appears that the economy of mountain hamlets has moved ever further away from the logic of the local people's life.

In both of the descriptions above, it appears as though the people of the mountain hamlets had no other choice. But even if they were under pressure from an overwhelmingly powerful external force, was there really no other choice? In other words, is it absolutely necessary that the economy of mountain hamlets must continue to deviate from the logic of the local people's life?

In this respect, Miyamoto states: 'Mountains cannot be effectively used solely by the local people's resources.' This is because 'forestry resources are needed more by people outside mountain hamlets than by people living there. Mountain people have cut down mountain trees in response to demands from the outside, and this will continue in the future' (Miyamoto 1976). As Miyamoto predicted, mountain hamlets have continued to react to external demands, reacting to the tourism boom of the 1980s, then to the current ecology boom.

Nevertheless, there have been some changes since Miyamoto's research. For example, he says: 'Mountains provide resources for trade rather than resources for meeting local demands for living necessities. Many of the mountain products are convertible into cash' – this is no longer the case. But this only serves to reinforce his claim that: 'If mountains cannot be made use of, the mountain people will become worse off. If mountains can be made more effective use of, they will be assured of an affluent life,' but 'the use of mountains is not very effective.' Yet as he says, 'it is never wise to develop mountains by simply constructing golf courses because there is no other use for the mountains.' He believes that 'the use of land other than mountains has made considerable progress up to the present, but the use of mountains is far behind the level' it was in the late 1920s. Thus, he argues that we must now reconsider how to use the mountains.

Miyamoto's perspective – that effective use of the mountains requires the resources of people from outside the mountains – is important. So let us turn to a discussion of the outside view of mountain hamlets.

Mountain hamlets and development plans

Let us begin with a review of changes in Japan's Comprehensive National Development Plans (CNDP) in an effort to understand the government's view of mountain hamlets, which has caused significant changes in their landscapes.

The First CNDP was announced in 1962, when the postwar economy was getting back on the road to recovery (Economic Planning Agency 1962). This plan aimed at the

> well-balanced development of all regions through effective use of natural resources existing in Japan and appropriate distribution to all regions of capital, labor, technology and other resources, while taking into account overgrown cities and reduction of regional

disparities, in accordance with the National Income Doubling Plan.

Although mountain hamlets were about to be swept up in a nation-wide trend towards rural depopulation, the First CNDP does not mention mountain hamlets. Instead, it defines mountains as places where dam projects should be developed to ensure adequate water resources, flood prevention and the provision of electrical energy. At the same time, the plan also defines mountains as tourist resources as well as a source of lumber through advanced forestry production. In this context, the plan aimed at rationalizing forest road development and small forest management in close association with the modernization of agriculture and establishing economically-viable agroforestry management.

The Second CNDP was announced in 1969, at the peak of the rapid economic growth, when its negative impacts began to emerge in forms such as severe pollution (Economic Planning Agency 1969). This plan had four principal aims: 'protecting and preserving nature to permanently satisfy people's craving for nature, which is expected to become even more intense with future progress of urbanization'; 'expanding and equalizing development potential throughout the country' to avoid unbalanced use of the nation's land; 'reorganizing, and improving efficiency of advanced use' through developing each region in such a way as to make effective use of local characteristics; and 'developing and maintaining safe, comfortable and cultural environmental conditions in both cities and rural villages.' Unlike the First CNDP, this plan emphasizes measures against the rapid progress of overpopulation and depopulation.

With respect to the areas surrounding mountain hamlets, the Second CNDP considers it necessary to construct large-scale, in-tensive recreational facilities for nature sightseeing and to develop area-wide sightseeing routes. It also emphasizes the need to develop large-scale water resources to meet the excessively high demand for water in cities. For local communities whose community functions had deteriorated due to depopulation, the plan mainly provides for protecting the living environment by measures such as relocating and consolidating communities. With respect to forests, it specifi-cally proposes to convert the existing natural forests into commer-cial plantations, in furtherance of the First CNDP.

The depopulation trend had not yet been clearly established when the First CNDP was developed, but was unmistakable by the time the Second CNDP was formulated. Hence, the Second CNDP's policies and measures for mountain hamlets and forests determined the subsequent landscape of mountain hamlets.

The Third CNDP was issued in 1977, after Japan had experienced an oil crisis and entered the so-called period of low economic growth (National Land Agency 1977). The aim of this plan was, 'on the basis of limited land resources,' to 'systematically develop a comprehensive environment for human living, which should be healthy, cultural and stable, based on harmony between people and nature as well as on historical and traditional culture, by making good use of local characteristics.' This aim was to be achieved through the Integrated Residence Policy (IRP; *teijūken kōsō*). To realize the IRP, the plan proposed the integrated management of water systems, which we might refer to as the 'basin area policy.'

Based on the idea that a whole basin area should be regarded as a single unit, mountains were incorporated into the Third CNDP as part of the geographical areas which would play a central role in the efforts to conserve water. The mountains were expected to provide recreational spaces for basin residents. More specifically, the plan proposed constructing nature trails as places for human contact with nature. With respect to mountain hamlets, the plan considered it necessary to construct comprehensive facilities that would make good use of local characteristics. The plan emphasized the relationships between and among these facilities and other elements of a basin unit. With respect to forests, similarly to the Second CNDP, the Third CNDP lists the following factors: comprehensive assessment of their diverse functions, natural environment protection and national land conservation, and recreational functions. Again, what is important here is the position of forests in the basin.

Had the Third CNDP's Integrated Residence Policy been realized, the landscapes of mountain hamlets might look different today. The greater portion of the IRP, however – at least the policy on mountain hamlets – ended up merely as empty slogans.

The Fourth CNDP was developed in 1987, when Japan entered a period which later came to be called a 'bubble economy.' This plan was developed in accordance with slogans of 'multipolar dispersion country' and 'exchange networks.' In many respects this plan appeared to be a major backslide from the Third CDNP (National Land Agency 1987).

With respect to mountains, while the Fourth CNDP aimed at the comprehensive management of water systems and, like the

Third, the multipurpose development of local areas making good use of local characteristics, it also proposes developing large-scale, long-stay resorts. This plan resulted in the development of large-scale resorts and golf courses all across the mountains of Japan. Areas that did not pursue such developments suffered further depopulation and desolation of the mountain environment. Other policies proposed by the plan include: public participation in the development of forests; ecological education; and conservation of resources to be inherited by future generations. None of these policies were realized.

In 1998, the Fifth CNDP – a plan for the next decade – was announced (National Land Agency 1998). This plan aims to conserve and maintain land by focusing on basin units, as well as constructing a multipolar system for the nation's land. In this respect, it represents the revival of the Third CNDP, which was not realized.

With respect to mountains, the Fifth CNDP aims to develop residential areas surrounded by a rich natural environment and at 'mitigation.'[4] As for forests, the plan aims to develop forest and wood culture, which is intended to conserve forests and woods upstream of or around mountain hamlets while enjoying the benefits of those forests. The plan also aims to revitalize the forestry and lumber industries in each basin.

As was the case with the Agricultural Basic Law, the above CNDPs were all clearly headed in directions that ensured further destruction of the economy of symbiosis by promoting further monoculturalization. This has resulted in further destruction of the landscape of symbiosis in mountain hamlets. The Fifth CNDP aims to revive the landscape of symbiosis and ways of life based on symbiosis, although it is as yet unknown whether this can be achieved.

Mountain hamlets from the perspective of downstream cities

The environmental movement to protect the Yahagi River, which arose in areas along the river, later came to be known across the country as the Yahagi River method. In Toyota City, too, various groups emerged in the mid-1970s with the aim of protecting the environment of the Yahagi River. Among them was one that published a journal titled '*Gekkan Yahagi-gawa* (The Monthly Yahagi River)' (1977–1985). Let me review the perception of mountain hamlets from the perspective of the people who live in cities downstream.

While 'The Monthly Yahagi River' group was primarily focused on conservation of the Yahagi River, the journal also devoted a considerable number of pages to discussing the upstream mountain hamlets. Simply put, these articles present clear representations of such mountain hamlets. After 1976, the Toyota City government established a water source conservation fund. Prior to this, in 1976, the group proposed to set up a water source conservation fund based on the prefectural government's draft plan (Gekkan Yahagi-gawa Dōjin (The Monthly Yahagi River Club) 1977). The main purpose of the government's draft plan was flood control. At this point, 'The Monthly Yahagi River' group argued strongly against constructing a dam; and conserving the catchment-area forests surrounding the upstream hamlets was consistent with their goal of stopping the dam construction.

The group had not yet discussed any specific details concerning the catchment-area forests at this point. The mountain hamlets were considered to be closely related to the water source of the Yahagi River. At the group's discussion meeting in November 1984, however, interesting changes are evident. Allow me to quote a rather lengthy excerpt from the minutes of this meeting:

B: When we hear we have to plant trees on the mountains because we don't have enough water, people often say "people living upstream should not pollute river water" or "they should produce water." But these opinions are forcing responsibility onto the people living upstream. If these people make an effort, who'll benefit from it? That's only cities from midstream to downstream. There is the "water source fund," but I think it is a mere pose. In a certain country in Europe, their approach is to return a certain percent of water charges to communities on the mountains. Like this, I think that if we force such obligation and responsibility onto mountain people, the time must come that we pay them fitting compensation for their effort....

E: The water source fund is encouraging tree planting.

C: The water source fund is used in really funny ways. If someone plants Japanese cedars, the fund pays for it. That's actually the opposite of what you should do to produce water. If you plant Japanese cedar or cypress, the mountains release less water than otherwise. Miscellaneous trees can hold more water....

A: All trees on the mountains were cut down during the war, and they thought they had to plant trees on the ruined mountains and started planting only conifers. That's where the mistake started.

From the latter half of the 1970s, there was a national trend for establishing water source funds. The above remarks were made at a time when people began to realize that these funds offered a way out of the economic impasse of artificial afforestation.

The *Monthly Yahagi River* suspended publication in July 1985, after issue No. 100. In the earlier issues the journal represented mountain hamlets and their forested landscapes as a 'green dam.' However, over time, as the club's data collection progressed, the journal began to explore the relationship between forests and the people living in mountain hamlets, and their arguments shifted from the concept of 'green dam' – a view of forest resources that was prevalent in the mid-1970s – to other concepts, including discussions about the culture of the mountain hamlets. Although the language used differed from the CNDPs, these later discussions were in effect a revival of the understanding of the importance of a landscape of symbiosis for functioning mountain hamlets.

Mountain hamlets from the perspective of forest owner-managers
The local forest owner-manager, A, continues to believe that forestry can be a viable local industry and that they should pursue its potential as an industry as long as they continue to live in the mountain hamlet. Although social forestry[5] has been touted by the government and environmental groups, A firmly believes that it only makes sense if there are forest owner-managers; he is sure that social forestry without forest owner-managers will not last long.

The rest of this section is an account of A's opinion about the potential of forestry as a local industry:

> The water source fund makes no sense in the existing circumstances. It can do little more than provide subsidies to forestry associations, which only helps forestry to continue as subcontract work. They construct forestry roads, but those roads are being constructed just to spend money, rather than constructing roads appropriate for each mountain. It is not uncommon for tenders to be called for before the route has been decided. Having to spend these subsidies from the national government has become a burden on our community that it can no longer bear.
>
> If they have to provide subsidies after all, there is no point in doing so unless they do it in a manner that enables forestry to become a viable local industry. To make forestry a viable local industry, about fifty trees must be brought down per day per worker, so forest owner-managers cannot rely solely on their own mountains. Moreover, con-

sidering how we should bring down trees and where we should carry them to, we probably should not confine our business to the Yahagi River basin. Our forestry would not be a viable local industry unless we form something like a forestry zone with the Toyo River basin.

Sub-conclusion

As can be seen in the photos at the beginning of this section and through the history discussed above, the commonly shared perception of mountain hamlets as densely forested landscapes was only created after the war – in fact, quite recently. Before then, mountains had been used in various ways. In particular, the grassy mountains surrounding mountain hamlets had been most commonly used to obtain grass clippings, and for rice and vegetable fields. This had created landscapes similar to those found in the flatland forests used by nearby communities.

The schematic layout of mountain hamlets had changed from 'settlements; cultivated lands; and grassland, firewood or charcoal supplying forests' before the war to 'settlements; cultivated lands; and commercial plantations' after the war. Furthermore, recent decades have seen the desolation of commercial plantations. It has been noted that 'neglected bamboo thickets are expanding on hills and terraces in all parts in and west of the Chūbu region of Japan' (Tabata 1996). This type of landscape is not only expanding on hills and terraces, but also on the slopes of neglected mountains, at least in the upper reaches of the Yahagi River.

Landscapes are created, but natural cycles are faster. Remote from nature, human beings can only live with plants and animals by taming them.

Looking at the four photos now, the places that remain unchanged in the landscape of this mountain hamlet that has changed so much in four decades are the places of gods – Shinmei-san and O-dō – where a balanced relationship has been maintained between people and nature. Nevertheless, the neglected nature that has been allowed to run wild is closing in on them. Once tamed, nature requires continual care.

A would say that the revival of the landscape of mountain hamlets – a symbol of the landscape and economy of symbiosis – cannot be successful without forest owner-managers. The economy and landscape of symbiosis is an idealistic ambition. To make it a realistic ambition, with commercial plantations already standing for nearly four decades, it is necessary that the harvesting of these commercial plantations becomes a viable local industry. This is what is required to 'look after' them. And to make this sustainable, in turn, means changing the basis for constructing local people's way of living, as argued by Tsuneichi Miyamoto. The basis for constructing their way of living has not collapsed, but has shifted. This can be seen in the above photos, in the landscapes around the shrine and the small Jizō shrine, which remain well looked after.

Because he knows that the basis for constructing people's way of living is safe, A confidently predicts that the forests in his area will be beautiful once more, once there is a good prospect for successfully transforming local forestry into a viable local industry. When this occurs, we will begin to see a landscape of symbiosis again.

Modern forest management and native thoughts

'The tragedy of the commons' metaphor

'The tragedy of the commons,' a metaphor used by Garret Hardin (1968), has been accepted by many specialists involved in environmental issues as a model for explaining the destruction of an environment. It can be summarized as follows.

A pasture of fixed size can be maintained as long as it is grazed by a suitable number of cattle. For each person who grazes his/her cattle there, however, the most reasonable option is to maximize his/her profit, which simply means increasing the number of cattle even if only by one. The person will thus receive an increased return from their investment. The pasture, however, will have lost the amount of grass eaten by the additional cattle, but this 'cost' is shared by all of the people who graze their cattle there. Subsequently, all grazers will fall into a cycle of increasing the number of their own cattle in attempts to maximize their own profit. As a result, the pasture will be overgrazed and destroyed.

Clearly, no one set out to destroy the pasture. Each simply pursued his/her own best interest. Nonetheless, the whole system broke down. This is the gist of the metaphor. It is based on the premise that the pasture is open to everyone. Of course there can be no such pasture. When we apply this metaphor to the air, the ocean, or forests under a free-market economy, however, it takes on very real dimensions.

Hardin's metaphor has provided a foundation for the ever expanding logic of global forest protection. From this perspective, if Himalayan forests, for example, are left open to 'common' usage, they will be over-harvested and destroyed, so we must protect them. It is true that Himalayan forests, which were maintained for a very long time, have been degenerating over the past several decades. Why has this happened? Is it because the Himalayan forests are commons that are open to all people?

To begin with the conclusion, the Himalayan forests have not been commons to which everyone has free access. The forests were controlled by forest protection systems maintained by small communities of local people. The forests were used and maintained based on those systems. Breakdown of these systems led to the encroachment of forests. Local people gave up their own forest protection systems because of external pressure – a worldwide trend for forest protection – and a new forest protection system was introduced to their communities. As a matter of fact, it was not only the forests that were encroached upon: since forest protection was part of the local people's everyday living system, I would argue that negative impact on the forests followed significant changes to their entire system of everyday life. What is at stake here, then, is the local people's system of everyday living, which has entailed changes in the local people's relationship with nature. Hence we should not make an issue of local population increase or deforestation, as Hardin discussed. We must instead problematize the fact that the past several decades have been characterized by strong forces which have prompted these changes.

In this section, I take two villages inhabited mainly by Sherpas – Junbesi in the Solu region and Namche Bazaar in the Khumbu region, both in the Himalayas, Nepal, as my examples. I will discuss how the local living systems changed and how these changes effected the management of pastures, forests and other local resources – in short, the relationship with nature.

Logic of forest protection in the Himalayas

Discovery and conservation of landscapes
Deforestation, particularly of tropical forests, had begun to attract attention long before global environmental issues came to the fore. The total extent of forests on Earth has rapidly decreased due to a number of factors, including harvesting lumber for market exchange, slash-and-burn agriculture and land clearing for farmland. It is anticipated that if the diminution of forests continues unabated, the impact on the global environment will be severe. It is certainly a devastating sight to see bare mountains whose forests

have been cleared. The Himalayas are no exception. For several decades, Himalayan forests have decreased at a tremendous pace. At least this is how many lovers of the Himalayas understand the situation.

Of the highland peoples of the Himalayas, the Sherpas are among the most well known. They believe in the spirits of mountains and, out of awe and respect, fear defiling the mountains. As discussed in Chapter One, the beauty of Sherpa villages was 'discovered' in 1951 by Sir Edmund Hillary, the Everest pioneer, along with other landscapes of the Himalayan Mountains. Subsequently, the beauty of these villages was made widely known by a large number of climbers and tourists. The village of Namche Bazaar (hereinafter referred to as 'Namche') became the base of tourism around the region. Residents of Namche earned cash-income by providing guide services and accommodation to tourists. The changes in their living conditions drove local people to reckless deforestation. It was also Hillary who 'discovered' the piteous sight of the once beautiful forests, after they had been cut down and reduced to bare slopes. In 1976 the region was designated as a national park and logging was restricted. Since then the region has been under protection.

Hillary's two 'discoveries' were only twenty-five years apart. When I first visited Namche in 1989, the village had been under the protection of the national park for fifteen years. I began my research in the village the following year. As I continued interviewing the local people, I noticed extremely conspicuous 'enclosures' within the villages. As I listened to what people told me about these 'enclosures,' I learned that they had something to do with Hillary's discovery. The 'enclosures' surrounded reserves that were established by the park.

From an outside perspective, a series of events occurred – the discovery, destruction, and protection of these beautiful landscapes. Yet within these communities are residents who have experienced what may be called the modern history of these landscapes. What did this series of events mean to them? I would like to discuss the modern history of landscapes, based on the history of Namche for the fifty years after Hillary's first discovery.

Landscapes in Namche
When I return to Namche to conduct my fieldwork, I board a seventeen-seat twin-engine Twin Otter airplane at Kathmandu Airport. Once airborne I enjoy a view of terraced fields extending from the bottom to top of the mountains. After a mere one hour

flight, the plane lands at Lukla Airport, although it seemed like we were going to crash into the cliff. From the airport to Namche, I enjoy mountain hiking. Turning right and left, I repeatedly weave around the swift river Dudh Kosi, which is rather cloudy. The name Dudh Kosi literally means 'milk river.' The cloudiness of the river, which is fed by melted water from glaciers, is probably unchanged since antiquity.

After crossing a large bridge that has recently been constructed over the river, I travel up and up along a steep trail. Moving away from the river, I eventually reach a tea booth on the ridge. Moving leftward around the ridge, in about fifteen minutes the forest abruptly comes to an end and the entire village of Namche comes into view. Houses form rows and appear to be clinging to a very steep, curved wall. From this perspective, the village appears to be so steep that the roofs of the houses in one row seem to be lower than the foundations of the houses in the immediately adjacent row above.

I walk on. Shortly before the village, I pass a place where there are several houses on both sides of the trail running tea stalls. Then I enter the village through an archway called *kani*. There is a watering place close by. From the archway a *stupa* is visible. Immediately above the *stupa* is a small cabin with a *mani* prayer wheel attached to it. The wheel is spun by running water. It is believed that each turn of the prayer wheel means that the mantra inside has been recited, and religious merit is obtained.

To get to the place where my colleagues and I usually set up our tents and open a medical clinic, I must climb the steep trail running between the houses for another fifteen minutes or so. The place is called Zolkan and is located at the highest part of the village. In Zolkan there are barracks of soldiers as well as the local offices of the national park.

The village has about one hundred houses in rows. Both sides of the village site seem to be steep grassland. Conspicuous in the grassland are several enclosures which stand sharply outlined against the grassland. During my first year in the village I wondered what they were for, but they soon blended into the familiar background and I forgot even having wondered what they were.

When I visited Namche again in the summer of 1990, however, my first thoughts turned, once again, to wondering what those enclosures were for. One large enclosure is clearly visible from the spot where the village first comes into view. It is shaped something like a whale. What in the world is that? Is it a special holy place or something similar? I assumed this might be the case because it seemed to have been built to enclose a big rock on which prayer flags were flying.

The enclosure is a stone wall surrounding a piece of grassland. Viewed from a distance, the grassland inside these enclosures seems a little less green, a little less grassy. A closer inspection reveals that the entire slope beside the village has been planted with trees that are about one meter tall and that, although they are still small, they have grown thick and are a deep green. The enclosures that appear to be less green either have very small trees, or the trees are dead.

Looking around, I realize that there are scarcely any trees in or near the village of Namche, except for those planted trees that are still small. Considering that the surrounding areas are still covered by intact forests, the extent to which they have cut down the forests is rather surprising. Those one-meter tall trees were reportedly planted ten years ago. How long will it take for them to grow to the size of trees in the surrounding areas? It seems somewhat ironic that the word '*namche*' literally means 'forest.'

On his first visit to Namche in 1951, on his way to Mount Everest, Hillary wrote, 'The whole region (of Namche) was dense with greenery. Below the village, giant conifers soared.' Twenty-five years later, Hillary wrote in grief, 'I repeated this very same journey. The valley of the Dudh Kosi River was still very beautiful, but the forest was woefully thinned by the axes and saws of the Nepalese who had been cutting timber for buildings. The trees below Namche Bazar had been scarred by the heavy knives of Nepalese porters taking branches and bark for fuel and gummy heartwood for torches and lighting fires' (1984: 12). Hillary succeeded in reaching the summit of Everest in 1953. This was a few years before the Tibetan revolt, and before refugees flooded from Tibet into the Khumbu region, including Namche.

Refugee families account for about 20% of all families in Namche today. The refugee families tend to be larger than local families, though, so the refugee population is closer to thirty percent. Hillary's impressions of Namche were thus formed a few years before this increase of refugees. Since then, Namche has been continuously opened more and more to the outside world, beginning with the opening of the Nepalese mountains to climbers, followed by the Himalayas climbing boom in the 1970s, and the trekking boom in the 1980s which marked the beginning of general tourism. Nearly half of the families in Namche today run tourist lodges as their main business. Other sources of cash income include providing trekking guide services.

There is cultivated land, but the amount of land available for farming is very limited on the steep slopes. There are barely enough meadows to feed their livestock. More than a few villagers have accumulated wealth by trading with Tibetan villages, including Tingri. All of these circumstances seem to have accelerated the change of the villagers' livelihood from subsistence farming to guiding treks and lodge management.

It has been fifty years since Hillary first saw Namche (needless to say, he visited the village countless times thereafter). During these four decades, the village underwent all of the changes described above. I believe that the changes to the villagers' livelihoods changed the landscape of the village more than the population change. Villagers cut down trees to build lodges, and then cut down more trees to supply fuel for trekkers.

Upon 'discovering' the extent of this deforestation, Hillary said it was primarily his fault: 'In the early sixties I made an effort to assist my friends the Sherpas by building schools, hospitals, bridges and water pipelines.' Additionally, 'To help in the transport of building materials we constructed an airfield at Lukla. But the airfield had an unexpected effect: it gave much easier access to the Everest area, and increasing numbers of trekkers and tourists accelerated the demand for fuel' (Hillary 1984: 12).

Thus were the forests destroyed. To protect them the village was soon enclosed in the national park.

Establishment of the national park

Let us briefly review the circumstances under which the national park was established. In 1972, the Nepalese government and the local office of the FAO (United Nations Food and Agriculture Organization) agreed to establish four national parks in Nepal. One of them was the Sagarmatha National Park. For this park, they decided to promote a project with support from the New Zealand government. Around that time, Hillary 'was sure that some sort of control would have to be exerted if the Khumbu District were not to become a treeless desert.' To this end, he believed that 'The answer seemed to be the establishment of some form of National Park, initially financed by foreign aid.' In 1973 Hillary visited Nepal to make advance arrangements. At the same time, he approached the Minister of Foreign Affairs of New Zealand with a proposal. As a result, the New Zealand government formally decided to provide assistance. In 1974, an investigation was conducted by a New Zealand investigation team led by P. H. C. Lucas. The report submitted by the team provided the foundation for future policies. The team conducted investigations for only a month or so, but this had been preceded by numerous investigations and reports sponsored by the New Zealand government in the late 1960s and early 1970s.

Lucas's report integrated the preceding reports and their recommendations. The report was written in response to a sense of crisis that the world's most precious natural heritage would be lost, with a potentially catastrophic impact on the Sherpa communities, unless the changes in the Sherpa communities could be halted – particularly the reckless deforestation due to increasing numbers of climbers.

In response to this report, the New Zealand government decided, in 1975, to invite Nepalese to New Zealand for basic forest protection training. It also decided to provide financial aid for the following five years. Thus, the national park was formally established in 1976.

Not surprisingly, this national park project was resisted by villagers concerned that their firewood supplies would be restricted, that they might lose the pastures for their important yak livestock, and that they might be driven out of the national park.

At the same time, several points of conflict emerged within the New Zealand government and between the government and Hillary. One of these was about the amount of financial aid that should be provided. Some members of the government insisted that the planned aid was only intended to provide an impetus to promote self-sustaining development by the Nepalese government. They argued that the New Zealand government should therefore only provide a portion of the necessary amount (NZ$820,000 over the five years up to 1980, based on the initial investigation), while their opponents argued that this aid was urgent and should therefore be provided in full.

Another conflict arose over the initial plan to exclude the village from the national park. That is, the plan was to create a national park without any human residents. Hillary objected that such a plan was entirely unfeasible. The outcome of these disputes was that the financial aid was reduced to NZ$300,000 and the village was included in the park (Naylor 1976, and other New Zealand government documents).

This dispute over the amount of financial aid was typical of all proposals for this type of project. Such aid issues invariably raise a particularly interesting and complex problem, already evident in Hillary's aid to the Sherpa community – which included the construction of schools and hospitals through a foundation established independently by Hillary. If we consider the changes in the Sherpa community in the context of modernization, deforestation and the construction of the school and hospital were all products of the same trend. In this respect, Hillary's contribution to the Sherpa community was unavoidably paradoxical, as he recognized himself (see his comments cited above).

That is, the establishment of the national park failed to stop the major trend of change – the move to a tourism-oriented economy – that had occurred in Namche, even though this was the 'cause' of the deforestation.

Oddly enough, every person I interviewed responded that the forest views around Namche have not changed much over many decades. Even the most elderly made no mention of the dramatic changes that Hillary described. Surely there were more trees when they were young, than when Hillary first visited the village. Nevertheless, only a small number of people responded that there might have been more trees before.

What, then, has changed most in the village's landscape? The villagers say that it is simply that everyone has a new house and there are more lodges. Logging to obtain lumber for construction has been prohibited in the national park. Lumber for the construction of new lodges now has to be brought from far down the mountain, from outside the national park, at great expense. Nevertheless, new lodges continue to be constructed – a building boom in response to an ever increasing number of trekkers. Villagers say that with rising construction costs, an increasing number of lodges have been constructed by those people who have formed management partnerships with foreigners.

Another significant change in the village's landscape is the conspicuous enclosures mentioned earlier. According to the villagers, the first enclosure was constructed about eight years ago. This is confirmed by photos taken in 1982, which show only one of the two current enclosures. The other was obviously constructed later. The villagers say that another enclosure is to be constructed in 1991. These enclosures are nurseries for seedlings, looked after by the national park. The nurseries are surrounded by stone walls to prevent the seedlings from being trampled by people and livestock. Whether from a distance or up closer, however, the trees inside the enclosures seem to be growing more slowly than those outside, where livestock and people have access. I asked the villagers why.

They replied that it is because yaks are not allowed in there, so the grass that would otherwise be eaten by the animals has overgrown and there are probably not enough nutrients left for the trees. A quick visual inspection reveals that, indeed, the grass has grown thickly within the enclosures, and is a somewhat lighter shade of green than the evergreen trees. Trees outside of the enclosures have grown somewhat faster, which makes the areas outside of the enclosures look darker green. The difference in tones is not very clear in black-and-white photos, but from color photos the difference is obvious.

According to Hillary, these seedling nurseries were established around 1981, when the New Zealand government had completed their initial five-year project and was about to withdraw from the region. The seedling nurseries were the centerpiece of the national park and were the hub of a promising plan to restore the forests within the national park. After the New Zealand government's withdrawal, financial problems in the restoration of the forests were settled by the Himalayan Trust, a foundation set up under at Hillary's initiative, which continued to provide NZ$15,000 each year.

Since the village is within the Sagarmatha National Park, it seemed rather odd that enclosures had been constructed *in* the park. Villagers seem to be divided over the enclosures, with about half in favor and half opposed. They are not particularly bothered by the enclosures, but nor do they think that the enclosures will help trees to grow. Either way, the enclosures probably do not bother them, since tourism has become their main business.

Village forest management and the villagers' view of nature
Currently, most of the villages in this region, including Namche, are included in the national park. Looking around the village of Namche, it seems certain that forests have been cut down and converted to grassland. If this is true, we must ask: Why did these people, who had long maintained the forest as integral to the village, engage in haphazard and reckless deforestation? Were there any changes in their understanding of the forests?

To begin, villagers had never been allowed to cut down trees at liberty. Sherpa villages, including Namche, traditionally had officers called *nawas*, as discussed in Chapter One. There were two types of *nawas*: *nawas* of the forests, who controlled logging, and *nawas* of livestock, who controlled the movement of yak and other livestock. The *nawas* played very important roles in their villages.

Controlling logging and livestock movement meant controlling fuel and livestock feed. Practically, they were authorized to manage the central part of the business of their communities. However, the role of the *nawas* of the forests was assumed by the national park around 1982. The former *nawas* were employed by the park as public officials responsible for forest management. In other words, forest management was no longer under the villages' control.

At the same time, the *nawas* of livestock remained responsible for the movement of yak from the village to the pastures above the village in June, after the village's annual festival called *dumjee*. To prevent the animals from returning to the village and trampling over the barley and potato crops, the *nawas* of livestock remain with the yak until they return with the animals to the village in winter. The *nawas* of forests and livestock were equally important in traditional village life. Both forests and yak were regarded as common property to be managed by the entire village. In fact, in the village of Thame, located above Namche, two *nawas* of forests and two *nawas* of yak continue to be elected at the annual meeting each June, and continue to perform their traditional roles.

Turning the *nawas* of the forests into public officials was part of the national park project from the beginning. The plan developed in 1975 by the New Zealand government included provisions to provide Nepalese with training in New Zealand. Accordingly, a Sherpa named Mingma Norbu traveled to New Zealand for such training. He returned to Nepal in 1981 after five years of training to become the first senior ranger of the national park.

Through this process, forest management was transferred from the village to the national park. This, of course, was the reason for creating the national park. As Hilary put it, 'some sort of control would have to be exerted.' Like Hilary, the New Zealand government believed that if nothing was done to stop the deforestation, the region would eventually lose all of its forests. The government had become aware of the *nawas*' existence during its initial investigation in the 1970s, but believed that they were not capable of implementing the necessary 'control.' They believed that the forests in the national park had to be managed according to different principles than those upon which the village-based *nawas* had customarily managed their forests. To prevent deforestation and to protect the Himalayan forests, they believed that it was necessary to reorganize forest management from the viewpoint of the Himalayas as a whole. More precisely, the government considered forest protection from the perspective of the natural

Photo 5.5: A mandala *(thanka, or Buddhist painting)*

environment. In contrast, the *nawas* had managed the forests from the perspective of the needs of everyday life in each individual village. In this context, the needs of everyday life are not reducible to mere economic considerations, but refer to life as a whole.

Many of the norms in Sherpa communities are derived from Lamaism (Tibetan Buddhism). The photo above is of a *mandala* painted by a young Sherpa man who lives in a village located about a half-day's walk above Namche. *Mandalas* are based on traditional interpretations of Buddhist scriptures. While this painting follows those traditional interpretations to some extent, it also includes the painter's personal interpretations. At the center of the painting is Mt Khumbila, whose name means the god of Khumbu (the name of this region). From this mountain the god Khumbila appears on the back of a horse. The villages of the Khumbu region are built around the mountain. Each village has a Lamaist temple. The god appears in many places other than the temples, too, such as the flags on the roofs of houses and the *stupas*. The large sacred trees surrounding the temples are also believed to embody the god.

The fundamental characteristic of Tibetan Buddhism as it has generally been understood is as follows:

> The new Buddhism did not attempt to suppress the local people's belief – a belief which has an inclination toward incantation and seems to believe that a god or spirit exists in every object, including a mountain, river, grass and a tree, and in every natural phenomenon, such as wind, rain, thunder and lightening – but, rather, interacted and syncretized with it. (Nagao 1989)

Certainly, the local people do believe that there is a god present in every object – whether animal, plant, rock or mountain – and prayer for all these gods underlies their life. Their belief that a god resides in every object means that they have no framework for distinguishing between themselves and nature. This is a belief system that views nature in continuity with human beings, rather as opposed to human beings. The local people's concept of nature is not limited to natural objects and phenomena, either. Note a small airplane is in the lower right of the *mandala* above, and thus incorporated into their traditional world. This is their view of nature.

Environmental issues and modern history of landscapes
I mentioned that while Hillary claims that the forests of Namche had significantly receded, the villagers' do not confirm this. This does not, however, seem to be because one or the other have a faulty memory. Although Hillary was an outsider, he had visited Namche many times and must have seen bountiful forests with his own eyes. Yet it seems unlikely that the villagers have forgotten what the trees were like – since trees have always been an important life

resource for them. So, to what can we attribute the differences in their impressions of the forests?

The answer seems to be the same as to the question of the enclosures within the enclosure (national park). That is, the forests that Hillary saw are not the same as those seen by the villagers. In other words, Hillary and the villagers saw the same forests from different perspectives. Hillary saw them as part of the Himalayan landscape – a beautiful natural landscape rivaled by few in the world. More specifically, he took a macroscopic view of the Himalayas as a whole, and positioned Namche and its forests within this view. In contrast, the villagers regard the forests as a life resource situated within their life-world. They see the forests as a place that they have entered, pruned branches from, and cut the undergrowth. Further, they see the surrounding forests from the village of Namche, rather than seeing the forests and Namche from the outside. The enclosures for seedlings within the national park are derivative of Hillary's perspective (or rather, Hillary's perspective, and the one that informed the builders of these enclosures within an enclosure are derived from the same source). This perspective can only develop by positioning Namche and the forests on a par.

Hence the different accounts of the state of the forests can be explained by the fact that the entire framework of the villagers' life-world differs from Hillary's. As J. J. Gibson (1979) explained, even if the affordances provided by the forests are the same, the viewers have different niches, or different ecological positions. It follows that the desire to 'protect' the Himalayan forests is easy for us to understand because we view them from a position similar to Hillary's. In contrast, the Sherpas view the forests from their own – quite different – ecological position.

It is certainly not my intent to belittle Hillary's affection and contribution to the Himalayas, particularly the Sherpa communities. There can be no doubt about his propriety and good intentions. Yet, this provides a potent example of the danger that responses to current environmental issues, particularly global ones, may cause problems in people's lives on levels quite distinct from propriety and good intentions. This danger is perhaps most acute if we insist – whether consciously or unconsciously – on the propriety of our perspectives. Protection of forests is a global cause, but we must also protect people's ways of life. Namche's enclosures are not an important issue under the current circumstances. But if the grass and trees in the enclosures were essential to the people's everyday lives, the global cause of forest protection would be sharply opposed to the security of the local people's livelihood.

We can put this the other way around: if the residents of Namche continue to cut down trees, the forests will be destroyed, which will contribute to the destruction of the global environment. If we carry this logic to extremes, it may lead to extremely radical views and the practice of *natural* environmental protectionism, but it would also lead to self-denial. In contrast, hard-core *living* environmental protectionism has long been seen as simple egoism. Examining the history of Namche, however, it is apparent that the people of Namche have not cut down forests thoughtlessly. They managed forests using the *nawa* system. This system has only failed to work in the past few decades. The change in the villagers' business from trade and agro-pastoral farming to tourism undermined the *nawa* system, at least to some extent. When the national park was established, it practically eliminated the system.

The beautiful landscape of Namche was discovered, ravaged, and then enclosed to protect and restore its beauty. This is a microcosm of modernity, as experienced in many other landscapes. Yet this is not only an issue of landscapes. A landscape represents the entirety of the local people's way of life. The history of a landscape, therefore, represents both the history of the 'discoverer's' mind as well as that of the local people.

Even if the forests are 'restored' and the landscape resumes its former beauty, people in Namche, who may appear to continue to live undisturbed, cannot return to their former 'idyllic' life – as perceived by outsiders. The more the local people attempt to 'get rich(er),' the more complicated their problems will become. At the same time, the 'discoverer' of the landscape will have to accept the history of his or her own mind while struggling with the paradox of development and protection. No matter how we attempt to protect a landscape, we cannot take responsibility for it in its entirety – that is, including the history of the local people's way of life.

The environment protection system

Resource control in the Nepalese Himalayas

The Solu and Khumbu regions in Nepal are inhabited mainly by the Sherpa people. In particular, Namche in Khumbu makes an excellent base for Sagarmatha (Everest) climbers and was frequented by trekkers in the 1970s. Trekkers generally go from Kathmandu to Jiri by bus. Junbesi in Solu is another large village that these trekkers pass through on their way to Everest Base Camp. Namche and Junbesi are located at altitudes of 3400 meters and 2700 meters, respectively. Junbesi also has several lodges for trekkers, although not as many as Namche.

The Solu region, including Junbesi, is still densely forested. The forests and the pastures spreading across the cirque above the timberline are still used for transhumance – a livestock farming system involving seasonal movements of livestock.

The Sherpa people have basically made their living through agriculture, livestock farming and trade with Tibetan communities. Their lifestyle is based on livestock management, and livestock movements have determined their relationship with nature. Sherpas have at least three dwellings – summer pastures (*yersa*), winter pastures (*gunsa*), and houses in the villages – which they move between seasonally. In the rainy season they produce potatoes, barley and other crops for home consumption around their houses in the villages. During this period, they drive their livestock out of the villages to the higher summer pastures. The high pasture plants die in their snowy winter, so they move down with their livestock to less snowy pastures nearer to the villages. They also have grassland to produce hay to feed the livestock in early spring when there is not enough grass left in the winter pastures. They cut hay in autumn and dry it on the ground floors of their houses. These three types of pastures are not enough to provide for their livestock's needs, though. So, in the forest areas between these pastures, they feed leaves to their livestock. Forest grazing is an important part of their livestock farming.

To maintain this lifestyle, each community has had to control the order and timing of their space utilization. This must be carried out in a closed system that is exclusive to the members of each community. If the spaces of one community were open to others, the resources of those spaces could not be effectively managed. This is how the Sherpa people have maintained their commons without inviting tragedy.

Let us briefly examine the Khumbu and Solu regions to attempt to understand how they order their space and time, and how they have maintained this order. Solu and Khumbu have different bodies for managing their pastures and forests. In Khumbu, the villages manage the pastures; in Solu, patrilineal clans called '*ru*' possess the pastures and forests. A *ru* is an exogamous group. The Sherpa people are divided into nearly twenty *ru*. In Khumbu, each village has more than one *ru*, whereas in Solu, each village generally consists of a single *ru* (Table 5.1). But this does not mean that the villages effectively manage their pastures, for some villages have more than one *ru*. For example, Pankarma has two *ru*, each of which uses its own pastures.

The Basa Valley, stretching northward from Junbesi, is dotted with eight settlements, including Junbesi (twenty-nine families) and Pankarma (thirteen families). Junbesi and Pankarma each consist of a single clan called Lama and Salaka, respectively. Other settlements also consist mainly of Lama or Salaka. The forests and pastures along this valley are divided into areas that are each 'owned' by a particular *ru*. In each of these areas, only the *ru* that owns it is authorized to use it. Members of a *ru* are basically free to use the land possessed by the *ru*.

However, whether and when livestock are allowed on the land is regulated by the *ru*'s rules (called *tsai keku*). In relatively large areas, the clan uniformly restricts the periods when pasture is available for grazing. For example, Basa and Chalunka are the Lama clan's summer pastures located in the upper part of the valley. The days when the land in or above Basa (there is a fence along the lower part) is available for grazing are strictly determined by the clan (for further details, refer to Inamura and Furukawa 1995). The forests near a settlement and cultivated fields are not possessed by any clan, but are open to all villagers.

It is not known when this management system began. When land registers were established in 1952 by Nepalese law, these lands were registered but no changes were made to the management system. In 1994, however, the state declared that all lands, except for cultivated lands and houses, belong to the state. The forests were declared to be 'everyone's forests,' and, at least in the eyes of the law, the clans lost their lands. In 1995, the state delivered land registers to individuals who owned land. For people owning livestock, this sudden change caused enormous trouble – there was no way for them to implement such a change.

The region is not without signs of change, however. Around April 1994, when residents became aware that forest management would be put under state control, the communities in the region were disturbed by massive logging by some of the community members for commercial purposes. Practices began that would never have been allowed in earlier times. Another problem is a decreasing number of livestock farmers and their successors. The regular movements of livestock have thus far resulted in the successful monitoring of the forests and restrictions on their use.

Table 5.1: Clan composition in Solu and Khumbu

	Solu							Khumbu		
	Junbesi	Nauje	Pankarma	Mophun	Sunjima	Pukmuche	Ukpa & Indima	Namche Bazaar	Khunde	Dimboche
Old clan										
Thaktkwa								5	3	7
Paldorje								2	3	9
Nawa										13
Shire								3	3	5
Chawa								6		1
Pinasa				3				2		1
Taksindok								3		
Langkal									3	
Gardza									1	1
Lama	26			1						1
Salaka			11	17	6	2	5		1	
Goparma			2				4			
New clan										
Chusherwa								14	10	8
Shangku									5	5
Lhukpa									7	3
Sherwa									4	5
Mendewa								3		3
Ronserwa								11		2

Table 5.1: continued

	Solu							Khumbu		
	Junbesi	Nauje	Pankarma	Mophun	Sunjima	Pukmuche	Ukpa & Indima	Namche Bazaar	Khunde	Dimboche
Khampa or propertied Tibetan refugees										
Gurung								8		
Tamang								1		1
Newar										1
Dokpa									1	
Pelukpa								1		
Tibetan refugees, Kamba								11	7	4
Unknown										
Tasanga								1		
Kami										
Biswakarma	3							6		
Total	29	4	13	21	6	2	9	77	48	70

Data for Khumbu were collected in 1990 (Tsukihara and Furukawa 1991). Data for Solu were collected in 1994 (Inamura and Furukawa 1995)

If the livestock movements stopped, the forests would be simply reduced to unrestricted timber storage. It is possible that the forests of Solu may soon face a similar situation.

As mentioned, in Khumbu the land is not owned by clans, but by the village. Each village has its own pastures. For example, the village of Khumjung has pastures on the hill to the west of Dudh Kosi. Between the rivers Imja Khola and Khumbu Khola are pastures that belong to the next village, Khunde. A close examination of the distribution of the clans and their land use, however, seems to indicate that in earlier times the clans did control these lands, also (Brower 1991).

Movement of livestock and the use of forests were controlled by the *nawas*, appointed by each village. The village of Khumjung in Khumbu had two osho (livestock) *nawas* and three to four *shingo* (forest) *nawas* (Fürer-Haimendorf 1964).

As previously mentioned, at the beginning of June each year, the *osho nawas* drove the livestock out of the village after the annual festival called *dumjee*. Villagers were only allowed to bring their livestock back to the village after the potatoes and barley were harvested. In the meantime, the path from the village to the pastures was typically blocked by a small wall, and not a single animal was allowed in the village. Brower reports the only exception that he ever heard of was a case in 1985, when one zopkio (a cross between a yak and a cow) was allowed to stay in the village due to a broken leg (Brower 1991). This indicates how strictly this rule was enforced. Offenders would have had to pay a fine to the *nawas* – usually in the form of a set quantity of an alcoholic drink called '*chang*.'

Thus, removing livestock from specific places during periods determined by the village was the most important mechanism for managing resources. Removing the livestock from the village protected the crops in the fields. Similarly, by allowing animals into the village when there were no crops in the fields allowed the grass in the pastures to be fully grown before grazing began.

The main duties of the *shingo* (forest) *nawas* included granting permissions to villagers to cut a designated number of trees for specified purposes (such as house building and cremation) and checking the amounts of firewood the villagers kept in stock in their houses. As in Solu, only dead trees could be collected from the forests near the village, except for on certain special occasions. Offenders were subject to fines, which were normally paid in *chang* (Fürer-Haimendorf 1984).

Thus, it appears that, while the resource management systems differed slightly between Solu and Khumbu, the local people of both regions had maintained their respective systems over a long period of time in order to conserve their resources. These management systems, though, as we have seen, underwent significant changes in the 1970s. These changes were particularly dramatic in Khumbu, triggered by the designation of the entire region as a national park.

As discussed, in 1976 this entire region, including Namche, Khumjung and Khunde, was designated as the Sagarmatha National Park. By then, an airport had been constructed in Lukla, from where one can travel to Namche in two days. In 1972, another airport was constructed in Syangboche, the village immediately above Namche. The Nepalese government regarded these changes as an opportunity to increase tourism revenue, and wanted to establish a national park so it could charge admission. The New Zealand government, as we have seen, also wanted a national park, to protect the environment from the steadily increasing number of tourists. The Nepalese government then began to loudly spread the news about the dramatic environmental deterioration in the region. Several investigations of the environment in the region were conducted to provide background information, typically drawing conclusions such as: the natural environment enjoyed by early visitors to Khumbu is now on the verge of being lost because of uncontrolled grazing coupled with deforestation (Brower 1992).

The Sagarmatha National Park was soon established. The former *nawa* system was abolished and replaced by forest protection officers. Areas around the villages were soon enclosed for afforestation projects. Logging was (almost) totally banned (each resident is only permitted to cut down three trees in his/her lifetime to build a house). The park managers purchased all of the goats in the park and expelled them, on the grounds that goats eat saplings (Brower 1992; Furukawa 1991, 1992).

As discussed, the Sherpas' way of life was primarily based on raising livestock. Livestock and resource (such as grass and forest) management were inseparable. Their system of resource management was only possible through the villagers' joint efforts. The *nawa* system had been the basis of this management system, and its abolition inevitably changed the villagers' entire way of life.

Aid to the Nepalese Himalayas
Around the time that the Sagarmatha National Park was established, campaigns to draw attention to the environmental crisis in the

Himalayas intensified. They began to make noises about a crisis in the Himalayas, making various claims such as that the deforestation in the Himalayas would result in soil loss resulting in severe flooding in Bangladesh. These campaigns were always based on three points: (1) There has been excessive deforestation by villagers, so tree felling should be restricted and trees should be planted; (2) There has been overgrazing, so the number, kinds and movements of livestock should be restricted; and (3) The population has increased, so birth control should be introduced and practiced (Brower 1992). These analyses and their corresponding solutions do not hold true – at least not in the Solu and Khumbu regions, as demonstrated by the villagers' traditional resource management systems outlined above.

Nonetheless, these campaigns, coupled with broader ecology movements, became yet more powerful in the 1980s. The Solu and Khumbu regions were virtually overrun by international environmental protection and aid projects.

Since Hillary reached the summit of Everest in 1953, a series of aid measures had been granted to Sherpa communities under Hillary's auspices, mainly in Solu and Khumbu. In fact, the changes in the Khumbu communities, the establishment of the national park, and subsequent international aid – were all extensions of Hillary's initial aid efforts (Table 5.2).

Hillary's successful climb of Everest brought the Himalayas into the spotlight as a breathtaking tourist destination. Lukla Airport was constructed with Hillary's support, and made Himalayan trekking more accessible, leading to an inundation of tourists from all over the world. Undoubtedly, the growth of tourism changed the environment in Khumbu. More importantly, it changed the Sherpa people's way of life. Tenzing Sherpa was the man who accompanied Hillary to the summit of Everest, which made it known all over the world that Sherpas are competent assistants for Himalayan climbers. Providing guide services to tourists became an important business for Sherpas in Khumbu. English education at the schools established by Hillary for the Sherpas played a significant role in this.

These changes in the Sherpa communities led, in a way, to an over-reliance by the Sherpa communities on foreign aid. They also caused some dissolution of the Sherpa communities. For one thing, it has become common for tourists to become patrons of individual Sherpas, or whole families, and to finance the construction of their

Table 5.2: Aid to Khumbu

Period	Aid and investigation project	General movement in Khumbu
1920s		Sherpa assistants play important roles in British Everest climbers' teams
1950s		Hillary and Tenzing climb to the summit of Everest
		Many first successful climbs to the summits of Himalayan mountains
		A large number of Tibetans flow in as a result of the Tibetan revolt
1960s	A school is established in Khumjung	(Himalayan climbs banned during 1965–1968)
	An airport is constructed in Lukla	
	A hospital is constructed in Khunde	
	A watering place project	
1970s	A bazaar system is established	Himalayan trekking becomes a tourist attraction
	An airport is constructed in Shamboche	Many local people work as guides or porters or run lodges
	The Everest View Hotel is built	
	Forest investigation by New Zealand	*Bhatti* (teahouses) increase along the Everest trail
	Designation as a national park	Many local people flow out to Kathmandu.
1980s	A hydroelectric project (lighting available for four hours)	ODA aids are expanded
	Creation of no-go areas starts	
1990s	The *nawa* system is restored	The Panchayat system is abolished
	A water system construction project (water supply to each house)	
	An electrification project (electricity available twenty-four hours)	

Other new establishments include millitary and police forces, banks, post offices and health posts (Furukawa 1992).

lodges or their overseas study. For another, there has been a great increase in the number of local students who attend universities in Kathmandu or India as a result of the education they receive at the Hillary Schools. These students often stay in Kathmandu and find employment or travel abroad to work; they rarely come back to their home villages to live in.

This is not only the case with Namche but also Junbesi, despite the fact that the latter has had less tourism development. As of 1994, though, most of the children of the thirty-six families in Junbesi had left the village upon becoming adults and lived in Kathmandu. Moreover, as many as twelve former residents had taken up residency in foreign countries, including the U.S. and Japan (six in the U.S., three in Japan, and three in other countries).

The 'Hillary syndrome' and environmental issues

I have discussed changes in resource management in the context of modernization and foreign aid. The meanings of these events can be clearly understood by taking a bird's-eye view of the changes as events that occurred in only three or four decades of the Sherpa's long history.

According to our values, Sherpa communities have clearly become richer. In Nepal, one of the poorest countries in the world, some of the Sherpa communities are now among the wealthiest in the country. This is the result of aid they have received from all over the world, beginning with Hillary. These communities now have high literacy rates and excellent sanitary conditions. These are both results of the Hillary Schools and Hillary Hospitals. In the course of a very long history, in only three decades or so, huge amounts of aid were granted, resulting in the lives they now live. In the process, however, they became incapable of supporting themselves without that aid. Their former industries are on the verge of collapse. The bountiful nature that once surrounded them is being lost. It is no exaggeration to say that the Sherpa communities have been devastated. How long will these contradictions continue – destroying their communities on one hand, while continuing to provide aid on the other? We know that the aid provided by Hillary and the rest of the world was given with warmth and good intentions. However, good intentions do not always produce the intended results. It has become increasingly apparent that this aid and these good intentions were all based on 'Western' values. How will the Sherpa people earn a living once the aid stops? I call this kind of intervention – based on different values from those of the target community (whether with good or bad intentions) – the 'Hillary syndrome,' which entails the resultant changes that occur.

The changes to the Sherpa resource management systems clearly demonstrate the fact that aid will always require more aid, unless aid providers have a clear and correct understanding of how the local resource management systems work in the context of the local culture before aid is given. Failure to comply with these procedures will simply produce more communities in perpetual need of aid. To break the cycle of the Hillary syndrome, I believe that we must spend time in retelling the various ways and means of life embedded in the local communities in the context of a holistic or integrated way of life.

Conclusion: Towards Neo-Communalism

Small communities as the focus of observation

In macroscopic social change, societies have frequently marginalized small communities as passive entities. The fundamental purpose of this work has been to study the processes through which such communities actively and creatively respond to such changes, and thus present a new perspective for future studies of rural communities.

People who live in a community for a long time create social bonds based on common ties to their region or on blood relationships. They then establish relationships with other communities based on their own community-based identities. The nature and processes of community formation certainly vary, depending on historical conditions, the ecological environment and cultural contexts. There is, however, at least one point that they all have in common: every community includes a group of people who share a sense of membership in their particular community and who are well-versed in its history, including the histories of each of its member families. In Japan, the term '*mura*' corresponds to this group. I have referred to such communities throughout this work. Similar small communities are also found at the foot of the Himalayas, as discussed in the latter part of Chapter Five, albeit in a quite different historical and cultural context than Japanese villages.

The present study has focused on these small communities, emphasizing the importance of elucidating the historical and social bases of their potential for active adaptation to social change. I have argued that any discussion of this potential must be preceded by a thorough study of the processes through which such communities have emerged, with particular emphasis on the initiative that they have shown. This perspective may be termed 'neo-communalism.'[1]

Communitarianism is a powerful concept that emphasizes the importance of re-creating strong communities in contemporary societies. It developed primarily as a critique of liberalism. Liberalism emerged in the early modern era as a response to various forms of suppression and social inequality, placing the highest value on the rights and freedoms of self-regulating individuals. It was perhaps a necessary response to broad social changes such as the rapid dissolution of 'intermediate' forms of social organization (e.g., families, churches and neighborhood associations) and the increasing independence of individuals from social organizations.

The term liberalism refers to a broad spectrum of social philosophies, ranging from the libertarianism advocated by authors such as Nozick (1974) and Friedman and Friedman (1980) – who argue that individual freedom is primordial, and therefore social organization should be left to market mechanisms without any government intervention – to the egalitarian liberalism advocated by Rawls (1971), Dworkin (1977, 1989) and Sen (1982) – which imposes conditions on individual freedom, such as 'equal concern and respect' (Dworkin) or equal 'basic human capabilities' (Sen). Nonetheless, these liberal philosophies share an assumption that the individual exists as an isolated entity independent of society.

Communitarians reject this atomistic or monadic view of the human being, locating human identity in cooperative social activities. It has played an important role in countering the excesses of arguments for the right to self-determination in modern society, by highlighting the interdependency of the individual self on/with others – arguing that the construction of the self necessarily entails communal bonds.

On this basis, it would seem that the concept of the 'small community' advocated in this work belongs to the family of communitarianism. I prefer the term neo-communalism, however, due to considerable discomfort with communitarianism, primarily because the idea of community in communitarianism is quite vague. It vaguely subsumes the communal qualities and senses of community found in a broad range of social strata, from families to small neighborhood groups, organizations such as schools and churches, as well as municipalities, ethnic groups, nation states and the global family. It is thus understandable that many liberals fear that communitarianism could be reduced to yet another sect of narrow racialism or nationalism. In contrast, the type of community embraced by this work is the world of everyday life, in which the members of the community share a mutual understanding of their community's history and a specific sense of the community throughout its history. This is quite distinct from the vague notion of community found in communitarianism and is much closer to communalist philosophies.

Communalism is an idea that has been refined through studies of South Asia.[2] In this context, it emerged from India's struggle for independence from Britain, conceptualized through discussions of how each of the many heterogeneous groups would be able to maintain its own identity in a unified nation-state. The initial arguments were dominated by critics who emphasized how detrimental and backward such communalism would be to the construction of a nation-state, as the power elite aimed to establish a secular and homogeneous nation which denied the claims of separate identities by Hindu and Islamic groups, different castes, and numerous ethnic groups with distinct linguistic cultures.

However, this idea of a homogeneous nation of self-regulating individuals – which came to dominate independent India – was merely an imitation of the modern European nation-state. Opponents of this idea claimed that in a society as heterogeneous as India, there was nothing wrong with promoting the distinct identity of each of those groups whose members had shared a sense of community and a common history. They advocated communalism. Unlike communitarianism, the type of communalism they advocated entails a clear notion of a parent body to which members belong. This notion of communalism is much closer to the idea that I have advocated in the present work. In my view, however, the parent body is limited to *mura* as a dense accumulation of real-life activities, and excludes ethnic, religious and other 'imagined communities' whose members are highly anonymous. This is why I prefer the term 'neo-communalism.'

The communities that form parent bodies in this sense are not fixed or closed systems. Through various historical changes, they have been organized and re-organized for the changing convenience of their members. To develop an accurate picture of these communities, I have focused on analysis and description of the processes through which these *mura* communities emerged as independent bodies in the local society, although this may appear to be a somewhat roundabout approach. To put it plainly, my central task was to reconsider what *mura* is. In order to understand the processes by which a *mura* is organized in response to changes – whether internally or externally stimulated – I have embraced and attempted to deepen the 'living-based theory' and the 'interconversion theory' proposed by Aruga.

Let us briefly revisit Aruga's living-based theory.[3] Aruga restricts sociology to the study of social relationships and regards social relationships as 'direct intermediation' between the individual person (individual) and the group (collective). He does not consider social relationships to be fixed and argues that we must 'understand the process of formation and the formulated facet in association with each other.' These two aspects can exist only through intermediation. Specifically, in a social relationship, the process of formation (i.e. the historical aspect) and the formulated facet (i.e. the social aspect) intermediate.

Aruga defines the nature of life phenomena as follows:

> Since the nature of a certain practice in life is related to the nature of cultural phenomena in general, the nature of the practice must include that it is a social and historical phenomena. Therefore, its nature is nothing other than [the particular way] that the various forms of the practice are socially and historically related with each other. (1943: 21)

Therefore, the nature of a phenomenon in life must be defined so as to elucidate the 'social and historical interrelationships among the various forms by identifying social conditions occurring at moments of development' (Aruga 1943: 21). The historical perspective underlying this definition of nature is an important characteristic of Aruga's living-based theory.

Aruga's theory was constructed to define the nature and types of ethnic practices. His typological concepts (such as *dōzoku* and *kumi*) and the interconversion theory are thus structured to understand the characteristics of social relationships in this context.

According to Aruga, types are created by 'eliminating specific differences from individual social relationships [that are similar to] a certain extent.' Importantly, Aruga does not regard these types as predetermined by social evolution but as interconvertible depending on particular conditions. He thus opens the possibility for sociological studies of history by stating, 'The interrelationship or interconvertibility between different types of social relationships of the same kind remains unchanged throughout historical periods under certain conditions.'

Hence, the living-based theory can be summarized thus: life is a process continuously generated by interconversion between individual creativity and group norms (the living-based theory). The various practices and groups thus generated do not evolve in a predetermined direction but are interconvertible depending on conditions (the interconversion theory). From this change of perspective (i.e. rejecting the theory of evolution and accepting that social norms socialize individuals), we obtain the ideas of creativity and the unrestricted plasticity of people's lives, as well as the idea that a society or group controls and molds individuals according to internal principles.

Aruga astutely observed that *ie* – as an organizational unit specific to Japanese society – is a life community (rather than a prescriptive kinship community). He then conceived *mura* to be an accumulation of *ie*. I have called this view the 'living-based theory,' following Torigoe (1977). Based on this theory, various social systems can be flexibly and freely changed to improve and reform everyday life. This was made clear by considering examples of religious organizations in which such systems were believed to have worked in a fixed manner. This study has demonstrated that even fixed religious organizations such as *miyaza* have changed throughout their history in accordance with the logic of life.

By examining the processes of this change we revealed the communities' identity and its active resistance or adaptation to macro-level changes. As described in Chapter Two, since the beginning of the Meiji Period Japanese villages have been in danger of losing their autonomy as they were subsumed by the state's tax collection systems. As evident in the case of Chinai Village, however, villagers were not always open in their opposition to the state's impositions. Yet they maintained their independence by modifying their internal systems to resistant forms, clearly distinguishing what must be changed from what should be maintained.

From the perspective of protecting the living environment, the history of *mura* from the Meiji Period to the present can be regarded as a history of filling gaps – the gap between protecting particular territory and modes of production and protecting human life; gaps which gradually widened as religious affairs were increasingly divorced from administrative affairs and everyday life. Responsibility for protecting the local environment was increasingly assumed by the government. Moreover, centralized land improvement projects contributed to the individualization of farm management. In the process, the protection of territory and modes of production became independent from local communities. In other words, many areas of everyday life that were previously deemed to be village affairs became individual household affairs. At the same time, growing numbers of part-time farmers and non-farmer residents exacerbated the situation. Communities have attempted to maintain their local living environments by diversifying their modes of production (e.g., in Chinai, fish-farming and tourism have been developed). In the process, however, their community and their territory are no longer as integrated as they were when their way of life was inseparable from their mode of production. Their 'territories' have been reduced from a particular source of livelihood to a more abstract 'domain.'

The potential of everyday life knowledge

People must nevertheless continue to protect their living environment in some form or another in order to continue living in the same place. Unless each of us imagines himself/herself to be totally independent of all others – and leave all aspects of social life to the government – we must maintain community life in one form or another. Communities have sustained their frameworks of communal life though various means. In maintaining these frameworks, they have, in turn, continued to protect their living environment.

Communities' protection of the living environment is only possible via the everyday life knowledge embedded within the communities, as discussed in Chapters Four and Five. In this context, protecting the living environment means maintaining the independence of a small community to the extent necessary for its members' to live. These chapters revealed that in water use, the *mushi-okuri* ritual and forest management practices, organizations were established, routine procedures followed and sanctions imposed according to the particular conditions of the respective communities. We have seen that the everyday life knowledge in such communities includes mechanisms for preventing organizations, routine procedures and sanctions from becoming 'fixed' norms – that is, norms that are relative rather than absolute. Everyday life knowledge includes mechanisms for flexibly adapting local organizations, routine procedures and sanctions according to changes in both internal and external conditions. Conversely, adapting to internal and external conditions means flexibly adapting their everyday life knowledge whenever necessary, rather than holding fast to existing norms. Sometimes they may introduce something totally new, but they may also abandon it if it does not work out. This is part of the everyday life knowledge of a small community.

The potential of everyday life knowledge is seen in some of the events we have reviewed: the confusion immediately following the replacement of the traditional water supply and drainage systems by modern tap water systems in Chinai; the abandonment of the *mushi-okuri* for pesticides; and the replacement of the *nawa* system with the warden system in the Himalayan forests, where the former was a comprehensive system for managing livestock, forests and cultivated land while the latter is a monological scientific system of forest management. In basic terms, everyday life knowledge is specific rather than abstract, multi-functional rather than monological, and clearly aims at protecting the way of life of the people within the community rather than being value-neutral. It is also variable rather than fixed and is illogical in the sense that its diverse parts cannot be reduced to words. It is a body of knowledge that is constantly generated and modified through the interactions of all aspects of everyday life and with all of the environments surrounding everyday life. It is a comprehensive body of knowledge whose structure is difficult to understand – especially when one attempts to understand it using the 'scientific' methodology of reducing it to its constituent elements. In all of these respects, it is essentially the opposite of scientific knowledge, which is abstract, monological (i.e. it has a single function), (supposedly) value-neutral and – because it is communicated only linguistically – fixed. As a result, the life skills produced by everyday life knowledge are embodied in forms that are quite distinct from scientific skills. In recent years there have been various attempts to apply everyday life knowledge to scientific (technological) fields, as it becomes increasingly obvious that science is but another ideology and, as such, is not immune from history.

Life-environmentalism and the logic of small communities

Life-environmentalism, as detailed in Chapter One, intends to emphasize and take into account, in dealing with environmental issues, the ingenuity of people's efforts to live (everyday life knowledge) in small local communities. Everyday life knowledge is often embodied in frivolous, minute actions or in inconsistent, illogical words and deeds. The various social science disciplines have, to date, taken very little notice of these everyday life activities because they seem to be irrelevant to the concepts of development and protection encapsulated in clear and rational explications of the world.

Life-environmentalists have focused on the inexplicit systems embedded in community life, believing it to be impossible to discuss the protection of the global environment and the development of local economies without understanding how people maintain everyday life within their communities. This idea has certainly attracted criticism, including the claim that life-environmentalism is simply another logic of development that emphasizes the conservation of traditional ways of life in small communities; and that its methodology is faulty, since it is impossible for researchers to actually put themselves in the shoes of community members. I addressed the latter in Chapter One. The former critique also suggests that life-environmentalism lacks a position from which to criticize authority. This accurately highlights life-environmentalism's delicate position.

Life-environmentalism began, however, from a growing discomfort with the way that macroscopic critiques of authority have increasingly tended to diverge from the concrete lives of community members. Life-environmentalists intentionally emphasized the creativity that underlies everyday life logics and the rebellious spirits embodied in the traditions that have been unconsciously developed by ordinary people. They did so to highlight the fact that a grand theory, no matter how clear and rational, or how radical and critical it may appear, is merely a variant of modern epistemology. Whether for 'development' or 'protection,' the various arguments mounted about environmental issues have invariably been based on rational, systematic ways of thinking originating in modern Europe. Such arguments undervalue the everyday life of ordinary people living in local communities, neglecting the tacit understandings, knowledge and concrete practices of environmental protection that have developed 'on the ground,' so to speak. That is, they fail to appreciate the inexplicit, unscientific knowledge and practices of the people living in geographical areas with environmental problems. This is the attitude that Hillary displayed when, in his attempt to protect the forests of Namche, he invited villagers to New Zealand for education in the 'science' of forest management.

Japanese rural communities have been considerably restricted by external forces, particularly since the early 1980s. In this book I have attempted to demonstrate the potential of independent spirits by outlining various aspects of the everyday life practices of communities as they respond to external pressures. Their micro-level everyday life practices (everyday life knowledge) are not maintained by simply ignoring or directly resisting external pressures but employ a variety of other strategies, such as reorganizing or redirecting the focus of these pressures. I believe that the accumulation of the effects of this kind of practice will gradually break through the restrictions these pressures impose. In fact, there seem to have been a few cases where this kind of practice has begun to be taken into account in the development of environment policies.

At the same time, micro-level everyday life practices continue to generate independent bodies that create their own ways of life. In this sense, we could say that there are interactions between a communities' plasticity, its independence and its everyday life knowledge.

Various scholars have argued that small communities, where this sort of everyday life knowledge is still in practice, ought to be positioned as the main players in environmental protection. Such arguments have been developed by, among others, Hiroyuki Torigoe (1997a) and Yukiko Kada (1995). Although the present work has focused primarily on developments that occurred before Japan's rapid economic growth in the latter half of the twentieth century – partly due to the availability of reference materials – I believe that small communities still retain the potential for creating a new public spirit. I hope to further develop my arguments on this point by continuing my fieldwork and the search for new materials.

When dealing with environmental issues in the future, we must be fully self-aware of the kind of self-righteous authority that lurks in modern understandings of environmental issues, whether we accept or reject the approach of life-environmentalism. This must be the starting point for environmental sociology in the twenty-first century. Such self-awareness can only be realized through the spirit of criticism developed through fieldwork.

Notes

Introduction

1 I conducted fieldwork in this mountain village in Asahi-chō, Higashikamo County, Aichi Prefecture between 1992 and 1996 and was involved in the formulation of a regional development plan for the five adjacent municipalities.
2 Ken'ichi Miyamoto (1973) discusses the development process and social meanings of large-scale development projects.
3 This dispute has generated a mountain of literature. Kōhei Aoki (2002) and Takashi Kawamoto (1995) provide good introductory overviews.
4 Matsuda and Furukawa (2003) suggest the possibility of developing small community-ism into neo-communalism.

Chapter 1

1 For the history of studies in environmental sociology, please refer to: 'Kankyō mondai no shakaigaku-teki kenkyū (A sociological study of environmental issues),' in Nobuko Iijima (ed.) (1993) *Kankyō Shakaigaku* (Environmental sociology); Iijima (1998); and Saburō Horikawa (1999). For the basic concepts of environmental sociology, please refer to, for example: Hiroyuki Torigoe (1996, 1999); Saburō Horikawa (1996); and Shinji Katagiri (1995a). For an overview of the results of environmental sociology research, see 2001 *Kōza: Kankyō shakaigaku* (A seminar in environmental sociology) (five vols); and Shirīzu, 2000–2003, '*Kankyō shakaigaku* (Environmental sociology series) (six vols), Shin-yo-sha.
2 These are Minamata disease, Niigata disease, Yokkaichi asthma and itai-itai disease.
3 Examples of such movements include: the campaign in Ishigaki Island, Okinawa Prefecture to protect the coral reefs, the national trust movement in Tenjinzaki, Wakayama Prefecture, the campaign to protect the virgin beech forests in the Shirakami Mountains in Aomori and Akita Prefectures, and environmental movements for the Otaru Canal in Hokkaido and Odagahama beach in Imabari, Ehime Prefecture
4 See for example, 'Kankyō undō to NGO (Environmental movements and NGO),' in *Journal of Environmental Sociology*, issue 4.
5 For example, the following works had an enormous influence on sociological studies of environmental issues: Hikaru Shōji and Ken'ichi Miyamoto (1964) *Osorubeki kōgai* (Terrible pollution), and (1975) *Nihon no kōgai* (Pollution in Japan); Jun Ui (1971) *Kōgai genron* (The principles of pollution) (republished in a single volume in 1988); Muneaki Tajiri (1972) *Yokkaichi: Shi no umi to tatakau* (Yokkaichi: A battle against

death); Masazumi Harada (1972) *Minamata-byō* (Minamata disease); Yuzuru Hanayama (1978) *Kankyō seisaku wo kangaeru* (Thinking of environmental policy); Yoshiyuki Tsurumi (1982) *Banana to nihonjin* (Bananas and Japanese); and Daikichi Irokawa (ed.) (1983) *Minamata no keiji* (Revelation of Minamata) (two volumes).

Chapter 2

1 See for example, Yukiko Kada (1991), and Torigoe and Kada (eds) (1984).
2 See for example, Kazunori Matsumura (1995), and Matsumura and Aoki (eds)(1991).
3 Here Kawamoto is restricting production activities to land as fishermen who live on boats are uncommon in Japan and non-existent on Lake Biwa.
4 These three periods can each be associated with turning points in legislation, primarily concerning river and drainage management in rural communities. From this perspective, the first period is characterized by the 'Amendment of the Ward, Town and Village Council Act' (1884) and the 'River Law' (1896); the second period by the integration of forestlands in rural communities through revisions to the city-town-village system (1911) and a 'Supplementary guide to improvement of major drainage' (1923); and the third period by various measures taken by the agricultural administration, beginning with the 'Agricultural Basic Law' (1961), and the 'New River Law' (1964).
5 See Kada (1991) for a discussion of changes after 1907.
6 The title '*Kiroku*' by Chinai Village appears in Toshinao Yoneyama's (1967) *Nippon no mura no hyakunen* (One hundred years of Japanese villages). Although Yoneyama claims that the oldest volume of the Chinai *Kiroku* dates from 1859, my search of the documents found one dating from 1745. The *Kiroku* materials are of a subtle nature, being neither official documents nor personal diaries. Because it is not an official record, it was continuously maintained even after Chinai Village ceased to officially exist. Because it is not a personal diary, it had to be kept continuously up-to-date. It is therefore a highly valuable collection of documents. The greater part of the *Kiroku* dated before 1945 has been typed in collaboration with Yasuhiro Itō (Furukawa and Itō 1987–1993). We are currently reading and interpreting documents written during the last days of the Edo Period (1600–1868), which are difficult to read, and are compiling a database of all documents.
7 Chinai Village became part of Momose Village along with other villages. As the result Chinai Village is officially named Momose Ōaza Chinai.
8 Unless otherwise noted, all quotations in this work are from Furukawa and Itō (1987–1993). The code '/' means beginning of a new line in the original *Kiroku*. '??' signifies an unknown letter. Some personal names have been fictionalized.
9 Note a potential confusion in translation here, for the *osabun/kumigashira* translated as 'council of elders' here is composed of villagers who are members (*kyōgiin*/councilors) on account of the scale of their land-holdings. As we will see, though, in the 1902 revisions to these bylaws, this

system of privilege is abolished in favor of a council of elected members (*kyōgiin*), which we will refer to as the 'elected council.'
10 In the next section I outline the structure of rural communities in China, with a particular focus on *miyaza*.
11 *Miyaza* whose membership is held exclusively by certain privileged villagers are called *kabuza* (privileged union), while those whose membership is open to all villagers are called *muraza* (village union).
12 Although spelled with different *kanji* characters, both terms are pronounced the same.
13 The members of Chinai's *moroto* and *osabun* were extracted and compared from *Moroto kōmeichō* (Moroto register) (1898–1943) and *Kiroku*, respectively.
14 There were two ways to pay for village dues. First, villagers would attempt to pay by physical labor, and if this were not possible, they would pay by cash.Being unable to fulfill duties through labor does not signify poverty; rather, it indicates that there is no-one available to provide physical labor at that house. If a villager neither had money nor labor-power, he would be demoted to a lower class of villagers as a form of sanction, but have total exemption from village dues.
15 *Mizunoe* monkey indicates one specific year in the sixty-year Sexagenary (ten stems combined with twelve branches known as the Chinese zodiac).
16 That is, at each year's ritual, the *tōya* is appointed for the subsequent year, and will officiate at the next annual ritual, before being replaced, and so on.
17 Not all men are *yoboshi* members, only the first son is. When a boy is born, his name will be listed on a *yoboshi* note, making him a member of the village and locating him in the hierarchy of male villagers. We find this tradition relatively often in Shiga prefecture.
18 Major = head family, Middle = one of the oldest cadet families, and Minor = other cadet families. *Nengyōji* was chosen only from members of Major and Middle families, therefore we can say that the *nengyōji* was appointed according to 'class.'
19 This idea was inspired by Kyōko Ueda, particularly: 'This request as a social existence for protection of daily life by creating *mura* (village) can be understood as an aspiration for the village's function to provide security in villagers' daily life to the extent that each household is unable to do so.' (Ueda, Summary report at the 75th conference of the Japan Sociological Society, the 16th of November, 2002.)
20 Recent years have seen further individualization, such that even the household (family) is now seen to be endangered, reducing 'household affairs' to 'private affairs.'
21 Chinai River is situated on the village border of Chinai and Nishihama, thus fishing rights have been a source of conflict for years. The rights alternated between Chinai and Nishihama (decided upon by the Magistrate's office).
22 Note that documents related to lobbying and discussions during the period between 1873 and 1875 are contained in another volume.
23 *Chinai Gyogyō Kumiai enkaku shi* (History of Chinai Fishermen's Association), February 1905. The publisher and other details of this document are not known.

24 The business is called '*hinmin gyogyō sei* (the poor's fishing system) in the application for the establishment of the Chinai Fishermen's Association in 1889.
25 The Code of Savings Association was enforced in 1889. It is thus likely that when the general meeting was held in 1885, the part mentioning the Code of Savings Association at the end of the quotation did not exist.
26 *Kanoto* sheep indicates one specific year in the sixty-year Sexagenary (ten stems combined with twelve branches known as the Chinese zodiac).
27 According to a list in the *Kiroku* dated 1880, the village's total land value and other details are as follows:
   - Total value and acreage of the village's land: Acreage: 221.4 acres/ Land value: 39,319 yen 76 *sen*
   - Land tax: 1,171 yen 59 *sen* 3 *rin* (in 1875 and 1876; 3%)
   - Land tax: 980 yen 49 *sen* 6 *rin* (from 1877; 2.5%)
   - Breakdown: rice field, 162.7 acres/other fields, 26.8 acres/housing land, 5.9 acres/shrine land, 3.4 acres/temple land, 0.7 acres/reedland, 6.0 acres/grassland, 7.7 acres/bushes, 1.2 acres.
   - Others:/cemetery, 0.8 acres/swamp, 1.5 acres.
28 In 1915, the 'Momose Mura buraku yū zaisan touitsu ni kansuru kyōteisho (Agreement on integration of property owned by Momose Village communities)' was executed, but it did not go so far as to effect changes to the use of property exclusively owned by particular villages, such as Hiratoyama.
29 'Community dues' are collected from all villagers and 'community membership' dues are collected from those who have community membership. Both are used for the benefit of the village in the same way.
30 The term *sonmin* (villagers) first appeared in the *Kiroku* in 1881: '(after completion of shrine roof repairs) *sonmin were treated to rice cakes and sake*.' Before this term was first used, terms such as *murakata ittō* (all villagers) or *hyakushō ittō* (all farmers) had been used to mean roughly the same membership. The term *ittō* (literally: 'all' or 'everyone') was used until 1913, in such variations as 'Ōaza *ittō*' (all people in Ōaza) or *kumin ittō* (all residents in the district). The term *sonmin* was used until 1944 (or 1954, in the form of *sonmin zei* (villagers' tax). After that, the term *kumin* (district residents) was mainly used in place of *sonmin*.

Chapter 3

1 '*Dōzoku*' – literally: 'kin,' but member families are not necessarily related by blood; the system is characterized by vertical relationships between a head family and branch families.
2 Masao Gamō passed away before he was able to fully develop the conception of a '*tōya* community.'
3 Whether *miyaza*'s seniority system exists only within *miyaza* or reflects the broader community structure must be decided by future studies.
4 '*Sō-shō*' is a union of two or more *sō-son* formed within a manor.
5 In this respect, Andō (1984: 180) classifies *miyaza* as:
   - *Shō-miyaza* ("*shō*" – literally: 'manor'): One *miyaza* was formed for each manor. This type of *miyaza* had an extremely medieval character,

in that there were classes within *miyaza* and that disputes on *miyaza* among farmers were brought into *miyaza*.
- *Mura-miyaza*: One *miyaza* was formed for each village. This type of *miyaza* was formed with the formation of "*sō-son*" or "*gō-son*," after the start of the early-modern times. There were no classes within *miyaza*, and disputes on *miyaza* among farmers were not brought into *miyaza*.
- Composite *miyaza*: A *miyaza* system where *mura-miyaza* were formed in villages governed by a *shō-miyaza*.

This classification offers very important clues to understanding *miyaza*. How to deal with it in terms of rural community structure, however, must await future analysis.

6 As Gamō argues:
> The system in a "vertical community" under which the social status of its members is generally determined by birth and remains unchanged throughout their life seems to clearly show the inherent ideology of "adaptability to circumstances." On the other hand, the system in a "seniority community" under which the social status of its members changes as time passes cannot survive without the ideology of "adaptability to circumstances."

He adds that in a *tōya* community, 'rotational *tōya* is obviously based on the ideology of "adaptability to circumstances"' (Gamō 1979: 42–3).

7 Based on the historical record of studies conducted so far, it is safe to assume for our purposes that *miyaza* is typically seen in the Kinki region. However, as I intend to use *miyaza* as an important indicator of community types, I need to confirm exactly which regions *miyaza* are typically found in and its distribution. In this respect, Andō makes a notable comment: 'if rural communities in a feudal society are seen with a central focus on *miyaza*, they can be divided into *miyaza* communities and non-*miyaza* communities.' This is an attempt to understand *miyaza* as an analytical concept, rather than getting bogged-down in the subtle differences among different *miyaza* in specific arguments about its historicization. Andō seems to make an important point for linking historical science and sociology in *miyaza* studies.

8 So named by Kazuhiko Sumiya in 1968 in the title: 'Nihon no ie to kazoku – Aruga-Kitano ronsō no mondaiten (*Ie* and *kazoku* in Japan – The issues in the Aruga-Kitano Controversy),' *Shisō*, vol. 527 pp. 135–46.

9 Teizō Toda explains the characteristics of family as a group. 'Regardless of institution, family arises from the characteristics of a group, based on people's internal behavior' (1937) (*Kazoku kousei* (Family structure): 20). Also '[f]amily is fusion of personalities based on affection of couple, parent-child and close relatives and it is the relationship of subordination and collective production formed by these emotional fusion' (same as above: 48).

10 Takashi Nakano (1956) details the involvement of Aruga, Kitano and Hiroshi Oikawa at the beginning of *dōzoku* studies.

11 Yoshikazu Hasegawa argues that one issue remains unclear in Aruga's argument on the relation between the landlord-tenant relationship and *dōzoku*, and discusses this point in detail. According to Hasegawa (1981,1983), Aruga's theory on *ie* and *dōzoku* was constructed based on his research of Ishigami Village where the *nago* system – 'a typical

social system under which the landlord-tenant relationship overlaps with the *ie* relationship or *dōzoku* relationship' – had remained strong, and this prevented Aruga from clarifying differences between the landlord-tenant relationship and the *dōzoku* relationship. Hasegawa, who argues that differences between these two relationships must be clarified, claims that the differences are based on whether or not the members are related by blood. This point is a central part of Aruga's theory as well. In short, blood relations is not a factor that determines the way a specific member participates in the operation of *ie* or *dōzoku*.

12 The terms 'life community' (*seikatsu shūdan*) and 'kinship group' (*shinzoku shūdan*) are used here following Aruga's and Kitano's respective uses of these terms.

13 It seems inconsistent for Kitano to call *ie* and *dōzoku* kinship organizations (*shinzoku soshiki*) while admitting the existence of non-blood-related *ie* members and non-blood-related branch *ie*. This is a matter of how one understands the term 'kinship organization.' As Takashi Nakano puts it: 'If the concept of non-monophyletic kinship community, which includes the two types of "adoption" – adoption as relatives and adoption as non-relatives (live-in servants brought up and trained from childhood) – becomes widely used in the academic world, then I will not have to worry about being misunderstood when I say *dōzoku* is a "non-monophyletic kinship community"' (1981: 839). Kitano has roughly the same concept of *shinzoku* (kinship), and thus sees no inconsistency in calling *ie* and *dōzoku* kinship organizations.

14 The outline of the methodology that follows is a summary of 'Shakai kankei no kiso kōzō to ruikei no imi (The basic structure of social relationships and the meanings of types)' (Aruga 1947). Reference notes are omitted.

15 To oppose the concept of 'type' (*ruikei*), Aruga uses the term 'model' (*tenkei*), defining it as a form understood using 'individual, historical' concepts (1948c: 353).

Chapter 4

1 Iijima is a rare exception to this 'rule,' attempting to include the pollution of the feudal era within the history of pollution, stating, 'similarities to pollution cases in later periods…are seen in the nature of pollution and victims' behavior' (1984a).

2 Recall from Chapter Two that Chinai Village is divided into a lakeside area (Shimo-chinai) and an inland area (Age-chinai).

3 *Utetenai*: 'not hit' indicated that the water was drinkable, but hard. People used the word 'hit' because this type of water was not 'hit,' or 'pounded,' enough by nature (lake bottom, stones, shore, wind, etc) so it was not soft (therefore not tasty) water for them.

4 *Ike gumi* (*Ike* group) is an official unit name. Basically *Ike gumi* and *Ike nakama* are the same thing but people who belong to the *Ike gumi* call each other *Ike nakama*.

5 Sake has an important place in the cooperative activity of Japanese villages because, after cleaning the *ike* together, there is a feast followed, of course, by sake drinking.

6 This tax is not paid in cash: *Ike nakama* rent the land in common ownership. The rental rate is 80 *bu*, which is 80 *sen* (according to interview); a very cheap tariff compared with the normal rate. There are no precise rules regarding how to organize, manage and participate in *ike*. Ike have been used for more than 100 years, so *ike* membership is fixed.
7 Ōtsuka Minzoku Gakkai (Ōtsuka Folklore Society) (1972) *Nippon minzoku jiten* (Dictionary of Japanese folklore), Tokyo: Kobundo.
8 Torigoe explains the distinction between the 'world of self' and the 'world of others' as follows:
> People often do not interpret a matter or concern in the same way but choose to form different worlds of interpretation/meaning. H, if one refers to an individual's world of interpretation/meaning as the "world of self," the world consisting of individuals or groups whose worlds of interpretation/meaning are different can be referred to as the "world of others." (1989)

In this context, Torigoe asserts that the criterion for distinguishing between the 'world of self' and the 'world of others' is the 'attributes' of members constituting each group, in that they are observable by researchers. Motoji Matsuda has further developed this concept of 'attributes' (Matsuda 1985).
9 In Japan the first universal suffrage took place in 1890, but only rich men over twenty-five years of age could vote at the time. From 1925, all men older than twenty-five years of age could vote. Women had to wait until 1945.
10 See Nakayama, *Social History of Science and Technology*, vol. 1, on the occupation forces' instructions to replace light traps with DDT.
11 Chinai Shore can be found in Makino-cho Ōaza Chinai.

Chapter 5

1 Photos 5.1 and 5.2 were both taken near the Shinmei shrine (located near A's house), looking westward. The 1998 photo was taken from a site a bit further north of the location from which the 1950s photo was taken, because trees obstructed the view from the original site. In the mid-1950s, there were very few trees on the ridges on the left of the photo, but in 1998 many trees have grown in-between the planted trees, forming dense forests. The white structure below the dense forest in the upper center of the 1950s photo is a small shrine for Jizō, where the Shintō ceremony of *hikiri* (fire kindling) is performed.
2 Photos 5.3 and 5.4 were taken from the small Jizō shrine (seen in Photos 5.1 and 5.2), looking eastward. Again, the 1998 photo was taken from a site considerably higher than that from which the 1950s photo was taken, because trees now obstruct the view from the original location. The ridges in Photos 5.1 and 5.2 can be seen at the center-right of Photo 5.3. The Shinmei shrine can be seen at the center, where trees were cut back to form a clearing. A similar clearing can be seen in the 1998 photo (Photo 5.4).
3 A system in which a person (forest manager) other than the landowner plants, grows and otherwise manages trees, and the earned income is shared in a defined ratio between the forest manager and the landowner.
4 'Mitigation' means to relieve the anticipated negative effects of development and other human actions on the natural environment by means such as avoidance, minimization or replacement.

5 Contrary to Industrial Forestry, Social Forestry aims to develop both economy and the preservation of natural resources by giving local people living in rural areas the ownership and management of forestry in order to meet their demands.

Conclusion

1 My argument has been inspired by discussions with Hiroyuki Torigoe, Yukiko Kada and Motoji Matsuda. Their arguments presented have some common bases, although they also have subtle differences. My path to assuming a communalist position is described in detail in Furukawa and Matsuda (2003) and Matsuda and Furukawa (2003). In those works I explored the controversy between liberals and communitarians, referring to both primary and secondary sources. Secondary sources that I found particularly helpful include those by Kawamoto (1995), Aoki (2002) and Saitō (2000), which clearly and lucidly explain the controversy, and those by Fujiwara (1993), Tsuchiya (1996) and Mamiya (1999), which helped me to locate it in the context of the actual situation of small local communities.
2 My understanding of the communalism found in South Asia studies is based on the works of Kotani (1993), Dumont (2001), Basu (2000) and Sharma ((ed.) 1998). Note, however, that the term 'communalism' has also been variously defined. For example, Bookchin (1994) developed it as a movement aiming for communes. For present purposes, I use the term only in the context of South Asia studies.
3 Torigoe (1977) provides a highly informative account of Aruga's living-based theory.

Bibliography

Andō, Seiichi (1960) *Kinsei miyaza no shi-teki kenkyū* (A historical study of early-modern *miyaza*), Tokyo: Yoshikawa Kōbunkan.

Andō, Seiichi (1984) *Kinsei nōson-shi no kenkyū* (A study of the early-modern history of rural communities), Osaka: Seibundō Shuppan.

Aoki, Kōhei (2002) *Komyunitariarizumu he – kazoku, shi-teki shoyū, kokka no shakai tetsugaku* (Toward communitarianism: Social philosophy of family, private property and the state), Tokyo: Shakai Hyōronsha.

Ariès, Philippe, Toshio Nakauchi and Nobuko Morita (eds) (1992) *L'histoire des Mentalites; Problemes de L'education*, Tokyo: Fujiwara Shoten.

Aruga, Kizaemon (1943) 'Nihon kazoku seido to kosaku seido (Japanese family system and tenancy farming system),' in *Aruga Kizaemon chosaku shū* (Collection of Kizaemon Aruga's works), vols 1 and 2, Tokyo: Miraisha.

Aruga, Kizaemon (1947) 'Dōzoku to shinzoku (*Dōzoku* and kinship),' in *Aruga Kizaemon chosaku shū*, vol. 10, Tokyo: Miraisha.

Aruga, Kizaemon (1948a) 'Sonraku seikatsu – mura no seikatsu soshiki (Rural community life: Life organizations in rural communities),' in *Aruga Kizaemon chosaku shū*, vol. 5, Tokyo: Miraisha.

Aruga, Kizaemon (1948b) 'Toshi shakaigaku no kadai (Topics in urban sociology),' in *Aruga Kizaemon chosaku shū*, vol. 8, Tokyo: Miraisha.

Aruga, Kizaemon (1948c) 'Nihon kon'in-shi ron (Discussion on history of the Japanese marriage system),' in *Aruga Kizaemon chosaku shū*, vol. 6, Tokyo: Miraisha.

Aruga, Kizaemon (1952) 'Nihon no ie (*Ie* in Japan),' in *Aruga Kizaemon chosaku shū*, vol. 7, Tokyo: Miraisha.

Aruga, Kizaemon (1960) 'Kazoku to ie (Family and *ie*),' in *Aruga Kizaemon chosaku shū*, vol. 9, Tokyo: Miraisha.

Aruga, Kizaemon (1962) 'Dōzoku dan to sono henka (*Dōzoku* groups and their changes),' in *Aruga Kizaemon chosaku shū*, vol. 10, Tokyo: Miraisha.

Aruga, Kizaemon (1965) 'Ie no rekishi (History of *ie*),' in *Aruga Kizaemon chosaku shū*, vol. 11, Tokyo: Miraisha.

Aruga, Kizaemon (1966) 'Shinpan no jo (Preface to the new edition),' in *Aruga Kizaemon chosaku shū*, vol. 1, Tokyo: Miraisha.

Aruga, Kizaemon (1974) 'Ie to hōkōnin (*Ie* and servants),' in *Sonraku kōzō to shinzoku soshiki* (Rural community structure and kinship organization), Tokyo: Miraisha.

Asahi-chō Shi Henshū Kenkyū Kai (Study Group for the Edition of History of Asahi-chō) (1981) in *Asahi-chō shi* (The history of Asahi-chō), Asahi-chō.

Basu, Sajal (2000) *Communalism, Ethnicity and State Politics*, Jaipur: Rawat Publications.

Bookchin, Murray (1994) *What is Communalism? The Democratic Dimension of Anarchism*, An Online Research Center on the History and Theory of Anarchism.

Brower, Barbara (1991) *Sherpa of Khumbu*, Delhi: Oxford University Press.

Brower, Barbara (1992) 'Crisis and conservation in Sagarmatha National Park, Nepal,' in Messerschmitt, D.A. and Rai, N.K. (eds), *Social Forestry and Natural Resource Management for Nepal*, Kathmandu: HMG Ministry of Agriculture-Winrock International, pp. 171–85.

Catton, William R., Jr. and Riley E. Dunlap (1978) 'Environmental sociology: a new paradigm,' *The American Sociologist*, 13: 41–9.

Dumont, Louis (1967) *Homo Hierarchicus: Essai sur le Système des Castes*, Paris: Gallimard.

Dunlap, Riley E. (1980) 'Paradigm change in social science: From human exemptionalism to an ecological paradigm,' *American Behavioral Scientist*, 24: 5–14.

Dworkin, Ronald (1977) *Taking Rights Seriously*, Cambridge: Harvard University Press.

Dworkin, Ronald (1989) 'Liberal community,' *California Law Review*, 77: 479–504.

Emori, Itsuo (1976) *Nihon sonraku shakai no kōzō* (The structure of Japanese rural communities), Tokyo: Kōbundō.

Fisher, James F. (1990) *Sherpas: Reflection on Change in Himalayan Nepal*, Delhi: Oxford University Press.

Friedman, Milton and Rose Friedman (1980) *Free to Choose: A Personal Statement*, New York: Harcourt Brace Jovanovich.

Fujimura, Miho (1996) 'Shakaigaku to ekorojī – R. E. Dunlap no riron no kentō (Sociology and ecology: A study on R. E. Dunlap's theory),' *Kankyō shakaigaku kenkyū* (Journal of Environmental Sociology), vol. 2, Tokyo: Shin-yo-sha.

Fujiwara, Yasunobu (1993) *Jiyūshugi no saikentō* (A review of liberalism), Tokyo: Iwanami Shoten.

Fukutake, Tadashi (1948) 'Waga kuni nōson shakai no ni ruikei (The two types of farming communities in Japan),' republished as 'Dōzoku ketsugō to kōgumi ketsugō (*Dōzoku* bond and *kōgumi* bond)' in *Fukutake Tadashi chosaku shū* (Collection of Tadashi Fukutake's works), vol. 4, Tokyo: University of Tokyo Press.

Fukutake, Tadashi (ed.) (1965) *Chiiki kaihatsu no kōsō to genjitsu* (Plans and realities of regional development), vols 1–3, Tokyo: University of Tokyo Press.

Funabashi, Harutoshi, Kōichi Hasegawa, Munekazu Hatanaka, Harumi Katsuta (1985) *Shinkansen kōgai – kōsoku bunmei no shakai mondai* (Shinkansen pollution: Social problems in the age of high speed), Tokyo: Yūhikaku.

Funabashi, Harutoshi, Kōichi Hasegawa, Munekazu Hatanaka, Takamichi Kajita (1988) *Kōsoku bunmei no chiiki mondai – Tōhoku shinkansen no kensetsu, funsō to shakai-teki eikyō* (Regional issues in the age of high speed: Construction, dispute and social consequences of Tōhoku Shinkansen), Tokyo: Yūhikaku.

Funabashi, Harutoshi (1993) 'Shakai seigyo to shite no kankyō seisaku (Environment policies as social control),' in Nobuko Iijima (ed.), *Kankyō shakaigaku* (Environmental sociology), Tokyo: Yūhikaku.

Funabashi, Harutoshi (1995) 'Kankyō mondai he no shakaigaku-teki shiza – shakai-teki jirenma ron to shakai seigyo shisutemu (A sociological perspective on environmental issues: The social dilemma theory and social control systems),' *Kankyō shakaigaku kenkyū* (Journal of Environmental Sociology), vol. 1, Tokyo: Shin-yo-sha.

Funabashi, Harutoshi and Nobuko Iijima (eds) (1998) *Kōza shakaigaku 12: Kankyō* (Sociology lecture 12: Environment), Tokyo: University of Tokyo Press.

Funabashi, Harutoshi, Kōichi Hasegawa and Nobuko Iijima (eds) (1998) *Kyodai chiiki kaihatsu no kōsō to kiketsu – Mutsu Ogawara kaihatsu to kaku nenryō risaikuru shisetsu* (Plans and results of large-scale community development: The development of Mutsu Ogawara and its nuclear fuel recycling facilities), Tokyo: University of Tokyo Press.

Fürer-Haimendorf, Christoph Von (1964) *The Sherpas of Nepal: Buddhist Highlanders*, London: Jon Murray.

Fürer-Haimendorf, Christoph Von (1975) *Himalayan Traders: Life in Highland Nepal*, London: Jon Murray.

Fürer-Haimendorf, Christoph Von (1984) *The Sherpas Transformed*, Delhi: Sterling Publishers Pvt. Ltd.

Furukawa, Akira (1983) 'Kogan shūraku no dentō-teki yō haisui shisutemu (Traditional water supply and drainage systems in lakeside communities),' in Hiroyuki Torigoe (ed.), *Kohan jūmin no seikatsu hensen to Biwa-ko no imēji* (Changes in the life of lakeside residents and the image of Lake Biwa), Shiga Ken Biwa-ko Kenkyū-jo (Lake Biwa Research Institute, Shiga Prefecture).

Furukawa, Akira (1984) 'Kawa to ido to mizuumi – kogan shūraku no dentō-teki yō haisui (Rivers and wells and the lake: Traditional water supply and drainage in lakeside communities),' in Hiroyuki Torigoe and Yukiko

Kada (eds), *Mizu to hito no kankyōshi – Biwako hōkokusho* (The history of the environment for water and people: Lake Biwa report), Tokyo: Ochanomizu Shobō.

Furukawa, Akira (1985) 'Mizu no fūkei (Landscapes of water),' in *Kokoku to bunka* (The lake state and culture), vol. 35, Shiga Ken Bunka Taiiku Shinkō Jigyō Dan (Cultural Promotion Corporation, Shiga).

Furukawa, Akira and Yasuhiro Itō (1987–1993) 'Kō-shū Chinai-mura "Kiroku" 1745–1945 Mura no nikki (1)–(12) ("Kiroku (Records)" of Chinai Village, Kō Province, 1745–1945, Village diaries (1)–(12)),' *Chūkyō Daigaku Shakaigakubu kiyō* (Bulletin of Chukyo University School of Sociology), 2–1 through 8–1.

Furukawa, Akira and Yasuhiro Itō (1989) 'Mura kiyaku – Kō-shū Chinai-mura "Kiroku" (ho) (Village bylaws: "Kiroku (Records)" of Chinai Village, Kō Province, (Suppl.)),' *Chūkyō Daigaku Shakaigakubu kiyō*, 4–2.

Furukawa, Akira (1990) 'Himaraya kōchi jūmin no kankyō ninshiki kenkyū nōto (Research notes on environmental awareness among Himalayan highlanders),' *Himaraya-gaku shi* (Himalayan studies monographs), vol. 1, Kyoto Daigaku Himaraya Kenkyū Kai (Society for Himalayan studies, Kyoto University).

Furukawa, Akira (1991) 'Sagarumata Kokuritsu Kōen no seiritsu to jūmin no kankyō mondai – Himaraya kōchi jūmin no kankyō ninshiki kenkyū nōto (The establishment of the Sagarmatha National Park and residents' environmental issues: Research notes on environmental awareness among Himalayan highlanders),' *Himaraya-gaku shi* (Himalayan studies monographs), vol. 2, Kyoto Daigaku Himaraya Kenkyū Kai.

Furukawa, Akira (1992) 'Himaraya shinrin keikan ron – fūkei to kankyō mondai (A study on landscapes of Himalayan forests: Landscapes and environmental issues),' in Akira Furukawa and Yukio Ōnishi (eds), *Kankyō imēji ron – Ningen kankyō no jūsō-teki fūkei* (Studies on images of the environment: Multilayered landscapes of the human environment), Tokyo: Kōbundō.

Furukawa, Akira and Yukio Ōnishi (eds) (1992) *Kankyō imēji ron – Ningen kankyō no jūsō-teki fūkei* (Studies on images of the environment: Multilayered landscapes of the human environment), Tokyo: Kōbundō.

Furukawa, Akira (1994) 'Futatsu no miyaza no hen'yō katei – miyaza-gata sonraku ron (The transformation process of two *miyaza*: A study on rural communities with *miyaza*),' in Tadashi Inoue, Osamu Soda and Katsuyoshi Fukui (eds), *Bunka no chiheisen* (The horizon of cultures), Kyoto: Sekai Shisōsha.

Furukawa, Akira and Motoji Matsuda (2003) 'Kankō to iu sentaku – kankō, kankyō, chiiki okoshi (Tourism as a choice: Tourism, environment and community development projects),' in Akira Furukawa and Motoji

Matsuda (eds), *Kankō to kankyō no shakaigaku* (Sociology of tourism and environment), Tokyo: Shin-yo-sha.

Gamō, Masao (1958) 'Shinzoku (Kinship),' *Nihon minzokugaku taikei* (An anthology of Japanese folklore studies), vol. 3, Tokyo: Heibonsha.

Gamō, Masao (1979) 'Nihon no ie to mura (*Ie* and *mura* in Japan),' *Sekai no minzoku 13: Higashi ajia* (Peoples of the world 13: East Asia), Tokyo: Heibonsha.

Gamō, Masao (1982) 'Nihon no dentō-teki shakai kōzō to sono henka ni tsuite (The traditional structures of Japanese communities and their changes),' *Meiji daigaku seikei ronsō* (Collection of works of the School of Political Science and Economics, Meiji University), pp. 55–6.

Gekkan Yahagi-gawa Dōjin (The Monthly Yahagi River Club) (1977–1985) *Gekkan Yahagi-gawa* (The Monthly Yahagi River), Nos.1 through 100, Gekkan Yahagi-gawa Dōjin.

Gibson, James J. (1979) *The Ecological Approach to Visual Perception*, Boston: Houghton Mifflin.

Graner, Elvira (1997) *The Political Ecology of Community Forestry in Nepal*, Saarbrücken: Verlag für Entwicklungspolitik.

Hagiwara, Tatsuo (1962) *Chūsei saishi soshiki no kenkyū* (A study of medieval ritual organizations), Tokyo: Yoshikawa Kōbunkan.

Hagiwara, Tatsuo (1978) *Kamigami to sonraku* (Gods and rural communities), Tokyo: Kōbundō.

Hanayama, Yuzuru (1978) *Kankyō seisaku wo kangaeru* (Thinking of environment policy), Tokyo: Iwanami Shoten.

Hara, Hiroko (1979) *Kodomo no bunka jinruigaku* (Cultural anthropology for children), Tokyo: Shōbunsha.

Harada, Masazumi (1972) *Minamata-byō* (Minamata disease), Tokyo: Iwanami Shoten.

Harada, Rie (1997) 'Minamata-byō kanja dai-ni sedai no aidentiti – Minamata-byō wo katari hajimeta "kibyō no ko" no seikatsu-shi yori (The identity of second-generation patients of Minamata disease: From the life history of "children with a rare disease" who began to talk about Minamata disease),' *Kankyō shakaigaku kenkyū* (Journal of Environmental Sociology), vol. 3, Tokyo: Shin-yo-sha.

Harada, Toshiaki (1975) *Mura no saishi* (Religious rituals in villages), Tokyo: Chūō Kōronsha.

Harada, Toshiaki (1976) *Mura matsuri to za* (Village festivals and *za*), Tokyo: Chūō Kōronsha.

Hardin, Garrett (1968) 'Tragedy of the commons,' *Science*, vol. 162, 13th of December, pp. 1243–8.

Hardin, Garrett (1974) 'Life boat ethics: The case against helping the poor,' *Psychology Today*, September: pp. 39–43, 123–6.

Hasegawa, Kōichi (1996) *Datsu-genshiryoku shakai no sentaku – shin-enerugī kakumei no jidai* (A choice for a post-nuclear society: The age of the new energy revolution), Tokyo: Shin-yo-sha.

Hasegawa, Yoshikazu (1981 and 1983) 'Dōzoku dan no shogen-teki keitai to futatsu no kakeifu (Original forms of *dōzoku* groups and the two family trees),' *Kōbe Daigaku Bungakubu kiyō* (Bulletin of the Faculty of Letters, Kōbe University), vols. 9 and 10.

Higo, Kazuo (1941) *Miyaza no kenkyū* (A study of miyaza), Tokyo: Kōbundō.

Hillary, Sir Edmund (1984) 'Learning about the problems,' in Sir Edmund Hillary (ed.), *Ecology 2000*, London: Michael Joseph.

Hirano, Toshimasa (1981) 'Aruga Kizaemon no ie riron (Kizaemon Aruga's theory on ie),' *Kazoku-shi kenkyū* (Family history studies), vol. 4, Tokyo: Kōbundō.

Hiraoka, Yoshikazu (1993) 'Kaihatsu tojō-koku no kankyō mondai (Environmental problems in developing countries),' in Nobuko Iijima (ed.), *Kankyō shakaigaku* (Environmental sociology), Tokyo: Yūhikaku.

Hiraoka, Yoshikazu (1996) 'Kankyō mondai no kontekusuto to shite no sekai shisutemu (The global system in the context of environmental issues),' *Kankyō shakaigaku kenkyū* (Journal of Environmental Sociology), vol. 2, Tokyo: Shin-yo-sha.

Horikawa, Saburō (1996) 'Kōgai/kankyō mondai to kankyō shakaigaku (Pollution/environmental problems and environmental sociology),' in Arisue Ken, Shimono Toshiaki, Sekine Masami (eds), *Shakaigaku nyūmon* (An introduction to sociology), Chapter 10, Tokyo: Kōbundō.

Horikawa, Saburō (1999) 'Sengo nihon no shakaigaku-teki kankyō mondai no kiseki – 1945–1998 nen wo chūshin ni shita kenkyū dōkō (The history of sociological studies on environmental issues in postwar Japan: Research trends mainly seen in 1945–1998),' *Kankyō shakaigaku kenkyū* (Journal of Environmental Sociology), vol. 5, Tokyo: Shin-yo-sha.

Humphrey, Craig R. and Frederick R. Buttel (1982) *Environment, Energy and Society*, Belmont: Wadsworth Publishing Company.

Iijima, Nobuko (ed.) (1977) *Kōgai/rōsai/shokugyō-byō nenpyō* (The chronological table of environmental pollution, industrial accidents and occupational disease), Kōgai Taisaku Gijutsu Dōyū Kai (Association of Environmental Pollution Control Technology).

Iijima, Nobuko (1984a) 'Kōgai-shi (The history of pollution),' in Nihon Kankyō Gakkai Henshū Iinkai (Editorial Committee, Japan Association for Environmental Studies) (ed.), *Kankyō kagaku e no michi* (The road to environmental science), Tokyo: Yūhikaku.

Iijima, Nobuko (1984b) *Kankyō mondai to higaisha undō* (Environmental issues and victim movements), Tokyo: Gakubunsha.

Iijima, Nobuko (ed.) (1993) *Kankyō shakaigaku* (Environmental sociology), Tokyo: Yūhikaku.

Iijima, Nobuko and Harutoshi Funabashi (eds) (1999) *Niigata Minamata-byō mondai – kagai to higai no shakaigaku* (The issue of Niigata Minamata disease: Sociology of perpetrators and victims), Tokyo: Tōshindō.

Iijima, Nobuko (1998) 'Sōron: Kankyō mondai no rekishi to kankyō shakaigaku (Overview: The history of environmental issues and environmental sociology),' in Harutoshi Funabashi and Nobuko Iijima (eds), *Kōza shakaigaku 12: Kankyō* (Sociology lecture 12: Environment), Tokyo: University of Tokyo Press.

Ikeda, Kanji (1996) 'Kankyō shakaigaku no shoyū-ron-teki pāsupekutibu – "gurōbaru komonzu no higeki" wo koete (A perspective from environmental sociology in the context of ownership theories: Beyond the "tragedy of the global commons"),' *Kankyō shakaigaku kenkyū* (Journal of Environmental Sociology), vol. 2, Tokyo: Shin-yo-sha.

Inamura, Tetsuya and Akira Furukawa (1995) 'Nepāru, Himaraya, Sherupa zoku no kankyō riyō – Junbeshi-Basa dani ni okeru toransuhūmansu (Utilization of the environment by the Sherpas in the Himalayas, Nepal: Transhumance in Junbesi, Basa Valley), *Kankyō shakaigaku kenkyū* (Journal of environmental sociology), vol. 1, Tokyo: Shin-yo-sha.

Inoue, Makoto (1995) *Yakihata to nettai-rin – Karimantan no dentō-teki yakihata shisutemu no hen'yō* (Slash-and-burn and tropical forests: Changes in the traditional slash-and-burn system in Kalimantan), Tokyo: Kōbundō.

Inoue, Shun, Chizuko Ueno, Masachi Ōsawa, Munesuke Mita, and Shunya Yoshimi (eds) (1996) *Iwanami kōza, gendai shakaigaku 25: Kankyō to seitaikei no shakaigaku* (Iwanami's lectures, contemporary sociology 25: The sociology of environment and ecosystem), Tokyo: Iwanami Shoten.

Inoue, Takao (1996) *Shirakami Sanchi to Seishū Rindō – chiiki kaihatsu to kankyō hozen no shakaigaku* (The Shirakami Mountains and Seishū Forestry Road: Sociology of regional development and environment protection), Tokyo: Tōshindō.

Inoue, Tatsuo (1986) *Kyōsei no sahō – kaiwa to shite no seigi* (Proper manners of coexistence: Justice as conversation), Tokyo: Sōbunsha.

Irokawa, Daikichi (ed.) (1983) *Minamata no keiji (jō, ge)* (Minamata Revelation vols. 1 and 2), Tokyo: Chikuma Shobō.

Itō, Yasuhiro (1984) 'Gyojō sōron (The controversy over fishing grounds),' in Hiroyuki Torigoe and Yukiko Kada (eds), *Mizu to hito no kankyōshi – Biwako hōkokusho* (The history of the environment for water and people: Lake Biwa report), Tokyo: Ochanomizu Shobō.

Iwamoto, Yoshiteru (1985) 'Senzen ni okeru nōsei to sonraku (Agricultural administration and rural communities in prewar times),' Sonraku Shakai Kenkyū Kai (Japanese Association for Rural Studies) (ed.), *Sonraku shakai kenkyū* (Journal of Rural Studies), vol. 19, Ochanomizu Shobō.

Kada, Yukiko (1984) 'Mizu riyō no henka to mizu no imēji (Changes in water use and the image of water),' in Hiroyuki Torigoe and Yukiko Kada (eds), *Mizu to hito no kankyōshi – Biwako hōkokusho* (The history of the environment for water and people: Lake Biwa report), Tokyo: Ochanomizu Shobō.

Kada, Yukiko (1991) 'Kankyō kanri shutai to shite no sonraku soshiki to sono hen'yō – Biwa-ko gan no mura no hyakunen no rekishi kara (A rural community organization as the environment manager and its transformation: From the one-hundred year history of a village on the shore of Lake Biwa),' in Sonraku Shakai Kenkyūkai (Japanese Association for Rural Studies) (ed.), *Tenkanki nōson no shutai keisei – sonraku shakai kenkyū* (Establishment as actor of rural communities at their turning point; Rural studies), vol. 27, Nōsangyoson Bunka Kyōkai (Rural Culture Association).

Kada, Yukiko (1993) 'Kankyō mondai to seikatsu bunka – mizu kankyō osen wo tegakari ni (Environmental issues and lifestyles: Using water pollution as a lead),' in Nobuko Iijima (ed.), *Kankyō shakaigaku* (Environmental sociology), Tokyo: Yūhikaku.

Kada, Yukiko (1995) *Seikatsu sekai no kankyōgaku* (Environmentology in the world of everyday life), Nōsangyoson Bunka Kyōkai (Rural Culture Association).

Kankyō Chō (Environment Agency) (ed.) (1998) *Kankyō hakusho (sōron, kakuron)* (White paper on environment (general and particular)), Ōkurashō Insatsukyoku (Printing Bureau, Ministry of Finance).

Katagiri, Shinji (1995a) 'Kankyō (Environment),' in Takashi Miyajima (ed.), *Gendai shakaigaku* (Modern sociology), Chapter 7, Tokyo: Yūhikaku.

Katagiri, Shinji (1995b) *Shakai undō no chū-han'i riron – shigen dōin ron kara no tenkai* (Middle-range theory of social movements: An approach from the resource mobilization perspective), Tokyo: University of Tokyo Press.

Kawamoto, Akira (1972) *Nihon nōson no ronri* (The logic of Japanese rural villages), Tokyo: Ryūkei Shosha.

Kawamoto, Akira (1983) *Mura no ryōiki to nōgyō* (The territory and farming of the rural community), Ie-No-Hikari Kyōkai (Ie-No-Hikari Association).

Kawamoto, Takashi (1995) *Gendai rinrigaku no bōken – shakai riron no nettowākingu he* (An adventure of modern ethics: Towards networking among social theories), Tokyo: Sōbunsha.

Keizai Kikaku Chō (Economic Planning Agency) (1962) *Zenkoku sōgō kaihatsu keikaku* (Japan's Comprehensive National Development Plan), Ōkurashō Insatsukyoku (Printing Bureau, Ministry of Finance).

Keizai Kikaku Chō (1969) *Shin zenkoku sōgō kaihatsu keikaku* (Japan's New Comprehensive National Development Plan), Ōkurashō Insatsukyoku.

Kitagawa, Takayoshi and Kiyoshi Ishikawa (1965) 'Kōgyōka no shinten to chiiki shakai no henka – Shizuoka-ken Mishima-shi chōsa hōkoku (Industrialization and community change: An investigation report of Mishima-shi, Shizuoka Prefecture),' *Shakai rōdō kenkyū* (Society and labour), vol. 11, no. 3, pp. 41–83.

Kitano, Seiichi (1939) 'Kōshū sanson no dōzoku soshiki to oyakata-kokata kankō (*Dōzoku* system and *oyakata-kokata* in mountain communities in Kōshū Province),' *Minzokugaku nenpō* (Annual bulletin of ethnology), vol. 2.

Kitano, Seiichi (1941) 'Dōzoku soshiki to oyakata-kokata kankō shiryō (Materials on the *dōzoku* system and the *oyakata-kokata* custom),' *Minzokugaku nenpō* (Annual bulletin of ethnology), vol. 4.

Kitano, Seiichi (1951) 'Dōzoku soshiki to hōken isei (*Dōzoku* system and remnants of the feudal system),' *Ie to dōzoku no kiso riron* (Basic theories of *ie* and *dōzoku*), Tokyo: Miraisha.

Kitano, Seiichi (1959) 'Oyabun-kobun (*Oyabun-kobun*: A pseudo parent-child relationship),' in *Nihon minzokugaku taikei* (An anthology of Japanese folklore studies), vol. 4, Tokyo: Heibonsha.

Kitano, Seiichi (1962) 'Nihon no mura to ie (Villages and *ie* in Japan),' *Shakaigaku nenpō* (The annuals of sociology), vol. 12, Sōdai Shakai Gakkai (The Waseda Sociological Society).

Kitano, Seiichi and Kanji Masaoka (eds) (1971) *Ie to shinzoku soshiki* (*Ie* and kinship systems), Tokyo: Miraisha.

Kitano, Seiichi (1981) 'Oyakata-kokata kankei ron no mondai ten (jō) (Issues in arguments on *oyakata-kokata* relationship (vol. 1)),' *Kazoku-shi kenkyū* (Family history studies), vol. 4, Tokyo: Kōbundō.

Kitō, Shūichi (1996) *Shizen hogo wo toi naosu – kankyō rinri to nettowāku* (Reconsidering nature conservation: Environmental ethics and networks), Tokyo: Chikuma Shobō.

Kokudo Chō (National Land Agency) (1977) *Dai-san-ji zenkoku sōgō kaihatsu keikaku* (The Third Comprehensive National Development Plan), Ōkurashō Insatsukyoku (Printing Bureau, Ministry of Finance).

Kokudo Chō (1987) *Dai-yo-ji zenkoku sōgō kaihatsu keikaku* (The Fourth Comprehensive National Development Plan), Ōkurashō Insatsukyoku.

Kokudo Chō (1998) *Dai-go-ji zenkoku sōgō kaihatsu keikaku* (The Fifth Comprehensive National Development Plan), http://www.mlit.go.jp/kokudokeikaku/zs5/index.html.

Kotani, Hiroyuki (1993) *Rāmu shinwa to meushi – Hindū fukko shugi to isuramu (Korekara no sekaishi 5)* (The Ram myth and cow: Hindu reactionism and Islam (World history for the future 5)), Tokyo: Heibonsha.

Kuhn, Thomas Samuel (1962) *The Structure of Scientific Revolutions*, Chicago: University of Chicago Press.

Kunwar, Ramesh Raj (1989) *Fire of Himal: An Anthropological Study of the Sherpa of Nepal Himalaya Region*, New Delhi: Nirala Publications.

Mamiya, Yōsuke (1999) *Dōjidai ron – shijō shugi to nashonarizumu wo koete* (Contemporary arguments: Beyond supremacism and nationalism), Tokyo: Iwanami Shoten.

Matsubara, Haruo (ed.) (1971) *Kōgai to chiiki shakai – seikatsu to jūmin undō no shakaigaku* (Pollution and communities: Sociology of living and public movements), Tokyo: Nihon Keizai Shimbun, Inc.

Matsubara, Haruo and Kamon Nitagai (eds) (1976) *Jūmin undō no ronri – undō no tenkai katei, kadai to tenbō* (The logic of public movements: The development process of, problems in and prospects for movements), Tokyo: Gakuyō Shobō.

Matsuda, Motoji (1985) 'Afurika ni okeru dentō no hi renzokusei ni tsuite (The discontinuity of tradition in Africa),' *Jinbun kenkyū* (Studies in the Humanities), vol. 37, no. 2, Faculty of Literature and Human Sciences, Osaka City University.

Matsuda, Motoji (1989) 'Hitsuzen kara bengi he – seikatsu kankyō shugi no ninshiki ron (From necessity to convenience: Epistemology of living environmentalism),' in Hiroyuki Torigoe (ed.), *Kankyō mondai no shakai riron – seikatsu kankyō shugi no tachiba kara* (Social theories on environmental issues: From the perspective of living environmentalism), Tokyo: Ochanomizu Shobō.

Matsuda, Motoji (1996) *Toshi wo kai narasu* (Taming cities), Tokyo: Kawade Shobō Shinsha.

Matsuda, Motoji and Akira Furukawa (2003) 'Kankō to kankyō no shakai riron – shin komyunarizumu he (A social theory on tourism and environment: Toward neo-communalism),' in Akira Furukawa and Motoji Matsuda (eds), *Kankō to kankyō no shakaigaku* (Sociology of tourism and environment), Tokyo: Shin-yo-sha.

Matsumura, Kazunori (ed.) (1997) *Sanson no kaihatsu to kankyō hozen – rejā supōtsu ka suru chūsankan chiiki no kadai* (Development of mountain villages and environment conservation: Tasks for intermediate and mountainous areas being converted to leisure resorts), Tokyo: Nansōsha.

Matsumura, Kazunori and Shinji Aoki (eds) (1991) *Yūki nōgyō undō no chiiki-teki tenkai – Yamagata Ken Takahata-machi no jissen kara* (Local development of organic farming movements: From the practice in Takahata-machi, Yamagata Prefecture), Tokyo: Ie-No-Hikari Kyōkai (Ie-No-Hikari Association).

Matsumura, Kazunori (1995) 'Yūki nōgyō no ronri to jissen – 'karada' no fīrudo wāku he no kikyū (Thought and Practice in the Japanese Organic Farming Movement: Toward an alternative approach to fieldwork which would lead to a change in the attitudes of sociologists as a socially constructed "body"),' *Shakaigaku hyōron* (Japanese Sociological Review), vol. 45, no. 4.

Mitsuyoshi, Toshiyuki (1970) 'Shinzoku kankei (Kinship relationship),' in Shūhei Yamamuro and Tsutomu Himeoka (eds), *Gendai kazoku no shakaigaku – seika to kadai* (Sociology of the modern family: Outcomes and tasks), Tokyo: Baifūkan.

Miyamoto, Ken'ichi (1973) *Chiiki kaihatsu wa korede yoika* (Have we done regional development right?), Tokyo: Iwanami Shoten.

Miyamoto, Ken'ichi (1989) *Kankyō keizaigaku* (Environmental economics), Tokyo: Iwanami Shoten.

Miyamoto, Tsuneichi (n.d.; republished in 1972), 'Yamaoku to ritō to (Isolated mountains and islands),' *Miyamoto Tsuneichi chosaku shū* (Collection of Tsuneichi Miyamoto's works), vol. 12, Tokyo: Miraisha.

Miyamoto, Tsuneichi (1972) (republished in 1973), 'Kaso to hekichi kyōiku (Depopulation and remote area education),' *Miyamoto Tsuneichi chosaku shū* (Collection of Tsuneichi Miyamoto's works), vol. 13, Tokyo: Miraisha.

Miyamoto, Tsuneichi (1976) 'Atogaki (Postface),' *Miyamoto Tsuneichi chosaku shū*, vol. 23, Tokyo: Miraisha.

Miyauchi, Taisuke (1998) 'Jūsō-teki na kankyō riyō to kyōdō riyō ken – Soromon Shotō Maraita Tō no jirei kara (Mixed use of the environment and collective usufruct: case study in Malaita, the Solomon Islands),' *Kankyō shakaigaku kenkyū* (Journal of Environmental Sociology), vol. 4, Tokyo: Shin-yo-sha.

Murakami, Yōichirō (1974) 'Kagaku, gijutsu to kindai no rinen kōzō (The ideal structure of science/technology and modern times),' *Sōgō kōza: Nihon no shakai bunka-shi 5* (Comprehensive series: The sociocultural history of Japan 5), Tokyo: Kōdansha.

Nagao, Gajin (1989) 'Chibetto bukkyō gaikan (An overview of Tibetan Buddhism),' *Iwanami kōza, tōyō shisō 11: Chibetto bukkyō* (Iwanami's lectures, Oriental thoughts 25: Tibetan Buddhism), Tokyo: Iwanami Shoten.

Nakamura, Hisashi and Yoshiyuki Tsurumi (eds) (1995) *Komonzu no umi – kōryū no michi, kyōyū no chikara* (The sea of commons: Means of exchange and power of sharing), Tokyo: Gakuyō Shobō.

Nakano, Takashi (1956) 'Dōzoku dan kenkyū no kiten to kadai (The starting point of and tasks in studies of *dōzoku* groups),' in Tadashi Fukutake (ed.), *Hayashi Megumi kyōju kanreki kinen ronbun shū: Nihon shakaigaku no kadai* (Festschrift for the 60th birthday of Professor Megumi Hayashi: Topics in Japanese sociology), Tokyo: Yūhikaku.

Nakano, Takashi (1981) *Shōka dōzoku dan no kenkyū, dai-2 han (jō, ge)* (A study of *dōzoku* groups constituting merchant families, second edition (vols 1 and 2)), Tokyo: Miraisha.

Nakano, Yasuto, et al. (1996) 'Shakai-teki jirenma to shite no gomi mondai

(The waste problem as a social dilemma),' *Kankyō shakaigaku kenkyū* (Journal of Environmental Sociology), vol. 4, Tokyo: Shin-yo-sha.

Nakaoka, Tetsurō and Kōhei Hanazaki (1986) 'Shūhen kara – 'henkaku' no vijon no tameni (taiwa) (From the periphery: The vision for a "change" (dialogue)),' *Shin Iwanami kōza: Tetsugaku geppō 16* (New Iwanami's lectures: Monthly philosophy bulletin 16), Tokyo: Iwanami Shoten.

Nakata, Minoru (1993) *Chiiki kyōdō kanri no shakaigaku* (Sociology of communal management), Tokyo: Tōshindō.

Nakata, Minoru (1995) 'Kankyō mondai to kankyō shakaigaku (Environmental problems and environmental sociology),' *Shakaigaku hyōron* (Japanese Sociological Review), vol. 45, no. 4.

Nakayama, Shigeru (1995) *Kagaku gijutsu no sengo-shi* (The postwar history of science and technology), Tokyo: Iwanami Shoten.

Nakazawa, Hideo, Sung Won Cheol, Naoto Higuchi, Kazunori Kado, and Hiromitsu Mizusawa (1998) 'Kankyō undō ni okeru kōgi saikuru keisei no ronri – kōzō teki sutorēn to seijiteki kikai kōzō no hikaku bunseki (1968–82) (The logic of protest cycle formation in environmental movements: Comparative analysis of structural strain and structure of political opportunities),' *Kankyō shakaigaku kenkyū* (Journal of Environmental Sociology), vol. 4, Tokyo: Shin-yo-sha.

Naylor, Reynolds (1976) *The Everest National Park*, Ministry of Foreign Affairs: New Zealand.

Nihon Jinbun Kagakkai (Japanese Association for the Humanities) (ed.) (1955) *Kindai kōkōgyō to chiiki shakai no tenkai* (Modern mining and manufacturing and the development of local communities), Tokyo: University of Tokyo Press.

Nozick, Robert (1974) *Anarchy, State, and Utopia*, New York: Basic Books.

Ōhashi, Kaoru (1953) 'Dōzoku narabini sono ruien sho gainen no saikentō (A review of *dōzoku* and similar concepts),' *Soshioroji* (Sociology), vol. 4.

Ōishi, Kaichirō (1961) *Nihon gyō-zaisei-shi josetsu* (An introduction to the history of Japanese administration and public finance), Tokyo: Ochanomizu Shobō.

Ōkawa, Masahiko (1999) *Seigi* (Justice), Tokyo: Iwanami Shoten.

Ortner, Sherry B. (1978) *Sherpas through Their Rituals*, Cambridge: Cambridge University Press.

Ortner, Sherry B. (1989) *High Religion: A Cultural and Political History of Sherpa Buddhism*, Princeton: Princeton University Press.

Ōshima, Mitsuko (1989) 'Mura to ie no hō seido (The legal system for villages and *ie*),' in Fukuju Un'no and Mitsuko Ōshima (eds), *Ie to mura* (*Ie* and villages), Tokyo: Iwanami Shoten.

Ōshima, Mitsuko (1990) 'Ishin to jiyū minken (The Restoration of freedom and people's rights),' Nihon Sonraku-shi Kōza Henshū Iinkai (Editorial

Committee for Nihon sonraku-shi kōza) (ed.), *Nihon sonraku-shi kōza 5: Seiji 2* (Lectures on the history of Japanese rural communities 5: Politics 2), Tokyo: Yūzankaku.

Ōtsuka, Yoshiki (1998) 'Idenshi kumikae sakumotsu wo meguru kankyō mondai to kagaku gijutsu no sōgo-teki kōchiku (Mutual development of environmental issues and modern technology surrounding genetically engineered crops),' *Kankyō shakaigaku kenkyū* (Journal of Environmental Sociology), vol. 4, Tokyo: Shin-yo-sha.

Ōtsuki, Emi (1984) 'Suikai to gyorō (The hydrosphere and fishery),' in Hiroyuki Torigoe and Yukiko Kada (eds), *Mizu to hito no kankyōshi – Biwako hōkokusho* (The history of the environment for water and people: Lake Biwa report), Tokyo: Ochanomizu Shobō.

Polanyi, Michael (1958) *Personal Knowledge: Towards a Post-Critical Philosophy*, London: Routledge and Kegan Paul.

Polanyi, Michael (1967) *The Tacit Dimension*, New York: Anchor Books.

Rawls, John (1971) *A Theory of Justice*, Cambridge, Massachusetts: Belknap Press of Harvard University Press.

Saitō, Jun'ichi (2000) *Kōkyōsei* (Publicness), Tokyo: Iwanami Shoten.

Sakurai, Atsushi (1984) 'Kawa to suidō – mizu to shakai no hendō (Rivers and water service: Changes in water and society),' in Hiroyuki Torigoe and Yukiko Kada (eds), *Mizu to hito no kankyōshi – Biwako hōkokusho* (The history of the environment for water and people: Lake Biwa report), Tokyo: Ochanomizu Shobō.

Sen, Amartya Kumar (1982) *Choice, Welfare and Measurement*, Cambridge: Harvard University Press.

Sharma, Sita Ram (ed.) (1998) *Anatomy of Communalism (Historical Perspectives on Communalism, vol. 1)*, New Delhi: A.P.H. Publishing Corporation.

Shōji, Hikaru and Ken'ichi Miyamoto (1964) *Osorubeki kōgai* (Terrible pollution), Tokyo: Iwanami Shoten.

Shōji, Hikaru and Ken'ichi Miyamoto (1975) *Nihon no kōgai* (Pollution in Japan), Tokyo: Iwanami Shoten.

Stevens, Stanley F. (1993) *Claiming the High Ground: Sherpas, Subsistence and Environmental Change in the Highest Himalaya*, Los Angeles: University of California Press.

Sumiya, Kazuhiko (1963) *Kyōdōtai no shi-teki kōzō ron* (A theory on the historical structure of communities), Tokyo: Yūhikaku.

Sumiya, Kazuhiko and Seiichi Kitano (1968) 'Taidan: Nihon no ie to kazoku – Aruga-Kitano ronsō no mondaiten (Dialogue: *Ie* and *kazoku* in Japan: Issues in the Aruga-Kitano Controversy),' *Shisō* (Thought), vol. 527, Tokyo: Iwanami Shoten.

Sumiya, Kazuhiko (1982) *Nihon no ishiki – shisō ni okeru ningen no kenkyū*

(The consciousness of Japan: A study of humans in thoughts), Tokyo: Iwanami Shoten.

Tabata, Hideo (1996) 'Satoyama no hozen (Conservation of rural woodland),' in *Kōza: Bunmei to kankyō* 9: Mori to Bunmei (Series: Civilization and environment 9: The forest and civilization), Tokyo: Asakura Shoten.

Tabeta, Masahiro, Akira Fujimori, Toshiko Masugata and Yūko Kubota (1986) *Chiiki jikyū to 'nō' no ronri – seizon no tame no shakai keizaigaku* (Regional self-sufficiency and the logic of 'farming': Social economics for survival), Tokyo: Gakuyō Shobō.

Tajiri, Muneaki (1972) *Yokkaichi: Shi no umi to tatakau* (Yokkaichi: A battle against pollution), Tokyo: Iwanami Shoten.

Takahashi, Tōichi (1978) *Miyaza no kōzō to henka – saishi chōrō sei no shakai jinruigaku-teki kenkyū* (The structure and changes of *miyaza*: A social anthropological study of the gerontocratic ritual system), Tokyo: Miraisha.

Takata, Akihiko (1995) 'Kankyō mondai he no sho apurōchi to shakai undō ron (Environmental sociology and the theory of social movements),' *Shakaigaku hyōron* (Japanese Sociological Review), vol. 45, no. 4.

Takeda, Chōshū (1977) *Sonraku dōzoku saishi no kenkyū* (Studies on the *Dōzoku* rites and festivals), Tokyo: Yoshikawa Kōbunkan.

Takeuchi, Yoshirō (1986) 'Bunka no henkaku (Cultural changes),' *Shin Iwanami kōza: Tetsugaku 12* (New Iwanami's lectures: Philosophy 12), Tokyo: Iwanami Shoten.

Takubo, Yūko (1996) 'Kariforunia shū "genshiryoku anzen hō" no seiritsu katei – fukusū no arīna kan no sōgo sayō to shite no seiji katei (Process of enactment of California's "Nuclear Safeguards Initiative": Political process as interaction between arenas),' *Kankyō shakaigaku kenkyū* (Journal of Environmental Sociology), vol. 2, Tokyo: Shin-yo-sha.

Takubo, Yūko (1997) 'Makimachi "Jūmin Tōhyō wo Jikkō suru Kai" no tanjō, hatten to seikō (Creation, development and success of the "Local Referendum Initiative Group" in Makimachi),' *Kankyō shakaigaku kenkyū* (Journal of Environmental Sociology), vol. 3, Tokyo: Shin-yo-sha.

Tamanoi, Yoshirō, Tadao Kiyonari and Hisashi Nakamura (eds) (1978) *Chiiki shugi – atarashii shichō he no riron to jissen no kokoromi* (Regionalism: A theory and trial practice of a new thought), Tokyo: Gakuyō Shobō.

Taniguchi, Yoshimitsu (1996) 'Jūmin no risaikuru kōdō ni kansuru kikai kōzō ron teki bunseki – Nichibei hikaku chōsa wo motoni (An analysis of residents' recycling behavior from the perspective of opportunity structure: Based on a Japan–US comparative survey),' *Kankyō shakaigaku kenkyū* (Journal of Environmental Sociology), vol. 2, Tokyo: Shin-yo-sha.

Taniguchi, Yoshimitsu (1998) 'Amerika kankyō shakaigaku to paradaimu ronsō (American environmental sociology and the paradigm dispute),' *Kankyō shakaigaku kenkyū*, vol. 4, Tokyo: Shin-yo-sha

Terada, Ryōichi (1995) 'Saisei kanō enerugī gijutsu no kankyō shakaigaku – kankyō minshu shugi wo tenbō shite (Environmental sociology on renewable energy technology: Toward environmental democracy),' *Shakaigaku hyōron* (Japanese Sociological Review), vol. 45, no. 4.

Torigoe, Hiroyuki and Yukiko Kada (eds) (1984) *Mizu to hito no kankyōshi – Biwako hōkokusho* (The history of the environment for water and people: Lake Biwa report), Tokyo: Ochanomizu Shobō.

Torigoe, Hiroyuki (1977) 'Aruga shakaigaku ni miru seikatsu haaku no hōhō (Methods of understanding living seen in Aruga's sociology)' (published as 'Aruga riron ni okeru seikatsu haaku no hōhō (Methods of understanding living in Aruga's theories)' in Torigoe (1992).

Torigoe, Hiroyuki (1982) *Tokara Rettō shakai no kenkyū* (A study of society in the Tokara Islands), Tokyo: Ochanomizu Shobō.

Torigoe, Hiroyuki (1983) 'Ie to yashiki (*Ie* and premises),' in Ajio Fukuta and Noboru Miyata (eds), *Nihon minzokugaku gairon* (An introduction to Japanese folklore), Tokyo: Yoshikawa Kōbunkan.

Torigoe, Hiroyuki (1985) 'Kankyō mondai to nichijō seikatsu (Environmental issues and daily life),' *Kwansei Gakuin Daigaku Shakaigakubu kiyō* (Kwansei Gakuin University School of Sociology journal), vol. 51.

Torigoe, Hiroyuki (ed.) (1989) *Kankyō mondai no shakai riron – seikatsu kankyō shugi no tachiba kara* (Social theories on environmental issues: From the perspective of living environmentalism), Tokyo: Ochanomizu Shobō.

Torigoe, Hiroyuki (1997a) *Kankyō shakaigaku no riron to jissen – seikatsu kankyō shugi no tachiba kara* (A theory and practice of environmental sociology: From the perspective of living environmentalism), Tokyo: Yūhikaku.

Torigoe, Hiroyuki (1997b) 'Komonzu no riyō ken wo kyōju suru mono (Those who enjoy the right to use commons),' *Kankyō shakaigaku kenkyū* (Journal of Environmental Sociology), vol. 3, Tokyo: Shin-yo-sha.

Torigoe, Hiroyuki (1999) *Kankyō shakaigaku* (Environmental sociology), Hōsō Daigaku Kyōiku Shinkō Kai (The Society for the Promotion of the University of the Air).

Tsuchiya, Keiichirō (1996) *Seigi ron/jiyū ron – muen shakai Nippon no seigi* (A theory of justice/freedom: Justice in Japanese society with no personal relationships), Tokyo: Iwanami Shoten.

Tsuchiya, Toshiyuki (1991) 'Sanson (Mountain villages),' Nihon sonraku-shi kōza Henshū Iinkai (Editorial committee for Nihon sonraku-shi kōza) (ed.),

Nihon sonraku-shi kōza 3: Keikan 2 (Lectures on the history of Japanese rural communities 3: Landscapes 2), Tokyo: Yūzankaku.

Tsukihara, Toshihiro and Akira Furukawa (1991) 'Kunbu, Tinrī ryō chihō no seigyō kūkan hensei – kachiku shu kōsei kara mita dentō to hen'yō (The composition of occupational space in the Khumbu and Tingri regions: Tradition and changes in the composition of livestock species),' *Himaraya-gaku shi* (Himalayan studies monographs), vol. 2, Kyoto Daigaku Himaraya Kenkyū Kai (Society for Himalayan Studies, Kyoto University).

Tsurumi, Kazuko (1996) *Naihatsu-teki hatten ron no tenkai* (Developments of the spontaneous development theory), Tokyo: Chikuma Shobō.

Tsurumi, Yoshiyuki (1982) *Banana to Nihon-jin* (Bananas and Japanese), Tokyo: Iwanami Shoten.

Tsurumi, Yoshiyuki (1990) *Namako no me* (Sea cucumbers' viewpoint), Tokyo: Chikuma Shobō.

Uchiyama, Takashi (1989) 'Sanson rōdō ryoku no hen'yō to chiiki shakai (Changes in labor power in mountain villages and local communities),' in Takashi Uchiyama (ed.), *'Shinrin shakaigaku' sengen* (A declaration of forest sociology), Tokyo: Yūhikaku.

Uchiyama, Takashi (1998) 'Kindai-teki ningen kan kara no jiyū (Freedom from the modern view of human beings),' in Takashi Uchiyama, Takashi Ōkuma, Shūichi Kitō, Shigemitsu Kimura, and Jun'ichi Shinmura (eds), *Rōkaru na shisō wo tsukuru* (Creating local thoughts), Nōsangyoson Bunka Kyōkai (Rural Culture Association).

Ueno, Kazuo (1981) 'Ōmi Kotō no miyaza saishi – Echi-gawa ryūiki no futatsu no jirei wo chūshin ni shite (Rituals by *miyaza* in Kotō, Ōmi: Based on two cases in the basin of the Echi River), in Hirofumi Tsuboi (ed.), *Saishi-teki sekai to sonraku* (Ritual world and rural communities), Tokyo: Kōbundō.

Ui, Jun (1971) (bound in one volume in 1988), *Kōgai genron* (The principles of pollution), Tokyo: Aki Shobō.

Ukai, Teruyoshi (1992) *Okinawa: Kyodai kaihatsu no ronri to hihan* (Okinawa: The logic and criticism of large-scale development), Tokyo: Shakai Hyōronsha.

Umino, Michio (1993) 'Kankyō hakai no shakai-teki mekanizumu (Social mechanisms of environmental destruction),' in Nobuko Iijima (ed.), *Kankyō shakaigaku* (Environmental sociology), Tokyo: Yūhikaku.

Un'no, Fukuju and Mitsuko Ōshima (eds.) (1989) *Ie to mura* (*Ie* and villages), Tokyo: Iwanami Shoten.

Yamamuro, Atsushi (1998) 'Genshiryoku hatsudensho kensetsu mondai ni okeru jūmin no ishi hyōji – Niigata Ken Makimachi wo jirei ni (Residents' declaration of intention on the issue of nuclear power plant construction: A case study, Makimachi, Niigata Prefecture),' *Kankyō shakaigaku kenkyū* (Journal of Environmental Sociology), vol. 4, Tokyo: Shin-yo-sha.

Yamamuro, Shūhei (1970) 'Kazoku riron (1) (A theory of family (1)),' in Shūhei Yamamuro and Tsutomu Himeoka (eds), *Gendai kazoku no shakaigaku* (Sociology of the modern family), Tokyo: Baifūkan.

Yanagita, Kunio (ed.) (1938) (reprinted 1975), *Sanson seikatsu no kenkyū* (A study of mountain village life), Toshokankōkai.

Yoneyama, Toshinao (1967) *Nihon no mura no hyakunen* (One hundred years of Japanese villages), Tokyo: NHK Books.

Yorimitsu, Ryōzō and Yūko Kurisu (1996) *Gurīn tsūrizumu no kanōsei* (The potential of green tourism), Tokyo: Nihon Keizai Hyōronsha.

Yorimoto, Katsumi (1990) *Gomi to risaikuru* (Waste and recycling), Tokyo: Iwanami Shoten.

Name Index

Andō, Seiichi, 40, 136–145, 150, 273–274
Aruga, Kizaemon, 151–169, 263–265, 274–275, 277; see also Aruga-Kitano Controversy

Dunlap, Riley E., 48–49, 52

Emori, Itsuo, 132–135

Fukutake, Tadashi, 54, 131–132, 135, 145
Funabashi, Harutoshi, 39, 45–47, 54–57

Gamō, Masao, 96, 130–131, 133–135, 147–149, 152, 273–274
Gibson, James J., 250

Hagiwara, Tatsuo, 136–138, 140–142, 147
Hanayama, Yuzuru, 271
Harada, Masazumi, 271
Harada, Rie, 60
Harada, Toshiaki, 136–138, 140–142, 146–147
Hardin, Garret, 238–239
Hasegawa, Kōichi, 55–57
Hasegawa, Yoshikazu, 274
Higo, Kazuo, 73–74, 136–137
Hillary, Sir Edmund, 25–29, 31, 240, 242–246, 249–250, 258–260, 268

Hirano, Toshimasa, 165
Hiraoka, Yoshikazu, 45, 60
Horikawa, Saburō, 270

Iijima, Nobuko, 17, 39–42, 44–45, 49–51, 54–56, 270, 275
Inoue, Makoto, 58
Inoue, Takao, 59
Irokawa, Daikichi, 39, 271
Ishikawa, Kiyoshi, 54, 60
Iwamoto, Yoshiteru, 126–127

Kada, Yukiko, 21, 32, 39, 47, 58, 65–66, 68, 172, 177, 188, 202, 269, 271, 277
Katagiri, Shinji, 56, 270
Kawamoto, Akira, 58, 63–67, 106, 270–271, 277
Kitagawa, Takayoshi, 54
Kitano, Seiichi, 151–169, 274–275; see also Aruga-Kitano Controversy
Kitō, Shūichi, 59
Kuhn, Thomas Samuel, 170

Matsubara, Haruo, 54, 56
Matsuda, Motoji, 36, 58, 102, 199, 270, 276–277
Matsumura, Kazunori, 59–60, 271
Merton, Robert K., 39, 55
Mitsuyoshi, Toshiyuki, 153
Miyamoto, Ken'ichi, 47, 270
Miyamoto, Tsuneichi, 228–231, 238

Murakami, Yōichirō, 171

Nakata, Minoru, 45, 51–52, 59
Nakayama, Tarō, 137
Nakayama, Shigeru, 276
Nakazawa, Hideo, 57
Nitagai, Kamon, 56

Ōhashi, Kaoru, 152
Oka, Masao, 131
Ōshima, Mitsuko, 108, 124
Ōtsuka, Yoshiki, 60

Polanyi, Michael, 195–197

Sakurai, Atsushi, 191, 198
Shimazaki, Minoru, 54
Shōji, Hikaru, 270
Sumiya, Kazuhiko, 146, 152, 274

Tajiri, Muneaki, 270
Takahashi, Tōichi, 145–146, 149
Takeda, Chōshū, 137, 141–142, 144
Takubo, Yūko, 60
Toda, Teizō, 151, 153, 274
Torigoe, Hiroyuki, 11, 21, 32–34, 39, 58–59, 68, 106–107, 161, 165, 169, 177, 188, 194–196, 265, 269–271, 276–277
Tsuchiya, Keiichirō, 277
Tsuchiya, Toshiyuki, 224–225
Tsurumi, Kazuko, 39
Tsurumi, Yoshiyuki, 24, 58–59, 271

Uchiyama, Takashi, 96–97, 107, 227
Ueno, Kazuo, 146–147, 149

Ui, Jun, 270
Umino, Michio, 46–47, 57, 108

Yamamuro, Atsushi, 60
Yamamuro, Shūhei, 153
Yamazaki, Masakazu, 11
Yanagita, Kunio, 216, 219
Yoneyama, Toshinao, 271

Subject Index

administrative
  affairs, 13, 74–75, 89, 91–92, 94, 96, 124–125, 200–201, 205, 265
  control, 65, 76
agricultural affairs, 205, 208
Agricultural Basic Law, 234, 271
Aruga-Kitano Controversy, 129, 151–154, 159, 274

beneficiary/affected zones, 39, 52
Biennial Trap Fishing Act, 102
boundary, 53, 100, 137, 195, 212
breakdown of the farmer class, 140
buji (safety), 96
bylaws
  1890, 70–71, 92, 123
  1897, 71, 91–92, 94, 122–123
  1902, 93, 95, 122–124

canals, 209, 270; see also drainage canals
centrality of 'convenience,' 11
coexistence with nature, 3, 5, 9–10
collaborative work, 124
collective community property, 57, 64
common
  forests, 214
  wells, 177

commons, 58–60, 185, 238–239, 252
communalism, 12, 261–263, 270, 277
commune, 159
communitarianism, 12, 261–263
community
  co-management theory, 59
  development, 10, 56, 59
consolidation of towns and villages, 117
construction of modern water supply systems, 172, 186, 190, 198
constructionism, 53
controversies between objectivism (universalism) and relativism, 170
convenience of rural life, 5
creativity, 1, 8, 15, 36, 169, 264–265, 268
criticisms of Japanese capitalism, 163
cross-cultural analytical concept, 153–154, 165, 167, 169
cultural contexts, 261

daily
  visit card, 125, 128, 211
  water, 172–173, 179, 182, 184
deforestation, 16, 26–27, 30, 43, 239–240, 243–247, 257–258

297

denunciation model, 43
depopulated areas, 6, 8, 10, 206
depopulation problems, 5, 228
destruction of
  everyday lives, 33
  nature, 46, 52
development
  and protection, 29, 32, 251, 267
  assistance, 15
  of depopulated areas, 6
  of tourism, 26, 212
developmentalism, 27, 36
disaster, 68, 95–96, 98–100, 104–106, 109–110, 119–120, 122–123, 125, 209, 214
disputes, 11–12, 67, 100, 121, 145, 244, 274
  over fishing rights, 120
domestic wastewater, 43, 175, 185–187, 192
double equality structure, 132, 135, 145, 148–149
dōzoku (quasi-kin relationships),14, 135, 151–169, 264, 273–275; see also arguments on *ie* and *dōzoku*
drainage, 14, 21, 111–113, 122, 139, 172–174, 184–187, 190–192, 198, 267, 271; see also traditional drainage systems
  canals, 186, 192, 198
duality of land ownership, 63

economy of circulation, 228
ecotourism, 9
elders, 70–72, 74–76, 78, 82, 84–87, 89–90, 97–99, 111, 146, 271

empiricism, 33
environment protection system, 251
environmental; see also theories on the generation of environmental issues
consciousness, 4, 17, 44, 53
policy, 45–46, 271
pollution issues, 37
protection, 5–6, 9–10, 13, 15, 22, 27–28, 30–32, 43, 58–60, 63, 66, 258, 268–269
protectionism, 251
environmentalism, 18, 129, 170; see also global environmentalism, life-environmentalism
estimate, 94
everyday life, 16, 22, 24, 28–35, 37–38, 53, 55, 58–59, 78, 107, 123, 125, 145, 171–172, 195, 199, 250, 263, 265, 267, 269; see also protecting everyday life
knowledge, 14–15, 170–173, 191, 193–194, 198–199, 266–269
logics, 268
practices, 13–15, 43–44, 268–269
-related environmental issues, 42–44, 53
exclusive fishing rights, 105

family classes, 136–137, 148–150
feudal-type ruling body, 140
fieldwork, 240, 269
First Meeting Day, 71
fishing rights, 100, 120; see also disputes over fishing rights, exclusive fishing

Subject Index

rights, poor's fishing system
flood, 99–100, 103, 119, 123, 232, 235
   damage, 92–93, 109, 123, 201
forest
   management, 2, 15, 28–30, 218–19, 232, 238, 246–247, 253, 257, 266–268
   protection, 27–29, 238–239, 244, 247, 251, 257
   views, 245

genealogical relationships, 152–153, 155–158, 163–164, 166
global, 16–19, 25–27, 38, 43–44, 46–47, 49, 60, 63, 238–239, 250–251, 262, 268
   environmental issues, 16, 38, 42–44, 46, 52, 239
   environmentalism, 16–19, 24, 28
grassland, 224, 227, 237, 241–242, 246, 252, 273
green tourism, 8–9, 11; see also ecotourism

hare (temporal), 216
hashi (pier), 152, 183–185
hekichi (remote rural area), 228–229
Hillary syndrome, 260
hinmin-kasegi (the poor's business referred to as the 'poor's fishing system'), 104
historical context, 167, 199
horizontal union, 96, 131–132
household affairs, 13, 76–77, 98, 265, 272

huge developments, 7
Human Exceptionalism Paradigm, 48

ie (family), 14, 135, 151–169, 191, 265, 274–275
   and *kazoku*, 151, 153, 164, 274
   arguments on *ie* and *dōzoku*, 154, 162, 164
   associations, 162; see also two types of *ie* associations
   concept of, 159
   definition of members, 162
   origins of, 156
   property of, 156, 159–160
iibun (argument), 194–196, 198
ike (ponds), 177–185, 275–276
ike gumi (*ike* group), 178, 182, 275
industrial pollution issues, 18, 43, 53
interconversion, 166, 263–265
internal equality, 141, 144, 146–147, 149
interrelationship, 166, 264
isolated type, 143

Japan's Comprehensive National Development Plans, 231
Japanese capitalism; see criticisms of Japanese capitalism
Japanese culture, 157, 160, 169
Jizō Bon, 180–183

kabuza (exclusive union), 81, 91, 136, 141–142, 146–147, 149, 272

kannushi (shrine guardian), 73, 79, 81–82, 91
ke (ordinary times), 216
kinship
  community theory, 163, 165
  organizations, 163–164, 169, 275
  -based theory, 129, 151, 165–168
Kiroku (village diary), 13–14, 67–70, 74, 79–80, 92, 97, 100–103, 107, 109, 111–119, 122–123, 125, 127, 191, 201–202, 204, 207, 211, 213, 215, 271–273
kumigashira (head of the village), 71, 74, 93–94, 99, 107–108, 113, 119–121, 271
kyōgiin (councilors), 70, 75, 91, 93, 271–272

lagoons, 175–176, 184–188
lake basin, 32
land belonging to nobody, 121
Land Tax Reform, 63, 118, 120–122, 127, 213
landscape, 218–219, 222, 226–227, 233, 237, 243, 245, 250–251
  of symbiosis, 15, 226–228, 230, 234, 236–238
large-scale development, 46, 56, 270
liberalism, 262
libertarianism, 262
life
  and culture studies, 47
  community, 159–160, 162–163, 167–168, 265, 275
  community theory, 162–163, 165
  skills, 227, 267
  -environmentalism, 12, 16–17, 31–36, 39, 52, 58–59, 267–269
lifestyle, 3, 6, 10, 18, 53, 252
livestock management, 252
living
  relationships, 157, 159
  system, 33, 107, 146–147, 239
  -based theory, 129, 151, 165–167, 169–170, 263–265, 277
local
  contexts, 198
  government administration system, 107
  industry, 230, 236–238
  initiatives, 1–2
  knowledge, 3, 12–13, 15, 28–30

macroscopic critiques of authority, 268
middle range theory, 39, 55–56
miyaza (form of ritual organization), 14, 73–74, 76, 79–81, 87–89, 91, 96–97, 129–150, 265, 272–274; see also original form of *miyaza*, studies on *miyaza*
  as a feudal-type ruling body, 140
  as a *za*-like union, 140, 142
  as a religious body for worshipping guardian gods, 140
  -type, 96
modern
  civil society, 3, 5, 24–25
  history of landscapes, 240, 249

technology, 28, 32, 171
water supply systems; see construction of modern water supply systems
modernist ideology, 19
monocultures, 15
monograph, 157
moroto (members of *miyaza*), 73–76, 80, 88–92, 94–95, 97, 122–123, 125, 148, 272
mountain hamlets, arguments on, 228
mura-kasegi (village business), 103–104
muraza (village union), 73, 81, 136, 138, 141–143, 146–147, 149, 272
mushi-okuri (annual torch procession for driving away noxious insects), 199–200, 202–205, 211, 213, 266–267

natural and living environments, 12
natural cycles, 227, 237
nature; see views of nature
nature conservation, 26–27, 37, 45–46, 97; see also coexistence with nature
nature of phenomena, 166
nawa (Sherpa officer), 28–29, 246–248, 254, 256
nawa system, 28, 30, 251, 257, 259, 267
neo-communalism, 261–263, 270
New Comprehensive National Development Plan, 6
New Ecological Paradigm, 48
non-blood-related persons, 151, 160–161, 275

northeastern Japan-type, 132

objectivism; see controversies between objectivism (universalism) and relativism
Ōaza Chinai Kiyaku (Ōaza Chinai bylaws), 71
ohimachi (sunrise-waiting party), 90
okonai (event), 14, 73, 80–85, 87–88, 95, 125
organic agriculture movements, 60, 62
organization theory, 33
original form, 91–92, 159, 165, 169
  of *miyaza*, 141
osabun (decision-making body), 70–75, 89–94, 97–99, 111, 113, 116, 118–119, 122–123, 125, 271–272
osho nawas, 256
ownership, 13, 63, 101, 104, 106–107, 119, 121, 128, 148, 276–277
oyakata-kokata (pseudo parent-child) relationship, 151, 155, 157–159, 161, 164

pasture, 225, 238–239, 244, 247, 252–253, 256
permanent shrine guardianship, 79, 81, 108, 147, 213
perpetrator-victim dichotomy, 16–17, 39, 42–43, 51, 57, 59
  perspective, 51
political structures, 54
pollution; see industrial pollution issues

poor's fishing system, 13,
    103–107, 273
positivism, 24, 36
practical usage, 44
preferential right to use or
    occupy common land, 106
private
  and collective ownership, 63
  land, 63, 106
  wastewater tank, 175, 185
product protection, 64, 66–67
property ownership, 106, 121
protecting
  and serving, 158
  everyday life, 32–33
  human life, 265
  the living environment, 67,
    73
  the natural environment, 8
protective management, 65
publicness, 55–56

rapid economic growth, 15,
    42, 59, 67, 206, 227, 232,
    269
rational understanding, 29
recognition
  as a local issue, 194, 197–198
  as an environmental issue,
    194, 197–198
regionalism, 17, 52, 59
relativism, see controversies
    between objectivism
    (universalism) and
    relativism
religion, 74, 128
religious
  body, 73, 78–79, 97, 137, 140,
    142–143, 150
  gerontocracy, 146
remoteness, 230
research methods, 35, 57–58

residents'
  knowledge, 193, 195–196,
    199
  perspectives, 42
  perspectives from their
    everyday lives, 33
resort development, 5–7
resource management, 28,
    257–258, 260
restrictions on river use, 174
retrospective history method,
    166
right to use, 228
ritual organizations, 2, 12, 14
river
  basin, 32, 237
  fish trap, 100
  management, 65, 173–174
River Law, 271
rotating shrine guardianship,
    79, 81, 108
rotational duty systems, 73
rural communities, 1–10,
    12–14, 34, 54, 58, 62–67,
    69–70, 73–74, 76, 80, 91,
    96, 98, 127, 129–135, 138,
    140–141, 143–145, 148–151,
    154, 162–164, 168, 172,
    200, 208, 216, 219, 261,
    268, 271–272, 274
rural
  development, 5–6, 8–10
  life; see convenience of rural
    life
  residents, 10, 12
  studies typology of
    communities, 80
rural community; see
    also studies of rural
    communities
  structure, 14, 129–131, 144,
    148–149, 274

studies, 13–14, 62–63, 151
typology, 80, 96

safety of village, 97, 105, 107
Sagarmatha National Park, 243, 246, 257
scientific knowledge, 14–15, 25–26, 30, 170–172, 197, 199, 267
scientific technology, 172
secular type, 143
self-enlightenment model, 43
self-interest, 17
sen'nichi nissan (one-thousand-day daily visit), 125
seniority system, 82, 88, 131–133, 136, 146, 149, 273
sewakata (managers), 81–88
Sherpa people, 25–29, 31–32, 239–240, 243–252, 257–260
shingo (forest) *nawas*, 256
Shinpū association, 90, 125–126
Shinto affairs, 13, 74–75, 88, 91–95, 98
small community, 13, 15, 154, 262, 266
social
  change, 39, 261
  dilemma theories, 52
  forestry, 236, 277
  relations theory, 165
  research, 35–36
sōdai (community representative), 64, 70, 77–78, 113–116, 120, 124, 183, 203, 208
sō-shō (union of two or more *sō-son*), 140, 273
sō-son (everybody's village), 138–141, 144, 147, 273–274

sō-son-miyaza type of community, 144
southwestern Japan-type, 132–133
space managed by a rural community, 65
spontaneous development theory, 39, 52, 58–59
structure of damage, 52, 54
studies of rural communities, 261
studies on *miyaza*, 73, 150
studies on *ie* and *dōzoku*, 151, 162
sufficient sources of livelihood, 1
support, 27, 45, 104, 161, 212, 243, 258

tōya (head family), 81–87, 96, 130, 133–136, 142–143, 146–150, 272–274
tacit knowledge, 195–196
theories on the generation of environmental issues, 52
theory of power, 33
thinking in the everyday life-world, 21
tokobori (river dredging), 22, 174–175, 209
tourism; see development of tourism
traditional drainage systems, 172–173, 187, 190
turnaround culture, 36
two types of *ie* associations, 163

ujigami (guardian gods), 140, 142, 147
ujiko (shrine parishioner), 140–144, 147–148, 208

underground drainage, 111–112
universal justice, 29
urban messages, 5
urban people, 18

vertical
  and horizontal systems, 131
  and seniority systems, 132
  communities, 131–132, 134
  or master–servant relationships, 152, 155
victims, 12, 16, 18, 41–43, 52–55, 60, 125, 275
victims' movements, 54
views of nature, 200, 202, 204–206, 246, 249
village
  affairs, 13, 77, 87–88, 91, 94–95, 98, 265
  bylaws, 69–70, 89, 92, 94, 98
  diary, 67–68; see also *Kiroku* (village diary)
  duties, 77
  head, 79, 99
  sense of autonomy, 116
  territory, 117–118, 121–122

Ward, Town and Village Assembly Act, 115, 124, 127
ward-district system, 109, 114–115
warden system, 28, 267
wastewater; see domestic wastewater, private wastewater tank
water supply/drainage systems, 190–191
water supply practices, 124
weak's right to subsistence, 105–107

world
  of others, 195, 276
  of self, 194, 276
worldview, 29, 32, 48–49, 97, 199–200, 205–206, 216

Yahagi River method, 234

za (union), 80, 136–142, 144–146
za-like nature, 142